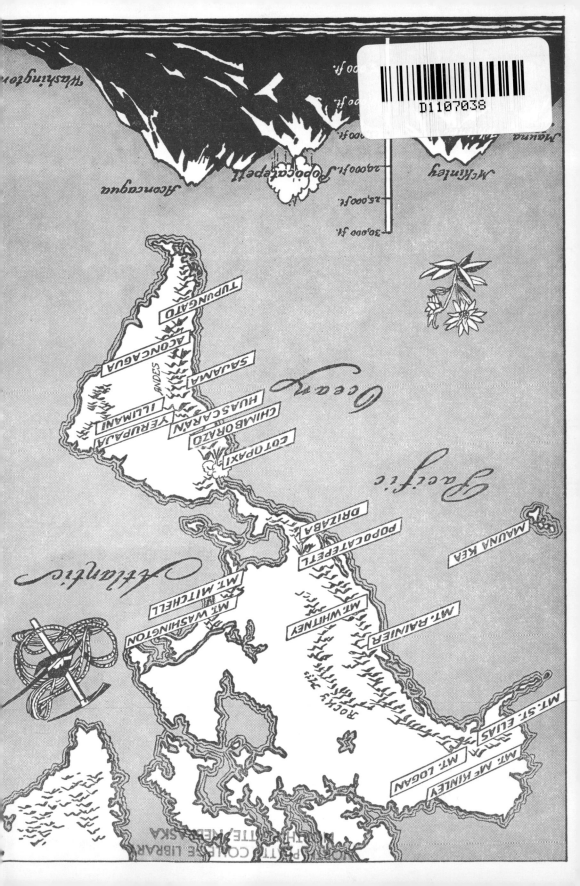

NORTH PLATTE COMFE LIBRARY
NORTH PLATTE, NEBRASKA

THE AGE OF MOUNTAINEERING

Books by James Ramsey Ullman

AMERICANS ON EVEREST

WHERE THE BONG TREE GROWS

FIA FIA

DOWN THE COLORADO

THE DAY ON FIRE

TIGER OF THE SNOWS

BANNER IN THE SKY

THE AGE OF MOUNTAINEERING

THE SANDS OF KARAKORUM

ISLAND OF THE BLUE MACAWS

WINDOM'S WAY

RIVER OF THE SUN

THE WHITE TOWER

HIGH CONQUEST: The Story of Mountaineering

THE OTHER SIDE OF THE MOUNTAIN:
An Escape to the Amazon

MAD SHELLEY

KINGDOM OF ADVENTURE: EVEREST (Editor)

THE AGE
OF MOUNTAINEERING

BY

James Ramsey Ullman

Ullman, James Ramsey, 1907-1971.
The age of mountaineering.

G510 .U38 1964

RSN=00013771

J. B. LIPPINCOTT COMPANY
PHILADELPHIA AND NEW YORK

Copyright, 1941, 1954, © 1964 by
James Ramsey Ullman

Printed in the United States of America

Second Printing

This book is based on the author's earlier
book HIGH CONQUEST and continues the
story of mountaineering through the postwar
years and the climbing of Mount Everest.
For this new edition, a supplementary final
chapter has been added, carrying the story
through to 1964, and the Appendices have
been brought up to date. No changes have
been made in the body of the text.

Library of Congress Catalog Card Number: 64-24035

TO
THE HEROES ON EVEREST
AND
THE DUBS ON OLD BALDY

Have we vanquished an enemy?
None but ourselves.
George Leigh-Mallory

ACKNOWLEDGMENT

The stories related in the following pages have, for the most part, been taken from the original accounts of those who lived them, and my debt to these men and their writings is as great as it is obvious. Also—and specifically—my thanks for their kind helpfulness are due to Helen I. Buck, Eaton and Georgia Cromwell, Norman G. Dyhrenfurth, David Harrah, Charles S. Houston, Gail Oberlin, Paul Petzoldt and Bradford Washburn—mountaineers all.

CONTENTS

ILLUSTRATIONS

MAPS AND SKETCHES

FOREWORD

THIS BOOK derives from my earlier story of mountaineering, *High Conquest,* and carries on from the point where it left off. Specifically, that point was the year 1941, and in the interval, mountains, no less than the world at large, have seen their full share of history.

During the war, to be sure, there was little climbing activity, except for military purposes, and an inevitable lag followed before it was again possible to mount large and ambitious expeditions. By the late 'forties, however, a new mountaineering era had opened, and already it has become the most active in the history of the sport.

Pre-eminent, of course, has been the climbing of Everest—that soul-stirring climax to one of the great adventures of modern man. But Everest did not stand, or fall, alone. In the past few years three other Himalayan giants have been conquered: Annapurna by the French, Tirich Mir by Norwegians, and Nanga Parbat by a group of Germans and Austrians. Also there have been unsuccessful attempts on four more of earth's highest summits—by Americans on K2, Swiss on Dhaulagiri, Japanese on Manaslu, British on Cho Oyu—plus two Everest ventures by the Swiss and one by Russians. Note that on eleven expeditions nine nationalities were represented; add the fact that the conquerors of Everest were a New Zealander and a Himalayan native; and it becomes obvious that mountaineering is now among the most worldwide of human activities.

American climbers have played a full part. Besides the near-miss on K2, earth's second highest summit, they have made two notable first ascents in the Peruvian Andes—of Yerupajá and Salcantay—and scaled a whole host of peaks in Alaska and the Yukon. Since 1941 Mount McKinley, the rooftop of North America, has been climbed eight times, as against a total of twice in all the years preceding. Logan and St. Elias, ranking only slightly below it, have both been topped for the second time, and the remaining virgin peaks of the continent have been falling at the rate of at least one a year.

The techniques of mountaineering are constantly being refined, and there have been great improvements in climbing apparel and equipment. The plane, the radio, oxygen, the nylon rope, new fabrics, alloys and food concentrates, have all played a part in recent high-mountain ventures, helping the weak flesh to goals that would have been unattainable in an earlier day. Annapurna—Nanga Parbat—Everest the King: one by one the giants are toppling, as mountaineering enters its period of maximum efficiency.*

These are what might be called the "headline stories" of the past few years. But in America, at least, there has been still another story, and one that is perhaps even more important and significant. This is the tremendous increase of interest in mountaineering, which has brought it out from the province of the specialized few into the ken of almost everyone. Among the causes, of course, have been the great and dramatic ascents, and the subsequent books and motion pictures that have told of them. But this is by no means the whole of it. One contributing factor has been the introduction to climbing, during the war, of many young men who served with our mountain troops. Another, the great popularity of skiing, which has brought people to the mountains in ever-larger numbers. Still another, the continuing development of transportation facilities, which turns the wilderness of yesterday into the vacation playground of today. Strongest of all, perhaps, there has been, not an outward, but an inward cause: the deep and growing need of us all to offset the pressures and strains of modern living by some measure of contact with the simplicity and beauty of the natural world.

In any case, it seems to me that the events of recent years—and the widespread interest in them—are enough to warrant an up-to-dating of the story of mountaineering. And here it is. Some of the material is old; some new. The original cast of characters remains, and many other names have been added. The drama plays on as it began: a drama of aspiration and struggle, triumph and tragedy, set against the most spectacular stage setting that the earth provides.

Now the curtain rises. The axes and ropes are ready. The sky is bright. The peaks are waiting.

> Berg heil!
> A la montagne!
> Good climbing!
>
> J.R.U.

---

* The "period of maximum efficiency" referred to above has, in the decade since the lines were written, borne fruit that even the most optimistic could hardly have foreseen. In this new edition of *The Age of Mountaineering* a final supplementary chapter has therefore been added, continuing the story from 1954 to 1964.

THE AGE OF MOUNTAINEERING

NORTH PLATTE COLLEGE LIBRARY
NORTH PLATTE, NEBRASKA

1

GODS, DEMONS — AND MEN

THE SUN IS DOWN. Purple shadows race swiftly across the desolate Tibetan uplands, and the buildings of the ancient monastery in the valley are soon almost indistinguishable from the mountain rock. Presently, across the valley, there sounds the blare of trumpets—an eerie, monotonous note, long sustained, reverberating from the valley walls and the ice-fields far above. It is answered by a clash of cymbals and the tiny tinkling of prayer wheels. Men sit cross-legged and motionless on the terraces of the monastery, beside rough piles of stones in the surrounding waste, and at the mouths of caves cut in the living rock. They are yellow, weatherbeaten men in homespun robes and pointed hats: holy lamas of the Buddhist faith. They sit quietly while the dusk deepens, their eyes raised to the mountain that looms white and gigantic above them.

It is a magic mountain at which they are gazing—a sacred and supernatural mountain, ringed with mystery and a fear as old as night. It is the abode of spirits and demons. Great shadowy shapes with flaming eyes prowl the glaciers and, on the gaunt heights beyond, the ghosts of the departed hold black communion with the howling wind. The Evil Ones are there—Sukpas and Zhidags and Nitikanji—lurking in blue crevasses and behind the walls of precipices; and the bloodthirsty Snowmen, with long hair and tails, roam the high ridges under the stars. Woe to the mere mortal who would venture into this ice-shrouded world

15

5108

above the world. Woe to him who would violate the demon-guarded sanctuary of the mountain goddess.

The lamas of the Rongbuk Valley gaze up at the monstrous white pinnacle above them and slowly turn their prayer wheels. "Chomo-lungma," they murmur, "Goddess Mother of the World—"

The long shadows race swiftly up the mountainside. They fall on glacier and snow-field, precipice and ice-wall, and now at last on a sky-line ridge, ten thousand feet above the valley, where the tiny fig-ures of two men are moving upward toward the darkening sky. These men move with infinite slowness, their feet dragging on the ice-en-crusted rocks, their bodies bent almost double against the fury of snow and wind. Their faces are not yellow, but white, beneath their frosted beards; and on their heads, instead of pointed lamas' hats, are helmets of leather and fleece. Dark goggles cover their eyes, and they carry packs on their backs and ice-axes in their mittened hands. For a dozen steps they struggle on, then for another dozen, while their hearts pound to bursting, their lungs gasp for air, and the last light of day drains slowly from the sky. Then, suddenly, they stop. For a long while they stand motionless, leaning on their axes, staring upward.

Above them the desolate ridge twists on into space. Their eyes, strain-ing through the dusk, perceive neither beast nor demon nor goddess, nor do their ears hear the cries of the departed and damned. All that they see is the brown, snow-flecked rock slanting endlessly away; the only sound is the deep moaning of the wind. Yet the two men go no farther, for they know that to go farther is to die. The night is at hand; they have given to the last measure of their strength and will; and it has not been enough. The great white pinnacle of the mountain still looms above them in the darkness, inviolate as it has been since the beginning of time. One of the men starts slowly down. The other lingers for still another moment, gazing upward. Pain, exhaustion and disappointment lie on him like a leaden weight, but his eyes, behind their snow-fogged goggles, fix the summit with the deep, quiet chal-lenge of the undefeated.

"Just wait, old thing," he mutters between cracked and frozen lips, "we'll get you yet!"

More than thirty years have passed since a young Englishman named Geoffrey Bruce stared up at the unconquered crest of Mount Everest and spoke these words. But in the long-gone moments of that Himalayan dusk—and in the minds and hearts of those who watched it—lies the very essence of the story of mountains and men.

Why do men climb mountains?

The simplest, if perhaps an evasive, answer is that most men don't. Mountains are as old as the earth, mankind's contact with them as old as the race, but the compelling urge to climb and conquer is something very new under the sun. Ancient man did not climb. Primitive man does not climb. To the western mind the superstitions and rituals of the Rongbuk lamas, murmuring over prayer wheels as they gaze at their Chomolungma, may appear to bear slight relation to the world of fact and reality in which we live our lives. Actually, however, they spring from one of the most ancient and deep-rooted of all human attitudes, and the weight of history, of tradition, of the folkways of centuries lies behind them. It is not the Tibetan lamas, turning their wheels, but the men of the West, struggling up the mountainside high above them, who are the exotic and alien ones—the bearers of "a banner with a strange device."

The spirit of exploration and adventure is so ingrained a part of our modern western civilization that we are apt to take it for granted. Is there an unknown continent? We discover it. An unsailed sea? We cross it. A mysterious jungle or desert or mountain peak? We journey to the ends of the earth to find and know them and make them ours. These things have come to seem to us almost as natural and inevitable a part of life as eating and begetting and building shelters against the cold. Yet for the mass of mankind, down through the ages, this has not been the case at all. The unknown, the remote and inaccessible places of the earth have, to be sure, always had the power to stir the human imagination, but far more often to awe and dread than to inquiry and action. Modern man, staring at the horizon, sees beyond it a challenge and a promise; his ancestors, with rare exceptions, saw only darkness. The cross-legged Buddha was born into the world long before the wandering Faust.

Mountains and mountain ranges are the most impressive things that nature has created upon the earth, and from time immemorial they have been objects of superstition and fear. Among ancient peoples the world over, as among primitive people today, they were looked upon less as part of the actual earth than as a separate supernatural realm between the earth and sky—the half-world of gods and demons, the dwelling place of the dead. And though the legends and mythologies surrounding them varied greatly among different races and different eras, one belief remained constant: they were no place for mortal men. Long after the deserts and jungles and ocean wastes of the earth had given up their secrets the great peaks and ranges were still untouched, unvisited and unknown. They remained—and many of them remain today—the last frontier of our planet.

As recounted in the pages to come, the story of mountaineering will appear principally in the guise of physical adventure. It will be told in terms of where and when and how, of practical men and their practical problems, of rock and ice, ropes and axes, cold and storms and avalanches. And, indeed, it is of these things that mountain climbing largely consists. But it consists of something else besides, and without that "something else" its exploits would not have been worth the doing or its history worth the telling. Bruce on the wild northeast ridge of Everest and the lamas in the valley below were separated by far more than those ten thousand feet of precipices and glaciers. Other things than belays, barometers and lung-capacity are involved when what moves one man to nameless terror moves another to mutter defiantly: "We'll get you yet!" The history of mountaineering is not merely a story of the conquest of mountains, but of the conquest of fear. It is not merely the record of stirring deeds, but of a great adventure of the human spirit.

The mountains surrounding the Mediterranean basin were famous landmarks of the ancient world, and the records which have come down to us from olden times abound in references to great peaks and ranges. In some instances these are factual and historical; more often they are grounded in religion and mythology. But in virtually every case it is the spiritual rather than the physical nature of mountains with which the accounts are concerned.

Many of the most famous biblical stories have a mountain background: Noah on Ararat; Moses on Sinai and Pisgah; Jesus Himself going up into the mountain to pray and facing the supreme moments of His life on the Mount of Olives and Golgotha. The old Greek gods —though not the Greeks themselves—were mountaineers of the first order, and their fabled dwelling places, Olympus, Parnassus and Helicon, were among the most celebrated localities of early western civilization. Farther afield were the Atlas Range of Africa, where the Titan whose name they bore was reputed to carry the sky upon his shoulders, and the mysterious Caucasus, where Prometheus first stole fire from heaven. Indeed, there was scarcely a mountain in the known world of ancient times which the imaginations of men did not invest with an aura of legend.

Actual authenticated ascents, however, were few and far between. We know that the philosopher Empedocles ascended the volcano Etna, in Sicily (though he did not, as the story has it, kill himself by leaping into its crater); and during the period of the Roman Empire the same summit was surmounted by many climbers, among them the Emperor Hadrian. Philip V of Macedon climbed one of the peaks of the rugged Haemus Range and met the not-uncommon mountaineer's fate of finding only mist where he had hoped for a view. But aside from these and a few other sporadic ascents, the ancients were content to gaze up at their mountains from the plains below. They marveled at them; they worshiped them; they created great imaginative legends about them. But they did not climb them.

The long years of the Middle Ages, the Renaissance and the two centuries following it saw little change in the relationship between mountains and men. The horizons of mankind, to be sure, were slowly being pushed back, and factual knowledge was gradually impinging on the legends and superstitions of the ancient world; but the earth's high places still held their grip on the human imagination as realms of awe and dread. As late as the middle 1700's adventurous travelers would solemnly commend their souls to their Maker before risking the crossing of what today are considered the most prosaic Alpine passes, and to the occasional unhappy wanderer on the higher slopes it was merely a question of whether a bandit, a three-headed dragon or the ghost of Pontius Pilate would waylay him first.

It was no accident that men first began climbing mountains in the late eighteenth and early nineteenth centuries. On the contrary, it was a direct result of the profound changes that were occurring in the world and in men's ways of looking at it. This was the era of Napoleon and Goethe and Beethoven, of the American and French Revolutions, of the birth of science and democracy and the beginnings of industrial civilization. In every sphere of human thought and activity the bonds of ancient tradition were being broken; frontiers were pushed back with dazzling rapidity; and in the province of physical adventure, no less than in politics, science and the arts, man looked about with fresh and eager eyes. The Alps, towering above the very nub of Europe, had for unnumbered centuries moved him only to awe and terror. Now, suddenly, they were a challenge, beckoning him to try his new-found knowledge, skill and courage.

And the story of mountaineering began.

The climbers of the world's great mountains have been drawn from many nations and diverse backgrounds. The great majority, however, have been men of standing and achievement in fields far removed from mountaineering, and there are few among them who could fit the conventional mold of the professional athlete. Edward Whymper, A. F. Mummery and George Leigh-Mallory, three of the greatest figures in climbing history, were respectively an artist, a businessman and a member of the faculty at Cambridge University. De Saussure, who, if anyone, merits the title of "the father of mountaineering," was one of the foremost scientists of his time, as was John Tyndall, conqueror of the Weisshorn and many another Alpine summit; and a listing of those who have followed them would read like a complete roster of the arts and professions. To single out a few of more recent years, almost at random: Charles S. Houston, the outstanding American Himalayan climber, is a physician; Paul Bauer, of Kangchenjunga, a lawyer; N. E. Odell, of Everest and Nanda Devi, a geologist; Maurice Herzog, of Annapurna, an engineer. Among the others are clergymen, writers, teachers, nuclear physicists, university presidents and major generals. Perhaps the most intriguing of alter egos is that of Sir Edmund Hillary, conqueror of Everest, who is—of all things—a professional beekeeper.

One of the most active climbers in the Alps around the turn of the century was a young Italian priest named Abate Achille Ratti, who was later to become Pope Pius XI. Kings and princes have also been proud to count themselves among the mountaineers, notably the Duke of the Abruzzi, of the former royal house of Italy, who stalked great peaks across the world from Alaska to Central Africa, and, in later years, King Albert of the Belgians. It was as a climber, indeed, that Albert

perished, falling to his death while scaling a cliff in his native countryside. Other well-known men who have followed the mountain way
include the scientist Julian Huxley, the historian and United States
Senator Hiram Bingham, the conductor Dimitri Mitropoulos, and Supreme Court Justice William O. Douglas.

With certain notable exceptions, the earliest climbers were prepon-
derantly British, and Englishmen have maintained their key position in
the sport all the way to the summit of Everest. Over the years, however, the lure of the mountains has made itself increasingly felt throughout the world, until today there is scarcely a country that does not have
its devotees and experts, clubs and expeditions. In the Himalayas alone,
which even in the air age are scarcely on most nations' doorsteps, there
have, in the past few years, been climbing parties from almost every
country in western Europe, plus the United States, Latin America, Russia, Poland, Japan and New Zealand. Most significant of all, perhaps,
is that those greatest of mountain-fearers, the Himalayan natives themselves, have at last begun to climb—and no longer only for pay from
western employers, but because they too have felt the challenge of the
peaks. In gaining the top of Everest with Edmund Hillary, Tenzing
Bhotia, the Nepalese hillman, did far more than climb the highest summit on earth. He caused millions of his fellow-men to raise up their
eyes, for once, not in dread, but in joy and pride, and helped lift from
them the burden of centuries of superstition and ignorance.

From de Saussure to Tenzing, from peasants with hand-hewn staffs
to atomic scientists with radio-telephones and tanks of oxygen: these
are the men who have climbed to the earth's high places. In origin and
personality, way of living and way of climbing, they have differed
widely, one from another. So too have their goals and achievements.
With scarcely an exception, however, it has been the same questing
spirit, the same love of mountains, that has motivated them all; and,
taken together, they form as gallant and adventurous a company as
has existed in the modern world.

But why? the valley-goer still asks. Why do men deliberately turn
their backs on the hard-won security of their usual lives to face storm
and cold, hardship, danger and often death itself on lonely and savage
heights? Why walk when you can ride, climb when you can fly, struggle
when you can rest? What is the lure of Old Baldy, Knob Hill, Storm

King, Washington, Rainier, the Matterhorn, McKinley, Aconcagua, Annapurna, Everest? The ascent of Old Baldy and of Everest are very different things, to be sure; yet inwardly, in their essence, they are the same thing, and if the one baffles you, so too, in all likelihood, will the other.

The surest way *not* to understand a mountaineer is to suspect him of an ulterior and practical motive. Certainly it is not money that impells him, for no fortune was ever made on peak or glacier. Nor is it fame, for how many of even the greatest climbers are known by name to the general public? It is not power, nor prestige, nor—except on Hollywood mountains—the hand of a heroine. In a world full of golf courses and gymnasiums, it can scarcely be mere exercise; nor, in the air age, "the view." It is not even that most revered of modern sacred cows—science. True, research of various kinds has been a by-product of many mountain ventures. It has helped pay the way and presented a cloak of respectability for the eyes of "practical" onlookers. But one may be very sure that men who aspire, struggle and suffer as have those whose stories are told in this book are driven by far deeper and more human forces than a scholarly interest in rock strata, oxygen consumption or trigonometrical surveying.

It is not an incidental, but a fundamental, aspect of mountaineering that it is, by pragmatic standards, "useless." That its end is neither money nor fame nor power nor knowledge nor even victory. That it is one of those rare and precious human activities that man performs for their own sake, and for that alone. "Have we vanquished an enemy?" George Mallory once asked himself, standing with his companions upon a high, hard-won summit and looking down at the long way they had come. And there was only one answer: "None but ourselves."

The men of the mountains have climbed because they needed to climb; because that was the way they were made. Scanning the heights, they saw more than rock and ice and snow and the immense blue emptiness of the sky. They saw, too, a great challenge to their own qualities *as men;* a chance to conquer their own weakness, ignorance and fear; a struggle to match achievement to aspiration and reality to dream. In that struggle they have learned things about their own bodies and minds that most men can never know in their standardized routine of living. They have found the divine harmony and simplicity of the natural world, and themselves alive in it, a part of it. They have climbed up out of the valleys, not only to the outposts of our planet, but to new frontiers of human experience.

The mountaineering spirit is the possession of no small and specialized group of experts. It can be found equally in the words of Geoffrey Bruce, gasping and defiant on the heights of Everest, and in the whistling of two Sunday companions heading up toward Old Baldy for a look into the next county. It lies not in what men *do,* but in what they *are*—in the raising of their eyes and the lifting of their hearts.

2

AN ADVENTURE BEGINS

The Winning of the Alps

ALPS—1. *A range of mountains in Europe*
    2. *Any large range of mountains*
ALP—1. *Any mountain in the Alps*
    2. *An upland meadow or pasture*
    3. *Any mountain*
ALPINE—1. *Pertaining to the Alps*
    2. *Pertaining to any mountain*
ALPINIST—1. *A climber of the Alps*
    2. *A climber*
    (derivation uncertain)

THUS, IN EFFECT, the dictionary. And if the definitions add up to something less than conciseness, they still make one fact abundantly clear: the Alps—as a place, as a descriptive term, as an idea—are inseparable from the whole subject of mountains and mountaineering.

Furthermore, in a very real sense, they are inseparable from the history of western civilization. For uncounted centuries they formed the great natural rampart of the ancient world, separating the advanced nations of the Mediterranean basin from the barbarian hordes of the North. In later times they served as the rugged highroad of conquest, the steppingstone of Hannibal and Alaric the Goth and Napoleon in their wide-ranging forays which changed the map of the world. Towering between the plains of Germany and Italy, they were, only yesterday, the Mountains of the Axis.

This is the political history of the Alps. Happily, however, they have also another history—one that unfolds without benefit of kings and generals, clanking armies and rumbling caissons, and dictators plotting in the Brenner Pass. It is a story of men and the spirit of men and the interplay of that spirit with the physical world in which they live. It is a story of the slow, painful conquest of fear, of the gradual spread of knowledge, of the awakening of the world to the challenge of new frontiers. The Alps were the birthplace of mountaineering and the first great range of the earth to be climbed. This in itself is not important. What is important is that they were the first place where it ever even *occurred* to men to climb mountains—where not merely a sport was born, but an idea.

Two centuries ago scarcely a peak in Europe had been ascended; today scarcely one remains that has not, and the high white world above the valleys that was once a shunned and unknown wilderness has become rich in human associations. The winning of the Alps has been a struggle, to be sure—what meaningful human activity has not? It has been marred by pettiness and bitterness, ugly rivalries and jealousies, defeat and tragedy; for mountaineers, no less than kings and generals, are only human. But, in its essence, it has been a struggle not of man against man, nor even of man against the obstacles of the physical world, but of man against his own ignorance and fear.

This is the second history of the Alps. It is less familiar than the first; less important, no doubt, by the usual standards of men. The impression persists, however, that it is a history which does rather more credit to the human race.

In point of sheer size the Alps are not among the pre-eminent mountains of the earth. They do not compare to the Himalayas of Asia in height nor to the Rockies or Andes of the New World in extent. From the French Riviera to the environs of Vienna their over-all length is somewhat less than six hundred miles, and the elevation of their loftiest summits is in the 15,000-foot class, or roughly half the height of Everest.* What the Alps lack in sheer mass, however, is more than offset in beauty, variety and sharp dramatic impact. Their valleys and

* For the altitudes of the principal Alpine peaks see Appendix IV.

forests, twisting trails and plunging streams present an ever-changing panorama of soft loveliness and rugged majesty; their great peaks, passes and glaciers remain today, as they have been since men first climbed, the unrivaled paradise of mountaineers. "The Playground of Europe," the English climber-philosopher, Leslie Stephen, called them long ago. He might as rightly have called them the playground of the world.

It is a common supposition among many Americans that the Alps lie wholly, or almost wholly, in Switzerland. This, however, is far from the case. Only about one-third of the range is Swiss, another third is Italian, and the rest is divided equally between France and Austria, with a small segment of the latter section extending into southeastern Germany. Also, the Alps are by no means a continuous and unbroken chain, but are repeatedly split into sub-chains and lesser ranges by deep passes and valleys and even, in some instances, by open plains. The various districts thus formed are apt to differ greatly, one from another —in terrain and geological structure, in the nationality and language of their inhabitants, in the height of their peaks and their attractions for mountaineers. No true climber would make the mistake of returning home from a vacation and announcing to his colleagues merely that he had been climbing in the Alps. The answer would inevitably be: "What Alps?"

The southwesternmost spurs of the range rise from the Mediterranean Sea along the French and Italian Rivieras. Roughly paralleling the frontier of the two countries, they are known successively as the Maritime and Cottian Alps and, together, extend northward for some hundred miles to the pass of Mont Cenis. The average elevation of this region is not high, and there is little to attract the mountaineer, with the exception of Monte Viso, in the Italian Cottians, one of the most beautiful of all Alpine peaks.

Northwest of the Cottians rise the Dauphiné Alps, centering about Grenoble and wholly French. This is a district of steep uplands and bold rock-towers which in recent years has become a favorite climbing ground for expert cragsmen and has been the scene of some of the most difficult and sensational ascents ever made. The most famous summits are Mont Pelvoux, Les Ecrins and La Meije, the last-named having been among the latest of the major Alpine peaks to be conquered.

The Graian and Tarentaise Alps lie northeast of the Dauphiné, between Mont Cenis and the Little St. Bernard Pass, the former on the French-Italian border, the latter altogether in France. There are many fine mountains in this region—notably the Grand Paradis, the Grande-Casse and the Grivola—but they are rather difficult of access and have been infrequently climbed.

Beyond the Little St. Bernard, near the point where France, Italy and Switzerland come together, the mountains suddenly expand on to the grand scale. Here towers the Mont Blanc range, topped by the great peak itself, which, at 15,782 feet, is the highest of the Alps. This vast massif presents so many claims to fame in the history of mountaineering that it is virtually impossible even to list them. It was the scene of the first extensive mountain explorations, of the first major ascents, of the development of modern rock-climbing, and of many of the most famous climbing exploits of the last seventy-five years. It was here that the profession of guiding had its beginnings. It was here that almost every noted European climber from de Saussure to the present day served his apprenticeship and, in many cases, performed his finest feats.

The Mont Blanc range is unsurpassed in Europe for the grandeur of its scenery and in the whole world for the quality and variety of the climbing which it affords. The main peak itself is predominantly a snow-mountain, presenting today more than twenty recognized routes of ascent of all degrees of difficulty. Crowded around it is a veritable army of lesser summits—domes, knobs, towers, spires—some of them also snow-covered, more rising in bare bristling granite from their skirts of glaciers. Most notable of all, perhaps, are the famous and aptly named *aiguilles* (or needles) of Chamonix: du Plan, du Midi, de Triolet, d'Argentière and the rest, topped by the fabulous Aiguille Verte. Others are the Grandes Jorasses, the Charmoz, the Grépon, Mont Dolent, the Dru, the Géant, the Requin—the list is all but endless; and every one is of such structure and form that it might almost have been built to specification for mountaineers. All these lie close within the shadow of Mont Blanc, ranging like great spiky sentinels around the famous glacier of the Mer de Glace. Further afield, across the valley of Chamonix, a smaller but equally fine chain of peaks known as the Aiguilles Rouges runs northward along the French-Swiss border toward the uplifts of the Buet and the Dents du Midi.

Beyond Mont Blanc, however, the main backbone of the Alps makes a right-angle turn and sweeps eastward in the towering chain of the

THE ALPS

High above the heart of Europe the most famous mountains in the world sweep in a great bow six hundred miles long—from the French Riviera to the environs of Vienna. The Alps are by no means synonymous with Switzerland. Their ramparts rise from the soil of five different nations: France, Italy, Switzerland, Austria and Germany. Their loftiest peaks, however, are concentrated in a comparatively small area between Innsbruck, on the east, and Chamonix, on the west. Here rise the three greatest sub-ranges of the Alps—the Mont Blanc uplift, the Pennines and the Bernese Oberland—containing hundreds of the most celebrated and most frequently climbed mountains on earth.

Pennines. Bounded by the famous passes of the Great St. Bernard and the Simplon, this range boasts the highest average elevation of any in the Alps and presents a galaxy of world-famous peaks. Here rise the Breithorn, the Lyskamm, the Grand Combin, the Dent d'Hérens, the twins Castor and Pollux, the gigantic snow-dome of Monte Rosa and the incomparable Matterhorn *—a towering international rampart with its northern slopes in Switzerland and its southern in Italy. Slightly to the north and wholly in Swiss territory are a host of others no less impressive: the Obergabelhorn, the Zinal-Rothorn, the Dent Blanche, the Strahlhorn, the Weisshorn—the picture-book mountain—and, loftiest of all, the great mass of the Mischabel, which in itself comprises a whole sub-range of peaks, topped by the Täschhorn and the Dom. The principal climbing centers in this region are Zermatt, on the Swiss side, and Breuil, on the Italian, and over a period of three-quarters of a century they have witnessed many of the most celebrated exploits in mountaineering history.

North of the Pennines and separated from them by the upper Rhone valley lies the jumble of peaks, valleys, passes and glaciers known as the Bernese Oberland. This is the heart of Switzerland, and though its summits are not quite so high as those of Mont Blanc and the Pennines, it yields to neither in majesty of scenery or attraction for the mountaineer. The most famous summits, many of them rising like the walls of an amphitheatre about the little town of Grindelwald, include the Schreckhorn, the Wetterhorn, the Finsteraarhorn, the Blümlisalp, the Aletschhorn, the Bietschhorn and, pre-eminently, the great triumvirate of Jungfrau, Mönch and Eiger. The imagination can spin drama out of the very names of these three—the Virgin, the Monk and the Ogre. The Oberland, lying within easy traveling distance of Interlaken and Lucerne, is more accessible from northern Europe than most sections of the Alps and over the years has probably been the scene of greater climbing activity than any other high mountain region in the world.

Mont Blanc, the Pennines and the Oberland are the culminating points of the Alps. Further east, the range still sweeps on for hundreds of miles—to the Adriatic, to the outskirts of Munich and Vienna—but it never again quite matches the height and grandeur of these three huge uplifts.

---

* The French called the Matterhorn Mont Cervin; the Italian Monte Cervino. The English, however, and climbers generally, know it by its German name.

Even more than in the west, it now spreads out into separately designated sub-ranges. In the south the Lepontine Alps continue the rampart begun by the Pennines along the Swiss-Italian frontier, extending for some seventy-five miles from the Simplon to the Splügen Pass and cut in two by the celebrated St. Gotthard. The outstanding summits here are Monte Leone, Pizzo Rotondo and the Rheinwaldhorn. Still further on are the Albula, Bergamasque and Rhaetian ranges, the last-named distinguished by the magnificent isolated peak of Monte della Disgrazia, and beyond them the Dolomites, the Carnic Alps and the Julian Alps, curving down in a great horseshoe toward the Adriatic. Of these, the Dolomites, centered about the Italian town of Cortina, are of special interest. Formed of a peculiar type of limestone, known likewise as dolomite, they are bold in outline, strikingly reddish in hue, and present a rough, almost sponge-like outer surface unmatched anywhere else in the Alps. Mountaineering on this range is limited in its scope, as there is virtually no ice or snow, but some of the most sensational rock-climbing of recent years has been accomplished upon its precipices, chimneys and giddy pinnacles.

The Bernina and Silvretta Alps, a northward continuation of the Rhaetians, lie east of the Lepontines between the Splügen Pass and the Austrian border. This is the region known as the Engadine, and its center is the international resort of St. Moritz. The Berninas are for the most part massive snowpeaks, better suited to ski mountaineering than to the more usual forms of climbing. Among the outstanding summits are the Piz Bernina, itself, Piz Roseg, Piz Scersen and Piz Palu, the last-named ranking among the most photographed mountains of the world. The Silvretta group, farther to the north, culminate in the impressive summit of Piz Linard, and beyond it the range fans out into the numerous, but less important, chains of northeastern Switzerland.

The Austrian Alps sweep eastward from the Swiss border, past Innsbruck, toward Salzburg and Vienna. They completely fill the narrow corridor between Italy and Bavaria, and are cut laterally into two roughly equal sections by the broad gash of the Brenner Pass. West of the Brenner the principal peaks are, from north to south, the Zugspitze, the Wildspitze, the Weisskugel and the great massif of the Ortler, perhaps the finest uplift of the eastern Alps. Actually, neither the first nor last of these lies in Austrian territory—the Zugspitze is just over the line in Bavaria, and the Ortler since the First World War has been

wholly Italian—but both are nevertheless part and parcel of the Tyro-
lese chain. East of the Brenner are the Zillerthal mountains and the
outstanding massifs of the Gross Venediger and the Gross Glockner;
then, finally, comes the outpost peak of the Hohe Dachstein, and great
ranges slope gradually away into the rolling forest-land of central
Austria.

These are the Alps. For some thirty thousand centuries their white
crests loomed above the heart of Europe, as remote from the tides of
life as if they stood upon the surface of another planet.

Indeed, it is hard to say just when what we may call their human
history began. The ancient Romans were familiar with them, of course,
and many records have come down to us of their legions marching
through the passes of the Brenner and the St. Bernard; but there is no
indication of their having ascended, or even attempted, any of the
actual peaks. In fact, Monte Viso, the great white watchtower at the
source of the Po, is the only Alpine summit to be mentioned by name
in all the surviving writings of the old historians. The Romans were
conquerors and explorers, but they were no mountaineers.

Then came the Middle Ages and silence.

A few accounts exist of sporadic ventures in the foothills of the Alps
during the thirteenth and fourteenth centuries, but the first complete
and authenticated ascent of a peak did not take place until late in the
fifteenth—in fact in the significant year 1492. This was the climbing
of Mont Aiguille in the Dauphiné by one Antoine de Ville of Grenoble.
Undertaken at the command of King Charles VIII of France, it was a
truly remarkable exploit, for the Aiguille, though not high, is a steep
and formidable rock tower. Even today its ascent is considered a fairly
difficult one; four hundred and fifty years ago it was all but miraculous.

The sixteenth century was the age of the High Renaissance and, as
might be expected, marked the beginnings of the first fairly systematic
exploration of the Alps. In the forefront of the pioneers was no less a
figure than Leonardo da Vinci, that universal genius who made the
whole realm of human knowledge his own; and we find him, as early
as 1500, venturing high on the southern slopes of the Pennines in the
interest of meteorological investigation. More truly mountaineers, however, were a group of men who a few years later began climbing and
exploring among the ranges of northern Switzerland. Their leading

WORLD ABOVE

From the very nub of Europe rises the white wilderness of the Alps. This is a winter scene in the Pennines, with the Matterhorn, the Dent d'Herens rising massively in the middle distance.

Instituto di Fotografia Alpina "Vittorio Sella"

THE APEX OF EUROPE

The huge white mass of Mont Blanc, rising above the French valley of Chamonix. Beginning with the famous early ascents, this is the side of the mountain that has been most frequently climbed.

Photo by Burton Holmes from Ewing Galloway

spirits were Conrad Gesner and Josias Simler, professors at the University of Zurich, and their writings are the first of which we have any record that exhibit an interest in mountains and mountain climbing for their own sake. The actual ascents made by Gesner, Simler and their followers are unimportant—the highest was probably the 7,000-foot Pilatus on the shores of Lake Lucerne—but they did more than anyone before them to dispel the age-old fear with which men regarded the high places of the Alps.

The next two hundred years, however, saw little progress, and as late as 1725 "authoritative" guides to Switzerland were being published which included detailed descriptions and classifications of Alpine dragons. Then gradually, in the middle of the eighteenth century, a profound change began to occur. It was a change, to be sure, that extended far beyond the province of mountains and mountaineering, into the whole fabric of men's lives and ways of thought. The American and French Revolutions were in the making; democracy, capitalism, science, the industrial revolution—a thousand new concepts and institutions were evolving slowly out of the doldrums of an outworn and stagnant civilization. And, in key with the times, men presently found themselves eyeing the Alps with a new perspective and a clearer vision. Travelers on the celebrated "Grand Tour" no longer gazed up from their valley inns with horror, but with admiring awe. Naturalists and other curious wanderers pushed up toward the treeless slopes and the high glacial passes. Books and pamphlets were circulated in ever-increasing numbers, dealing not with dragons, but with climate, flora, fauna, rock structure, glaciers. Strongest and clearest of all was the voice of Rousseau, the impassioned prophet of the new order. His *La Nouvelle Héloïse,* in fact, published in 1769 and devoted largely to the glorification of untamed nature, had perhaps the widest circulation and greatest influence of any book of its time.

The horizons of the world were expanding again, as they had during the Renaissance and in the golden age of Greece. All Europe was astir with ideas and events, and great exploits were at hand—in the Alps as elsewhere.

England has its 1066, the New World its 1492, the United States its 1776. The first great date in the story of mountaineering is 1786, the year of the climbing of Mont Blanc.

Mont Blanc is not only the highest of the Alps; it is the highest mountain in Europe west of the Caucasus. Situated some fifty miles southeast
of Geneva, on the high frontier where France, Italy and Switzerland
meet, its summit is wholly French, but its slopes build up from the territory of all three nations, making it one of the most truly international
of mountains. It is as impressive as it is huge. A snow-peak rather than
a rock-peak, it rises from an enormously broad base in a great sweep of
glaciers, soars for thousands of feet in a maze of plateaus and ice-walls,
ridges and sub-peaks, and culminates in a massive buttressed summit like
the dome of a cathedral. Seen from whatever side, it completely dominates its surroundings, appearing from the distance less a mountain
among mountains than a single blindingly white mass suspended in the
sky.

Unlike most of the world's great peaks, Mont Blanc has long been
familiar to men. Many of the ancient trade routes of Europe passed
within view of its shining summit, and as early as the eleventh century
a priory had been established in the French valley of Chamonix at its
very base. Like all other mountains, however, it remained for hundreds
of years an object of fear and superstitious legend, and it is not until
after 1700 that we have any record of men approaching even so far as
its lower slopes and glaciers. These earliest pioneers were crystal-seekers
and chamois-hunters, and, while they contributed little to the actual
exploration of the mountain, they at least brought back the cheering
tidings that the expected demons and dragons had failed to materialize.
Soon others were following where they had blazed the way—scientists,
travelers, adventuresome spirits from all parts of Europe. By the middle
years of the eighteenth century the terrain surrounding Mont Blanc had
been fairly well explored, its great snow-dome was established as one
of the celebrated "sights" of the continent, and Chamonix was already
on its way to becoming the famous international resort it has remained
ever since.

Scientist, tourist and peasant alike, however, were content to go
about their business in the valleys and gaze up at the mountain from
afar, and it remained for one man to look upon it and feel its challenge
and say to himself the magic words: "I must get to the top." The man
was Horace Bénédict de Saussure, and he was to become the first, and
one of the greatest, of mountaineers.

Looked at from the perspective of almost two centuries, de Saussure is a remarkable figure. A native of Geneva, he was both a man of wealth and social position and a scholar whose researches in the natural sciences had made his name known throughout Europe. Visiting Chamonix in 1760 in pursuance of his study of glaciers, he conceived the idea, undreamed of by any others, that Mont Blanc could—and should —be climbed, and a great part of his labors and energies for more than a quarter of a century thereafter were devoted to that end. To be sure, there was no such thing as a mountaineer at the time; neither the word nor the idea existed. De Saussure himself, in almost all his writings, refers to his great project as a purely scientific venture, devoted to geological study and observation. But only one kind of man could have known feelings such as he recorded after one of his many visits to Chamonix. "It became for me a kind of illness," he wrote. "I could not even look upon the mountain, which is visible from so many points round about, without being seized with an aching of desire."

Whether or not the word then existed, de Saussure was a mountaineer.

Chiefly as a result of his enthusiasm and planning, several attempts were made on Mont Blanc between 1775 and 1785. All of them, including one by de Saussure himself, fell far short of the goal; but each successive venture added something to men's knowledge of the mountain and, more important still, resulted in the development in Chamonix of a sizable group of skilled and experienced climbers—the forerunners of the professional Alpine guides. By the summer of 1786 de Saussure was no longer alone in his belief that the mighty summit could be attained. The mountain had at last fired the imagination of others, and the struggle for its conquest began in earnest.

As it turned out, it was to be a struggle that is unique in mountaineering annals. The records of most great climbs are concerned primarily with physical obstacles met and overcome—with glaciers, precipices and ridges, cold, altitude and storms. The conquerors of Mont Blanc, to be sure, encountered their full share of these, and their exploits bear full witness to their skill and courage. But the basic drama of the story is concerned with the characters and personalities of the men involved. For in its whole subsequent history it is doubtful if mountaineering supplies a more pointed example of both the good and the bad that it can generate in its followers.

De Saussure was the motivating force behind every attempt to climb the mountain and the dominant figure in its conquest. But the men who were the first to stand upon its summit were Michel Gabriel Paccard and Jacques Balmat. Paccard was a physician of Chamonix, Balmat a peasant guide and crystal-hunter. Despite great differences in background and education, however, the two men were as one in their love of mountains, and both had been fired by de Saussure's enthusiasm to vanquish the great peak that overlooked their native valley. Over a period of several years each on his own had made extensive reconnaissances of the approaches to the summit. Then at last, on the morning of August 7, 1786, they set out together to reach it.

The external facts of their epoch-making ascent are simple and well known. Ascending steadily all through the first day, Paccard and Balmat worked their way up the great glaciers that buttress the Chamonix face of the mountain. After several hours they traversed to the more stable footing of the so-called Montagne de la Côte, a long tongue of solid ground running far up into the higher slopes, and, following it to its top, came out on the jagged prominence where the oft-visited Grands Mulets hut stands today. Near here they spent the night, improvising a tiny shelter. The next morning, frostbitten but undaunted, they pushed on, passing in turn over two great tilted snow-fields known as the Petit Plateau and the Grand Plateau and then inching up a precarious snow-ridge between two bands of outcropping rock.* This passage, as it turned out, was the crux of the ascent. There remained only the gentle white slopes of the summit dome, and at six-thirty in the evening the two adventurers were standing, exhausted but triumphant, on the highest pinnacle of the highest mountain in the Alps. Forty-eight hours later, after an arduous descent, they stumbled into Chamonix, to be greeted as heroes by their rejoicing fellow-townsmen.

Thus was Mont Blanc won; but the real struggle over its winning was yet to come. The peasant Balmat was unfortunately a man whose head was easily turned by success and fame, and he promptly began boasting to all who would listen that it was he and he alone who deserved credit for the great ascent. Paccard, he claimed, had been merely

---

* These rock-bands, immediately beneath the summit dome, are called the Rochers Rouges and are a distinguishing feature of the upper mountain as seen from Chamonix. Paccard's and Balmat's route passed between them, but de Saussure, on his ascent, followed the snow above the upper band. This latter route was soon to become one of the most famous in the Alps and is known today as the *"Ancien Passage."*

excess baggage. It had been he, Balmat, who had discovered the route to the summit, hacked out the laborious way and, indeed, all but carried the poor doctor on his shoulders during most of the climb. It was not long before rumors were circulating to the effect that Paccard had not reached the summit at all.

It is doubtful if much credence would have been given Balmat's tale had it not been for the entrance into the controversy of still another figure—one Marc Théodore Bourrit. Bourrit was a Swiss writer and journalist of some note at the time and a recognized authority on Alpine exploration. For years past he had been among those who believed that Mont Blanc could be climbed and had, indeed, made several attempts of his own to gain the summit. All of them had been complete failures, but he nevertheless clung to the hope that he would be the first to reach the famous summit, and he watched his various rivals with a sharp and jealous eye. The result was that when Paccard, whom he particularly resented, won the coveted prize, he threw himself vigorously into the work of discrediting him. Soon after the ascent he published a pamphlet which supported, and even elaborated, Balmat's story, and for years thereafter lost no opportunity to minimize the doctor's role in the exploit.

Indeed, Bourrit may be said to have established what is probably an all-time endurance record for spite, for, as late as 1832, when he was an old man of seventy, we find him repeating his story to no less a personage than Alexandre Dumas the elder. Dumas took his account at its face value, and his subsequent "history" of the conquest of Mont Blanc, based on Bourrit's version, enjoyed world-wide circulation and went unchallenged for many years. It is only comparatively recently that historians of mountaineering have uncovered the authentic records of the venture, which indicate that Paccard was not only its moving spirit but the pathfinder and leader through most of the ascent.

In pleasant contrast to the machinations of Bourrit and Balmat was the conduct of de Saussure. Disappointed though he must have been at not being the first to the summit, he was generous in his praise of the victors and in the following summer of 1787 returned again to Chamonix for yet another try on his own. He was not even to be second up, however, for in early June of that year, while he was still busy with preparations, Balmat again reached the top of Mont Blanc, this time in company with two fellow-guides. Nevertheless, de Saussure proceeded with his plans and at last, on the first of August, set out on his long-dreamed-of venture.

From the strictly mountaineering point of view de Saussure's ascent of Mont Blanc is of interest today chiefly as a curiosity. The huge climbing party consisted of no less than twenty persons: the scientist himself, eighteen guides headed by Balmat, and—of all things—de Saussure's valet, who had never been on a mountain in his life. They were loaded down with an enormous quantity of provisions and heavy scientific instruments, as well as much primitive climbing equipment and large crepe masks to shield their eyes from the sun's glare; and through much of the ascent were strung out haphazardly along the steep slopes in a fashion that would cause a present-day Alpinist to shudder. The glimpses we are given of de Saussure himself show him plodding upward between two guides, one hand resting on an alpenstock which they hold between him and the precipice as a railing. There were constant minor mishaps, long arguments as to routes and campsites, threatened mutinies and desertions. But in the end de Saussure's resolute spirit prevailed, and late afternoon of the second day found virtually the entire party crowded exultantly together on the summit. A full four and a half hours were spent there, devoted to scientific observations and recordings; then through the two succeeding days the caravan staggered triumphantly down to the valley.

Almost without exception it is the first ascent of a mountain that becomes the famous ascent. This was not, however, to be the case with Mont Blanc: de Saussure's climb was destined not only to eclipse that of his predecessors but to become, in a historical sense, one of the most important single events in the history of mountaineering. Paccard and Balmat were obscure French villagers, and their exploit was of small interest to a world that had not yet awakened to the challenge of mountains. De Saussure, on the other hand, was both an aristocrat and an internationally known scientist. All Europe, figuratively, watched and held its breath as he struggled to the summit of the highest Alp, and his success and subsequent writings about it had the effect of wiping away, almost in one stroke, the age-old terror and superstition with which men regarded the high places of the earth. . . . "Lift up thine eyes unto the hills," adjure the Scriptures. Now at last, with de Saussure's conquest of Mont Blanc, the world lifted them for the first time without fear.

The true birth of mountaineering as a sport was, however, still far in the future. For more than half a century ninety per cent of the climbing in the Alps consisted of endless ascents and reascents of Mont Blanc, and although a few new trails were blazed and various improvements made in technique and equipment, the majority of climbers were content to follow the routes and methods of the pioneers. The fourth ascent of the peak was made by an Englishman, Colonel Beaufoy, less than a week after de Saussure's successful climb, the fifth by another Englishman, Woodley, the following year. Woodley was accompanied on his ascent by the journalist Bourrit, but the latter gave out when only a few hundred feet from the top. Indeed, it is an ironic instance of poetic justice that he never succeeded in reaching it.

The French Revolution and the Napoleonic Wars put a pause to climbing for a considerable period around the turn of the century, but after 1818 activity was resumed and increased steadily thereafter. Among the milestone-ascents were that by the first American party, in 1819, and that by the first great woman-mountaineer, Henriette d'Angeville, in 1838. Although no one knows how often Mont Blanc has been scaled in the past hundred-odd years, it is safe to say that the figure runs into the tens of thousands—the climbers running the gamut from children to graybeards and from Pope Pius XI to John Barrymore.

It is elsewhere, however, that we must look for the next early developments in the struggle between mountains and men. While the great snow-peak of Chamonix basked in the spotlight and drew the tourists, a small group of adventurous men were gradually filtering into other and less-known regions of the Alps, exploring the passes and glaciers, working their way ever higher and higher toward the peaks. Outstanding among these were the members of a wealthy Swiss merchant family named Meyer, who ranged widely through the Bernese Oberland during the early years of the nineteenth century and among other exploits accomplished, in 1811, the first ascent of the famous Jungfrau. Another important pioneer was J. D. Forbes, who, though actually a Scot, may yet properly be called the first true British mountaineer. Between 1827 and 1844 Forbes visited virtually every district of the Alps, from the Dauphiné to the Dolomites, crossing the high passes and glaciers, cir-

cling the peaks, breaking new ground wherever he went. His record of
first ascents, like that of the Meyers, was impressive, but even more
important, perhaps, was the interest which his expeditions aroused
among his fellow-countrymen. It was he, in fact, more than any other
man, who was responsible for the development of that whole school of
British climbers who were soon to make the realm of the Alps so completely and brilliantly their own.

As the century grew older other influences were also at work, turning
the eyes and ambitions of men toward high places. The industrial revolution had created in Europe an upper-middle class with the means and
leisure for extended journeys. Furthermore it had provided railroads
which put the Alps within easy traveling distance of the great cities of
the North, and each year such resorts as Chamonix, Zermatt and Grindelwald were thronged with larger crowds of tourists. The work of
the Swiss-American naturalist, Louis Agassiz, focused the attention of
science on the geology of mountains and the movements of glaciers; in
the field of literature, John Ruskin, picking up the torch where Rousseau had dropped it, preached eloquently not only of the physical, but
the spiritual grandeur of the great peaks and ranges; and on every hand
pamphlets, guidebooks and travel-brochures on the Alps were making
an appearance and gaining wide circulation.

To all this was presently added the phenomenal influence of one Dr.
Albert Smith. Smith, by profession, was an English physician, but in
inclination and talent he was a showman and high-pressure publicity
agent. Having made the ascent of Mont Blanc in 1851, he conceived
the idea of making a good thing of it commercially, and accordingly,
the following year, produced at a London theatre a show purporting to
be based on his experiences. The show, which took the form of an illustrated lecture and featured the wildest kind of melodrama, was an
instant and huge success, running for six consecutive years and bringing
mountains and mountaineering to the attention of a wide public which
would never have heard of them through a hundred years of scientific
treatises and literary essays. Indeed, not a few of the earliest English
climbers themselves, who were for the most part highly educated men,
were by their own admission first exposed to the lure of the Alps
through the medium of Dr. Smith's penny-dreadful thriller.

At all events, the tide was rising, and the time was at hand when it
was to be in flood.

By the middle of the century a total of perhaps a hundred Alpine peaks had been ascended. These included, besides Mont Blanc and the Jungfrau, such famous summits as the Ortler, the Finsteraarhorn, the Gross Venediger, Mont Pelvoux, and all but the very highest pinnacle of Monte Rosa, as well as many others slightly less celebrated. But the climbing had been done by only a few scattered enthusiasts over a long period of years, and it remained for the 1850's to witness the first large-scale invasion of the mountains and the emergence of climbing as a recognized and widely practiced sport.

1854 is generally accepted as the date on which the so-called "Golden Age" of mountaineering began. Almost as if by a prearranged signal, a throng of ambitious and accomplished climbers made their appearance in the Alps during the summer of that year, reconnoitering, exploring, wandering far and high afield into the realms of rock and snow where no men had ever been before. In 1855 their number was larger, in 1856 still larger, and throughout the next decade the invasion swelled by leaps and bounds. One by one, ten by ten, finally hundred by hundred, the great summits began to fall before the onslaught, among them vast, awe-inspiring mountain-masses which until a few years before had seemed destined to remain unclimbed until the end of time. The outstanding conquest of 1854 was the Wetterhorn. The following summer came the highest point of Monte Rosa; in 1857 the Mönch; in '58 the Dom; between '59 and '64 the Bietschhorn, the Aletschhorn, the Grand Combin, the Dent Blanche, Monte Viso, the Schreckhorn, the Lyskamm, Disgrazia, the Grandes Jorasses, the Täschhorn, the Weisshorn. The list, indeed, is almost endless, and in 1865, when the tide culminated in the conquest of the fabled Matterhorn, only a negligible handful of virgin summits remained throughout the length and breadth of the Alps.

The climbers of this halcyon period were almost exclusively English. Forbes, who may well be called the godfather of them all, had retired from active mountaineering some time before, but there were now hundreds of his countrymen ready to take up where he had left off, and during the years that followed one might almost have thought the Alps were actually British, rather than Swiss and French, Italian and Austrian. The great names among these early climbers were legion, and scant justice can be done most of them in a record that must perforce skip over decades in seven-league boots. Outstanding among them were the Reverend Charles Hudson, Alfred Wills, Leslie Stephen, John Tyndall, A. W. Moore, F. F. Tuckett, E. S. Kennedy, and pre-eminently, Edward Whymper, who was to become one of the most dramatic figures in the history of mountaineering. Many of these men are best remembered for the conquest of one or more specific peaks—Wills for the Wetterhorn, for example, Tyndall for the Weisshorn, Whymper and Hudson for the Matterhorn. But few of them, it should be noted, were mere one-peak adventurers like the majority of their predecessors on Mont Blanc. They were mountaineers in the truest sense—wide-ranging, catholic in their interests, loving the mountains for their own sake as well as for such triumphs as they could win from them—and their legacy to the infant sport of climbing was far more than a statistical record of "famous firsts."

Indeed, the whole term "Golden Age," signifies much more than a lot of men climbing a lot of peaks at random. Mountaineering was still primarily an adventure—in any age and under any circumstances it is primarily that—but the conquerors of the Alps were not long in discovering that it could also be a craft, a science and an art. Each year, during the 'fifties and 'sixties, climbers came to know more about the structure and behavior of mountains, about glaciers and crevasses, sound rock and rotten rock, stonefalls and avalanches, and the other phenomena of the high, untrodden world above the trees. Route-finding, bivouacking and the use of alpenstock and rope were brought to a new degree of efficiency. The ice-ax, second in importance only to the rope among the climber's tools, was devised and perfected. The profession of guiding developed rapidly, not only in the number of practitioners but in standards of performance. Guidebooks and maps were published, routes marked out, huts and shelters built. And, with the formation in 1857 of the Alpine Club of London, a means was provided for the promotion and collation of mountaineering knowledge and the future of the newborn sport was assured.

So many noteworthy climbs were made during this prodigal period that it is almost impossible to single out any of them as being of greater interest or importance than the others. Wills' conquest of the Wetterhorn stands out not so much because of its actual difficulties, but because it headed the parade. In 1855 came one of the historic exploits of Hudson and Kennedy—the climbing of Mont Blanc by a new route and without guides. The ascent of Disgrazia in 1862, by Stephen and

Kennedy, was a remarkable feat; so too was that of the Lyskamm, a year earlier, by a party of no less than fourteen members. Perhaps the greatest of all—also accomplished in 1861—was the magnificent struggle of Tyndall and his guide Bennen up the huge pyramid of the Weisshorn—a peak whose reputation for invincibility was second only to that of the terrible Matterhorn.

Yet the true significance of the period is to be found less in such individual exploits, extraordinary though many of them were, than in the cumulative results of them all. At its inception ninety per cent of the great Alpine summits were still untouched, unknown, as they had been for three million years. At its close ninety per cent had been ascended. Before 1854 a man climbing a mountain was simply—a man climbing a mountain. A decade later he was a mountaineer. The Alps had been won, a sport born.

A MOUNTAIN AND A MAN

The Ascent of the Matterhorn

LATE IN THE MORNING of July 15, 1865, three dazed, exhausted men stumbled down from the glaciers into the Swiss village of Zermatt. They were returning from the conquest of the most famous mountain of Europe, but there was no spring to their step, no light of victory in their eyes. Swiftly and silently the villagers gathered around them, and in the eyes of all there was but one sombre question:

"Where are the other four?"

It was then that Edward Whymper told the story of the climbing of the Matterhorn. And today, almost a century later, it is still one of the great, tragic adventure stories of the world.

There are hundreds of mountains higher than the Matterhorn; there are hundreds that are harder to climb. But there is none, anywhere in the world, which has so consistently and deeply stirred the imagination of men. Rising in an immense isolated pyramid on the frontier between Switzerland and Italy, it possesses not only the dimensions, but the stark simplicity, of greatness, and its sprawling neighbor-peaks, some of which actually exceed its 14,782-foot altitude, seem to shrink into insignificance beside it. Through all the centuries that men have known the Alps their eyes have been drawn irresistibly upward to its savage, soaring pinnacle. Other mountains were—well—mountains. This mountain was beauty and magic and terror.

In the early 'sixties of the last century the Matterhorn was as famous as it is today—but for a different reason. The previous decade, as we have seen, had been the great age of Alpine mountaineering, and with the first ascent of the Weisshorn by Tyndall in 1861, virtually all the great peaks of the range had fallen. All, that is, save one, for the Matterhorn still towered into the sky, untouched and unchallenged as it had been since the beginning of time. But men scarcely counted it in their reckonings. The Swiss and Italian peasants of the surrounding valleys looked up at its cloud-hung battlements with superstitious awe and spoke fearfully of a ruined city on the summit where ghosts and demons dwelt. Even the unsuperstitious—travelers, scientists and mountaineers from all over Europe—stared at it in fascination, shook their heads, and turned away. True, there had been a half dozen or so attempts to gain the upper reaches of the peak, but all had been utterly defeated, and none who returned held out any hope for future success. The Matterhorn, men were agreed, was not only an unconquered mountain. It was unconquerable.

They did not know that in the summer of 1860 Edward Whymper had made his first visit to the Alps.

In that year Whymper was only twenty and had as yet made none of the ascents which were to make him the foremost mountaineer of his day. Indeed, he did not know that he was a mountaineer at all. An artist and illustrator by profession, he came to Switzerland from England for a few weeks of sketching and intended to do no more climbing than was necessary to find vantage points for his easel and brush. But the great peaks cast their spell upon him, and the fever to climb and conquer came into his blood. Alone and with local guides, he made many notable climbs, but, once his eyes had feasted on the fabulous Matterhorn, all else became of secondary interest to him. Here, he told himself, was a mountain fashioned for an artist's dream: the unclimbed mountain, the unclimbable mountain. Staring up at it, he vowed that it would be his.

Thus began what remains to this day the most relentless battle ever waged between a mountain and a man. Seven times in five years Whymper attacked the Matterhorn, and seven times he was beaten back. The obstacles that confronted him were enough to have broken the spirit—not to mention the neck—of a lesser man. In addition to the natural perils of precipice and glacier, storm and avalanche he had also to contend with the stupidity, cowardice and duplicity of men. But he kept on, undismayed—dreaming, planning, attacking, counterattacking; on each of his seven unsuccessful attempts he made progress and learned a little more about his mighty antagonist than he had known before; and at last, on the eighth attempt, he went to the top. No mountaineer has ever had a greater triumph. Nor, as fate in the end decreed, a more bitter one.

On his first visit, in 1860, Whymper did not actually come to grips with the mountain, but contented himself with studying it, carefully and patiently. He saw that it was built in the shape of a colossal pyramid, with four principal faces and four well-defined corners, the whole mass thrusting skyward in precipice upon precipice to a height of some five thousand feet above its skirt of glaciers. Across this vertical mile the wind howled with unchecked fury, and down its chimneys and gullies roared endless avalanches of rock and ice. For the men who ventured into that savage, slanting world death would lurk not only in the abysses below; at every moment it would be clutching at their clothing or hanging invisible above them, poised, ready to fall.

The northern and western sides of the peak seemed to Whymper to be utterly inaccessible. He therefore did most of his reconnoitering from the south and east, chiefly in the region of the Theodule Pass, a great glacial bridge that connects the Swiss valley of Zermatt with the Italian Val Tournanche. The line-drawing on page 47 adapted from Whymper's own, shows the outlines of the Matterhorn from the summit of this pass, itself 10,900 feet above the sea. As can be seen, two possible routes suggest themselves: the northeast and southwest ridges, the former leading up from the direction of Zermatt, the latter from the village of Breuil in the Val Tournanche. Of the two, the northeastern seemed to Whymper the more direct, but he judged the southwestern to be less steep, and when he returned to England in the late summer of 1860 he had already determined that this would be his route of attack.

And so it was, through six fruitless attempts during the summers of 1861, 1862 and 1863. It was not until 1865 that Whymper at last turned to the northeast ridge—and to triumph and tragedy.

On the morning of August 29, 1861, Whymper set out from Breuil on the first of his great adventures. He was accompanied by a solitary

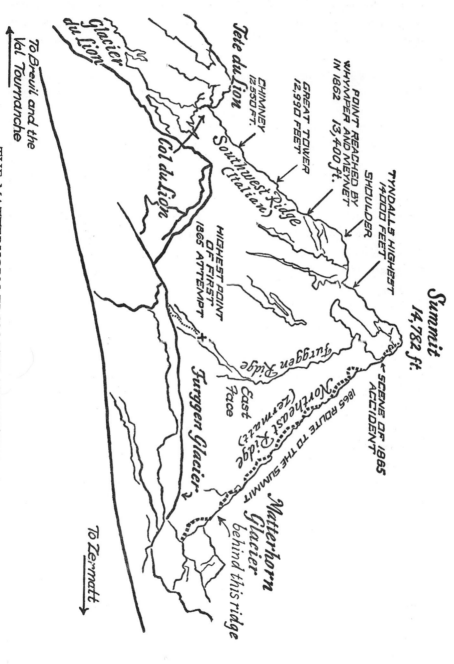

Summit
14,782 ft.

TYNDALL'S HIGHEST
14,000 FEET

POINT REACHED BY
WHYMPER AND MEYNET
IN 1862   13,400 ft.

SHOULDER

GREAT TOWER
12,990 FEET

CHIMNEY
12,550 FT.

Tête du Lion

Southwest Ridge
(Italian)

Glacier
du Lion

Col du Lion

HIGHEST POINT
OF FIRST
1865 ATTEMPT. ×

East
Face

Furggen Ridge

Furggen Glacier

SCENE OF 1865
ACCIDENT

1865 ROUTE TO THE SUMMIT

Northeast Ridge
(Zermatt)

Matterhorn Glacier
behind this ridge

To Breuil and the
Val Tournanche

To Zermatt

THE MATTERHORN FROM THE THEODULE PASS

guide—the only man in all the surrounding villages he could induce to go with him. They spent the first night in a shed in the highest pasture of the Val Tournanche, where their herdsmen-hosts spoke fearfully of the demons of the Matterhorn and pleaded with them to turn back. The next day, however, they pushed upward, ascending the Glacier du Lion and skirting the cliffs of the Tête du Lion at its head, until they reached a high, narrow saddle leading to the base of the Matterhorn's southwest ridge. On the snowy summit of this saddle, shown in the drawing as the Col du Lion, they pitched their tent.

They were now well within the domain of the great peak, almost a mile above Breuil. On one side of them steep slopes of glassy snow descended to the glacier they had crossed. On the other a sheer wall fell away to the Tiefenmatten Glacier, so far below that when they threw down a bottle no sound returned for more than a dozen seconds. At nightfall it grew bitterly cold; the wind howled and tugged against the canvas of their tent, and the water froze in a flask under Whymper's head. They succeeded, however, in dozing for a while, until "—about midnight there came from high aloft a tremendous explosion, followed by a second of dead quiet. A great mass of rock had split off and was descending toward us. My guide started up, wrung his hands and exclaimed, 'O my God, we are lost!' We heard it coming, mass after mass pouring over the precipices, bounding and rebounding from cliff to cliff, and the great rocks in advance smiting one another." Luckily only a few fragments fell near the tent, but there was little sleep for the two men the rest of that night. Whymper had had his first taste of the cannonading of the Matterhorn.

At dawn they began the ascent of the southwest ridge. The day was fine, the climbing was hard but in no way hazardous, and the heights above seemed very near. Pausing for a moment's rest, Whymper's heart pounded with the excitement of the artist and mountaineer.

"We overlook the Tête du Lion," he writes, "and nothing except the Dent d'Hérens stands in the way. The ranges of the Graian Alps, an ocean of mountains, are seen at a glance—how soft and yet how sharp they look in the early morning! The midday mists have not begun to rise; nothing is obscured; even the pointed Viso, all but a hundred miles away, is perfectly defined.

"Turn to the east and watch the sun's slanting rays coming across the Monte Rosa snowfields. Look at the shadowed parts and see how even they, radiant with reflected light, are more brilliant than man knows how to depict. . . . Then note the sunlight as it steals noiselessly along and reveals countless unsuspected forms—the delicate ripple-lines which mark the concealed crevasse, and the waves of drifted snow, producing each minute more lights and fresh shadows, sparkling on the edges and glittering on the ends of the icicles, shining on the heights and illuminating the depths, until all is aglow and the dazzled eye returns for relief to the sombre crags."

His joy and exhilaration were to be short lived. Less than an hour after leaving the Col du Lion they came to a point now known as the Chimney—a smooth, almost vertical slab of rock fixed between two other rocks, equally smooth. Bracing himself against the sides and using several tiny cracks for holds, Whymper succeeded in scrambling up, but his guide, after several unsuccessful attempts, suddenly untied himself from the rope and announced that he would go no farther. "I told him he was a coward," said Whymper, "and *he* mentioned his opinion of me." Argument, however, was fruitless; the guide insisted on going down, and the artist, frustrated and angry, had to follow.

"The day was perfect; the wind had fallen; the way seemed clear, no insuperable obstacle was in sight; but what could one do alone?"

Thus the first assault on the Matterhorn ended at a height of 12,550 feet.

Whymper did not attempt the mountain again in 1861, but the following summer he was back in full cry and launched no less than four separate attacks. Warned by his earlier experience, he had determined that in future he would not depend on the whims of a single guide. His first venture of 1862 was therefore undertaken with four companions: his friend and fellow-mountaineer, Reginald Macdonald, two Zermatt guides, Taugwald and Kronig, and, as porter, a little hunchback from the village of Breuil, Luk Meynet. Of these, strangely enough, it was Meynet who was destined to play the most heroic role in the arduous days to come.

In spite of the strong party and elaborate plans Whymper's second try was doomed to quick and complete defeat. A nasty fall by one of the guides delayed them while crossing the Glacier du Lion and dampened the spirits of the others. Then, no sooner had they reached the Col du Lion and made camp than a strong wind blew up, freezing

their hands and feet and causing them to spend a sleepless night holding their wildly flapping tent.

By morning a hurricane was howling at them from the great snow-
fields of Monte Rosa, to the east. Taking advantage of a brief lull they
made a start up the southwest ridge, only to have the gales whip back
at them with renewed frenzy. "Advance or return," wrote Whymper,
"were alike impossible; the ridge was denuded of its debris, and we
saw stones as big as a man's fist blown away horizontally into space.
We dared not attempt to stand upright and remained stationary on all
fours, glued, as it were, to the rocks."

It was all they could do, in the next lull, to make the return to the
tent, and even their diehard leader had to admit defeat. Battered and
chagrined, they descended to Breuil.

Whymper's next attempt—his third—is noteworthy in that it marked
the beginning of his association with the great guide, Jean-Antoine
Carrel. Carrel was famous throughout the Alps as a climber of skill
and daring, and, in addition, he was perhaps the only mountaineer in
the world, outside of Whymper, who believed the Matterhorn *could*
be climbed. It had been his lifelong dream that he should be the first
to stand upon the summit of the peak—for the honor of Italy and his
native Val Tournanche—and for years past he had explored the mountain and sought vainly to conquer it. Whymper had met him in 1860
and 1861, but until now all the artist's efforts to secure him as guide
had failed. Proud and strong-willed, Carrel resented the intrusion of an
outsider on what he considered his own personal preserve, and indeed,
in 1861, had not only refused to accompany Whymper on his first attempt but had made a separate attack of his own on the very same day.
Now at last, however, he came to the decision that it was wiser to fight
with this determined Englishman than against him. The greatest climber
and the greatest guide in Europe joined forces, and a strange relationship of friendship and enmity began.

Whymper wasted no time between his second and third attempts on
the mountain. He met Carrel at Breuil the night of his return, won
him over, and the very next day set out again for the southwest ridge.
In addition to Carrel he was accompanied by his friend Macdonald and
a second guide called Pession. They followed the now-familiar route
up the glacier, around the cliffs of the Tête du Lion and onto the nar-

row snow-saddle of the col; but this time they did not camp there. Instead, following Carrel's advice, they went on up the ridge to the foot of the Chimney, where they found a tiny level space among the cliffs and set up their tent.

The day being fine, they then pushed on farther and within an hour came to the foot of a crag. This huge rock battlement, one of the most distinctive features of the southwest ridge as seen from below, was known as the Great Tower and, at 12,990 feet, marked the highest point on the mountain which anyone had ever reached before. Whymper and his companions studied the wilderness above, discovered what seemed a feasible route, and descended to their tent to rest for the great effort of the following day.

It was an effort, however, that never came off. No sooner had they left their camp at daybreak and begun the passage of the Chimney than the guide Pession complained of feeling ill and declared that he could not go on. There was a long wait, and long arguments, but the man refused to budge another step upward, and Carrel declined to go further as the only guide. Whymper and Macdonald were helpless. Instead of pushing on into the unknown world above they began the long, joyless descent to Breuil.

"Three times," wrote Whymper of this stage of his campaign, "I had essayed the ascent of this mountain, and on each occasion I failed ignominiously. I had not advanced a yard beyond my predecessors. Only 1800 feet remained, but they were as yet untrodden and might present the most formidable obstacles; no man could expect to climb them by himself. It was evident that a party should consist of three men at least, but where could the other two be obtained? Want of men made the difficulty, not the mountain."

There was reason for his pessimism. Macdonald had been called back to England, Carrel and the hunchback Meynet were busy with work in their village, and not a single other guide in either Breuil or Zermatt was willing to risk his neck and immortal soul on what had come to be known throughout the Alps as "that awful mountain."

After a week of galling inactivity Whymper returned to the southwest ridge alone. He himself declares that it was for the practical reason of looking after the tent, which had been left at the Chimney, but one suspects that by this stage of the game he simply could not stay away from the mountain of his dreams. At all events, he lingered on the heights, drinking in an artist's fill of beauty.

"The sun was setting," he relates, "and its rosy rays, blending with the snowy blue, had thrown a pale, pure violet as far as the eye could see, the valleys were drowned in purple gloom, while the summits shone with unnatural brightness; and as I sat in the door of the tent and watched the twilight change to darkness the earth seemed to become less earthly and almost sublime: the world seemed dead, and I its sole inhabitant—"

He spent the night there, wrapped in a spell of height and loneliness, and in the morning began inching his way upward alone. Soon he had reached the foot of the Great Tower, the highest point of his previous ascent. The monstrous rock mass above him "stood out like a turret at the angle of a castle, and behind it a battlemented wall led upward to the citadel." Whymper had ventured this far only to search for a possible spot for a new tent platform, but now, suddenly, temptation was too much for him.

Slowly and cautiously he worked his way up the Tower. The first step necessitated his jumping up, grasping a ledge eight feet above and pulling himself onto it by the sheer strength of his arms. Directly in front of him now was an overhanging rock wall and immediately to his left a precipice plunging to the glacier below. He bore to the right and in a moment found himself clinging to a sheer cliff, "fixed as if crucified, pressing against the rock, and feeling each rise and fall of my chest as I breathed." Making use of the tiniest cracks and ledges, he succeeded, however, in surmounting the Tower and came out on the ridge above.

Up to this point he had been climbing on firm, living rock. Now the upper reaches of the mountain soared above him in a fearful sweep of decay and ruin. For another half hour he crept upward, threading a path between huge, rotted blocks that appeared to him like the gravestones of giants. Then, at last, prudence returned and he started back. He was filled, nevertheless, with excitement and hope, for he had reached a height of 13,400 feet and was confident he had at last found the key to the summit.

Before that day's climbing was done Whymper was to have a painful, and almost fatal, object lesson in the perils of solitary climbing. Safely down the southwest ridge, he passed the col and began the now familiar passage of the snow-slope under the cliffs of the Tête du Lion. All the hazards of the mountain were apparently behind him, and he was descending rapidly, his thoughts on Breuil, a warm bath and bed—when suddenly he slipped and fell.

The slope beneath dropped steeply away, narrowing as it went, and came to an abrupt end in an opening between two walls of rock. Beyond this opening was a thousand-foot precipice, falling to the Glacier du Lion. Toward it—and almost certain death—Whymper now plunged as if down a funnel. He pitched first into a mass of rocks, then onto ice, flying head over heels as he gained momentum and spinning through the air in great bounds of thirty and forty feet. But the demons of the mountains were on his side that day. At the very neck of the gully he brought up against the rocks to one side of it, and his fall was stopped. Dazed and bleeding he clung there, two hundred feet below the point from which he had fallen, not ten feet from the lip of the precipice.

After several minutes he was able to creep to a place of safety, where he fainted. Night had fallen when he regained consciousness and, summoning his last reserve of strength, he continued the descent. Many of the villagers had already given him up for lost when, long past midnight, dazed and blood-soaked, he staggered into Breuil.

Another and yet another try at the Matterhorn Whymper was to have before the eventful summer of 1862 was done. No sooner had his wounds healed than he was back on the southwest ridge for his fourth campaign, accompanied this time by Carrel, little Meynet and a cousin of Carrel's called Caesar.

The four camped for a night at the base of the Chimney and the next day scaled the Great Tower and emerged on the savage upper ridge where Whymper had pioneered on his solitary climb. No sooner were they there, however, than a heavy mist descended upon them, and through it driving snow. Retracing their steps, they improvised a tiny platform among the crags at the base of the Tower and crept into their tent. Then occurred another of the bitter arguments which were constantly arising between Whymper and Carrel. The former, as usual, was hopeful and wanted to wait out the storm, which he thought would be of short duration. The latter insisted that the whole mountain would soon be coated with ice and that immediate retreat was their only sal-

vation. In the end the guide won out. They turned back, only to discover, to Whymper's intense irritation, that he had been right after all:
mist and snow soon blew away and the day shone clear and warm. But
it was then too late to retrace their steps.

This was nothing, however, to the vexation that was in store for him
next day. The four had agreed to set out from Breuil at dawn for yet
another try, but when the time came Carrel and his cousin were off
marmot-hunting. Only faithful Luk Meynet was on hand and ready,
and, with him as his only companion, Whymper set forth on his fifth
attempt on the Matterhorn.

The little hunchback of the Val Tournanche was as strange and lov-
able a man as has ever trod the high mountains. In spite of his affliction he was the sole support of his dead brother's widow and children,
and to earn bread for them he gladly followed Whymper into dangers
before which stronger men quailed. His loyalty and devotion were ab-
solute, and he looked upon the great peak that towered above his native
valley with an almost religious adoration. Whymper has given a touch-
ing picture of him as he stood upon the Col du Lion and for the first
time stared up and out at the unclouded view:

"The poor little deformed peasant," he relates, "gazed upon it silently and reverently for a time and then unconsciously fell on one
knee and clasped his hands, exclaiming in ecstasy, 'Oh, beautiful mountains!'"

Now, as the artist's sole companion, Meynet was to go higher on the
Matterhorn than men had ever gone before. Together the two labored
up the endless crags and precipices of the southwest ridge—past the
Chimney, up and over the Great Tower and onto the desolate heights
beyond. They passed Whymper's previous highest point and pushed on
until they were a bare half-dozen rope lengths beneath the great shoulder of the upper mountain. Here, however, the razor-edged ridge became so steep that it was unclimbable, and when they turned to the cliffs
on the right they found themselves "both spread-eagled on the all but
perpendicular face, unable to advance and barely able to descend." Further progress was impossible for the two men, but Whymper believed
that a larger party, aided by a ladder, would be able to go higher. As
quickly as possible he descended to Breuil to secure the ladder and again
enlist the services of Carrel.

His plans, however, were doomed to frustration, for during his absence on the mountain Professor John Tyndall and his famous guide, Bennen, had arrived in the village. The conqueror of the Weisshorn had made an attempt on the Matterhorn in 1860 and departed with the conviction that it was unclimbable. Two years, however, had apparently changed his mind, for Whymper found him now prepared for an immediate attack. To make matters even worse, he had a ladder with him and had engaged Carrel and Caesar to accompany him.

In an agony of disappointment and suspense Whymper fretted about Breuil, while his expert and well-equipped rival set out for the mountain. At sunrise of the second day the villagers claimed excitedly that they had seen a flag on the summit. Scanning the peak with his binoculars, Whymper determined that this was not so, but what he did see gave him little comfort: the climbers had passed his own highest point and even as he watched were disappearing over the great shoulder of the upper mountain. With sinking heart he resigned himself to the belief that his prize had been snatched from his grasp.

But the Matterhorn played no favorites. At sunset of that day Tyndall and his men returned to Breuil with "no spring in their step." They had gone to a height of almost fourteen thousand feet—less than eight hundred from the summit—but there they too had been turned back, defeated. Tyndall was completely discouraged. "Have nothing more to do with this awful mountain," was his parting word to Whymper.

As it turned out, Whymper did not have anything more to do with it that year, for a few days later his work called him back to England. But, unlike Tyndall, he was to return, and return again. For the Matterhorn was still there—the unconquered Matterhorn; *his* Matterhorn.

The following year, however, he made only one attack on the mountain—his sixth—and it met with speedy repulse. His party, which included Carrel, Caesar, little Meynet and two other porters, was the strongest he had ever had, and in addition he was supplied with a ladder and other equipment he had not had before. The chance of success seemed bright, but it was not to be.

The ascent of the glacier, the Col du Lion and the lower southwest ridge were made easily and in perfect sunny weather. At the foot of the Great Tower, however, the climbers felt a sudden warning rush of cold air and in a matter of seconds the sky had blackened and a storm descended upon them. Somehow they succeeded in pitching their tent and for twenty-six hours lay huddled under its frail protection while a gale-borne blizzard screamed against the mountain walls and thunder and lightning raged above their heads.

It was the most ferocious Alpine storm any of them had encountered, and it required all their remaining strength, when at last it blew away, to make the descent to Breuil. The weather was beautiful there, and the villagers looked skeptical when they heard the climbers' story. "We have had no snow here," said the innkeeper. "It has been fine all the time. There has been only that small cloud upon the mountain."

Small cloud or raging tempest, that night of terror put an end to Whymper's 1863 campaign. Again he returned to England, defeated and disconsolate. "But like a gambler," he said, "who loses each throw, I was only the more eager to have another try—to see if the luck would change."

A change of luck he was to have in full measure, but not only the change for which he hoped.

In 1864 Whymper, already one of the most famous mountaineers of his generation, made many notable ascents in the Alps, but it was not until a year later that he returned to his greatest struggle. This time he brought with him not only all his old skill, courage and determination, but a new, revolutionary plan.

Throughout his earlier attempts he had concurred in the general opinion that the Matterhorn could be conquered, if at all, only from the southwest. Now, however, he determined to turn his back on the great ridge, up which he had struggled so often in vain, and attack the mountain from the east. His decision was based not on mere whim, but on careful observation and reasoning. For one thing, he had noted in his many crossings of the Theodule Pass that the east face appeared much less steep when seen in profile than it did head-on from the valley of Zermatt. For another, he had observed that the rock strata of the peak sloped from northeast to southwest. This meant, he reasoned, that, whereas the rocks on the southwest sloped outward and down, those on the northeast must be tilted inward and up. As a seasoned mountaineer he knew that a narrow ledge or hold that sloped upward was easier and safer than a far wider one that sloped down; if his suppositions were correct, the east face of the mountain should be, in effect, a huge natural staircase.

A thorough reconnaissance in June of 1865 served to strengthen his new convictions, and a few days later he was ready to launch his first attack by a new route. His companions on this venture were Michel-Auguste Croz, a topflight Chamonix guide with whom he had made many difficult ascents, two other guides named Christian Almer and Franz Biener and—sole veteran of his previous attempts—faithful Meynet, the hunchback.

Following the plan which had been worked out by Whymper and Croz, these five approached the mountain from the Mont Cervin Glacier and began the ascent of a steep gully which led to the Furggen, or southeast, Ridge above. It was Whymper's theory that once they gained this ridge they could cross over onto the east face and continue up and to the right until they reached the northeast shoulder, just below the summit. The great danger, he realized, was that they might encounter avalanches in the gully, but he believed that they could minimize it by keeping well out on the gully walls and avoiding the center trough, which would be a natural chute for falling stones.

He was not long in being proved wrong. Pausing for lunch at a point about halfway to the ridge, their attention was suddenly drawn to an ominous trickle of small rocks skimming down the mountainside. An instant later there was a roaring on the heights above, and they looked up to see a huge welter of boulders and stones hurtling down upon them at projectile speed. Worse yet, they saw that the avalanche was not confined to the center of the gully, but was raking its sides as well, bounding from wall to wall in the wildest confusion. Dropping their food, the men dashed for cover, hiding under defending rocks while the cannonade of death crashed past them. Almost by a miracle none of them was struck, but, white-faced and shaken, they all agreed they had had enough of the gully. To have advanced farther in it would have been tantamount to sauntering toward the muzzle of a firing cannon.

Whymper, hoping against hope, clambered out of the gully and tried to reach the ridge by scaling the neighboring cliffs. Of his companions, only Meynet followed him, a grin on his homely face, the tent slung across his gnarled back. "Come down, come down!" shouted Croz from below. "It is useless!" Even Whymper, the eternal optimist, could see

that the guide was right, and after a few minutes' fruitless struggling
he turned back. His seventh assault on the mountain had, like all the
others, ended in failure.

Now at last began the strange and complicated sequence of events
by which fate set the stage and selected the characters for the last act
of the drama of the Matterhorn. No playwright has ever devised a more
triumphant and tragic final curtain.

Whymper had resolved to make his next attempt by the east face
and northeast, or Zermatt, ridge, and his companions of the gully were
ready to accompany him. A storm, however, delayed them, and before
they could make a start the guide Croz was called back to Chamonix
by a previous engagement. The artist accompanied him and, while Croz
was occupied elsewhere, made a notable first ascent of the Aiguille
Verte, in the Mont Blanc Range, with Almer and Biener. But the Matterhorn was in his blood. Too impatient to wait longer for Croz, he
returned to Breuil with the other two guides, only to have them back
down on him at the last moment.

"Anything but the Matterhorn," they implored him. *"Anything* but
that!"

Whymper was not unduly upset by their change of heart. Carrel was
available and eager for another go at the great peak, and of all the men
the Englishman had ever climbed with he respected this proud, self-
confident guide the most. After considerable argument Carrel agreed
to attempt the east face; Caesar and another helper enlisted for the venture, and it was agreed the assault would be made on the first fine day.

As it turned out, however, the first fine day brought no setting-out
for Whymper, but only anger and frustration. A few days previously
a large and well-equipped party of Italians had arrived in Breuil, with
the avowed intention of scaling the Matterhorn by the southwest ridge.
Now the artist was to suffer the ordeal of standing helplessly by while
Carrel pleaded "a previous engagement" and joined forces with his
rivals. Whymper knew that the previous engagement was a fiction and
that the real reasons for the guide's act lay deep in his proud and stubborn character. An Italian himself, he felt that his first duty was to his
fellow-countrymen, and although he had reluctantly agreed to try the
east face, his heart was set on conquering the peak from the side of his
native valley. But whatever Carrel's motives, the important thing to

Whymper was that his defection was an accomplished fact. Again, as on the day of Tyndall's attempt, he saw himself about to be cheated of his great prize. He had to act and act fast.

This was easier decided than done. Carrel apparently was not the only Italian patriot in the Val Tournanche, for not a man could be found who would agree to climb with him, or even to act as his porter across the pass to Zermatt. The crowning blow came when Luk Meynet turned him down; the little hunchback claimed to be in the thick of some cheese-making operations which it was impossible for him to leave. Whymper was desperate. The Italians, he knew, were burdened with ponderous equipment and were moving on the mountain very slowly. But he could not move at all.

In that dark moment fate intervened in the persons of two young men who came swinging down into Breuil from the Theodule Pass. One of them was a strong and adventuresome Englishman, Lord Francis Douglas, who had recently distinguished himself by several difficult Alpine ascents; the other was his porter, young Peter Taugwalder, son of one of the foremost guides of Zermatt. Whymper told Douglas his plight, and Douglas, for his part, said that he would like nothing better than a try at the Matterhorn. Furthermore, he declared that the elder Taugwalder, who had heard of Whymper's plans, agreed that the eastern face might be climbed and could undoubtedly be persuaded to accompany them. With high hopes the two Englishmen, with young Taugwalder as porter, raced over the pass to Zermatt. At the zero hour the fight for the Matterhorn had become an international rivalry.

But fate had yet stranger twists in store. Who should walk into the hotel in Zermatt that same night but Michel-Auguste Croz! He explained to Whymper that his employer in Chamonix had returned home earlier than expected and that he had subsequently been engaged by another climber—the distinguished clergyman-mountaineer, Charles Hudson. Hudson, with Croz and a young traveling companion named Hadow, had now come to Zermatt for the express purpose of attempting the Matterhorn. Whymper and the clergyman met after dinner that night and promptly decided to join forces.

It was therefore a party of seven that set out for the mountain the following morning. Whymper and Hudson shared the leadership; Douglas and Hadow, both of whom were only nineteen, were what

might be called the junior climbers; Croz and the elder Taugwalder
were the guides; the younger Taugwalder the porter. Of the seven only
Whymper and Croz had ever been on the Matterhorn before, and Croz
had been there only once, on the short-lived venture in the gully. But
the others were all strong, able men, and Whymper was satisfied with
them—and full of optimism.

Ascending steadily, they reached the foot of the northeast ridge before noon of the first day and a few hours later made camp on a ledge
at about eleven thousand feet on the east face. The route thus far had
been incredibly easy. During the afternoon, while the others rested,
Croz and young Taugwalder made a scouting trip high on the cliffs
above and returned in a state of great excitement. "Not a difficulty,"
they reported. "Not a single difficulty!" It was a lighthearted group of
mountaineers that huddled that night on their dizzy perch. "Long after
dusk," wrote Whymper, "the cliffs above echoed with our laughter and
with the songs of the guides, for we were happy and feared no evil."

Seven times in five years Edward Whymper had risked life and limb
in futile battle against the Matterhorn. Now, by a supreme irony, he
was to go to the top with almost ridiculous ease. The morning of July
14, 1865, dawned clear and still, and as soon as it was light enough to
see, the seven adventurers began the ascent. The precipices of the east
face towered above them three thousand feet into the sky, but, as Croz
and young Taugwalder had reported, there were no formidable obstacles. Whymper had been right. This side of the mountain was not
so steep as it appeared from the valley, and the upward tilt of the rocks
made it a giant staircase.

They gained altitude rapidly. Twice they struck the northeast ridge
and followed it for a little distance, but both times they soon worked
back onto the face, where the rock was firmer. Hadow, the least experienced climber among them, encountered some difficulty on the steeper
pitches; a helping hand, however, was all that was needed to get him
over them, and for the greater part of the way it was not even necessary
to take the precaution of roping up. At six-thirty they had reached the
height of 12,900 feet and at ten they were at fourteen thousand.

Above the point at which they now stood the last few hundred feet
of the east face shot up in an almost vertical wall. It was obviously unclimbable. Bearing to the right, they again worked over to the ridge,

crossed it, and crept out and upward onto the northern face. Here, for
the first time, the climbing was such as to call for all their mountaineering skill. The north wall of the mountain was less precipitous than
the east, but the rocks were covered with a thin film of ice and at their
backs was nothing but blue air and the Matterhorn Glacier four thousand feet below. Using the rope, they advanced one by one, Croz,
Whymper and Hudson leading and bracing themselves against a possible slip by those who followed.

This difficult section was of no great extent. They bore almost horizontally across the face for some four hundred feet, ascended directly
toward the summit for another sixty, then doubled back to the northeast
ridge. One last obstacle remained—a shoulder of rock that jutted out
into space at the uppermost extremity of the ridge. Carefully they edged
around it: two or three short sidling steps—one long step over the
abyss. An upward glance, and their hearts were suddenly pounding with
excitement. Above them was only a gentle snow-slope and beyond it
an empty blue dome of sky.

Whymper and Croz raced for the top and made it together. The Matterhorn was conquered.

But one great fear was still in all their minds: Were they the first?
Or had Carrel and the Italians, after all, beaten them to their prize?
Whymper almost ran along the narrow snow-ridge that formed the
summit of the mountain, searching for footprints. There were none.
Then from the extreme southern end, staring down, he saw a cluster
of tiny moving dots on the ridge far below. Up went Whymper's arms
in triumph. He and his companions shouted until they were hoarse;
they rolled rocks down the mountainside; and at last the defeated Italians paused and gazed upward at the victors. A few minutes later they
turned and began the descent of the mountain. Whymper and his men
were alone in their triumph.

Yet even in that most exalted moment of his life the conqueror of
the Matterhorn felt a pang of regret. "Still," he wrote later, "I would
that the leader of that party might have stood with us at that moment,
for our victorious shouts conveyed to him the disappointment of the
ambition of a life-time. Carrel was *the* man, of all who attempted the
ascent of the Matterhorn, who most deserved to be the first upon its
summit. It was the aim of his life to make the ascent from the side of
Italy, for the honor of his native valley. For a time he had the game

in his hand; he played it as he thought best; but he made a false move and he lost it." *

Secure in their victory, Whymper and his companions remained on the summit for an hour. They shouted and pummeled each other and danced for joy. Croz produced a tent pole, which he had carried on his back the whole way up, set it in the snow and tied his shirt to it as a flag. It was seen in Zermatt, in the Val Tournanche, in the valleys and towns of the Alps for miles around. At Breuil it was taken as a sign that the Italians had conquered, and there was great jubilation, only to be followed by bitter disappointment when their defeated champions returned. At Zermatt the excited villagers poured into the streets, staring upward at the tiny scrap of cloth that flapped triumphantly in the sky, speaking with awe of the heroes who had done the impossible. Everywhere men knew and rejoiced that the Matterhorn had been won at last.

Even nature itself seemed to be taking part in the celebration. The sun shone brilliantly; not a cloud or wisp of mist veiled the horizon; and from their perch in the sky the seven conquerors looked out upon a vast, glittering panorama of summits, snow-fields and valleys. "Not one of the principal peaks of the Alps was hidden," wrote Whymper. The gigantic shining dome of Mont Blanc loomed on the horizon to the west. The great crests of the Pennines and the Oberland tiered away endlessly to the east and north—Monte Rosa, the Mischabel, the Weisshorn, the Finsteraarhorn and hosts of others—incredibly white and vivid against the blue immensity of sky. They could even see Monte Viso, a hundred miles away, clear and gleaming in the crystal light. Their shouts stilled, they gazed out upon the gorgeous pageant, too moved for words. Long years have passed since that magic summer afternoon when they stood, the first of all men, on the summit of the Matterhorn, but it is doubtful if in the whole subsequent history of mountaineering men have ever again been granted so glorious an hour of triumph. Certainly it was the most glorious of their own lives.

For four of them it was also the last.

They had reached the summit at one-forty. At exactly two-forty they began the descent. In a moment or two they had come down the snow-slope and reached the beginning of the short "difficult section" on the

---

* Carrel reached the summit by the southwest ridge only three days later. But for all the joy it gave him it might as well have been a hundred years.

north face. Here they paused to rope up, and Whymper and Hudson worked out the order of descent. Croz went first and Hadow second. Then came Hudson and after him Douglas. Old Taugwalder, Whymper and young Taugwalder brought up the rear, in that order. In such a sequence the stronger members of the party were in a position to help the weaker—Hadow and Douglas—if they should encounter any difficulties. Or so they thought.

They rounded the jutting shoulder of rock and worked cautiously down the steep slabs on the other side. Only one man was moving at a time. A moment later—

"Croz had laid aside his ax, and in order to give Mr. Hadow greater security was absolutely taking hold of his legs and putting his feet, one by one, into their proper positions. As far as I know, no one was actually descending. The two leading men were partially hidden from my sight by an intervening mass of rock, but it is my belief, from the movements of their shoulders, that Croz, having done as I said, was in the act of turning around to go down a step or two himself. At this moment Mr. Hadow slipped, fell against him, and knocked him over."

There was a sharp, choked-off cry from Croz, and he and Hadow went flying downward. In an instant Hudson was dragged violently from his steps and Douglas after him. Whymper and the two Taugwalders braced themselves, clinging to the rocks. The rope spun out between Douglas and the elder Taugwalder, went taut with a violent jerk—

And broke.

"For a few seconds we saw our unfortunate companions sliding downwards on their backs, and spreading out their hands, endeavoring to save themselves. They passed from our sight uninjured, disappeared one by one and fell from precipice to precipice on to the Matterhorngletscher below, a distance of nearly 4000 feet in height."

Thus the Matterhorn adventure ended—in victory and appalling tragedy. The last great unconquered peak in the Alps had succumbed at last to the skill and courage and perseverance of men, but in the very hour of conquest it had exacted a frightful vengeance.

Whymper's descent of the mountain with the two Taugwalders was a waking nightmare such as few men have ever been called upon to endure. Even worse was the ordeal that awaited him below. It was presently disclosed that at the time of the accident the climbers had been using an old, frayed rope, although they had plenty of sound rope with them, and the surrounding countryside resounded with recriminations and accusations. It was even whispered that Whymper and the Taugwalders had deliberately cut the rope, consigning their companions to death to save their own skins. An official inquest cleared them; but what, a short time before, had been a joyous triumph ended in a sordid, miserable epilogue.

Croz, Hudson and Hadow were discovered lying on the great glacier and were buried in the churchyard in Zermatt. The body of Lord Francis Douglas was never found. As for Whymper, he lived on for almost half a century, but the memory of the disaster haunted him to the end. In 1874 he went back to Zermatt and made a second ascent of the Matterhorn—perhaps in an effort to exorcise its ghosts—and that was the only time he ever climbed again in Europe. He never married. He became a heavy drinker. Lonely and taciturn, he roamed the world and scaled its mountains: in the Andes, the Canadian Rockies, even Greenland. But the spell the Alps had cast upon him was never altogether broken, and in the end, an old and dying man, he returned at last to the scene of his early adventures, to pass his last days among the great peaks he loved the best of all.

In the years since Whymper the Matterhorn has become one of the most-climbed mountains in the world. Today it has been ascended by every ridge and every face, its more frequented routes bristle with fixed ropes and ladders, and scarcely a fine summer day passes that its summit does not do service as a picnicking ground for a party of tourists. The "awful mountain" has been tamed.

Yet its magic remains. It is still, as in days gone by, the most famous peak in the Alps, and it still possesses the power to move all who look upon it with wonder and excitement. For the Matterhorn is more than a mountain. It is a monument and a legend. And as long as men raise their eyes to its heights they will remember the time when Edward Whymper and his companions set out upon their great adventure—and struggled and won and lost.

"THAT AWFUL MOUNTAIN"

The Matterhorn from the northeast. The ridge in the center foreground is that climbed by Whymper and his six companions and is today the "usual" route from Zermatt. The ridge on the left is the Furggen, that on the right the Zmutt.

Ewing Galloway

WHITE DEATH
An avalanche thundering down a mountainside in the Bernese Oberland of Switzerland.
Ewing Galloway

NEW HORIZONS

1865-1954

WITH THE FALL of the Matterhorn the great period of Alpine first ascents came to an end. A few scattered peaks and peaklets lingered on unclimbed into the late decades of the nineteenth century, but the Golden Age of pioneering was gone. The Alps were known, their mighty summits conquered. And a new era in the history of mountaineering had begun.

One might suppose that the exhaustion of virgin peaks—and, on top of that, the widely publicized Matterhorn tragedy—would have caused a decline of interest and activity in climbing. But the effect was exactly the opposite. Whereas in the earliest days mountaineering had been the province of the select and initiated few, its popularity, after 1865, increased to such a phenomenal degree that within a few years it had become one of the foremost sports of Europe. The original Alpine Club of London, at its founding in 1857, had twenty-eight members. By 1875 it boasted ten times that many, and a variety of younger organizations, with less stringent admission requirements, numbered their adherents in the thousands. Nor was the expansion by any means limited to the pioneering English. The lure of the new sport spread with the speed of an epidemic; each summer saw more and more climbers of more and more nationalities swarming over the cliffs and glaciers of the Alps; and in seemingly no time at all Switzerland became in fact

"the Playground of Europe." Mountaineering is both by tradition and
its inherent nature a non-commercial sport, but its enormous growth in
the late years of the last century made it, willy-nilly, the father of one
of the most flourishing hotel industries in the world.

The majority of climbers, in the 'seventies and 'eighties as now, confined themselves to activities in which others had blazed the way. With
guide and guidebook they followed the famous routes to the famous
summits, and, before long, ascents which on their first achievement had
been considered almost miraculous were known, in Baedeker's immortal
phrase, as "an easy day for a lady." A few years before, climbs of any
of the major peaks had been looked upon as great and desperate adventures, usually preceded by a solemn making out of wills and followed, if successful, by band concerts and torchlight parades. Now
lofty summits like Mont Blanc, the Jungfrau and even the "awful"
Matterhorn were climbed a hundred or more times a summer, and in
fine weather it was a not uncommon occurrence for there to be fifteen
or twenty parties on one of them at the same time. A striking example
of the change in attitude appears in a well-known story about the French
guide, Père Gaspard. In 1877 Gaspard led the first ascent of the fearsome Meije, in the Dauphiné, in what was universally regarded as one
of the most hazardous exploits in Alpine history. But only a few years
later we find him approaching an inexperienced tourist with the casual
invitation: "Come up the Meije—all you need is an umbrella."

A natural result of the popularization of climbing was a boom in
the profession of guiding. Herdsmen and farmers in scores of Swiss
villages turned from their old pursuits to the more lucrative business
of leading sportsmen up Alpine walls, and in the big tourist centers
like Chamonix and Grindelwald virtually the whole adult male population were soon earning their living as guides. As in any profession,
most were of the journeyman variety, but a remarkable number, both
among the veterans of the pioneer days and the younger generation who
followed them, were mountain men of the very first rank. Jean-Antoine
and Louis Carrel, Jakob and Melchior Anderegg, Alexander Burgener,
Christian Almer, Mattias Zurbriggen, Franz Lochmatter, Josef Knubel,
Christian Klucker, Armand Charlet—these are names which will be
remembered and honored as long as the sport of climbing endures. It
was men such as these, together with the most illustrious of their em-

ployers, who painstakingly raised mountaineering from the realm of haphazard adventure to a science and an art. And it was their skill and pride and sense of responsibility in their profession, often passed on directly from father to son to grandson, that won for Alpine guiding the high standards of performance that it has maintained ever since.

Still it is not to the men who climbed for a living that we must look for the most notable advances in the field, but to the men who climbed because climbing was in their blood. As we have indicated, most amateurs of the late nineteenth century were content to follow where others had led. There remained, however, the skilled and ambitious few for whom routine activity and hand-me-down achievement were not enough and who longed, like the pioneers before them, for the challenge of the unknown and unconquered. The virgin summits were no more; a mountaineer could no longer come out at last upon a soaring rock-fang in the sky and feel his heart pound with exultation, knowing himself to be the first. So the second generation of Alpine climbers did the next-best thing. They set about conquering the old peaks by new routes.

Thus began a type of mountaineering, which has continued with ever-increasing ramifications to the present time. In the world's great unconquered ranges, to be sure, climbing is still primarily a matter of getting to the top in the quickest and easiest way; but since the 1880's the practice of the sport in the Alps has concerned itself less and less with the mere reaching of summits and more and more with the manner in which the summits are attained. Soon it was no longer "Have you climbed the Matterhorn?" but "Have you climbed the Matterhorn by the Zmutt or the Furggen Ridge?" Not "Have you ascended Mont Blanc?" but "Have you ascended it by the Ancien Passage or the Col de la Brenva?" As the interest in new routes grew it was soon discovered that there was not only one, but three or six or a dozen possible ways to most of the great summits and that peaks whose so-called "standard climbs" were an easy walk-up for a duffer might also possess ridges and faces to tax the powers of the most expert. And the experts were not long in answering the challenge. Only a few short years after the Alps had been considered won, the winning began all over again. The difference was that the important consideration was now no longer "what," but "how."

One name stands pre-eminent among the pioneers of the reborn sport

—that of Mummery. In his everyday, non-climbing life A. F. Mummery was a conventional and phlegmatic English businessman, but once he laced up his nailed boots and felt Alpine rock and ice beneath them he became mysteriously transformed into the very incarnation of mountaineering skill and daring. For more than twenty years between the 'seventies and 'nineties he ranged indefatigably through the length and breadth of the Alps. A "climber's climber" if ever there was one, he regarded mountains less as a playground than as a laboratory for the development of his craft, welcoming difficulty and hazard for their own stern sake, despising easy successes and the mere gathering of records. As a result, his name is perhaps less known to the general public than that of many of the other great men of mountaineering. But among climbers themselves he has grown with the years into an almost legendary figure, and there is no doubt that he did as much as any man before or since to raise the standards of Alpine achievement and technique.

Mummery's climbs were legion, and at one time or another during his career he pioneered new routes in almost every district of the Alps. But he was primarily what the old-school Alpinists called a "centrist," rather than an eclectic, and the center of his mountain world were the *aiguilles* of Chamonix. Here, on the needle-sharp rock-spires that rise in the shadow of Mont Blanc, we see Mummery the cragsman, at the peak of his powers—inching up the "impossible" walls of the Charmoz, the Grépon, the Aiguille du Plan, finding finger- and toeholds where there appeared to be only smooth slabs and glaring ice, pushing daringly, relentlessly on into new vertical worlds where no man had ever ventured before. If no known technique was adequate to a problem at hand, he would invent a new one. If a pitch or cliff-face offered no chance of ascent by standard methods he would devise one that was non-standard. Thus did he conquer the appalling north face of the Grépon by the perpendicular cleft now famous as the Mummery Crack. Finding that hands and feet alone were useless, he wedged as much of his body as he could into a narrow slit in the rock-wall and hoisted himself upward by the strenuous use of knees, shoulders, elbows and back. Today, such maneuvers as this, as well as many others which Mummery devised, are part of the bag of tricks of any experienced climber; but in his day they were sensational innovations.

Although indisputably the foremost figure, Mummery was by no means the only early practitioner of "new-route" mountaineering. Each year more and more adventurous spirits turned from the prosaic pleasures of routine climbs to the limitless field of trail blazing, and before long virtually every great summit in the Pennines, the Oberland and the Mont Blanc district had been ascended and reascended by a great variety of approaches. (Mont Blanc itself, for example, had by the turn of the century been climbed by no less than twenty different routes.) To attempt even to summarize the new ascents of old peaks which were made between 1865 and the outbreak of the First World War would be a hopeless task; they fill literally thousands of pages in every Alpine journal of the time. A few individuals, however, stood out above the rest—notably the Italian, Guido Rey, the German, Paul Güssfeldt and the Englishmen, A. W. Moore, Douglas Freshfield, Sir William Martin Conway, W. A. B. Coolidge and Geoffrey Winthrop Young.* Climbing year after year with ever-increasing skill and daring, these men, with their guides and companions, forged new trails up the ridges and precipices of scores of great peaks. Rey on the Grépon and the Furggen Ridge of the Matterhorn, Moore on the fearsome Brenva snow-ridge of Mont Blanc, Young on the Täschhorn, Freshfield and Conway on countless mountain walls between Chamonix and the Tyrol —theirs were exploits of the very first rank, and the ascents which they pioneered have since become the classic climbs of the Alps.

There was still another important contribution that Mummery and his contemporaries made to the development of mountain craft. This was guideless climbing. Skilled and resourceful though they were, few of the earliest generation of mountaineers would have dreamed of attempting a major summit without the advice and assistance of professional companions; but with the passing of the years expert amateurs tended more and more to break away from the old leading-strings and fare forth on their own. Not that even the greatest of them did not climb more often with guides than without: Mummery with Alexander Burgener, Moore with the Andereggs, Young with "Little Josef" Knubel and Franz Lochmatter are among the most celebrated teams in mountaineering history. In later phases of their careers, however, both Mummery and Young showed an increasing tendency to dispense with

---

* Young, among his other accomplishments, is one of the best writers on both the practical and spiritual aspects of mountaineering that the sport has produced. (See the Reading List.)

professional aid, and many others, following their lead, began also to learn the satisfactions and responsibilities of climbing on their own.

What is generally referred to as "modern" mountaineering dates from the end of the First World War. Its most spectacular development has been the expansion of the climber's domain from the boundaries of the Alps to those of the globe itself; but with the years there have also been many other changes—almost all of them reflecting similar changes in the world at large. As a technique, mountaineering has become more specialized, more mechanized. And as a sport, it has become more democratic.

The climbers of the last century, if not necessarily rich men, were almost all unmistakably of what was then called the gentry, and their standards were those of the time in which they lived. The line between employer and employee was hard and fast: on one side the amateur gentleman-sportsman and on the other the paid peasant-guide. Slowly and inexorably, however, the rigid distinctions began breaking down. The climbers became more heterogeneous, the guides better educated and less provincial, and what had once been virtually a master-and-servant relationship changed into that of client and professional expert. In the Alps today, *Herr* and *Führer* may still be distinguishable by clothing and speech, background and point of view, but the gap between them is nothing to what it was in the old days. In America, where such social distinctions never existed, about the only way to tell amateur from guide is by which is the better climber. . . . And even that does not always work.

Mountaineering is, of its very essence, an away-from-the-crowd activity. And as such, inevitably, it has its share of snobs. But one has only to spend a night at a mountain hostel or visit the base of an accessible peak on a fine summer Sunday to disabuse himself of the notion that it is a sport only for the privileged few. In the mid-twentieth century the average man of the West (unless he is unfortunate enough to live in some place like Uruguay or Kansas) can find his way to a mountain no less than to a beach or a golf course, a filling station or a frankfurter stand. Let us be honest: it is not *all* to the good. The earth's high places are not made for crowds, and no one in his right mind delights in heaps of tin cans, initials carved in rocks, and platoons of banana-eaters on summits where there should be only sky and space.

But surely these are lesser evils than the alternative. And whatever man in the mass has brought to the mountains, what they offer him in return is more than can be measured.

As for specialization—to the pioneer climbers it would have been a meaningless word. A mountain was a mountain and a man was a man, and when the two came to grips it was merely a matter of the skill and endurance of one pitted against the size and natural obstacles of the other. Of late years, however, there has been an ever-increasing tendency to break the sport down into its component parts, with individual climbers concentrating on one or a few highly technical aspects. Some are interested only in the most difficult types of rock-climbing—cragsmen, they call themselves, or "rock-engineers." Others specialize in snow and ice work, still others in ski mountaineering, exploratory mountaineering, high-altitude mountaineering. The result, by and large, has been an enormous advance in climbing technique and achievement—ascents are made today which would leave a Whymper, or even a Mummery, aghast—but, as usual, the price of specialization has been an unfortunate narrowing of interests on the part of the specialist.

In the matter of mechanical devices mountaineering has also kept pace with the times. Mechanization, as the term is employed in the sport, means the use of artificial aids to accomplish climbs that would otherwise be impossible, and its practice today is so widespread and highly developed that it may almost be said to constitute a new and separate phase of mountain craft. In the old days rope, ice-ax and the necessary boots and clothing constituted the sum-total of a cragsman's equipment, but in recent years these have been augmented by a variety of new instruments and appliances. Most important of these are the piton and the karabiner. The former is an iron or steel spike that may be hammered into tiny cracks in the rock to afford support to hand, foot or rope; the latter a snap-ring which when attached to a piton makes possible many ingenious manipulations of the rope. Using these devices and a number of more complicated derivatives, modern mountaineers have been able to effect ascents which a quarter of a century ago would have been utterly impossible. Holdless cliff-walls, bulging precipices and overhanging cornices, which could defy unaided climbers to the end of time, have been made to yield to man's mechanical ingenuity, with the result that the limits of the "possible" in rock-scaling have been pushed back until there are scarcely any limits left. Virtually

all the sensational new ascents in the Alps during the past decade have
been achieved only with benefit of piton, karabiner and the like.

No other aspect of mountaineering has been the subject of such long
and acrimonious argument as that of mechanization. The conservatives
of the sport—notably the leaders of the British Alpine Club—have
fought it relentlessly, claiming that mechanical gadgets have no place
on a mountainside and that their use merely debases the art of cragsmanship into a form of spectacular, acrobatic circus. Most continental
climbers, on the other hand, have welcomed each new development with
enthusiasm, and in the United States, too, a school of young and daring
cragsmen has grown up which scarcely considers any climb worth while
if it does not involve intricate equipment and manipulations. At its two
extremes the controversy can easily be reduced to absurdity. The conservative viewpoint, carried all the way, would outlaw rope, ax and boots as
"artificial aids"; the radicals' program could be extended to include the
use of motor-driven pulleys or even dynamite. Thus far, no one on
either side has suggested quite such fantastic measures, but within narrower limits the argument rages on, and the ideal of the Golden Mean
is no more easily found in mountaineering than in any other field of
human activity.

Climbing is fundamentally neither a standardized nor a competitive
sport, but in recent years, along with its other developments, it has had
a tendency to become so. One of the concomitants—part cause, part
effect—has been an elaborate system of grading ascents, which originated in the Alps in the 1920's and has since spread over most of the
world. By this method, climbs of all descriptions are ranked according
to their degree of difficulty, beginning with a First Degree for an easy
walk-up and culminating in a Sixth, which has been aptly defined as "an
ascent recognized as impossible until someone does it without being
killed." Inherently, perhaps, there is nothing wrong with such a system;
at least it helps a climber in the selection of his route and lets him know
roughly what he may expect. But it was soon perverted to the purposes
of competition, and by the 'thirties the Alps were full of glory-seeking
young climbers who looked down with contempt on anything less than
a certified Super-Sixth. The Eigerwand, the north wall of the Grandes
Jorasses, the north and west faces of the Matterhorn and various of the
rock-pinnacles in the Dolomites achieved a notorious celebrity as "im-

possible" ascents, and it was on them in particular that the new order of Alpine cragsmen concentrated and struggled—and often died.

Aiding and abetting this suicidal insanity was a rising tide of nationalism. To be sure, mountaineering, since its earliest days, has suffered from ugly and senseless rivalries (witness the stories of Mont Blanc and the Matterhorn), but the jingoistic fervor that developed in the decade before the Second World War touched new heights of absurdity. Inevitably, it was the Germans and Italians who carried it to its furthest extreme. Aflame with the hero-philosophy of Nazi-Fascism and egged on by flag-wavers and tub-thumpers at home, brown- and black-shirted young climbers began vying with one another in what they conceived to be feats of courage and skill. All or nothing was their watchword—victory or death. No risk was too great, no foolhardiness to be condemned, so long as their exploits brought kudos to *Vaterland* or *patria.*

As a result of all this, Alpine mountaineering—at least in its more "expert" phases—became an activity with scarcely any relationship to the usual concept of sport. Competition was everything: competition literally to the death. Each year saw scores of new attempts at "record climbs," hundreds of reckless youngsters clinging to precipices and cliff-faces which a centipede could scarcely have surmounted, much less a man. And each year, inevitably, the fatalities mounted, until two, three or four hundred lives a season came to be accepted as the usual toll. The Alps had once been looked upon as a playground; then as a laboratory. Now they had become a battlefield. Seldom has there been an unhappier example of how hysterical and perverted nationalism can infect even the most unpolitical of human activities.

One glimpse of this "all-or-nothing" type of climbing is more than enough. The time is mid-July of 1936; the scene the mile-high precipice of the Eigerwand—the Wall of the Ogre—that rises close by the Jungfrau in the heart of the Bernese Oberland. . . .

For years the Eigerwand had been famous throughout Europe as one of the few great unclaimed "prizes" of the Alps. Many parties of daredevil climbers—most of them Germans—had tried to force a way up its appalling pitches of rock and ice; but none had succeeded, and almost every venture had ended in the death of one or more participants. Still the suicidal attempts went on—"victory or annihilation"; "for *Führer* and *Vaterland.*" * And on the morning of July twentieth crowds of sightseers again thronged the terrace of the Kleine Scheidegg Hotel, in the valley below, staring upward through the telescopes. For yet another assault was underway.

High on the mountain wall the figures of the climbers could be seen, clinging to the rock like minute black insects. There were four of them —two Bavarians and two Austrians—all of them young, all with records of many sensational climbs behind them, all resolved to win fame and glory by accomplishing "the most difficult ascent in the Alps." By the time the telescopes picked them up on the morning of the twentieth they had already been on the precipice for two full days. Hour after hour they had inched their way upward, digging fingers and toes into tiny crevices, driving pitons where no crevices existed at all, dangling in space at rope's end as they struggled with vertical cliffs and bulging overhangs. The first night they spent standing upright, lashed to a rock-wall with pitons and rope. On the second a storm swooped down, and the whole mountainside around them was sheathed in a whirling fury of ice and snow. The watchers below gave them up as lost, but at daybreak they were still there alive—still able to move. And the third day began.

Throughout the morning they crept on and by noon were almost within a thousand feet of their goal. There, however, their good luck ended. Storm and cold and the savage, perpendicular wall must at last have taken their toll of the climbers' strength, for they were seen to remain motionless for a long time and then begin to descend. But their downward progress did not last long either, and presently they were motionless again—four infinitesimal specks transfixed against the wall. Apparently they were unable to move either up or down.

A council of war was held in the valley below, and four guides set out as a rescue party. Following the tracks of the Jungfrau Railway, which bores through the rock of the Eiger, they came out on the precipice through an opening in the tunnel wall and began working their way across it toward the point where the climbers were trapped. Soon they were near enough to see the four of them clearly. They were clinging to the merest wrinkles in the ice-coated rock-face, one above the other, tied together and supported by a mass of ropes and pitons. Their

---

* Hitler himself announced that gold medals would be awarded to the first scalers of the Eigerwand, in conjunction with the Berlin Olympic Games of 1936.

clothing was in tatters and their faces scarcely recognizable from the effects of exposure and exhaustion. Above them was a sheer, almost holdless wall, down which they had somehow managed to lower themselves. Below was an overhanging precipice and an abyss of blue space.

Slowly, with deliberation and care, the rescue party drew nearer, but while they were still some distance away the inevitable happened. The uppermost of the four Germans lost his hold and toppled backward into thin air, arms and legs twisting grotesquely. The coils of the rope, spinning down after him, caught the next man around the neck, almost wrenching his head from his shoulders, while a third, still lower, was struck by the falling body of his companion. Then the rope went taut and snapped. The first man plummeted on for four thousand feet to the valley below; the second and third stayed motionless where they had fallen, half lying, half hanging from the ropes and pitons. In five seconds it was all over. And one man was left alive.

Still the horrified guides kept on. Hacking their way diagonally across a sixty-degree ice-slope, they at last reached a point only a few yards away from the sole survivor—a Bavarian soldier named Kurz. But before they could begin the delicate work of rescue another storm bore down on the mountain, and they were forced to beat a retreat. Kurz was left to spend his third night on the precipice, his body suspended over space and tied to the corpses of two of his companions.

The next morning, miraculously, he was still alive, but so weak that he was scarcely able to speak or move. Again the guides began the grim work of reaching him and this time succeeded in establishing themselves on a narrow ledge some one hundred feet below his position. Farther, however, they could not go. The stretch that still separated them from Kurz was an ice-glazed overhang, and to have ventured so much as a step onto it would have been obvious suicide. They called up to Kurz to cut himself loose from the bodies of his companions. This he did, using the point of his ice-ax; then, summoning his last reserves of strength, he knotted several ropes together and lowered them to the guides. He was so feeble by this time that these two operations took him three hours.

On the ropes dangling from above the guides sent up a specially devised sling. As there was no possible way of their reaching him, it was up to Kurz to lower himself on it—if he had the strength left. Slowly and patiently he wrapped the coils about his body, leaned out into space, started down. The men below could hear his hoarse breathing and see his boot-nails scraping weakly against the rock. In a few moments he was so close that one of the guides, balancing on the others' shoulders, could almost touch his feet.

Then suddenly the rope sling jammed and Kurz's downward progress ceased. For a desperate, straining moment he clung with fingers and toes to the ice-smooth bulge of the overhang; but the last of his strength was gone. His ice-ax dropped from his hand and went spinning downward. An instant later he himself swung out from the mountain wall into space. And hanging there at rope's end, he died.

This miserable disaster was only one among many of similar nature that occurred in the Alps in pre-war years. The Eigerwand was finally climbed in the summer of 1938, and those other famous "impossibles," the north wall of the Grandes Jorasses and the northern and western faces of the Matterhorn, also yielded at last to climbers with more luck than sense. For each success, however, there were many failures and many lives lost; and, far from being deterred by the endless list of catastrophes, there appeared to be an ever-growing supply of young men eager to devise still more spectacular and gruesome ways of killing themselves. The coming of war had at least one good effect, in that it put pretty much of an end to this sort of lunatic extreme in mountaineering. True, there are still plenty of accidents in the Alps. "Impossible" ascents are still attempted, and occasionally made. But at least a measure of sanity has been restored; the hordes of storm-trooper heroes have disappeared, and the mountains are being given back again to those who understand and love them.

The Alps were the cradle of mountaineering and have remained through the years the great international center of the sport. But the day when they were the sum and circumference of the climber's world has long since passed. Whatever else it may signify to various individuals, the heart and essence of mountaineering is adventure, and adventure, by its very definition, means the pushing back of horizons, the search for the untrodden and unknown. During the Golden Age of the last century the province of the climber was limited to a few hundred square miles in Switzerland, northern Italy and southeastern France. Today it is limited only by the boundaries of the earth itself.

The earliest non-Alpine climbing, as might be expected, was confined to regions near the great population centers of western Europe. In this field, again, the British were in the forefront, and by 1900 every peak and sub-peak from northern Scotland to Land's End had been ascended dozens—in many cases even hundreds—of times. To be sure, the British Isles possess no summits even remotely comparable to those of the Alps. The highest of all—Ben Nevis, in Scotland—rises a mere forty-four hundred feet above the sea, and the other famous pinnacles—Scawfell, Great Gable and Pillar Rock, in the English Lake District, and Snowdon and Tryfaen, in Wales—can scarcely be called mountains at all. Yet climbing has persistently remained one of the most popular recreations in the country, and the record of achievement has been remarkable.

Because of the low altitudes and the nature of the terrain British stay-at-home mountaineering is limited almost exclusively to work on crags and cliffs. "Getting to the top," as an end in itself means nothing; at the top, as likely as not, the climber will find a sheep pasture, a resort hotel, or even a whole village. It is the matter of routes that is all-important—of climbing for its own sake and its own special problems and techniques. On some of the celebrated summits in the Lake District, for example, there are as many as a dozen recognized ways of ascent up a single rock-face, ranging from simple walk-ups to precipice-routes of the severest difficulty.

As all good Americans hope some day to go to Paris, so do all good Englishmen—at least if they are mountaineers—hope to go to Switzerland. To that end, and for its own sake as well, they have, in their native hills, developed rock-climbing to a point of high technical achievement. Virtually every British climber who has won a name for himself in the Alps or Andes, Caucasus or Himalayas began his career with a strenuous apprenticeship on the cliffs of Scawfell, Tryfaen or Ben Nevis, and these remain today, as they have been for years, an unexcelled schoolroom of mountaineering. A hundred-foot hillock can often be as effective as a 20,000-foot ice-peak in developing an acquaintance with those three prime elements of the climber's world—hard rock, thin air, a rope.

Western continental Europe abounds in mountain ranges, most of them of far greater height and extent than the English hills, but none approaching the grand scale of the Alps. Most famous, because of their long association with human history, are the Pyrenees, which form the high frontier between France and Spain, and the old, rugged chain of the Italian Apennines. Although ideal for walking tours or casual ascents, neither of these ranges presents first-class climbing problems, and their summits are within easy reach of anyone with a guidebook and a sound pair of legs. The same applies, by and large, to the Harz and Black Forest regions of Germany, the Vosges and Jura of France and the many sprawling ranges of central Spain. Almost all the larger Mediterranean islands are mountainous in character—notably Corsica, Sardinia and Sicily, with its fabled Etna—and offer a great variety of climbs in wild and unspoiled country.

The mountains of Norway and Sweden, though of no great height, cover an area of many thousand square miles and in recent years have become a playground second only to the Alps among the sports centers of Europe. The scenery is magnificent. Great rock-masses rise sheer from the deep, winding fiords that indent the coastline and the landscape alternates endlessly between frozen snow-peaks and the deep, green pockets of mountain valleys. Because of the high latitude of the range, glaciers and snow-fields are found at very low elevations, and in the northern sections conditions become truly arctic. Almost alone among the mountains of Europe, the Scandinavian highlands still offer a number of first ascents. There is also considerable exploration of a minor nature still to be done in the interior of Lapland, above the Arctic Circle.

The principal mountains of Central Europe are the Carpathians, fringing the borders of Poland, Hungary and Czechoslovakia. For the most part low and wooded, they culminate in one wild and spectacular sub-range, known as the High Tatra, which bristles with granite spires and offers ascents comparable to those on the *aiguilles* of Chamonix. Since they lie behind the Iron Curtain, however, they are at present not accessible to climbers from the western world. The Balkans, on either side of the Curtain, hold little for the mountaineer except the possibility of being shot at; but the ranges of Greece, to the southeast, are both accessible and attractive. Topped by 10,000-foot Olympus, they include also Parnassus, Helicon and many other summits, which, though of no great height or difficulty, are made interesting by their ancient fame in history and myth.

Most of European Russia is a vast unbroken plain, and its only two mountainous regions are on the borders of Asia. One of these, the Urals, is little more than a long chain of hills, but the other, the Caucasus, contains the highest peaks in Europe. Rising in the far southeastern corner of the continent, between the Black and Caspian Seas, they are remote from world trade routes and centers of population and, even in pre-Communist days, were rarely visited by climbers. Of those few who did come, most were not Russians but—as in the Alps—Englishmen, and it was they who, in the second half of the last century, made most of the important first ascents in the range.

After the conquest of the Matterhorn, as we have seen, Alpine mountaineering turned largely to the development of new routes, improved techniques and guideless climbing. But there were a number of accomplished and ambitious men who were not content merely to climb, however skillfully, where others had climbed before and who soon began scanning the horizon for new worlds to conquer. Pre-eminent among these was Douglas Freshfield, one of the greatest of English mountaineer-explorers, who was at that time at the beginning of his long and varied career.* In the summer of 1868 Freshfield, in company with A. W. Moore, C. C. Tucker and one Chamonix guide, undertook the first important expedition to the Caucasus, explored the great chain from end to end, and successfully climbed two of its major summits—Elbruz and Kasbek. The ascent of the former, though not in itself difficult, was nevertheless a significant event in the history of mountaineering. In the first place Elbruz, at 18,480 feet, is the highest summit of Europe. Also it had been famous for centuries, under its ancient name, Strobilus, as the legendary prison of the Greek Titan, Prometheus. And—most important of all in a strictly climbing sense—its conquest marked the beginning of the era of serious mountaineering on a world-wide scale.

The 1880's and 1890's saw the most active period of climbing in the Caucasus. Freshfield himself returned several times and a number of other leading Alpinists also tried their luck in the newly opened wilderness of rock and ice. Even Mummery tore himself away from his beloved Chamonix *aiguilles* long enough to scale the formidable walls of Dykhtau; and the other great peaks—Shkara, Koshtantau and Ushba—fell one by one to various parties of climbers.

In 1888 and 1889 Koshtantau was the scene of one of the most famous of mountaineering tragedies. Two well-known British climbers, W. Donkin and H. Fox, set out with two Swiss guides in the summer of the former year in an attempt to reach its then-unconquered summit and vanished without leaving a trace. Rumors began to spread that they

---

* Freshfield, whose climbing activity spanned a full half century, was one of the widest-ranging as well as one of the most competent of mountaineers. In addition, he was a prolific writer, and his books on the Caucasus, Himalayas and other great ranges have become classics in their field. (See the Reading List.)

had been kidnaped and murdered by bandits, and as the months passed the affair developed almost into a minor international dispute. Then, a year after their disappearance, Freshfield and his climbing-companion, Clinton Dent, went out to the Caucasus with a small party for the express purpose of trying to clear up the mystery. After weeks of reconnoitering and climbing, the detective-mountaineers made a dramatic discovery. High on a desolate ridge of the great peak they stumbled upon Donkin and Fox's last bivouac. Sleeping bags, rucksacks, cooking utensils, personal belongings of every kind—all were lying there neatly in the heart of that frozen, lifeless world, as if their owners had left them only a few hours before and would return to them again before sunset. The sorrowful remnants made one thing clear: the lost men had been the victims of a mountaineering accident and not of foul play. Long search by Freshfield and his companions, however, yielded no trace of the bodies, and where and how Donkin, Fox and their two guides died remains to this day a mystery.

By 1900 most of the major peaks of the Caucasus had fallen, and since the beginning of the First World War there has been no climbing by westerners in the range. Occasionally reports filter through of Soviet activity in the region, and it is apparent that it has been used as a training ground for expeditions to higher Asiatic mountains. But of the nature of these exploits—and indeed of Russian mountaineering in general—very little is known.

The first climbers of the Caucasus were the pioneers of the era of world-mountaineering. Just as Freshfield and his contemporaries had turned from the Alps to the sterner challenge of the Caucasus, so did these same men and their younger successors soon begin to wander still farther afield, searching for still greater prizes. Nor were they long in finding them. What the late fifteenth and early sixteenth centuries were to the exploration of oceans and continents, the last half century has been to mountaineering. Scarcely a year has passed in that time that some new peak or range or region has not been brought into the ever-widening field of activity, and the climber's world, once bounded by the Ortler on the east and Mont Blanc on the west, has gradually become synonymous with the world itself.

During a few years around the turn of the century the expansion took place on an enormous scale. Climber-explorers like Freshfield,

A. F. R. Wollaston and the Duke of the Abruzzi—to name only a few of many—pushed doggedly in toward the mysterious mountain-giants of Africa. Other adventures, with Freshfield again among them, undertook the exploration of the huge uplift of the Himalayas, in faraway India, blazing precarious trails toward the summits of the highest peaks on earth. Still others roamed the mountain wilderness of the New World, and fought their way to the pinnacles of the Andes, the Rockies and the sprawling, ice-sheathed ranges of Alaska. By the outbreak of the First World War there was scarcely a mountainous region left on earth—from Greenland to the Antarctic, from Norway to the South Sea Islands—that had not at least been visited and reconnoitered by the new order of globe-girdling climbers.

As might be expected, the great and famous ranges have drawn the lion's share of attention. But as horizons widened and ever more ambitious mountaineers entered the field, even the most remote and obscure corners of the world have become the scene of large-scale climbing ventures. The vast icecap of Greenland, studded with massive peaks, has been visited by expeditions of many nationalities, beginning as early as 1872, when the indefatigable Edward Whymper made ascents of several west-coast summits, and culminating in 1935 with the conquest of Mount Gunnbjornsfjeld (12,139 feet), the loftiest mountain in the Arctic.* The ranges of Spitzbergen have been systematically explored, notably by the far-ranging Sir William Martin Conway, who made two journeys to the island during the 'nineties of the last century. And, at the other end of the earth, even the storm-lashed mountains of Antarctica were not long to remain unknown. In the course of the Shackleton South Polar expedition of 1906 a small party of men made the ascent of the 13,300-foot active volcano, Mount Erebus, and were rewarded by the matchless sight of its huge crater—a boiling, steaming cauldron rising from the ice-fields of the coldest region in the world. Since then there have been few ascents of Antarctic peaks, but aerial surveys have shown that there are several summits ranging up to some fifteen thousand feet, the best known and probably the highest being Mount Markham, on the route from Erebus to the South Pole.

Meanwhile, the great uplifts of Central Asia, forgotten since the

---

* Mount Forel (11,100 feet) is Greenland's most famous peak, and until recently was believed to be the highest in the Arctic. It was climbed in 1938 by a party of Swiss.

days of Marco Polo and the Europe-Cathay caravans, came back into the ken of western explorers. Travelers like Sir Aurel Stein and Sven Hedin penetrated the trans-Himalayan fastnesses of Tibet, Mongolia and Turkestan and rediscovered the vast ranges of the Hindu Kush and Pamirs, the Nan Shan and Kunlun, the Altai and Altyn Tag. These are only a few of the dozens of great escarpments which rim the high plateaus of inner Asia, and their tallest peaks rank second only to the Himalayas themselves among the mountains of the earth. Indeed, for a time during and after the last war, there were recurrent reports of a summit even higher than Everest—a mysterious giant called Amni Machen, rising from the range of the same name in the remote wilderness of western China. Such grandiose claims for it have since been pretty well disproved, but there is no question that it is a huge mountain—perhaps twenty-five thousand feet or more in height. And there are many others in Central Asia not far below it.

Up to the present time exploration rather than mountaineering has been the goal of most of the expeditions to this region; perhaps a dozen peaks, all told, have been ascended in an area larger than the United States. And since China has followed Russia into communism there will be no further ventures in the foreseeable future—at least not by men from the West. It is known that the Russians, in the past few years, have sent out several Asiatic climbing parties, notably to Everest,* the Pamirs and the remote mountains of Kamchatka; but exactly what they accomplished—and what their plans are for the future—are among their innumerable guarded secrets.

In sharp contrast to the Atlantic shores, a large part of the continental coastline and most of the large islands of the Pacific Ocean are ruggedly mountainous in character. This is particularly true of Japan, which is itself the crest of a vast submarine uplift and whose ranges cover no less than three-quarters of the total area of the country. The most celebrated, as well as the loftiest, summit is, of course, the volcano Fujiyama, or Fuji-san, rising in flawless symmetry to a height of 12,400 feet above the near-by ocean. Fuji's fame, however, is not based on any difficulties of ascent, and between foreign sightseers and native pilgrims it has probably been climbed by as many people as any other peak of comparable size in the world. Far more challenging to the skilled mountaineer are many of the summits of the so-called Japanese Alps, farther

---

* See Chapter 14.

inland, which are said to bear favorable comparison even with the best of their European namesakes.

A great deal of climbing has been done in Japan both before and since the war—not only by western visitors but by the Japanese themselves. Several members of the imperial family—notably the late Prince Chichibu—have been devotees of the sport, and as a result it has become an activity of great repute among their prestige-loving countrymen. Huts and trails abound in most of the highland regions, trained guides are available, and climbing conditions in general resemble those of the Alps rather than those of the huge, wild ranges of continental Asia. If for nothing else, mountaineers owe the Japanese a debt of gratitude for originating a phrase that, in its simplicity and rightness, is worthy of becoming a universal climber's invocation: "May our five senses be pure," they request respectfully of their ancestral gods at the beginning of an ascent—"and may the weather on the honorable mountain be fine."

Southward from Japan, the large islands of the East Indies and Melanesia are all at least partly mountainous. The Philippines, Sumatra and Java abound in volcanos, and Borneo's fabled Kinabalu, The Mountain of the Dead, is only one of many little-known peaks that rise from the jungles of its interior. New Guinea, too, is traversed by lofty ranges, virtually *terra incognita* to mountaineers, but known to possess in Mount Carstensz, a summit more than sixteen thousand feet in height—the loftiest island mountain in the world. Still farther afield, the islands of Polynesia are for the most part boldly rugged in contour—notably, of course, the Hawaiian group, with its great volcanic trio of Mauna Kea, Mauna Loa and Kilauea.

Kilauea, one of the most famous volcanos in the world, is actually not a mountain at all, but simply a huge crater in the side of Mauna Loa. Mauna Kea, on the other hand, is not only one of the greatest of volcanic peaks, but, in a very real sense, the tallest of all mountains in the world. Its height above sea level is only 13,825 feet; its roots, however, spring from the ocean floor at a depth of eighteen thousand feet, and its seaward flanks rise in one unbroken slope of almost thirty-two thousand feet from base to summit.

Australia, strangely, has scarcely any mountains worthy of the name, Mount Kosciusko, the apex of the continent, being little more than seven thousand feet high. New Zealand, on the other hand, is practically a continuous chain of ranges, and for years past its great peaks and glaciers have drawn the attention and admiration of mountaineers. Among the first on the scene were two celebrated English climbers, the Reverend W. A. Green and Edward FitzGerald, who in 1882 and 1894, respectively, came to New Zealand accompanied by Swiss guides and pioneered a way to the summits of many of the principal peaks. The New Zealanders themselves, however, were not long in learning to appreciate the mountains of their homeland. Mount Cook, which, at 12,350 feet, is the highest point of the twin islands, fell to a local party in the same years as FitzGerald's expedition, and since then by far the greater part of New Zealand mountaineering has been carried on by residents of the country. Particularly since the last war, their climbers have ranked among the finest in the world, and it was one of them, of course—Edmund P. Hillary—who in 1953 became the co-conqueror of Mount Everest.

The New Zealand ranges themselves—designated, with a signal lack of imagination, the Northern and Southern Alps—have long held a reputation as a fine climbing ground. The peaks are bold and imposing, the glaciers, of which there are many, large and magnificent. Unfortunately, however, all the highland region is cursed with atrocious weather, one day of clear skies to five of fog and storm being the depressing year-in, year-out average. As the result of the heavy precipitation, combined with the islands' high southern latitude, snow and icefields abound, and pure rock-climbing, in the European sense, is almost unknown.

The six continents, the Arctic and Antarctic, the islands of the seas: all have been encompassed in the swift spread of mountaineering to the far corners of the earth. In the space of the few preceding paragraphs it has been possible to give merely the barest sketch of a great and infinitely detailed expansion; and in the chapters that follow the spotlight must perforce be focused on a select aristocracy of the greatest mountains and the greatest climbers. But before leaving the general for the specific, the world of mountains for the mountains of the world, it is important that we be mindful of a few fundamental facts.

The first is that the sport of climbing is still scarcely a hundred years old and climbing on a world-wide scale little more than fifty. Although almost all the great ranges of the earth have been opened up and many of the major peaks climbed, what has already been done is no more than what still remains to be done.

The second is that the famous mountains and mountaineers of which we are about to read—Everest, McKinley, Aconcagua, Annapurna; Abruzzi, Mallory, Washburn, Hillary—do not by any means comprise the whole story of twentieth-century climbing. They represent merely the bright, highlighted chapters of a history that is being written every day, all over the world, wherever there are mountains and men to climb them.

The third is that mountaineering is no mere vague term indicating any sort of going-up or going-down on the bumpy surface of the earth. It is a sport, possessed of a great body of history and tradition; and climbing as we know it today would not exist if it were not for the experience and experimentation of the past. Occasionally, as in the case of the "McKinley sourdoughs," we find great ascents made by men who know nothing more about mountains than that you have to go up to get to the top. But, for the most part, climbers the world over are consciously and proudly members of a craft. They use the same implements, the same techniques, the same rules and standards of conduct, and they are the inheritors of a common body of knowledge and tradition that originated in the Alps in the middle of the nineteenth century and have been painstakingly and lovingly developed ever since.

Mountaineering is more than a matter of individual climbers, individual expeditions, individual peaks. It is a way of acting, thinking and living. It is the fraternity of men who seek high adventure in high places.

HOME GROUNDS

Mountains and Mountaineering in the United States

MOUNTAINEERING IS SCARCELY an activity for stay-at-homes. The world's great peaks and ranges are scattered over the map with a fine disregard for the law of supply and demand, and no latter-day Mohammed has had any better luck in moving them than did the original. Man must still go to the mountain, and as often as not it is not only thousands of feet to its summit but thousands of miles to its base.

This is all well and good for the armchair mountaineer. Exploration and adventure are his for the opening of a book, and the pages carry him, as on a magic carpet, to the far and little-known corners of the earth. But what of those of us who want to do more than read? What of those of us who want to *climb ourselves?* Even in the air age, a jaunt to Uganda or Peru is no simple undertaking; an elaborate expedition to Kashmir or Nepal is apt to present a few too many problems. Our climbing, if any, must be done on a more modest scale and nearer home. Fortunately for us, great peaks and ranges are not a monopoly of the other side of the world. "From every mountainside, let freedom ring" is not from the national anthem of the Hindus, Tibetans or Tierra del Fuegans: our own country and continent have their mountains too.

And they are mountains of which we have no cause to be ashamed. True, they are not so high as the Himalayas or Andes, or so famous in mountaineering history as the Alps, but in extent and variety, sweep and grandeur, they need take second place to none. From Bay of Fundy to

Puget Sound, from Arizona's mesas to Carolina's green hills, they march in rank after rank, range after range—a sky-line frontier of wilderness above our whirring twentieth-century world of men and machines.

In recent years, more and more Americans have raised their eyes to their own mountains. Freedom rings from their sides, says the song. Beauty and strength and adventure are there too, for those who seek them.

The mountains of the eastern United States, known generally as the Appalachian Highlands, stretch in a series of ranges from Maine to Georgia, roughly paralleling the Atlantic coastline and from one to three hundred miles inland. They are one of the oldest uplifts in the world—weathered, rounded and heavily forested—and nowhere attain either the height or ruggedness of our western mountains. Only a handful of the loftiest peaks rise above timber-line, and none has glaciers or perpetual snow.

The best-known of the Appalachians, for climbing and hiking, are those of the New England states. Maine's Mount Katahdin (5,267 feet —with an added thirteen-foot cairn on top to raise it to an exact mile) stands some eighty miles north of Bangor, in the heart of the largest wilderness area remaining in the East. Its summit plateau, carpeted with arctic vegetation, was formerly the home of the last herd of caribou in the United States. And its topmost pinnacle is the first point in the country to receive, each morning, the rays of the rising sun.

Southwest of Katahdin, in northern New Hampshire, are the historic White Mountains, subdivided into the Presidential and Franconia Ranges. The White Mountains have been a famous summer playground for more than a century and, in recent years, have also become a popular center for winter and spring skiing. Mount Washington (6,288 feet), the highest elevation, boasts a hotel on its very crest, with both a motor road and a cog railway connecting it with the state highways below. For those who prefer their mountains unmechanized there is also a labyrinth of beautiful footpaths, both above and below treeline, and convenient shelters scattered along the slopes and ridges.

Except for infrequent and scattered cliffs neither the White Mountains nor any of the other eastern ranges provide climbing in the Alpine sense. Up to timber-line, at about five thousand feet, the going is principally through great slanting forests and along the rocky margins of brooks and rivulets; on the bare ridges above, it is over tumbled masses of broken boulders. The only hazard is the weather, which even at the comparatively low elevations of the Appalachians is subject to sudden and violent changes. Indeed, the meteorological station on the summit of Mount Washington has records of wind velocities up to the almost incredible figure of 231 miles per hour, this last—made on April 12, 1934—the highest that has been officially recorded anywhere in the world. Too many hikers and campers have met with accidents, and even death, through taking these unspectacular and usually gentle mountains too casually. Snow and lightning and winds of twice hurricane force are matters to be reckoned with, whether they are encountered on the fearsome crags of the Himalayas or on the familiar trails above Gorham and Pinkham Notch.

South and west from New Hampshire most states of the Atlantic Seaboard present at least one attractive mountain area. Vermont has its Green Mountains, Massachusetts its Berkshires, New York its Adirondacks and Catskills, Pennsylvania its Poconos and rambling Alleghenies. Below the Potomac River the Blue Ridge Mountains, famous for their Skyline Drive, sweep across all of western Virginia, merging with the Great Smokies along the Tennessee-North Carolina boundary. Here are found the loftiest mountains of the Appalachian chain, Carolina's Mount Mitchell, at 6,684 feet, being the highest elevation in the United States east of the Mississippi. Lying in a lower latitude than the New England ranges, the Smokies, despite their greater height, seldom rise above timberline. The surrounding country, however, is still in a primitive state and offers exceptional opportunities for the best sort of outdoor life.

Most of the expert climbing done in the eastern states does not involve the complete ascent of peaks, but is concerned rather with the mastery of short, difficult stretches on ridges and cliffs. Huntington Ravine, on Mount Washington, and the so-called "Chimney," on Katahdin, both present problems to test a cragsman's worth; and in New York State, areas like the Hudson Highlands and Shawangunks, though scarcely mountains at all, offer short routes of almost every degree of difficulty. On such terrain rock-climbing is practiced in its purest form —as an exercise performed simply for its own sake—and many of America's best mountaineers have served their novitiate and perfected their skills on hills not big enough to make a bump on the horizon.

Large sections of all the Appalachian ranges lie within the boundaries of National Forests or State Parks, and their maintenance in a state of wild and profuse nature, in the very heart of the world's greatest industrial region, is a heartening example of intelligent conservation. Perhaps the most remarkable feature of the whole area is the so-called "Appalachian Trail." This is a footpath extending from the summit of Mount Katahdin, in Maine, to the summit of Mount Oglethorpe, in Georgia, and traversing en route almost all the principal mountain regions of the East. Maintained jointly by the various state governments and many local climbing and hiking clubs, it avoids cities and highways and provides a wilderness thoroughfare more than two thousand miles in length.

Spreading from western Pennsylvania to central Colorado and from the Canadian to the Mexican border, the plains of the Mississippi Basin form one of the largest flat areas of the globe. They are broken in widely separated localities by small uplifts, such as the Black Hills of South Dakota and the Ozark and Ouachita Mountains of Missouri and Arkansas; but it is not until fifteen hundred miles have intervened that the earth again buckles upward into the second great highland area of our country. This is the realm of the Rockies, the Sierra Nevadas and the Cascades, and their relation to the Appalachians is almost literally that of mountains to molehills.

The ranges of the western United States are part of the longest continuous mountain region on earth, stretching from Arctic to Antarctic along the entire length of the hemisphere. They are not the highest of the chain, but they are by far the most numerous, most varied and most widely spread, and for grandeur and sheer extent can be matched only by the great ranges of inner Asia. Rising in rank upon rank from our northern to our southern boundaries, they spread over twelve states and more than a million square miles. The Rocky Mountains, Sierras and Cascades, vast as they are, are only three among the many great chains that comprise the whole, and they themselves are composed of many lesser chains and ranges. The Rockies alone contain more than a hundred separately defined and named groups. In the state of Colorado there are fifty-two peaks more than fourteen thousand feet high and some three hundred over thirteen thousand; in California fourteen and one hundred and fifty respectively.

Historically, these mountains have played a tremendous role in the making of our country. There would be no American West, as we know it, without its peaks, canyons, passes and great intervening plateaus. Yet we may read the records of a hundred and more years and find next to nothing of mountaineering as such. The explorer and soldier, the trapper, prospector, rancher and railroad-builder: all these have had a dominant part in the winning of the West. Of the climber—of the conquest of the high summits—there is scarcely a word.

There are two principal reasons for this. The first is that the early visitors to the West were pioneers, homesteaders, fortune-seekers, with other things on their minds than mountaineering. And the second is that, in most cases, the original climbing of a peak was not a particularly difficult or outstanding feat. Vast though they are, most of our western mountains are simple in contour and of subdued relief, and all but a very few have at least one easy route to the top. The early climbers naturally took these routes, and the majority reached their goal without trouble—and, for that matter, without even knowing the techniques of mountaineering. Not one of the first ascents of a mountain over fourteen thousand feet was a famous or significant event in climbing history.

As of today, with the approaches known and the trails blazed, the summits of most of our highest peaks can be reached by virtually anyone willing and able to make the effort of a stiff uphill walk. And this is how the majority of ascents are made: by hikers, campers and even casual tourists, who neither know, nor need to know, the technical lore of mountaineering. But this does not mean that there is not real climbing for those who want it. As in the Alps, almost all the great peaks can, be scaled by various routes, and these run the gamut from "nothing-to-it" to "next-to-impossible." Among climbers who take their sport seriously it is no longer simply a matter of going up Longs Peak or the Grand Teton. It is whether you did Longs by the East Face or "The Cable," the Grand from the north or the south. Of two parties on the same summit at the same time, one may have reached it by a leisurely stroll and the other by efforts that taxed their last resources of skill and endurance.

In a book of this scope, only a few of the western peaks and ranges can be dealt with—and these very briefly. The selection has been based not merely on their height or extent, but on their attractiveness to climbers. Almost all of them lie within, or include, areas that have been designated as National Parks or Forests, and detailed information about them—as well as about many others not included here—may be had from the National Park Service of the Department of the Interior and the National Forest Service of the Department of Agriculture.

Halfway between the Mississippi and the Pacific, stretching from Montana to New Mexico, are the ramparts of the Rocky Mountains. The Rockies are the heart of the West, and the broadest, most rugged section of the mountain backbone of North America. Unlike their Canadian continuation in the north, they are in no sense a single, unbroken chain of peaks, but rather a huge complex of many chains and ranges, often widely separated by great rolling tablelands. Considered as a whole, they form the principal natural division of the United States. The so-called "Continental Divide" roughly follows their highest crests, northwest to southeast, from the Canadian to the Mexican border, all the rivers of its eastern side draining to the Gulf of Mexico and all on the western to the Pacific Ocean.

In the northern Rockies, which comprise the ranges of Montana and northern Idaho, the most spectacular peaks and finest mountain scenery are to be found in the Lewis Range, which lies largely in Glacier National Park. Bold, rocky summits, together with many small glaciers and countless lakes, make this section one of the most attractive and frequented playgrounds of the West. Central Montana is a region of rounded and unimpressive uplands, but in the southern part of the state, northeast of Yellowstone Park, the Beartooth Mountains present a jagged uplift of great wildness and scenic splendor. Granite Peak (12,850 feet), their highest elevation, was not climbed until 1923 and is considered one of the most difficult ascents in the Rockies.

Yellowstone Park, in the northwest corner of Wyoming, is bisected by the Continental Divide, but is a great geyser basin rather than predominantly mountainous. Immediately south of it, however, the central Rockies thrust upward in a series of magnificent peaks known as the Teton Range.* The Tetons are not large in extent, covering only some four hundred square miles between Jackson Hole, Wyoming, and the Idaho state line; but they are considered by experienced mountaineers to offer the best rock-climbing of any range in the country. Their sum-

---

* It was the French who discovered and named the Tetons, and they bequeathed them the Gallic Touch. *Tetons,* in French, means *breasts,* and that is what the explorers decided they resembled, rising gracefully out of the Great Plains.

mits are bold, steep and closely grouped. Their granite is sound and solid. And, unlike most of the uplifts in the West, they present few, if any, walk-ups.

Capstone of the range is the celebrated Grand Teton, 13,766 feet high, which is by way of becoming the "classic" climb of the Rockies, as the Matterhorn is of the Alps. The top of the Grand can be reached by several routes: among them two from its south saddle (for the average climber), one on the east ridge (for the better-than-average), and one up the north face, that has been done only three times and ranks as perhaps the hardest high-mountain climb in the country. Other peaks in the group include the South and Middle Teton, Mount Moran and Mount Owen, Teewinot and Nez Percé. Like the Grand, all offer routes ranging from moderate to extremely difficult.

In recent years, the Tetons have become an active climbing center, comparable to certain of the famous resorts in the Alps. Each summer they play host, not only to many individual climbers, but to groups from various clubs, and they are also the locale of America's only civilian mountaineering school, operated by Paul Petzoldt and Glenn Exum, two of the foremost climbers in the country. At the present time an ambitious building and development program is underway in the neighboring Jackson Hole country, jointly sponsored by the Federal Government and the Rockefeller interests. This will serve to make the Tetons better known to the vacationing public (which is all to the good), but may also overcrowd them (which is something else again).

Not far away, in west-central Wyoming, lies the Wind River Range, one of the finest wilderness areas remaining in the country. Far larger in extent than the Tetons, the Wind Rivers contain a host of peaks that, because of their remoteness from towns and highways, are seldom visited, or even seen. Topping the range, in its northern section, are Gannett and Fremont Peaks, the former, at 13,780 feet, being the highest summit in the state. This is one of the most truly Alpine regions in the West and contains the largest glaciers east of the coastal Cascades. Gannett Peak was not ascended until 1922, decades after most of the Rockies had fallen, and there are still several lesser summits which have never been climbed. High, wild and unspoiled, the Wind Rivers are perhaps the most attractive of all the western ranges for mountaineers and trail-riders of the future.

Other important chains of the central Rockies include the Bighorn,

Absaroka and Medicine Bow Mountains of Wyoming and the Wasatch and Uinta Mountains of eastern Utah; but these do not offer climbing comparable to that in the Tetons and Wind Rivers. In southern Idaho, the Sawtooth Range, with its famous resort of Sun Valley, offers several peaks of interest to mountaineers, but is better known as a skiing area.

South of the Wind Rivers, the main backbone of the Rocky Mountains is cut by the broad plateau of the Wyoming Basin. This gateway between the ranges was the route of the historic Oregon Trail and is now traversed by the Union Pacific Railroad. Beyond it, the southern Rockies sweep on across Colorado and into New Mexico.

The mountains of Colorado are the highest and most extensive of the whole system, one range nudging and blending with the next in bewildering number and complexity. Here are concentrated more than three-quarters of the peaks in the country exceeding fourteen thousand feet in height,* as well as a host of others so numerous that even today many have not been named. Best known of the chains is the Front Range, a great mountain barrier extending from Rocky Mountain National Park, northwest of Denver, to Pikes Peak, near Colorado Springs. Pikes Peak, though 14,110 feet high, has an auto road to the top and is not a mountaineer's mountain; but the National Park section in the north, topped by Longs Peak, is one of the most popular climbing areas in the country.

Longs itself (14,255 feet) is a strangely contradictory mountain. By its so-called "Cable" and "Keyhole" routes it is an easy walk-up and has been ascended by as many as two thousand people in a single year; but its east face is a famous and formidable precipice which can tax the skill of the most expert rock-climber. The surrounding peaks also provide ascents of varying degrees of difficulty, and for the harder ones experienced guides are available at Longs Peak Inn, in the persons of Otto von Allmen and Bob Fagan. The one unattractive feature of the region, unfortunately, is its central village of Estes Park, which plays host each summer to hundreds of thousands of visitors and is less like a mountain resort than a transplanted Coney Island.

West of the Front Range are the Sawatch Mountains, which contain the highest peaks in Colorado, and also, in Mount Elbert (14,420 feet) the second highest in the country. Elbert and its neighbors, however,

---

* There are sixty-seven of these in all: Fifty-two in Colorado, fourteen in California and one in Washington.

rise gently from broad bases and offer little lure to the ambitious climber. Of more interest in this respect are the Elk Range, still farther west, and the Sangre de Cristo Range, to the south, both of which contain steep and challenging peaks; and best of all, perhaps, are the San Juan Mountains, in the southwestern part of the state, which rival the Wyoming Wind Rivers as a remote and unspoiled wilderness. Unlike most of the southern Rockies, the San Juans are sharp and spire-like. Notable among the summits are Uncompahgre, the Matterhorn (Colorado version) and Lizard Head, the last-named a particularly spectacular pinnacle which is dangerous, as well as difficult, because of its unsound rock.

The southernmost Rockies, in New Mexico, boast several sizable ranges, but few peaks of individual prominence, and have small attraction for mountaineers. And this is true, as well, of the great plateau region west of the Rockies, that sweeps across Nevada and Arizona and includes parts of Utah, Oregon and Washington. It is not until some five hundred miles have been passed and we are close to the Pacific that the earth again thrusts up into the second great mountain region of the West.

Here, in the northwest corner of the country, is the Cascade Range, sweeping through western Washington and Oregon and on into northern California. The connecting link between the Coast Range of British Columbia, to the north, and the Sierra Nevadas, to the south, the Cascade peaks are predominantly volcanic in origin, but all are either extinct or dormant. Receiving the full tide of the moist Pacific winds, they are densely forested on their lower slopes and, higher up, possess the largest glaciers and snow-fields to be found in the country. King of the range is Mount Rainier, a magnificent snow-dome whose 14,408 feet make it the third highest of our mountains. Rainier is famous not only as a peak for climbing, but as an all-year ski terrain, its summit icecap and encircling glaciers covering over fifty square miles. Because of its nearness to centers of population—particularly Seattle—it attracts a host of inexperienced visitors and has been the scene of an unfortunate number of accidents. To the uninitiate, snow- and ice-slopes may appear far less formidable than rocky precipices, but hidden crevasses and unpredictable avalanches can make them even more dangerous.

Other fine peaks in Washington include Mount Baker, in the far north, and Adams and St. Helens, south of Rainier. Beyond these, the

Cascades are cut through by the deep gorges of the Columbia River, and on the far side is Mount Hood (11,253 feet), the highest peak in Oregon. In California, at the southern end of the range, rise the graceful, snowy cone of Mount Shasta, beloved of postcard manufacturers, and, near by, Mount Lassen, whose eruptions in 1914 and 1915 make it the most recently active volcano in the United States.

This is the end of the volcanic zone, and of the Cascades. Stretching on to the south and lying wholly in California, are the granite peaks of the Sierra Nevadas. In the central part of the state, their focal point is around Yosemite Valley, a marvelously scenic region which is also easily accessible. The climbs in this area are of two extremes: either relatively easy, on well-trodden trails, or of the utmost difficulty, suitable only for experts. Some of the most sensational rock-climbing ever accomplished has been done on the sheer spires and domes that rise from the green floor of Yosemite Park.

Farther on are the Kings Canyon and Sequoia sections of the High Sierra, the latter culminating at 14,500 feet in the summit of Mount Whitney, the highest point in the United States.* Whitney and its neighbors, unfortunately, are not good "climber's mountains." On the west, the tree-line mounts to twelve thousand feet, there is little bare rock below the summit ridges, and the gradient is so gentle that one can ride a horse almost to the top. On the east, in sharp contrast, they rise in sheer, savage precipices, but for the most part the rock is so rotten and crumbling that it makes simply for dangerous, rather than challenging, climbing. "Schizophrenic Mountains," one disgruntled visitor called them. And not without reason.

Still the Sierras, over all, are perhaps the loveliest, as well as the highest, of our ranges. Their Pacific slopes are covered with the most magnificent timber in the country—notably the giant sequoia—and the upper valleys abound with lakes, cascades and waterfalls. In the eyes of John Muir, the famous naturalist and wanderer who first explored them, they ranked as the finest of all mountains, and there are today thousands of trampers, campers and fishermen who thoroughly agree with him. Not all of them are Native Sons, either.

Mountaineering, we have seen, is a sport that was long in developing.

---

* One of the interesting aspects of Whitney is that it stands only a few miles to the northwest of Death Valley, which, at 276 feet below sea level, is the lowest point in the Western Hemisphere.

In the United States it has been longer than elsewhere. The most obvious reason for this is our lack of a first-class, easily accessible mountain playground such as the Alps provide for western Europe; another, equally important, is that throughout most of our history we have been too occupied with combatting and taming the wild places of our country to think of them in terms of pleasure and recreation. To the pioneer, as to the peasant or tribesman, a mountain is an obstacle to be crossed, circumvented or ignored. Only to men of a highly developed civilization, possessed of leisure, imagination and a love of sport, does it become something to be surmounted as an end in itself.

Today, climbing is engaged in throughout the country wherever mountains exist—which means in some thirty-six states from Maine to California. It has, perhaps, still not attained the popularity it enjoys in Europe, and there are various problems to contend with—such as the greater distances involved in this country and the scarcity of mountain shelters and experienced guides. But the latter two, at least, are problems that can be solved, and as the appeal of mountaineering spreads, the supply of its requisites will gradually meet the demand.

Both a cause and an effect of this increasing interest are the many mountaineering clubs that now exist in the United States. The better-known among them include the American Alpine Club, with headquarters in New York City; the Appalachian Mountain Club, of Boston; the Sierra Club, of San Francisco; the Colorado Mountain Club, of Denver; the Mazamas, of Portland, Oregon; the Mountaineers, of Seattle; and there are also active climbing organizations at many eastern and western universities. Of these, the American Alpine Club most closely resembles the original Alpine Club of London, maintaining high standards of membership and sponsoring major expeditions. The others, mostly with much larger memberships, are concerned chiefly with close-to-home activities, but some have also begun to expand into a wider field. Almost all publish journals,* which, taken together, present a complete and up-to-date picture of climbing activity in this country.

Another great impetus was given to mountaineering by the formation, during the last war, of the first American alpine troops. Trained in the Rockies, Cascades and Alaska, these new and specialized units were brought together as the 10th Mountain Division, which served

---

* See the Reading List.

TWO FAMOUS "UNCLIMBABLES"

(*Left*) The pinnacle of the Grépon, most famous of the Chamonix *aiguilles*, first scaled by Mummery in 1881.

Photo by Bradford Washburn

(*Below*) The notorious Eigerwand—or Wall of the Ogre—towering above the Kleine Scheidegg Hotel in the Bernese Oberland. The route of most of the "suicide climbers" of the 1930's zigzagged up the center of the face.

Courtesy Swiss National Travel Office

Edward Whymper

A. F. Mummery

Duke of the Abruzzi

Alexander Burgener

MEN OF THE MOUNTAINS (I)

with distinction in some of the fiercest fighting of the Italian campaign, and many of its veterans have since taken their place among the country's finest climbers. Also, the troops themselves are still very much in existence, and their headquarters at Camp Hale and Camp Carson, in Colorado, are perhaps the best mountain training schools in the United States.

Here, as in other countries, mountaineering tends to divide itself into three rather distinct types. The first is concerned with expeditions—to Alaska, the Andes, the Himalayas, the world's great unclimbed mountains—and in this, as we will see, Americans are becoming ever more involved. The second and third are both for stay-at-homes, but there the resemblance between them stops. They might be called, respectively, "stunt climbing" and "normal, garden-variety climbing."

In discussing "stunt climbing" we are back again to the subjects of specialization and mechanization. Using many of the techniques first developed in the Alps, our own "rock-engineers" have in recent years developed them even further, until the scaling of sheer walls and precipices has become almost a separate branch of mountaineering—a sort of sport within a sport. If it can be called a sport, that is. To the average climber, let alone the non-climber, it seems more like an all-out form of masochism. But the *aficionado* of the vertical, time has shown, is a man who will not be denied, and year by year his methods become more ingenious and his list of "impossible" ascents grows longer.

That such a climber possesses great skill and courage is beyond argument; and let it be said for the American variety that there are no fanatically jingoistic overtones in his attitude. Also—and this is much to its credit—"rock engineering," as practiced in this country, has resulted in remarkably few fatalities. For one thing, most of the ascents undertaken here are not on the huge scale of the "suicide climbs" in the Alps, and, in the event of storm or other emergency, the climbers are usually able to lower themselves to safety. Furthermore, technical devices, both for climbing and protection, have been enormously improved. Contrary to appearances, the cragsman on his precipice is not hell-bent for self-destruction but merely enjoying himself in his peculiar fashion. Dangling from his pitons, wielding his rock drills and expansion bolts,* inching up like a spider over dizzying abysses—*but knowing at all times exactly what he is doing*—he is probably in less danger than the pop-eyed novice watching him from a near-by gentle ridge, who the

---

* For a description of technical climbing gear, see Chapter 16.

next moment may step carelessly on a loose rock and go plunging to his death.

The mechanized climber has borrowed from the Europeans the system of "graded" climbs—from First Degree to Sixth—and Sixth-plus is his metier. High summits, as such, do not interest him. His concern is with routes, and the harder the better. Thus, two of the most famous rock-climbs in the country are on uplifts that by no stretch of imagination could be called mountains at all. One is Shiprock, a sheer volcanic outcropping in the New Mexican desert, and the other the Devil's Tower, an almost vertical fluted shaft on the plains of eastern Wyoming, neither of which rises as much as two thousand feet above its base. Much climbing of this sort has also been done on the great rock faces of Yosemite Park, notably by members of the Sierra Club, who for several years have specialized in this sort of work and accomplished some almost incredible feats.

A composite of excerpts from recent accounts of such ascents will give the general idea:

". . . We started off carrying fifteen karabiners, ten horizontal pitons, eight angle pitons and twelve expansion bolts plus hangers; we also had a 300-foot rappel rope, a 120-foot climbing rope and a 120-foot hauling line for the packs." . . . "The chimney required a ladder of pitons up its full length, and I had the honor of exhausting myself on this lead. The top of the chimney was blocked by a horizontal overhang. Finding no usable cracks, I got around it with two expansion bolts." . . . "At the rate of four feet an hour, S. made twenty-five feet, using several pitons and bolts. One piton turned thirty degrees with his weight on it, but he quickly shifted his position and averted a fall." . . . "We made about 450 feet in over twenty hours' continuous climbing. The greatest difficulty was the lack of a suitable ledge for a bivouac; the night was passed on a tilted chockstone—crowded with two people, more so with four." . . . "In the prussik slings again, swinging slowly round and round in the air. At the high piton, rest again. Oh for a hold, a small tiny ledge for the fingers to grip! A slab of marble might have offered more holds." . . . "In the next section pitons had to be inserted while the climber was in a semi-layback position, holding on with one hand. This exhausting procedure resulted in one fall. The leader dropped from fifteen feet above his upper piton but was stopped by the dynamic belay of his second." . . . "On the morning of the fifth day we stood upon the summit. The 1500 feet had required twenty-five leads, nine bolts and over 150 pitons. Sometimes it seems odd that such torment of the body should afford such satisfaction. . . ."

Odd indeed.

Confronted with such performances, the average "garden-variety" climber blinks and looks elsewhere. It is not for him to pass judgment on his betters; and if the "rock-engineers" enjoy their agonies it is their privilege to pursue them, provided they do not kill themselves or—more important—cause others to be killed in trying to rescue them. Mountaineering, as has been said before, means different things to different men. There is the extreme of those who drill and hammer their way up precipices, and the other extreme of those who prefer to make their ascents by paved roads and cog railways. But the traditional mountain way lies somewhere in between; and it is a way which more and more Americans have been following in recent years.

This climbing is done without benefit of either hardware or engines. It involves no "famous firsts," no scaling the unscalable, no ordeals of the Sixth Degree, but merely a few congenial companions with stout boots on their feet, grub in their knapsacks and a handsome mountain before them that may be fun to surmount. Each year there is an increase in visitors to our great wilderness areas. And each year more of them are venturing high upon the hills: from Katahdin to Whitney, from Catskills to Tetons, from the bald knobs of the Smokies to the snowcap of Rainier. Perhaps they have not yet learned the difference between a crampon and a karabiner, a rappel and a prussik, but they have learned more important things than these. And having done so, they are perhaps on the road to being truer mountaineers than if they had spent a night lashed to a precipice with sixteen pitons and a prayer.

They know that the American out-of-doors is compounded of other things than motels, filling stations and clover-leaf intersections. They know what it is to stand on an island in the sky, while the sun goes down and the pinprick lights twinkle on in the shadowed valley below. They know the struggle of heart, lung and limb on the long upward pull and the sharp, sudden thrill of a summit gained at last. They know that the fabled ambrosia and nectar of the gods were really nothing more than a ham sandwich and canteen of water. They know what sleep can be, snug in a bed-roll, in the purple night. And knowing all this, they know the love of mountains, *for their own sake,* which is at bottom all that mountaineering has ever meant, or ever will.

THE GREAT ONE

The Story of Mount McKinley

IN THE FARAWAY frozen heart of Alaska stands the highest mountain in North America. We know it as Mount McKinley. Men of other races, however, have had other, and better, names for it. To many of the aboriginal Indian tribes of the region it was known as Denali— The Home of the Sun. Others referred to it as Tralaika, still others as Doleyka, and the Russians, when they came, called it Bulshaia Gora. Significantly these three names, in three different tongues, meant the same thing—The Great One.

For this remote snow-peak in our own Northwest is not merely the culminating point of the North American continent; it is also one of the greatest single mountains on earth. The giants of the Himalayas and Andes are higher—twenty-two thousand to twenty-nine thousand feet, as against McKinley's 20,300—but these figures indicate total heights above sea level, and the mountains usually rise from lofty plateaus that are themselves ten to fifteen thousand feet high. McKinley, however, has no such headstart. The valley of the Yukon River, from which its northern slopes spring, is a scant fifteen hundred feet above the sea, and the wilderness of forests and glaciers to the south is only slightly more elevated. The mountain soars up in one gigantic, unbroken sweep of rock and ice to its full height—three and a half miles straight up from base to peak.

But the greatness of McKinley is more than a matter of arithmetic. Every traveler who has laid eyes on it, from near or far, has declared it to be one of the most impressive sights in the world. From Cook Inlet on the Pacific, two hundred miles to the south, its snowy crest dominates the northern horizon; from Fairbanks, a hundred and fifty miles north, it appears like a great white giant crouched against the sky. Except for its immediate neighbor, 17,000-foot Mount Foraker, it has not a single rival. Its cloud-hung battlements tower, lone and immense, over three hundred thousand square miles of central Alaska.

This colossus among mountains has now been climbed ten times. The records of these ascents, together with those of the several near-misses, make a story that, for achievement and disappointment, tragedy and comedy, heroism and even villainy, are unsurpassed in the annals of mountaineering.

So far as we know, the first white man to look upon McKinley was the English navigator, George Vancouver. While exploring the southern coast of Alaska in 1794 he saw "distant, stupendous snow mountains" to the north. He did not, however, approach any nearer, nor did any other white men, so far as we know, for almost a hundred years. The Russians, who owned and occupied the territory for the first two-thirds of the last century, obviously knew of the peak, since they gave it a name, but there is no record of any exploration in its vicinity. In 1867 the United States purchased Alaska for what then seemed the enormous sum of $7,200,000—the famous "Seward's Folly." During the next twenty years traders and prospectors trickled in, and towns and trading posts were established. But they hugged the coasts. It was not until the 1890's that the interior wilderness began to be opened up, and Americans discovered that they had acquired not only a vast arctic storehouse of gold, fish and fur, but the highest mountain on the continent as well.

Most of the pioneers of central Alaska were men in search of gold. One of these, Frank Densmore, penetrated the McKinley region in 1889 and returned with such fabulous descriptions of the mountain that it was known for years among the Yukon prospectors as Densmore's Peak. Another, W. A. Dickey, followed in 1896, reaching the outer edge of the mountain's great skirt of glaciers. Presumably Dickey was ignorant of the already-existing names for the peak—or perhaps he was merely a good Republican. In either case, he named it in honor of William

McKinley, who was then candidate for President of the United States. And the name stuck.

In the next ten years several individuals and expeditions approached the mountain, among them George Eldridge and Robert Muldrow, of the U. S. Geological Survey, who measured it by triangulation and fixed its height at 20,300 feet. The first actual attempt at ascent took place in 1903. Under the leadership of Judge Wickersham, one of the foremost citizens of the new boom town of Fairbanks, a party of four men packed in to the base of the mountain and began to climb it. They were unfortunate in their choice of route, however, for they were halted almost immediately by unscalable walls of ice, and soon turned back. Thereafter Judge Wickersham was often heard to declare that the summit would never be reached except by an airplane or a balloon. Thereafter, that is, until it was climbed.

The next man to enter the expanding saga of McKinley was one of the strangest figures in the history of exploration and mountaineering. This was Dr. Frederick Cook, who was later to win world-wide notoriety as the bogus "Discoverer of the North Pole." At this time, however, Dr. Cook was concentrating on becoming the equally bogus "Conqueror of Mount McKinley." His first expedition to the mountain was in the same year as Judge Wickersham's, but it was little more than a reconnaissance of the surrounding passes and glaciers. Then in 1906 he returned and plunged energetically into the business of making his own particular brand of history.

Ironically, Cook's companions at the outset of this second venture were two men of complete honor and integrity. They were Herschel Parker and Belmore Browne, whose later battles with McKinley form one of the brightest, most heroic chapters of mountain history. On this occasion, however, they and Cook bogged down in the great wilderness south of the peak and were forced to withdraw without finding even a way of approach to the heights.

Then began Cook's audacious hoax. With only one companion, a packer named Edward Barrill, he returned to the base of the mountain, was unheard from for a few weeks, and reappeared with the claim that he had reached the summit. Neither Parker, Browne nor anyone else who knew McKinley believed him. He had not, for one thing, had enough time for the ascent, and, furthermore, his description of his experiences did not tally with their own observations. But Cook was a fraud who knew his business. Undeterred by suspicions and accusations, he returned to civilization and began systematically to reap the rewards of his "feat." He wrote a book called *To the Top of the Continent,* in which he described his struggles on the ascent and the magnificence of the view from the top. He showed photographs which he said he had taken on the summit. He lectured before public gatherings and learned societies. As far as the world was concerned, he was what he claimed to be—the "Conqueror of McKinley."

Seven years passed before the fraud was finally exposed. Parker and Browne could not conclusively prove their suspicions, and it remained for Hudson Stuck and his companions, who in 1913 made the true first ascent, to settle the matter once and for all. Stuck was Archdeacon of the Yukon, a man above suspicion in every way, and his description of McKinley refuted Cook's in countless details. From this point on the evidence piled up rapidly. Barrill, Cook's packer, after years of silence, signed a sworn statement that his employer's claims were untrue. An insignificant foothill peak was found, which coincided so completely with Cook's supposed photographs of McKinley's summit that it became obvious they had been made there. Within a short time the "conqueror's" claims were thoroughly discredited. Then, a few years later, came the still more sensational exposure of his faked discovery of the North Pole, and Cook's fantastic career reached its end. He dropped into obscurity—a dishonored, broken man.

Meanwhile the fight against The Great One went on. The bogus conquest had, if nothing else, aroused widespread interest in the greatest American mountain, and the attack was on in full force.

First in the field was a group of men who put even the incredible Dr. Cook to shame. They are known in climbing history as the Sourdough Expedition, and no stranger or more haphazard exploit than theirs has ever occurred on any major mountain in the world. By every accepted standard they should not only have made a fiasco of their attempt, but all should have been killed five times over. Instead, they missed immortality by a hairbreadth—or, to be accurate, three hundred feet—and, in addition, performed what is undoubtedly one of the greatest exploits in the annals of mountaineering.

The sourdoughs of McKinley were a half-dozen prospectors and miners of the vicinity of Fairbanks. None of them had ever been on a mountain in his life, but they were typical Alaskan frontiersmen, with frontiersmen's strength and pride, and when they heard of Cook's claims they snorted in disbelief and decided it was high time they took a hand in the affair themselves. "If McKinley is going to be climbed," they decided in effect, "we're the boys who are going to do it."

And in the spring of 1910, off they went.

The venture was organized in a way that would make a good Alpine Club member's hair stand on end. Or, rather, it wasn't organized at all. The $500 which was the bulk of their capital was put up by one Billy McPhee, a public-spirited saloonkeeper of Fairbanks. There was no leader, no prearranged plan of attack, and by the time they reached the base of the mountain half the party had come to blows with the other half and left for home. There was no scientific knowledge among them, no proper clothing or equipment, in fact nothing whatever of the things which a mountaineer is supposed to possess—save two. They had pluck and they had luck.

Their first great good fortune was in selecting the Muldrow Glacier as their way of approach. This vast tongue of ice extends from the northern foothills up into the very heart of the McKinley range, and, for forty years to come, it was the only practical route that was found giving access to the upper reaches of the mountain. The sourdoughs' experience was small, but their instinct was right. Day after day, they toiled up the gigantic ice-slope of the Muldrow, hacking steps, bridging crevasses, moving slowly on and up into a silent, frozen world where no living thing had ever moved before.

At last they reached the glacier's head. They were now eleven thousand feet above the sea, but barely at the base of the mountain proper, and above them the white ridges and precipices of McKinley towered almost another two miles into the sky. By this time only three members of the expedition were left—Pete Anderson, Billy Taylor and Charley McGonogol—but these three, as they were soon to prove, were men of herculean strength and determination. For several days they camped at the head of the glacier, studying the vertical wilderness above them and awaiting favorable weather. Then, at two in the morning of April tenth, they started off.

It should perhaps be mentioned, at this point, that an assault on a mountain as huge as McKinley is a vastly different proposition from climbing in a range like the Alps, where the distances are small and

huts and shelters abound. Here, climbing itself is only one of the problems involved; more than half the battle is the establishment of high
camps and the bringing up of reserve supplies, so that the climbers will
not starve or freeze to death in the event of a mishap or a storm. On
the great Himalayan peaks, as we shall see, one of the greatest difficulties has always been that of porterage. On McKinley, every normal
expedition has spent weeks preparing the way for the final assault. Such
finicky, tenderfoot precautions, however, were not in the line of the
Messrs. Anderson, Taylor and McGonogol. With the food and equipment that an average person might take along for a picnic lunch, they
climbed from their glacier camp to within three hundred feet of the
highest point of North America and back—*all in one day.**

The sourdoughs, unlike most mountaineers, have left no written
record of their venture, and the details of their astonishing ascent are
very vague. It is known, however, that their route was roughly that
followed by most subsequent expeditions: from the head of the Muldrow, up the great ice-spine that was later to be called Karstens Ridge,
and into the upper ice-basin near the mountain's summit. It was when
they reached this basin—now known as Harper Glacier—that they
made a choice that was to cheat them of world-wide fame. McKinley is
a mountain of two peaks—the south, or true summit, 20,300 feet high,
and the north, a scant three hundred feet lower. Standing between them
on that day, already at seventeen thousand feet and with victory in their
grasp, the sourdoughs chose the wrong one.

What prompted their choice has never been satisfactorily explained.
It may have been that they thought the north peak was the higher.
It may have been the knowledge that half the population of central
Alaska was watching through telescopes in Fairbanks, from which the
north peak alone is visible. At all events, the north peak it was. Mc-
Gonogol, near collapse, had to turn back within five hundred feet of
the goal, but Anderson and Taylor struggled on up the ice-slope, in
sub-zero cold, until they reached the top. There they unfurled the Stars
and Stripes on a fourteen-foot flagstaff they had miraculously carried
with them and planted it firmly on the topmost pinnacle. This done,
they started down, picked up the exhausted McGonogol, and descended
the nine thousand feet to the Muldrow Glacier without a single stop.

---

* In the Arctic, in spring and summer, the climbing day is limited only by the endurance of the climbers. Instead of darkness, nighttime brings merely a gray twilight,
and it is possible to climb safely at any hour.

And in another week or so they were safe and sound in Billy McPhee's Fairbanks saloon, telling all about it to anyone who would buy them a drink.

Confronted with a performance like this, the usual rules and standards of mountaineering collapse into the wastebasket. Indeed, the whole story of their ascent seemed so fantastic that for several years it was generally disbelieved—those same years, ironically, during which Dr. Cook was still a national hero. It remained again for Archdeacon Stuck to clear things up. In his ascent of the true summit in 1913 he had ample opportunity to view the top of the north peak, and what he saw completely vindicated the claims of the sourdoughs. The American flag was gone, to be sure, long since torn to shreds in the wild arctic winds; but the flagstaff was still there—"plain, prominent and unmistakable."

The sourdoughs never went back to McKinley. They were prospectors, not mountaineers, and one fling at The Great One was enough for them. That they could have reached the true summit had they tried no one who has known them or the mountain has ever doubted. But the fact remains that they didn't. The highest point in the continent still stood, lofty and untrodden, awaiting its next attackers.

And they were not long in coming.

Indeed, in the same year as the Sourdough Climb Herschel Parker and Belmore Browne were again in the vicinity of the mountain. As in 1906, they approached it from Cook's Inlet, on the south, fighting their way through almost impassable country, and this time they reached McKinley's base—only to find above them a sheer fifteen thousand feet of precipice and avalanche slope. Convinced that the peak could never be climbed from that side, they turned dejectedly away. And since then The Great One has never been challenged from the south.

But Parker and Browne were not through yet. McKinley had cast its spell upon them, and in 1912, six years after their first attempt, they were back again for their third and last. This time, profiting from experience, they approached McKinley from the north, by the same general route that the sourdoughs had used. But there any resemblance between their expedition and that of the doughty pioneers ended. Both of them were thoughtful, highly educated men—Parker, a physicist and university professor and Browne, a distinguished painter—and their attack was as reasoned and carefully planned as the sourdoughs' had been haphazard. For months in advance they pored over maps, planned their marches and camps, assembled their supplies and equipment. Then, with Merle La Voy and Arthur Aten, two Alaskans who had been with them in 1910, they set out for their goal.

From late February until late May they mushed in by dogsled from Seward, on the coast, to the inner fastnesses of the mountain. After much reconnoitering they found a pass through the northern ridge, came out on the Muldrow Glacier and began its steep, laborious ascent. The Muldrow was long and broad, but it could never be mistaken for a paved avenue. It lunged down from the heights like a colossal ski-jump, and its surface was an ice-choked wilderness of humps and hollows. In some places huge seracs, a thousand feet high, had to be surmounted; in others were yawning, seemingly bottomless crevasses that they circumvented. Often the sled-dogs would tumble headlong into them and hang howling by their harnesses until they were pulled out.

Back and forth, back and forth, went the men and dogs and sleds, establishing camps and bringing up supplies. But slowly they advanced, and at last, in the first week of June, they reached the head of the glacier. Here, at eleven thousand feet, the great northeast ridge of McKinley began its skyward climb. Leaving the dogs behind, with Aten to take care of them, Parker, Browne and La Voy set foot at last upon the mountain proper.

Almost immediately they encountered the frightful weather that was to plague them during their whole ordeal on the peak. A blizzard howled down, the ice-cliffs cracked and groaned, and avalanches roared about them like artillery. For four days the men huddled in their tent, rubbing one another's bodies to keep from freezing to death, clinging to the guy-ropes so that they would not be blown into eternity. When the storm had passed they resumed the ascent and for a week crept upward. Uncounted thousands of steps had to be hacked in the glazed snow of the ridge. Backbreaking loads had to be carried in relays to higher camps. At one point their food supply ran so low that they had to descend all the way to the glacier to replenish it. But they pushed on doggedly and at last gained the upper basin, at a height of about sixteen thousand feet.

Here another storm imprisoned them for days, but they bided their time hopefully, for they were confident that the worst of McKinley was beneath them. And, indeed, when the weather finally cleared, the last four thousand feet of the south peak appeared as merely a gentle slope into the sky, easy of access and presenting no major difficulties. At six in the morning of June 29 they began the summit dash with high hearts.

Dash, to be sure, is scarcely the word. It was still necessary for them to hack out footholds in the cone of ice and to halt every few steps, gasping, in the thin, freezing air. But they made steady progress and within four hours had gained half the distance. The summit point of North America stood out near and clear above them. "It rose," Browne declared later, "as innocently as a tilted snow-covered tennis court, and as we looked at it we grinned with relief—we *knew* the peak was ours."

Then the last blow fell. With paralyzing suddenness the wind sprang up into a howling gale, the sky darkened and the blizzard resumed. By the time they had struggled up another thousand feet they could no longer see one another at five yards through the blinding snow, and the sixty-mile wind threatened to hurl them at any moment from the mountainside. Bent double, frost-crippled, scarcely able to breathe, they still crept on until they reached the limit of human endurance. To have gone another step upward would have been suicide. At a height of twenty thousand feet—a mere three hundred from their goal—they turned back.

Somehow they succeeded in descending to their highest camp, and two days later they made a second attempt. But again the elements defeated them. A thick, freezing fog closed in about them, in which they could neither see nor breathe, and they were stopped at 19,300 feet. The next day, both their supplies and strength exhausted, they began the descent of the mountain. "I remember," said Browne, "only a feeling of dull despair."

Thus ended one of the most gallant unsuccessful ventures in the story of mountaineering. That it did not end in final and complete tragedy was merely a stroke of the greatest luck. For in that summer of 1912 the volcano Katmai, four hundred miles away, was in eruption, and the shock of its explosions was felt throughout the plains and ranges of central Alaska. Only a few days after they had descended to the lowlands, the weary, discouraged men were startled by a vast thunder of sound, so great that it seemed the earth itself were splitting open. And, indeed, it was. Behind them, as they watched, the whole north face and ridges of McKinley, on which they had so recently stood, gave a monstrous shudder, detached themselves from the main mass of the mountain and plunged wildly into the valleys below.

That was their last view of McKinley—roaring defiance at its challengers.

Mountains are not greatly concerned with human concepts of justice. Parker and Browne devoted years of their lives to the exploring and ascent of McKinley, only to meet ultimate defeat. Its next assailants spent a total of two months on its forbidding terrain—and conquered it.

Not that there was anything fortuitous in the triumph of Archdeacon Hudson Stuck. He and his companions were mountaineers of the first order; he had made many ascents in the American and Canadian Rockies, and for years past, during his journeys among the Indians of Alaska, he had seen McKinley from afar and yearned to climb it. Then, at last, in the spring of 1913 Stuck received leave of absence from his duties and set out from the mission station of Nenana to achieve his ambition. His companions were Harry Karstens, a sturdy sourdough who had come to Alaska in the Klondike gold rush and was later to become superintendent of McKinley National Park; Robert Tatum, a twenty-one-year-old missionary from Tennessee; Walter Harper, a strong, cheerful, young halfbreed, who had been Stuck's dog-driver and interpreter for several years; and two Indian youngsters from the Nenana mission school named Johnny and Esaias.

With dogs and sleds they mushed across the white plains of central Alaska, crossed the outer spurs and ridges that guard McKinley and came out at last on the Muldrow Glacier, as the other expeditions had done before them. Here Esaias, having done his bit, was sent back to Nenana, Johnny remaining to take care of the dogs. Slowly and carefully the little party threaded its way up the steep maze of the glacier, probing and zigzagging to avoid the great crevasses, suffering greatly from cold and snowstorms and the fierce wind that swooped down on them from the heights.

Presently, however, they reached the head of the glacier and stood staring upward at the huge white wilderness of the upper mountain. But, as they stared, they realized something was wrong. The great ridge which was to be their route was not at all as the previous expeditions had described it—a thin, clean knife-edge cutting into the sky. What they saw instead was an indescribable chaos of pinnacles and chasms and great tumbled ice-masses piled crazily upon each other as far as the eye could see. And then they realized what had happened. The great earth tremors of the previous year, from which Parker and Browne had barely escaped with their lives, had indeed blown to bits what had formerly been the northeast ramparts of the mountain. The ridge that the other parties had ascended had completely ceased to be. Instead of following a route which others had pioneered before them, they were faced with the necessity of becoming pioneers themselves.

What Stuck and his companions did then was quite simply this: they cut a three-mile staircase in the ice. With patience and endurance they hacked and chopped and clawed their way from the 11,000-foot altitude of the Muldrow's head to the 16,000-foot heights of the upper basin. They surmounted ice-blocks as large as three-story houses, they edged around cornices that hung in space a mile above the glaciers; they struggled up with their supplies on their backs, descended again, struggled up with more. None of them ventured to count the thousands or tens of thousands of steps they cut, but Stuck later estimated that each member of the party, in going back and forth, had climbed at least sixty thousand feet—or three times the total height of McKinley.

After days of toil the savage earthquake-shattered ridge was at last behind them. On June third they camped at 16,500 feet in the middle of the upper basin, between the twin peaks of the mountain, and three days later at eighteen thousand feet on the slopes just beneath the summit. And now the blessing that had been so cruelly withheld from Parker and Browne was granted to them: the day of the final assault was clear and fine.

They started at three in the morning and for hour after hour crept upward through the frozen gray silence of the arctic heights. Sometimes it was still necessary to hack steps with their axes; at other times their crampons sufficed, biting deeply into the hard-crusted slope. At eleven o'clock they passed the point at which Parker and Browne had been turned back by the blizzard. At one they stepped up upon the horseshoe ridge that forms the summit of the peak. And a few moments later—

"—there still stretched ahead of us," wrote Stuck, "and perhaps one hundred feet above us, another small ridge with a north and south pair of little haycock summits. This is the real top. With keen excitement we pushed on. Walter Harper, who had been in the lead all day, was the first to scramble up; a native Alaskan, he is the first human being to set foot on the top of Alaska's great mountain, and he had well earned the lifelong distinction. Karstens and Tatum were hard upon his heels, but the last man on the rope had almost to be hauled up the last few feet, and fell unconscious for a moment upon the floor of the little snow basin that occupies the top of the mountain."

Four men stood at last on the summit of North America.

Their first act was to thank God for permitting them to achieve their goal. "This prime duty done," to quote the reverend archdeacon, they set up the instruments that they had carried with them and took thermometer and barometer readings. Then they let their eyes sweep out over the stupendous panorama that no man had ever seen before—more than fifty thousand square miles of Alaska, peaks and ranges, glaciers and valleys, rivers and plains, from the ice-locked arctic interior to the sea.

But it is not alone for the sake of a "view" that men struggle up to the high places of the earth. Let us allow the conqueror of McKinley to describe the mountaineer's reward, for few men have described it better:

"Only those who have for long years cherished a great and almost inordinate desire, and have had that desire gratified . . . can enter into the deep thankfulness and content that filled the heart. . . . There was no pride of conquest . . . no gloating over good fortune that had hoisted us a few hundred feet higher than others who had struggled and been discomfited. Rather was the feeling that a privileged communion with the high places of the earth had been granted; that not only had we been permitted to lift up eager eyes to these summits, secret and solitary since the world began, but to enter boldly upon them, to take place, as it were, domestically in their hitherto sealed chambers, to inhabit them, and to cast our eyes down from them, seeing all things as they spread out from the windows of heaven itself."

They constructed a rough cross of birch staves which they had carried with them, thrust it deep into the snow, and, gathering around it, spoke the solemn, joyful words of the Te Deum. Then they started down, the tiredest and happiest of men.

For nineteen years after its conquest no one approached McKinley. Then, in the spring of 1932, two separate expeditions converged upon

it at the same time. One was successful in every respect. The other culminated tragically in the only deaths that have occurred on the mountain.

The successful party was composed of Erling Strom, a well-known
Norwegian-American skier, Alfred Lindley, a Minneapolis attorney,
Harry Liek, superintendent of McKinley National Park, and Grant
Pearson, a park ranger. They reached the upper basin by substantially
the same route as the earlier parties and successfully scaled both north
and south peaks, thus becoming the first party to reach both summits
of McKinley.

High on Karstens Ridge the Strom-Lindley party discovered a thermometer left by Stuck. It had been the archdeacon's belief that Mc-
Kinley, in winter, was the coldest place in the world, and on his descent
of the mountain he had cached a minimum thermometer at a point
where he hoped the next party would find it. The climbers of 1932
proved that he had been right. The indicator of the instrument had
dropped past the end of the scale, which was 95° below zero, and was
stuck in the bulb, where it could go no farther. It appeared obvious,
therefore, that at one time or another during the winters of the intervening years, the temperature had sunk to at least 100° below zero—
the greatest natural cold ever recorded anywhere on earth.

The second 1932 expedition to McKinley did not arrive on the scene
until the first was already high on the mountain. This was the so-called
"Cosmic Ray" expedition, which planned to undertake extensive scientific observations at great altitudes and was led by Allan Carpé, one of
the most accomplished young American mountaineers. These climbers
brought a startling modern innovation to the technique of mountaineering. And on the same day they found Stuck's thermometer on Karstens
Ridge, Strom and his companions stared down the face of a precipice
to see a plane landing supplies at the head of the Muldrow Glacier,
four thousand feet below. This was the first time in climbing history
such a feat had been attempted, much less accomplished.

During the next week, while the first party successfully scaled both
the north and south peaks, they saw nothing more of Carpé and his
expedition. When at last they descended to the head of the Muldrow,
the plane was gone, but two tents were standing near the former site
of one of their own camps. And the tents were deserted.

"Immediately," Strom had said, "we felt that something had gone wrong. Inside one tent we found two open sleeping bags and a pot half full of frozen mulligan stew. From the other tent, containing cosmic ray apparatus, we could hear a little mechanism slowly ticking."

From a diary found in one of the sleeping bags they learned that the only occupants of the tents had been Carpé and one companion, Theodore Koven. There being no sign of either man, they pushed on down the glacier, and it was not long before their fears were confirmed. A mile and a half below the camp they spied a tiny dark object against the white immensity of snow. It was Koven's body. One leg had been injured and also the side of his head. He had obviously fallen into a crevasse, but had managed to climb out again, only to collapse and die from exposure.

Carpé's body has never been found.

Few great mountains were climbed during the years of the Second World War, but McKinley was an exception. Indeed, it was climbed, not in spite of, but because of the war—as a military enterprise—at a time when Alaska was thought to be in imminent danger of invasion. Organized jointly by the U. S. Army and the American Alpine Club, the main purpose of the expedition was to test both men and equipment under the severest conditions that might prevail in arctic or mountain warfare. Reaching the top of McKinley was only a secondary aim, but this was accomplished for good measure.

The ascent took place in the summer of 1942, and seventeen men participated: a mixture of army specialists and trained mountaineers. Among the latter—and the expedition leaders in terms of actual climbing—were Bradford Washburn, Terris Moore, Robert Bates and Walter Wood, the four outstanding Alaskan climber-explorers of recent years. Organization was on an elaborate scale, and there was much experimentation with the parachuting of supplies from army planes. Some time was lost by the inevitable storms. Much more was spent in the testing of food, clothing and all manner of gear. But still the party made steady progress; presently they were strung out along the mountainside in the classic position for attack; and at last came the happy ending when a total of seven men reached the summit, on two successive days.

This was the first time that the American Army, as such, had ever come to grips with a great peak. And in doing so, it helped usher in

a new era of large-scale, scientific mountaineering. Surely, in all the
history of climbing, no greater contrast can be found than that between
this venture and that of the 1910 sourdoughs. Thirty-two years had seen
changes in the world—and on McKinley too.

For the next five years The Great One was left to its solitude. But
with war's end men were again able to turn their eyes to the mountaintops, and in the years since it has been climbed no less than seven times.
The first of these expeditions, in 1947, was jointly sponsored by the
strange combination of the New England Museum of Natural History
and RKO-Radio Pictures. The museum was interested in scientific research, the movie company in a mountain film it was preparing—which
passed on its name to the venture as "Operation White Tower." By no
coincidence at all, the director of the museum was Bradford Washburn,
already a McKinley veteran, and in the late spring of 1947 he was back
on the mountain, at the head of a variegated group of climbers, scientists, photographers and army "observers." Also in the party was
Mrs. Washburn, the first woman to enter the domain of Denali.

At the beginning the usual share of foul weather was encountered,
but the expedition was sufficiently big and well-equipped to wait out
storms that would have routed a smaller group; and as it moved higher
the skies cleared into a succession of flawless days that Washburn said
were the best he had ever seen on the mountain. This time, eight climbers went all the way, including Mrs. Washburn, who thereby scored
another "first." And she is still the only woman to have stood on the
top of the continent. In addition to the main south peak, several members of the party also scaled the north peak, marking the third ascent
of the Sourdough Summit.

The next two expeditions—one later in 1947, the other in 1948—
were on the smaller scale of the earlier, prewar climbs: but they were
both successful. Each was composed of students from the University
of Alaska, at Fairbanks, the first led by G. Herreid and the second by
Walter Gonnason. And both benefited by stores and equipment left on
the mountain by the "White Tower" party. On the 1947 ascent, three
men reached the top; in 1948, four.

All these ascents were made from the northeast, along the route originally found by the sourdoughs. For some forty years no one had tried
any other side of the mountain, and most climbers agreed with the

eloquent opinion of Fred Printz, a famous Alaskan old-timer who had accompanied two of the early expeditions on their search for other routes. Fred had said: "It ain't that we can't find a way that's possible, takin' chances. There ain't no way."

Bradford Washburn, however, had been forming other ideas. A pioneer in Alaskan aerial photography, he had made many flights over and around McKinley and became convinced that its far side was also vulnerable to attack. Accordingly, four years after "Operation White Tower," he returned to the mountain for the third time and, at the head of a party of eight, set out to climb the west buttress. This route, as Washburn was the first to point out, would have been extremely difficult without the use of a plane. The long wilderness trip around the mountain and a subsequent forty-four-mile grind up the huge Kahiltna Glacier would have exhausted a heavily laden expedition before it even reached the western base. But now it was 1951, not 1910 or 1913. Air transport was available. Four members of the party, bent on exploration and surveying, made the trip overland, but carrying supplies only for their own march. The other four were flown in all the way to the upper glacier, and so was every item of food and equipment for the climb itself.

No men had ever before stood at the foot of the west buttress, and the route they now followed had been planned entirely from aerial photographs. The camera had not lied; the buttress "went"; and for a week they steadily reconnoitered, climbed and packed their way upward. Profiting from the experience of previous expeditions, they dispensed with tents and slept instead in snow igloos, which both lightened their loads and gave far better protection against wind and cold. Between fifteen and sixteen thousand feet there was a difficult section of steep, snow-covered ice, on which each step required "twenty or thirty whacks with an ax." But they got by it safely and soon after reached Denali Pass, the 18,200-foot saddle between the north and south peaks. From here on, they were on familiar ground, and during the next few days all eight climbers reached the main summit, in three separate groups.

According to Washburn, this western route is easier than the traditional one from the northeast. The climbing itself is technically simpler; this side of the peak receives more sunlight than the other, and is therefore warmer; and, most important of all, the prevailing westerly winds are at a climber's back instead of cutting squarely into his face. The problem is getting to the route in the first place, and for this air support appears almost indispensable.

Five expeditions in a row—and every one successful. It might almost have seemed that McKinley was becoming "an easy day for a lady." But in 1952 and 1953 the mountain was challenged no less than six times, and only three of the attempts were successful. One of these was by a Mexican party, the other two by Americans, and all followed the traditional northeast route. Of the unsuccessful attempts, two also followed this approach, but were stopped by storms and dwindling food supplies. The third, a 1952 venture, tried the new western approach, but was refused the use of air transport by the National Park Service * and had to pack in across country. As Washburn had predicted, the journey was too long and too taxing, and the climbers had to turn back after barely setting foot on the west buttress.

Thus the story of McKinley to date. And as mountain stories go, it is a happy one: not only because it has been successfully climbed on ten occasions, but because these climbs, and the unsuccessful ones as well, have been accomplished with a minimum of misfortune. Carpé and Koven have been the only challengers to lose their lives, and not one of the many others has been seriously injured or disabled. On such a huge and formidable arctic peak, this is a record of which American mountaineers may well be proud.

The peak will be climbed again—many times. By old routes and by new routes. Bradford Washburn has already stated his belief that there are two likely ways up its northern flank, and these are sure to be tried, either by him or others. Granted, McKinley is no longer the inaccessible and mysterious goal it was in the old days. Science and experience, technique and equipment, plane and parachute have brought its top ever closer to the mountaineer's reach. But it is still no "tame" mountain, no walk-up; and the man foolish enough to hold it lightly is the man who will fail on it—if not die. Climbed, as unclimbed, it is still The Great One, still the summit of our continent: a mountain with a future as well as a past.

---

* The McKinley area has been a National Park since 1918.

7

TALL NEIGHBORS

Alaska - Canada - Mexico

McKINLEY IS THE northwestern outpost of the longest mountain chain in the world. South and east from it, a vast domain of peaks and ranges sweeps down across the length of North America. It covers all of southern and eastern Alaska, great areas of western Canada, and, broadening as it descends, spreads for a million square miles over the western third of the United States. In northwestern Mexico it thins and flattens out, but rises again in the great volcanic highlands of the south and continues, with only a few breaks, through Central America to Panama. There it merges with the northernmost spurs of the Andes, which continue the uplift along the entire length of South America, from Colombia to Cape Horn.

This gigantic highland region is almost ten thousand miles in length —more than three-quarters the distance between Pole and Pole. It covers approximately twenty per cent of the entire area of two continents. To be sure, it is divided into scores of ranges and sub-ranges, each with its own geological structure, its own climate, drainage and configuration; but fundamentally it forms a single connected chain, or cordillera. McKinley, near the Arctic Circle, and Sarmiento, beyond the Straits of Magellan, are almost literally half a world apart. Mount Logan and Aconcagua, the Canadian Rockies and the Sierra Madres of Mexico may seem as remote and disparate from each other as any mountains can be. But in the most basic sense they are only parts of a greater whole: vertebrae in the enormous rugged spine of the Western Hemisphere.

The mountains to the north and south of us are higher than our own. Most of them stand in wilder country and are far less frequently climbed. And those to the north, at least—in Alaska and parts of Canada—rank high among the most formidable mountains on earth.

The peaks of Alaska, like everything else in that land of superlatives, are on the grand scale. McKinley is the highest, but scores of its neighbors, too, are giants in their own right, and some have proven even harder to conquer. Their heights are defended not only by altitude and cold, but by a remoteness from civilization that makes it a major undertaking even to reach their bases. Food and equipment must usually be packed in over miles of wilderness; base camps and high camps must be established; vast areas of almost unknown terrain must be explored. Mountaineering here is far more than a matter of mere climbing. It is pioneering and exploration as well.

The Alaskan mountains are in every sense arctic mountains. Their rocky cores lie buried beneath enormous masses of ice and snow, and the glaciers that spill down from their slopes and fill the valleys between are far and away the largest in the world, outside of the polar icecaps. The Malaspina Glacier, which descends to the Pacific near Mount St. Elias is fifteen hundred square miles in area; the Hubbard, farther east, is over ninety miles long, and many others such as the Muir, Bering, Columbia and Kahiltna are on a scale so vast as to make the famous glaciers of the Alps seem miniatures in comparison. Pushing up them toward the inner fastnesses of the mountains, men reckon their journeys not in hours or days, but in weeks.

The peaks themselves comprise eight more or less separate ranges, or groups of ranges, strung out in a tremendous broken arc between the Yukon River, to the north, and the Pacific Ocean, to the south. Proceeding roughly from west to east, they are:

The Aleutian Range: Unlike the other Alaskan ranges, in that it is composed almost entirely of active volcanos. Among these is Mount Katmai, whose cataclysmic eruption in 1912 shattered the north wall of McKinley, hundreds of miles away. The area around it, now a National

Park, is a great steaming terrain of earth fissures and lava beds, known as the Valley of Ten Thousand Smokes. The peaks themselves, however, are low and truncated, and of small interest to mountaineers.

The Alaska Range: The gigantic uplift of south-central Alaska, of which McKinley is king. Closest rival of The Great One is Mount Foraker, fourteen miles to the southwest, whose 17,400 feet make it the fourth highest mountain in the Alaska-Yukon area. Other important summits are Mount Hunter (14,580 feet), Mount Hayes (13,740 feet) and Mounts Hess and Deborah, the last two known together as the Cathedral Peaks. Hunter and Deborah are today among the highest unclimbed mountains on the continent.

The Nutzotin Range: A continuation of the Alaska Range, curving southeast along the basin of the Tanana River. None of its peaks exceed ten thousand feet, but the country is extremely wild and rough. It is as yet little known to mountaineers.

The Chugach Range: A region of tremendous glaciers and snow-fields, bordering the coast to the northeast of the Kenai Peninsula. Its summits are somewhat higher than those of the Nutzotin group, but few have been climbed or explored on foot. An exception is Mount Marcus Baker, which, at 13,250 feet, is the highest in the chain.

The Wrangell Range: Extending from northwest to southeast between the Nutzotin and Chugach groups, but easier to reach than the others, by way of the Copper River. Some of the earliest Alaskan climbing exploits were in the Wrangells, and the principal summits have been reached. Great volcanic domes, they are easier to climb than any other mountains in Alaska, except the Aleutians.

The St. Elias Range: The mightiest mountain group in North America, exceeding even the McKinley uplift in everything except the altitude of its topmost summit. Its two greatest peaks are Mount Logan (19,850 feet) and Mount St. Elias (18,008 feet), respectively the second and fourth highest mountains on the continent—with Mexico's Orizaba ranking between them. The range straddles the international boundary between Alaska and Yukon Territory, its eastern section, including Logan, lying wholly in Canada. The western peaks front on the Pacific and were first seen and described by the earliest explorers of the Alas-

kan coast. Mount St. Elias, indeed, was named as early as 1741 by the
Russian navigator, Vitus Bering; but it was not until a century and a
half later that men penetrated up the great Malaspina Glacier and its
tributaries into the hidden, ice-shrouded wilderness surrounding Mount
Logan. In addition to Logan and St. Elias, this range contains a host
of other great peaks, and it has been the scene of many great mountaineering exploits.

The Fairweather Range: A southerly continuation of the St. Elias uplift, but lying wholly in Alaska. It is topped by 15,300-foot Mount
Fairweather, which has long been a famous Northwestern landmark
and is one of the highest coastal peaks on earth.

The Mountains of the Alaskan Panhandle: South of Mount Fairweather
the mountains extend in a broken chain along the lower coastal strip
of Alaska, becoming lower as they go and gradually merging with the
Coast Range of British Columbia. This region contains the historic
Chilkoot Pass, over which the hordes of prospectors struggled in the
Klondike gold rush of 1896. The Devil's Thumb and Kate's Needle,
near the town of Wrangell, are the most spectacular peaks in this area.

Great mountains, as we have already noted, are seldom climbed by
the men who live near them or by the first pioneers into the regions in
which they stand. Such men are usually engaged in too stern a battle
for the primary necessities of life—finding food, building shelter, getting to a destination—to go out of their way to seek hardship and adventure. This was the case in Alaska, where the early explorers and
settlers left the great peaks strictly alone, and the nineteenth century
had all but passed before the earliest mountaineering ventures were
launched. First of the major peaks to be attempted was Mount St. Elias,
rising like a great white beacon from the very shores of the Pacific. The
approaches to its heights were pioneered in 1890 and 1891 by an American university professor, Dr. Israel Russell; but the summit escaped
him, and it remained for the Duke of the Abruzzi, at the head of a
large and well-equipped expedition from faraway Italy, to carry the
campaign to its successful conclusion. St. Elias fell to him in 1897, in
one of the outstanding ascents of mountaineering history, and climbers
everywhere began turning their eyes to the other lofty snow-peaks of
the northwest.

The result was that during the past fifty years Alaska and the neighboring Yukon Territory of Canada have been the scene of as persistent and successful climbing as any wilderness mountain region in the world. In 1908, five years before the fall of McKinley, Mount Wrangell (14,000 feet), an active volcano in the range of the same name, was ascended by Robert Dunn and William Soule; and in 1912 the near-by Mount Blackburn (16,140 feet), also in the Wrangells, was conquered in a remarkable ascent led by a woman, Miss Dora Keen. In the same year as McKinley, Mount Natazhat (13,450 feet), in the St. Elias Range, was climbed by members of the Canadian Boundary Survey, and the following decade witnessed the ascent of several other virgin peaks and the exploration of great areas of theretofore unknown country. Then, in 1925, came one of the truly memorable feats of mountaineering history—the conquest of Mount Logan.

Second only to McKinley in all of North America, this colossus among mountains lies in such wild, inaccessible country that its existence was not even suspected until 1890. Seven years later the Duke of the Abruzzi and his companions gazed at it in awe from the summit of Mount St. Elias, but more than a quarter of a century was still to pass before men even approached its base. Then at last, in 1924, Captain A. H. MacCarthy, a noted Canadian climber, and H. F. Lambart, of the Canadian Boundary Survey, pioneered a way to its lower slopes, and the following year, under MacCarthy's leadership, a strong expedition of Canadian and American mountaineers set out to climb and conquer.

The first step was a remarkable expedition by MacCarthy and a renowned sourdough guide named Andy Taylor, who in the dead of winter, before the arrival of the rest of the party, fought their way up the great glaciers to the base of the mountain and established a long chain of camps and supply depots. This operation alone required seventy days of toil in sub-zero temperatures. In late May the expedition proper began, with nine men participating. The climbers were their own porters, and each carried a load of seventy pounds on his back, day after day, week after week. From the time they left timber-line behind, at a mere 3,000-foot altitude, they remained on ice and snow for forty-four consecutive days, without once setting foot on rock or earth. Worst of all, they were lashed by relentless blizzards and windstorms. Their undertaking combined the problems and hazards of mountaineering with virtually all the difficulties of polar exploration.

Logan, unlike McKinley, is not a single, isolated uplift, but almost a range in itself—more than twenty miles in length along the line of its summit ridge. Starting from the King Glacier, which pours down from the western flank of the mountain, MacCarthy and his companions found a way to this ridge, but once there, at a height of 14,500 feet, they were still separated from their goal not merely by a mile of vertical distance but by a seemingly endless succession of intervening peaks and cols. Over this jagged white sky-line they proceeded to fight their way. Day followed day while they hacked steps in the ice and floundered in snowdrifts up to their armpits. Almost every morning brought with it a fresh blizzard; at night the temperature frequently fell to as low as thirty below zero. But slowly they advanced, following the ridge up and down and then up again, and at last succeeded in pitching a tent at an altitude of 18,500 feet. This tiny shelter, known as the Eighteen-Five Camp, is still the highest ever made in North America.

The final dash from here to the summit and back was nothing less than a race with death. At four-thirty in the afternoon of June twenty-third, six of the climbers emerged on what they believed to be the highest pinnacle of the ridge, only to behold a still higher summit three long miles ahead. Night was coming on, and storm clouds were piling up ominously over Mount St. Elias, to the southwest; but the climbers were resolved that nothing would stop them now. For three and a half hours more they crept on, their hands and feet frozen numb, their lungs burning for want of air. And at last, at eight in the evening, victory was theirs: they were standing, the first of all men, on the 19,850-foot summit of Mount Logan, the highest point of all Canada and the second highest of the continent.

Not one among them, however, had the strength left to feel elation at their triumph, so severe had been their ordeal. And the ordeal had just begun. No sooner had they started the descent than the long-threatened storm closed in, and when darkness fell they were groping blindly in a blizzard. For more than an hour they floundered through the great drifts of the ridge, only to discover at last that they had not been heading toward camp at all, but back again toward the summit. Close to exhaustion and afraid to retrace their steps lest they plunge themselves ten thousand feet to the glacier below, they burrowed into the snow and huddled together through the murky twilight of the arctic night. In the morning the blizzard was still raging, but to remain where they were longer meant quick and certain death. On the ascent Andy Taylor had farsightedly planted a series of willow wands to mark the route, and they were now barely able to struggle from one to another as they descended. Reaching the Eighteen-Five Camp toward evening, they found it a shambles, but were luckily able to salvage some food and supplies. Then they spent a second night in the open.

The third day was again a nightmare of wind, snow and cold. By this time all the men were severely frostbitten, and some of them would have been unable to go on if their stronger companions, notably Mac-Carthy and Taylor, had not found the strength to help them. The faces and beards of all of them were so coated with ice that they could not recognize one another from a few feet away. Still they groped, floundered and hacked their way along the ridge, passing the ruins of their previous camps, stopping only when exhaustion compelled. This time they kept going not only all day but all the next night, for they knew that if they lay down to sleep again it would be never to awaken. And at last they reached their glacier base camp, just as the terrible three-day blizzard was blowing itself out. This camp had been wrecked, like all the others, but they managed to eke some warm food and shelter from the debris and a few days later were strong enough to begin the long trek toward civilization. They had achieved one of the genuinely great feats in mountaineering history. It was not their victory, however, that was in their thoughts as they turned their backs on tempest-crowned Logan; rather was it wonder and thankfulness that they had lived to tell the tale.

In the years that followed there was much climbing activity in Alaska and the Yukon, and almost every succeeding summer saw the conquest of one or more great peaks. During the 'thirties and early 'forties notable ascents were made, among others, of the following:

Mount Bona (16,420 feet) : in the St. Elias Range. Climbed in 1930 by Allan Carpé, Andy Taylor and Terris Moore.

Mount Fairweather (15,300 feet): the famous coastal peak in the range of the same name. Climbed in 1931 by Carpé and Moore, after two previous attempts had failed.

Mount Foraker (17,400): second peak of the Alaska Range, near Mount McKinley. Climbed in 1934 by a mixed party of American and English climbers. Its leader was the young American physician, Dr. Charles Houston, who was later to distinguish himself on Nanda Devi and K2.

Mount Crillon (12,725 feet): a neighbor of Fairweather, in the coastal chain of southeastern Alaska. Climbed in 1934. This was the first major venture of Bradford Washburn, whose total of twenty expeditions has made him the foremost Alaskan explorer and mountaineer of the present day.

Mount Steele (16,400 feet): in the eastern part of the St. Elias Range. Climbed in 1935 by an expedition headed by Walter A. Wood.

Mount Lucania (17,150 feet): one of the giants of the St. Elias Range; the second highest mountain in Canada and, at the time of its ascent, the highest unclimbed one in North America. Its top was reached in 1937 by Washburn and Robert Bates.

Mount Sanford (16,210 feet): highest summit of the Wrangell Range. Climbed in 1938 by Washburn and Moore.

Mount Hayes (13,740 feet): in the Alaska Range. Again by a Washburn expedition, in 1941.

Mount Wood (15,880 feet) and *Mount Walsh* (14,780 feet): in the St. Elias Range. Also in 1941, by Wood, Bates and others. This expedition was unusual, in that it was the first to receive aid, in transportation and supplies, from the U. S. Army.

During the war there was, of course, no high-mountain climbing in Alaska, other than the army-sponsored ascent of McKinley in 1942. But in the years since, full-scale activity has been resumed and many new peaks have fallen. These include:

Mount Vancouver (15,720 feet): still another peak of the St. Elias group, climbed in 1949 by a Walter Wood expedition. One of the climbers to reach the top was N. E. Odell, the English geologist, who had won fame on Everest no less than twenty-five years before.

Mount Hubbard (15,000 feet) and *Mount Alverstone* (14,560 feet): in the same range. Reached by a Wood-Bates party in 1951. This expedition was marred by an unusual and tragic accident, when a plane, flying out from the base of the mountains with Mr. Wood's wife and daughter, crashed in the wilderness. Although extensive searches were made, no trace of it has been found.

Mount Bear (14,850 feet): also in the St. Elias Range, and also climbed in 1951. The party was from Stanford University, and one of its members was Jon Lindbergh, son of the flier.

King Peak (17,130 feet): a part of the Mount Logan uplift, which, if considered as a separate mountain, was, since the conquest of Lucania, the highest virgin peak on the continent. In 1952 it was scaled twice, by two different parties—one from the University of Alaska and the other composed mostly of climbers from Seattle.

In addition to these, there have been several first ascents of summits only slightly less high; and three of the biggest peaks (other than McKinley) have been reclimbed. The summit of Mount St. Elias was reached for the second time in 1946, a half century, less a year, after the Abruzzi expedition, by a party from the Harvard Mountaineering Club. Among those to gain the top was Mrs. Betty Kauffman, the wife of one of the members. Then in 1950, after a twenty-five-year interval, Mount Logan was climbed again—not once, but twice, during a period of a few weeks. The first expedition was remarkable in that it was only a two-man affair, and doubly so because one of the two was Norman H. Read, aged sixty, who had been one of the mountain's original conquerors in 1925. The second Logan party was led by G. Herreid, of the University of Alaska, who had ascended McKinley three years before and thus became the first man to have climbed the two highest peaks in North America. Still another once-climbed mountain was reascended in 1951, when the Stanford expedition to Mount Bear also reached the top of near-by Bona.

Not the least result of these many Alaskan exploits has been the development of an ardent and expert group of American mountaineers. Men like Washburn, Wood, Bates and Moore are no mere haphazard adventurers, out to "do" a peak and then forget it. Washburn is the director of the Boston Museum of Science,* Wood of the American Geographical Society; Bates is a teacher at Phillips Exeter Academy, and Moore has for several years been president of the University of Alaska. They, and others like them, have explored and mapped as they went, and virtually every expedition has added its share to our growing knowledge of our last great frontier. Much geological work has been done on the glaciers. The cosmic ray has been studied. Military equipment has been tested. And some of the finest work yet done in aerial photography

---

* Formerly the New England Museum of Natural History.

has been accomplished over these peaks and snow-fields of the remote Northwest.

As we have seen on McKinley, the use of planes—in a variety of ways—has all but revolutionized Alaskan mountaineering. The approach can now be made in a few hours to peaks that, in the days of Stuck, Parker, Browne and the sourdoughs, required weeks of back-packing through the wilderness. The climbers are landed on a glacier close to their objective. Their supplies are dropped to them as they move upward. With them they have their aerial photos showing the route ahead. Not only can they climb more quickly and easily than would once have been believed possible, but more safely as well. In Alaska, in recent years, there have been fewer fatalities or serious accidents than in any other comparable mountain region in the world.

In addition to the climbers, the U. S. Air Force and U. S. Geological Survey have, since the war, carried out tremendous projects of surveying and mapping. Interior Alaska is no longer *terra incognita.* But it is still a long way from being a pastoral countryside. Thus far, only a few of the biggest mountains have been ascended more than once, or by more than one route, and uncounted hundreds remain which have never been attempted at all. Outstanding among these are a group of peaks adjacent to Mount Bona (tentatively called the University Peaks), which, at more than fifteen thousand feet, are today the highest unclimbed summits on the continent. Others, even more alluring to climbers because they rise as individual mountain masses, are Mount Hunter (14,-580 feet) and Mount Deborah (12,540 feet), in the Alaska Range near McKinley, and Mount McArthur (14,400 feet), in the Logan region. Of these, McArthur alone has been attempted—unsuccessfully, in 1953; but Washburn has worked out a detailed climbing route on Hunter, based on his aerial surveys, and it appears certain that it will be the goal of an expedition during the next few years. So, too, will other virgin peaks, as well as the summits of many climbed ones, by routes as yet untried.

The pioneering has been done; but the day is still far off when resort hotels will line the Alaskan glaciers and the white giants above them become a stroll for a tourist. The wilderness is still there—for anyone who hears its challenge.

Far different from the Alaska-Yukon ranges are the Rocky Mountains of Canada. Extending for some four hundred and fifty miles along the Alberta-British Columbia boundary, this magnificent chain of peaks has long been familiar to mountaineers, and virtually all its principal summits have been ascended, not only once but many times. Today it represents as close an approach as exists in the Western Hemisphere to the great mountain playground of the Alps.

The Canadian Rockies are of lesser extent than their American counterparts, partly because the name "Rockies," in Canada, is applied only to the easternmost range of the great western highlands. Also, they are less high, with only four summits rising to as much as twelve thousand feet. These deficiencies, however, are more than made up for by the fact that they lie farther to the north and, as a result, possess more high-alpine characteristics, such as large glaciers and snow-fields, than do most of the bigger peaks in the United States. No mountains, to be sure, are without flaw, and the Rockies of Canada have theirs: notably unstable weather and, in many areas, unsound rock. But in spite of this, they offer the ordinary non-expedition climber what is probably—for challenge, variety and natural beauty—the best terrain to be found on this continent.

Large sections of the range are easily accessible, being cut through, at two widely separated points, by the main transcontinental lines of the Canadian Pacific and Canadian National Railroads. Along these lines are many famous and flourishing summer resorts, notably Banff and Lake Louise on the C.P.R. and Jasper, one hundred and fifty miles farther north, on the C.N.R. Trails have been made and camps and shelters established throughout the more frequently visited sections; and in recent years a paved motor-highway has been completed between Lake Louise and Jasper, giving easy access to a vast, unspoiled region which before could be reached only by long pack trips.

An interesting enterprise of the railway companies was the bringing over, in the early 1900's, of many Swiss and Austrian guides, in an effort to attract visitors and make the region a true climbing center. The scheme was highly successful, and for many years the Canadian Rockies were the only mountains in North America where trained professionals were available. But as the original group grew old and died off, few new ones appeared to take their places, and it is now harder to find a guide in Banff or Jasper than in many comparable resorts in the United States. Fortunately, however, the gap has been at least partially filled by the activities of the Alpine Club of Canada. One of the leading mountaineering organizations on the continent, it focuses its attention particularly upon the Rockies and each summer sponsors large-scale climbing parties under expert leadership.

Most of the important first ascents in the range were made around the turn of the century, when the gradual opening up of the region caused an influx of many noted climbers. Not the least of these was Edward Whymper, who at the age of sixty-five, forty years after his conquest of the Matterhorn, had still not lost his love of mountains nor —more remarkable—the strength to climb them. Between 1901 and 1905 he traveled extensively in western Canada, and, although by this time he was less a mountaineer than a legend, he pioneered several lesser peaks and did much to bring this new alpine region to the attention of the public. His ascents there were his last before his death in Chamonix in 1911.

The majority of the climbs, however, were done by Canadians and Americans, in company with the Alpine guides; and by 1925 virtually every major peak in the range had been ascended, most of them on several occasions and by various routes. Though there are no giants to compare with McKinley and Logan, and only four summits of more than twelve thousand feet, there are no less than forty-seven above eleven thousand and almost seven hundred above ten thousand. Perhaps the best indication of the great mountaineering activity in this region is the fact that today not one of the Eleventhousanders remains unclimbed and only a few of the Tenthousanders—these chiefly in the outlying districts.

The chain of the Canadian Rockies is divided into almost equal thirds by the two railroad lines. North of Jasper, on the Canadian National, the country is still in a primitive state, and would-be climbers must be prepared for long pack trips and camping under canvas. This region is crowned by Mount Robson (12,972 feet), the monarch of the whole range and one of the most impressive peaks on the continent. After many unsuccessful attempts by earlier climbers the summit of Robson was first attained in 1913 by A. H. MacCarthy and W. W. Foster, later conquerors of Mount Logan, in company with the transplanted Austrian guide, Conrad Kain. Since then it has been often challenged, but only rarely with success, for Robson's steep ice-slopes, rumbling avalanches and ferocious storms make it a more difficult and dangerous adversary

BEACON OF THE NORTHWEST

Mount Ranier, third highest summit in the United States, as seen from the air beyond the harbor of Seattle, more than sixty miles away.

Photo by Bradford Washburn

TOP OF THE CONTINENT

Mount McKinley, looking up the Muldrow Glacier. All the parties except one that have reached the upper part of the mountain have made the ascent from this side. The South Peak, on the left, is the true summit.

Photo by Bradford Washburn

than many a higher mountain. Remarkably, it was climbed no less than five times in 1953—thanks largely to an unusual period of settled weather—but before that its summit had not been reached in fourteen years.

Between Jasper and the Banff-Lake Louise district the range continues in a succession of great massifs. This stretch comprises the heart of the Canadian Rockies, and in it are found the three peaks, besides Robson, which exceed twelve thousand feet in height—Mount Columbia, North Twin and Mount Clemenceau—as well as twenty-nine peaks over eleven thousand feet. One of the dominating features of the region is the Columbia Ice-field, unique among the great watersheds of the continent. Catching the outflow from scores of glaciers, the vast reservoir drains, in turn, to three different oceans: through the Columbia River to the Pacific, through the Athabasca to the Arctic, and through the Saskatchewan to Hudson Bay and the Atlantic. Until 1939 this wilderness of rock and ice had been seen by only a few surveying and mountaineering parties, but now it may be traversed by car along the Jasper-Lake Louise highway.

One of the most interesting ascents in the history of the Rockies was made in the Columbia Ice-field region. This was the climbing, in 1925, of 11,874-foot Mount Alberta—then the highest unscaled peak in the range—by a group of six Japanese mountaineers, accompanied by three Swiss guides. Reaching their goal, the party built a summit cairn, in which they planted an ice-ax, and in the years that followed the legend grew that the ax had been a gift to the expedition from the Emperor of Japan, and was made of silver. Several subsequent attempts were made to reach the top of the peak and verify the story; but Alberta is one of the most formidable mountains in Canada, and it was not until 1948 that it was climbed for the second time, by two Americans, Fred Ayres and John Oberlin. Sure enough, the ax was still there, after twenty-three years, but it was only a steel ax, not of silver. In an old tin can among the stones, however, Ayres and Oberlin found another, and perhaps even rarer, memento. It was an ancient slip of paper signed by the first climbers, and under their names they had written, in English: "We came from Japan so far called by this charming great mountain."

The best-known and most frequented district of the Rockies is the southern third of the range, bordering the Canadian Pacific line. Here hotels and camps abound, and the ascent of many of the peaks—as in the Alps—can be made in one day, from early breakfast in the dining room back to hot bath in the evening. Lake Louise is ringed by a magnificent chain of mountains which offer climbs of every kind and degree of difficulty. Among the more celebrated are Victoria, Lefroy, Temple, Hungabee and Mitre, all but the last more than eleven thousand feet high, which are climbed many times each season. Mount Louis, a sheer tower springing from the foothills near Banff, is considered one of the hardest climbs in America that can be done without benefit of "rock engineering." Further south, in wilder country that requires a two-day pack trip to reach, Mount Assiniboine (11,870 feet) rises in a spectacular, isolated pyramid reminiscent of the Matterhorn. This is the loftiest peak in the southern Canadian Rockies, but despite its height and appearance, it is one of the easier summits to climb.

Near Assiniboine stands the lower, but more formidable, peak of Mount Eon, whose first ascent, in 1921, was as tragic as Alberta's was romantic. The climbers were a Dr. W. E. Stone and his wife, who made their try for the mountain without guides or any other companions. A short way below the summit they reached a section that was too difficult for Mrs. Stone, and her husband, unroping, went on to the summit by himself. On the descent, according to Mrs. Stone, who could see him, he stepped on a loose rock and plunged down a precipice to his death. Mrs. Stone, alone and distraught, was able to get about halfway down to the base, but there her strength gave out, and for six days she remained on the mountainside without food or shelter. Amazingly, she was still alive when help at last reached her.

If the Canadian Rockies have been among the most-climbed of mountains, the ranges to the west of them have been, until very recently, among the least. These are a northern continuation of the more westerly American Rockies, but are known in Canada, collectively, as the Interior Ranges of British Columbia. Individually, the four principal groups are called the Purcells, the Selkirks, the Monashees and the Cariboos.

Because of their proximity to the Pacific Ocean they receive more rainfall and are more heavily forested than the Rockies, with dense underbrush and few trails in their lowland approaches. The region was wholly unexplored until the 1870's, and it was not until 1916 that it was first visited by mountaineers. But in recent years it has become an increasingly popular goal of ambitious climbing parties—particularly the Purcells and Selkirks, which are somewhat more accessible than the others. The peaks of the Monashees and Cariboos are, for the most part, still remote from road and railway; much back-packing is required even to reach their bases; and climbers setting out for them must be equipped as small—and sometimes not-so-small—expeditions.

Most of the higher summits of the four groups have now been attained, but hosts of lesser ones remain unscaled and unattempted. Topping the whole area is Mount Sir Wilfrid Laurier (11,750 feet), in the Cariboos, and next in rank is Sir Sandford, some hundred feet lower, in the Selkirks. One of the most attractive and frequented sections is a subrange of the Purcells called the "Bugaboos," whose spectacular rock-spires and towers offer a strong lure to expert cragsmen.

Even wilder than the Interior Ranges is the Coast Range of British Columbia, which borders the Pacific for nine hundred miles from the Alaskan Panhandle to Vancouver. The greater part of this chain is a virgin wilderness of peaks and glaciers, lakes and forest, as inaccessible and rugged, in many respects, as the Alaska-Yukon region to the north. Highest among its hundreds of summits is Mount Waddington (13,260 feet), an awe-inspiring steeple of ice-sheathed granite that was attempted no less than sixteen times before it was first climbed, in 1936, by Fritz Wiessner and William House, of the American Alpine Club. Another measure of its difficulty is that it has been surmounted only twice since; and in 1947 it was the scene of a fatality, when a climbing party was caught in an avalanche close below the summit.

A number of other ascents have been made in the Waddington area, which is in the southwestern part of the range, nearest the sea and the coastal settlements; but expeditions to the more northerly regions have been few and far between. Since the last war, however, planes have been brought into use—as in Alaska—both to land climbers on the wilderness lakes and drop supplies on the glaciers. Even the remotest sections of the Coast Range are now gradually being opened up, and its maze of peaks will offer new goals to mountaineers for years to come.

So much for the mountains to the north of us. To the south—in Mexico and Central America—there are many peaks and ranges as well, but utterly different in every respect. Forest and glacier, precipice and ice-ridge are gone; in their place are high, arid plateaus, long slopes of sunbaked shale and lava, and the high, symmetrical snow-cones of great volcanos.

The mountains of Mexico sweep southward from the United States borders in two roughly parallel chains—the Sierra Madre Oriental and the Sierra Madre Occidental. For some seven hundred and fifty miles they attain no great elevation or importance, but in the latitude of Mexico City the chains converge, and here there rises a group of tremendous volcanic peaks. The three principal ones are:

Orizaba (18,696 feet): the third highest elevation of North America, topped only by McKinley and Logan. Rising from the steaming tropical lowlands near Vera Cruz, its great height and almost perfect symmetry make it one of the most beautiful mountains in the world. Its last eruptive period was between 1545 and 1566, and it is now considered to be extinct. The Aztecs called it Citlaltepetl—Mountain of the Star.

Popocatepetl (17,883 feet): the famous "smoking mountain" of the Valley of Mexico, dominating the horizon of the capital. It is a quiescent, but not extinct, volcano and the fifth highest peak of the continent, only Mount St. Elias coming between it and Orizaba. "Popo," as it is known to all Mexicans, was one of the first of the world's great mountains to be climbed. Cortez partially ascended it in his journey of conquest in 1519, and a few years later a group of his soldiers pushed on to the summit to secure sulphur from its crater for the manufacture of gunpowder. This feat established a world's altitude record which endured for almost three hundred years—or until the early days of Himalayan exploration.

Ixtaccihuatl (17,342 feet): the immediate neighbor of "Popo," rising out of the same great volcanic uplift. Its tongue-twisting name—usually mercifully shortened to "Ixta"—is Aztec for "sleeping woman" and derives from the peculiar profile of its long summit ridge. "Ixta" is a thoroughly extinct volcano, not even a crater remaining.

Southern Mexico is largely mountainous country, but with few important peaks. In western Guatemala, however, the cordillera rises again in a great tangle of volcanic cones. None of them is as high as the giants of Mexico—Tajumulco, the loftiest, is about 13,800 feet—but they are far more numerous, and together form one of the most impressive groups of volcanos in the world. Many of them are active. Beyond Guatemala, various ranges extend southeastward through the rest of Central

America, but the cordillera does not again attain great heights until Panama is crossed, and South America and the Andes begin.

All the major volcanos of Mexico and Guatemala have long since been climbed. Few of them present any serious mountaineering difficulties other than that of altitude, and, owing to their gentle slopes, the ascent as far as the snow-line can usually be made on horseback. The most interesting feature of their ascents is the startling transition from tropical to arctic weather conditions in a few hours and a few thousand feet.

SNOW-PEAKS AND FIRE-PEAKS

The Andes of South America

THE CONTINENT of South America is built on a vast and simple scale, with three dominant physical features. Its central and northeastern interior comprises the greatest jungle area on earth: some three million square miles of tropical rain forest in the Amazon and Orinoco Basins. Its southeastern third extends unbroken through horizon after horizon across the flat, open pampas of the Argentine. And on the west is its backbone: the five thousand miles of continuous mountain ranges and chains which, taken all together, are called the Andes.

It is true that, strictly speaking, the Andes are not the only mountains of the continent. The back country of the Guianas, far to the east, possesses a wild highland region, topped by the mysterious, jungle-clad Mount Roraima; in the uplands of central Brazil there is a little-known range with the Land-of-Oz name of Serra Roncador—The Snoring Mountains; and the harbor of Rio de Janeiro, to be sure, boasts its fantastic fringe of rocky domes and spires. None of these isolated uplifts, however, is of any great extent or elevation. To all intents and purposes, the mountains of South America are synonymous with the word Andes.

This great range, or series of ranges, forms what is beyond comparison the longest unbroken mountain region in the world. Its northernmost spurs front the Caribbean Sea on the coasts of Colombia and Venezuela, and at Cape Horn, in farthest Tierra del Fuego, its gaunt headlands look south to the Antarctic Ocean. Between these two extremities stretch seventy degrees of latitude—the entire length of the earth's longest continent. In addition to their extent, the Andes are also among the highest of ranges, second only to those of Central Asia. The summit of Aconcagua, capstone of the Western Hemisphere, towers almost twenty-three thousand feet above the near-by Pacific, and scattered through Peru, Bolivia and along the Argentine-Chilean border are scores of other peaks exceeding twenty thousand feet in height.*

Extending from the tropics through the sub-tropics, the south temperate zone and almost to the Antarctic, the Andes vary enormously in formation and terrain, vegetation and climatic conditions. The region of the Atacama Desert, in northern Chile, is among the hottest and driest on earth, and one must ascend to twenty thousand feet, or the very tops of the highest mountains, before reaching the level of perpetual snow. In cold and stormy Patagonia, on the other hand, there are places where rain or snow falls on an average of three hundred days in the year, and the snow-line dips to a mere twenty-five hundred feet. Throughout Colombia, Venezuela and Ecuador the eastern flanks of the great peaks rise out of the equatorial rain forest of the Amazon and are covered in vegetation up to great heights. In the lake district of southern Chile the terrain and climate are similar to those of the Alps or our own Northwest. In the vast central Altiplano of northern Chile and Bolivia stretch thousands of square miles of peaks and plateaus boasting not so much as a tree, a shrub or a blade of grass. Many of the most important sub-ranges are volcanic in origin, and not a few of their greatest peaks are still active fire-mountains; separating them, however, are extensive areas where there are no volcanos whatever. In short, the Andes are as various as they are vast. Only one generalization will hold good for them all: they are big.

There is equal variety in their history and their effect on men and civilizations. Many districts, notably in the tropical north and the frozen, desolate south, are to this day among the most sparsely inhabited and least-known areas in the world. The great central highlands of Peru and Bolivia, on the other hand, have been thickly inhabited for uncounted centuries. It was here that Indian America reached its highest develop-

---

* As in the case of many of the world's great mountain ranges, the heights of most Andean peaks have not yet been exactly determined. In this and succeeding chapters the figures given are the most generally accepted estimates.

ment in the remarkable civilization of the Incas, and here too that the Spaniards first established dominion in their bloody conquest of the New World. The brown hills behind Cuzco were veined with trails and pitted with mine-shafts in the days when the Hudson and Mississippi valleys were still untouched, silent wilderness.

Today, as for the past four hundred years, the Andes are economically the most important mountain region in the world. The dry earth and rock of their central ranges are a virtually inexhaustible treasure-house of mineral wealth—gold, silver, iron, tin, copper—and since the days of the Conquistadores mining has been the foremost industry of Chile, Bolivia and Peru. The high peaks are, to be sure, devoid of life, as are all great peaks anywhere; but the plateaus and valleys that lie in their shadows swarm with men and machines. Indeed, this inhabited section of the range contains at the present time more than a quarter of the population and produces almost a third of the wealth of South America.

For the prospector, the miner and the exploiter the Andes have long been El Dorado. The mountaineer, however, has been slower in coming, and until recent years only a few of the greatest peaks had been climbed, or even attempted. As in the case of most of the world's big mountains, scarcely any of the first ascents have been made by natives of the surrounding country. The Andean peaks have, for the most part, fallen to Englishmen, Germans, Italians and, in later days, Americans—men from the nations in which the exploring and mountaineering instinct has become strongly developed. In the 1930's, during the period of Nazi expansion, the Germans were particularly—and significantly—active, sending out one expedition after another on ventures which had distinctly political overtones. Since the war, activity has been about equally divided between Europeans, North Americans and South Americans.

The early climbers concentrated on the great volcanos—particularly those which stand near the cities of the Pacific Coast and were therefore better known and more accessible. Then followed the peaks farther inland, or remote from roads and railways. And finally came what might be called the "hidden" ranges of the Andes: mountains so far off the beaten track that, in some cases, their existence was not even suspected until well into the twentieth century. Notable among these last are certain of the interior ranges of Peru, which have been the goal of several recent American expeditions and have proved to be the most impressive and difficult mountains on the continent.

The first of the Andes to be explored and ascended were the peaks of Ecuador. Here, in a compact area just south of the Equator, are clustered some of the loftiest volcanos in the world. More than thirty major peaks, spaced like sentinels, rise from the long rounded ridges of the cordillera, their flanks buried in green, primeval jungle, their snowcaps, white and remote, seeming to hang like great clouds in the blue, tropical sky. High above all their neighbors hang the summits of the two greatest: Chimborazo and Cotopaxi.

These are mountains with a history. Chimborazo—The Watchtower of the Universe, Simon Bolívar called it—has been a famous landmark since the earliest days of the Spanish conquest, and the region surrounding its base was well known to travelers and explorers of the Colonial period. Between 1736 and 1744 it was the site of what was probably the first major scientific expedition to any high mountain range—a large and well-equipped party of geographers and naturalists led by the Frenchmen Bouger and La Condamine and the Spaniards Ulloa and Juan Jorge. As a result of their investigations, made long before either the Himalayas or the higher southern Andes were known, Chimborazo was for almost three-quarters of a century ranked as the highest mountain in the world. In 1802, a still more distinguished visitor appeared on the scene in the person of the German naturalist, Alexander von Humboldt. Humboldt and his companions not only occupied themselves with scientific observations, but also made attempts on the actual summits of both Chimborazo and Cotopaxi. Although the ventures were unsuccessful, the subsequent writings of various members of the party served to place the two remote volcanos among the most famous mountains on earth.

Seventy more years were to pass, however, before either was climbed to the top. Then at last, in 1872, Cotopaxi fell to a German geologist, Wilhelm Reid, and his companion, A. M. Escobar; and in 1880 Chimborazo was conquered by no less an antagonist than Edward Whymper. Still a great mountaineer fifteen years after his epic struggle with the Matterhorn, Whymper was the first topflight European Alpinist to visit the high Andes, and his expedition to Ecuador provided the original impetus to organized climbing in the Southern Hemisphere. In addition

to Chimborazo, which he climbed twice, he reached the top of Cotopaxi
—the fifth ascent—and pioneered the way to some half-dozen lesser
summits in the surrounding ranges. Ironically, his principal helper and
companion on these climbs was Jean-Antoine Carrel, his brilliant guide
and bitter rival of bygone days in the Alps. It is surely not stretching
the imagination too far to picture these two old campaigners battling up
the last few feet of Chimborazo's icy crest, clasping numbed hands in
victory on its summit, and at that very moment thinking ruefully, each
to himself: "It might have been the Matterhorn."

Neither Chimborazo nor Cotopaxi has been climbed often in recent
years, and both remain among the more spectacular and difficult ascents
in the Andes. Of the two, Chimborazo is the higher—20,550 feet to
Cotopaxi's 19,335—but its high base and massive, irregular form somewhat detract from its impressiveness. Cotopaxi, on the other hand, is a
mountain of almost legendary beauty. Soaring a full ten thousand feet
above its green skirt of valleys, its cone is proportioned in measured
symmetry and its summit snowcap looms like a perfect white triangle
against the sky. Also it has the distinction of being a live volcano—the
only one in Ecuador and the highest active fire-mountain in the world.
When in eruption, molten streams of lava flow down its icy flanks and
vast jets of steam swirl like a veil over the whole upper face of the
mountain. Camping beside its crater rim while Cotopaxi was quiescent,
Whymper reported that even then the black ash was so hot that it
scorched the ground sheet of his tent.

North of Ecuador, the volcanic belt that includes Chimborazo and
Cotopaxi sweeps on across southern Colombia, culminating, near Bo-
gotá, in the 18,438-foot cone of Tolima—unclimbed until 1926. Beyond
it, the fire-peaks disappear, and the Andes of northern Colombia and
Venezuela spread out into various lesser groups that are little more than
outposts of the main cordillera. For the most part, they are typical equatorial mountains, rising out of jungle or semi-jungle country, heavily
forested, and with only a few of the highest summits reaching the level
of perpetual snow.

Unique among them is the range called the Sierra Nevada de Santa
Marta, which rise in the extreme north of Colombia, close to the Caribbean coast. For years the snowcaps of the Santa Martas have been seen
by tourists from the decks of cruise ships, but it was not until 1939 that

a small American party led by Walter A. Wood penetrated the intervening wilderness and scaled several of the highest summits. To the surprise of the climbers, they found many of the peaks to be more than
eighteen thousand feet high, an altitude which ranks them among the
tallest coastal mountains in the world. A few subsequent expeditions
have visited the range, but it is still imperfectly known and should prove
a rewarding objective for climbers of the future.

For mountains with a past, however—comparable to that of the
Ecuadorean volcanos—one must go thousands of miles to the south: to
Peru and Bolivia and the high frontier between Argentina and Chile. In
this last region, particularly, occurred one of the great events of early
Andean mountaineering: the first climbing of Aconcagua, the highest
summit in the western world.

Situated in the eastern section of its international range, the actual
peak of Aconcagua lies wholly in Argentina; but its vast western flanks
build up from the coastal lowlands of Chile, and its 22,835-foot snowcap can be seen from the Pacific Ocean, a hundred miles away, as a
white, sky-filling beacon, gigantic and alone. The Chilean cities of
Santiago and Valparaiso lie almost literally in its shadow, and the busy
transcontinental trade route between Santiago and Buenos Aires crosses
the Andes only a few miles to the south. As a result, it is not only the
greatest but perhaps the best-known landmark on the continent.

Aconcagua is of volcanic origin, but is not itself a volcano. Like many
of the great Andean peaks, it is enormous in extent as well as in height,
building itself up in interminable slopes of broken rock and debris and,
on its upper reaches, ice and snow. The reports of the various parties
who have battled their way to its summit are unanimous in declaring
that, from the point of view of climbing, it is one of the most unattractive mountains imaginable. In the alpine sense there are few, if any,
difficulties. There is little call for climbing skill or generalship. Yet its
altitude is so great, its cold so bitter, its storms so frequent and savage,
that the ascent ranks among the most grueling ordeals known to climbers. "An intolerably monotonous slag-pile"; "the dump-heap of South
America"—these are merely two of the more printable epithets hurled
at it by its battered and exhausted challengers.

The first attempt on Aconcagua was made in 1883. The leader of
the venture was Paul Güssfeldt, a well-known German Alpinist, and

the effort was a remarkable one, the climbers reaching a point only thirteen hundred feet below the summit before they were turned back by storms. In the succeeding years a few other attempts were made, but it was not until the winter (or, in the Southern Hemisphere, the summer) of 1896-97 that the goal was at last attained.

The victorious party was predominantly English. At its head was Edward A. FitzGerald, whose exploits in the Alps and New Zealand had made him one of the best-known mountaineers of his day. With him was a younger British climber, Stuart Vines, a small group of naturalists and a corps of Swiss and Italian helpers headed by the renowned Alpine guide, Mattias Zurbriggen.* They formed a strong, and well-equipped group, and it was well that they were. For Aconcagua was to prove one of the most stubborn antagonists against which mountaineers have ever pitted their strength and will.

Not the least of their problems was finding the mountain in the first place. Although Aconcagua, as seen from the Pacific, stands out bold and unmistakable, its base is almost lost among a vast jumble of lesser peaks, and the FitzGerald party, approaching it from the south and east, spent long weeks searching out a route to its lower slopes. The month was December, the beginning of the southern summer; the sun burned down relentlessly from a rainless sky, and the hot wind, blowing through the desolate valleys, almost overwhelmed them in stinging, choking dust. Trying first one way, then another, the climbers came at last into a deep ravine, known as the Horcones Valley, which seemed to twist up toward the very heart of the mountain. Then day followed day, while they laboriously ascended it. There was no shade, no moisture, no vegetation. Men and mules slid and slipped and floundered across interminable slopes of shale and rotting stone. In the parched, petrified world about them only one thing lived and moved—the giant Andean condors wheeling ominously through the sky.

Finally, a few days before Christmas, the valley was behind them, and they came out at the snout of the Horcones Glacier, near the western

---

* In the first days of high-mountain climbing practically all expeditions—even those to the farthest corners of the earth—took along one or more professional helpers. Whymper, as we have seen, was accompanied by Carrel on his ascents in Ecuador, and Conway's climbs in Bolivia and elsewhere were made in the company of Swiss guides. So too were most of the early ascents in the Caucasus and Himalayas. In later days, however, the tendency has been to dispense with this kind of professional assistance. On most recent expeditions the climbers have acted as their own guides, drawing on the native population for porters and helpers.

base of the great mountain itself. Here, at a height of fourteen thousand feet, they pitched their advance base camp. And here their first ordeal was to begin. Above them loomed the nine thousand feet of slanting, crumbling wilderness that formed the mighty cone of Aconcagua.

Elsewhere in this history there are references to "attacks" and "assaults" on mountains, to "rock scrambles" and "summit dashes." None of these spectacular activities, however, have any applicability to the experiences of FitzGerald and his men on the highest of the Andes. Day by day, hour by hour, yard by yard, they put one foot in front of the other—and, if they were lucky, a little higher; and day by day, hour by hour, yard by yard, the winds grew fiercer and colder, the valleys below receded into more shadowy darkness, and the great plain of the Pacific Ocean swung slowly upward above the horizon. The first ascent of Aconcagua can be described only as a siege. Its conquerors did not so much climb it or surmount it as they wore it down, and in the process they were forever desperately close to being worn down—and out—themselves.

Even at the advance base several of the party began suffering from exhaustion and mountain sickness, and soon only a handful of men were left with enough strength to go on. These included FitzGerald himself, Stuart Vines, Zurbriggen and an Italian porter-guide called Nicola Lanti. Launching their first effort, they crept painfully up the decomposed, rotting slopes above the glacier. Each foot of altitude was won only at the price of parched throats and gasping, burning lungs. For every three upward steps they slipped back two, as the debris of the mountainside gave way beneath their feet. And the wind, which lower down had been scorchingly hot, now lashed at them with icy fury. Still they kept grinding on. The second day brought them to a broad saddle high up on the western shoulder of the mountain, the third a scant five hundred feet higher on the summit ridge.

Here, at about nineteen thousand feet, FitzGerald, Vines and Lanti reached the end of their endurance. A freezing, sleepless night of coughing and choking left them too weak even to eat, let alone go on. Not so the iron-bodied Zurbriggen. Setting out by himself, he scouted upward across the wind-lashed slopes and after long hours of climbing reached a point only thirteen hundred feet below the summit. Here he made an exciting discovery—a man-made pile of stones amid the lifeless desolation. Beneath the stones was a tin box and in the box the card of Paul

Güssfeldt, who had made the first attempt on Aconcagua fourteen years before. The cairn marked the highest point that he had reached.

It was Zurbriggen's highest point too—at least for the present. Now close to exhaustion himself, he stumbled down to join his companions, and the next day all hands descended to the Horcones Valley to regain their strength and lay in fresh supplies. So ended their first attempt.

Their second carried them no farther. Days of renewed effort brought them again to their high camp at nineteen thousand feet, and on New Year's Day of 1897 all four went still higher, stumbling up the interminable stretches of broken rock and loose gravel. The westernmost of Aconcagua's twin summits was now clearly visible above them, but long hours of climbing seemed to bring it no nearer. Meanwhile the wind grew even colder and fiercer than it had been before, battering them almost to their knees, while at the same time bearing so little oxygen that it was almost impossible for them to breathe. All of them began to suffer from headaches, and their throats were bone-dry knots of pain. Finally, to complete their catalogue of woes, Zurbriggen's feet became so badly frozen that he could no longer climb. Turning back at last, it was all the others could do to get him safely down to the high camp.

Once more they descended to the valley, their fortunes now at their lowest ebb. Zurbriggen especially seemed to be in a bad way, suffering not only from his frostbitten feet but from a painful shoulder injury sustained in a mishap with a mule. Nevertheless, all were resolved on at least one more effort. For the third time they began the long upward push, and on the night of January twelfth, FitzGerald, Vines, Zurbriggen and Lanti again found themselves huddled in their 19,000-foot tent, while the winds of space howled through the darkness outside.

That night they were lucky—the temperature dropped to a mere zero. And the next day they again bent to their killing toil. To 20,000 feet they went; to 20,500, to 21,000, while the sun disappeared behind gray mists and the savage gales lashed down across the unprotected slopes of rotting stones. Then FitzGerald broke down. His parched throat was threatening to close and strangle him; his leaden feet would no longer obey his will. Barely clinging to consciousness, he stumbled and staggered down to the camp, with Vines and Lanti doing their feeble best to assist him.

Meanwhile Zurbriggen again went on alone. Detouring and zigzagging, he fought his way upward, passed his previous highest point at Güssfeldt's cairn, and came at last to a ridge from which he could view the whole summit of the mountain. But what he now saw filled him with dismay. The peak toward which they had striven so long, and which loomed now a scant few hundred feet above him, was not the summit at all. Beyond it, to the east, a jagged saddle of rock swung down, then rose again to a still higher peak beyond—the true pinnacle of Aconcagua. Struggling toward it, Zurbriggen made the saddle, but his strength would carry him no farther. Defeated, he began the descent, reaching camp after nightfall in a condition little better than FitzGerald's.

Another day, another try. This fourth time, however, all the climbers were soon overcome by dizziness and nausea, and a halt had to be called at twenty-one thousand feet. Back at their high camp they dug in for still another freezing, choking night. They had provisions left for one more day—and one more effort.

On the gray morning of January fourteenth they rested for an hour after breakfast, hoping that this would help their powers of resistance to the dread mountain sickness. Then, once again, they started up— through the crumbling shale; through the numbing cold; through the wind. This time they made better progress than ever before and by noon, after five hours of climbing, were within a mere thousand feet of the eastern, or true, summit. Here they rested again, contrived to build a tiny smudge fire and ate a little food. It was a disastrous mistake. No sooner had FitzGerald eaten than he was taken violently ill, and all his efforts of body and will could not get him back his strength. Again and again he strove to get to his feet and go on, only to fall back to his knees, gasping and retching. He was done in. With Vines and Lanti once more supporting him, he stumbled miserably down the mountain.

But all was not over yet, and that bitter, sunless day was still to end far differently from the others. For the third time Zurbriggen turned his face to the heights alone, and this time he made mountaineering history. Hour after hour, foot by foot, he went higher, his mind and senses growing numb, his feet thrusting forward like a relentless machine. . . . Then suddenly, miraculously, there was no place higher to go. All of the two Americas were beneath him. . . . In the fading light of evening he came down at last to rejoin his companions, leaving behind him his shining ice-ax, bearing with him a shining victory.

Aconcagua had been won; but the first Aconcagua adventure was not yet over. FitzGerald, Vines and Lanti still had their hearts set on reaching the top and during the weeks that followed launched two more efforts above their highest camp. On the first attempt they were overwhelmed by a blizzard, barely escaping with their lives. But on the second, Vines and Lanti plugged on irresistibly and late one February afternoon found themselves beside Zurbriggen's ax on the highest summit of the Andes. Poor FitzGerald alone was denied the ultimate satisfaction of personal victory. The originator and leader of the expedition, whose judgment and courage had been the mainstay of them all, he deserved the prize perhaps more than any of them. But on the final try, as on all the others, he collapsed from nausea and exhaustion and could not go on. Turning back for the last time, he descended the mountain—"with feelings," he records, "that I had perhaps better not try to describe."

In the years since 1897 Aconcagua has been reascended often. Men from many countries have participated in the ventures, making the tallest of the Andes one of the most "international" of mountains. And it has also been the scene of several unusual exploits. In 1934 an Italian party reached the top accompanied by two dogs, who thereby set a new, and probably permanent, canine altitude mark. In 1951 a small hut, the highest in the world, was built at almost twenty-two thousand feet by a group of Argentine Army climbers. And in the following year two priests carried up a statue of Our Lady of Carmel and implanted it on the very summit.

A mountain climbed is never so formidable as the same mountain unclimbed. But let no one assume that the Giant of the South has become an "easy" ascent. For every successful attempt during the past half century, there have been many that failed; and not a few of the failures have been disastrous—notably that of a large expedition in 1944 on which no less than four climbers died of exposure and exhaustion. Aconcagua is still the highest peak in the Western Hemisphere. It still consists of almost twenty-three thousand feet of slag and snow and ice and cold and wind. And he who would get to the top must still be—the Latins have a name for it—*mucho hombre.*

Aconcagua is usually thought of as lying in the far southern Andes, but beyond it the great range sweeps southward for another fifteen hundred miles. Along this enormous stretch there is, of course, great variety both of climate and terrain. In general, however, the weather is less dry and the mountains less lofty than in the regions farther north.

The hinterland of Santiago de Chile, bordering the transcontinental railway line, is, in a sporting and recreational sense, the most highly developed section in all the Andes. Lodges, inns, and resort hotels abound, and both climbing and skiing are practiced on a scale comparable to that in the Alps or our own Northwest. Mountaineers among the large German population of Santiago and Valparaiso have been especially active throughout this district in recent years, and almost all the important summits have been ascended.

Further south, the range resumes its usual aspect of uninhabited desolation. Here rises the massive, glacier-clad bulk of Tupungato (22,300 feet), first climbed by Vines and Zurbriggen in 1897, a few months after their ascent of Aconcagua; and beyond it begins the third great volcanic zone of the Andes, which extends for more than five hundred miles toward Patagonia. The major peaks range between twelve and eighteen thousand feet in height and include some of the most active fire-mountains in the world. Then abruptly, at about 40° south latitude, the range undergoes a startling change, as it enters the moist climate of the South Chilean lake district. Described on the travel-folders as "the Switzerland of South America," this region boasts more truly Alpine scenery and climbing conditions than are to be found anywhere else in the Andes. The peaks thrust up sharply in bold relief. Glaciers are numerous and superb. And, most remarkable of all, the surrounding slopes and valleys are carpeted with rolling forests and green meadows. Given ample moisture and a climate neither burningly hot nor arcticly cold, even the barren, brown Andes know how to bloom.

The lake district, like the section near Santiago, farther north, has in recent years become the site of many cosmopolitan resorts. In winter the mountainsides around Valdivia, Osorno and Bariloche swarm with skiers, in summer with climbers of many nations. During the 1930's the region was the scene of much competitive, "do-or-die" mountaineering of the sort then popular in the Alps. One peak in particular, the spectacular, 11,000-foot El Tronador, enjoyed a decade of notoriety as a sort of Andean Eigerwand or Grandes Jorasses, with numerous parties of Germans and Italians vying to see which could kill themselves off first on its bristling precipices. Tronador was finally conquered in the middle 'thirties, but many unscaled summits remain in the outlying areas of the district.

The zone of the Chilean lakes is the last outpost of the inhabited Andes. Beyond it lie almost a thousand miles of mountain wilderness, extending through Patagonia to the southernmost tip of the continent. This is a stretch of country as wild and savage as any left in the world today—a region of deep fiords and impenetrable black forests, ceaseless rain and storming winds. Of the hundreds of peaks, few are of great height, but all are inaccessible and girdled with great glaciers and snow-fields. Few of them have been mapped or named, much less climbed.

The Straits of Magellen cut their interoceanic way through ruggedly mountainous terrain. Leaping them, the Andes rise again, to march still farther southward along the western coastline of Tierra del Fuego. Here looms the last great peak of the continent, Mount Sarmiento—not high, compared with the giants farther north, but ranking among the most spectacular mountains in the world in its icy and forlorn grandeur. Almost alone among the southernmost Andes, Sarmiento has been attempted by climbers on several occasions, the first try having been made by the noted English mountaineer, Sir William Martin Conway, as early as 1890. But its precipitous, storm-lashed slopes have thus far repulsed every challenge, and its 7100-foot summit remains unconquered.

North of Aconcagua, the chain of the Andes sweeps up along the Argentine-Chilean border toward Bolivia and Peru. In this 800-mile section stand a whole host of peaks ranging up to 22,500 feet—among them Mercedario, Ojos del Salado, Dos Corros and the liquidly unpronounceable Llullaillaco—and most of them, like Aconcagua, are simply huge pyramids of weathered debris, volcanic in orgin, but long since extinct. In northern Chile the range crosses the wastes of the Atacama Desert, rivaled only by the Sahara as the driest place on earth. In many localities not a drop of rain falls from one year's end to the next; the land is carpeted only with gravel and broken rocks, and the peaks, rising in lonely, desolate masses, are perhaps as unalluring as any to be found in the world. There are no streams, no forests, no glaciers. And, in spite of their great altitude, they bear little snow on their summits. In the past two decades several of them have been climbed, but their as-

cents were exercises in endurance rather than in technical mountaineering.

Beyond the Atacama, the range crosses into Bolivia, where it is
known as the Cordillera Occidental. Here, too, it is grim and forlorn—
its brown flanks tilting upward from treeless wastes, its desolate summits hanging transfixed in a parched sky. The highest of the peaks in
this region, is white-hooded Sajama, which, at 21,425 feet, ranks as the
highest Bolivian mountain. After several unsuccessful attempts, Sajama
was climbed in 1939 by Joseph Prem, a German, and Piero Ghiglione,
an Italian, in a grueling siege involving great hardships and few mountaineering pleasures. There has been comparatively little climbing in
the surrounding area.

North and east of the Cordillera Occidental lies the great Bolivian
plateau, or Altiplano—the core of the Andes. Here, between the lati-
tudes of 15° and 20° south, the range attains its greatest breadth,
spreading in far-flung chains of peaks across an area of more than
seventy-five thousand square miles. The plateau itself, one of the highest inhabited districts on earth, is the site of Bolivia's highest cities and
of its important tin and copper mining industries; and the peaks rimming it on the north, called the Cordillera Real, are far better known
to mountaineers than are those to the south. Notable among them is
the famous Illimani, guardian sentinel of the capital city of La Paz.

Illimani is a mountain with a controversial history. After several unsuccessful attempts, it was first ascended in 1898 by Sir William Martin Conway, who scaled the more southerly of its twin peaks, in the
belief—which prevailed for the next fifty-two years—that it was the
higher of the two. But in 1950, observations by climbers who gained
both summits (the northern one for the first time) indicated that this
latter was some hundred feet taller—which, if true, would make Conway's ascent an "almost," comparable to the Sourdough Climb on Mc-
Kinley. Another, and uglier, storm blew over the mountain in 1938,
when a group of Germans raised a swastika flag on the south summit,
only to be followed in a few days by an English party, who promptly
tore it down. As indicated above, the exact height of the peak—or
peaks—is still in doubt, but it is somewhere around 21,200 feet.

North of Illimani, and slightly lower, is the huge mountain-mass of
Sorata, capped by the two peaks of Ancohuma and Illampu, which
were climbed, respectively, in 1915 and 1919. West of it lies Lake

Titicaca, which, at 12,500 feet, is the highest large body of water in the world. And beyond Titicaca stretch the Andes of Peru.

It is in this high land that was once the Incas' that the Andes attain their greatest complexity and variety. Peak crowds upon peak, range upon range, in a bewildering tangle that spreads over the full length and half of the width of the country. Some of the summits, though high, present few mountaineering difficulties and have long since been climbed. But more—and more than in any other section of the Andes—are extremely formidable and have only recently been attempted, or even approached.

Among the "easy" mountains are those in the extreme south, between Lake Titicaca and the Pacific. Known as the Cordillera Occidental (there is at least one Cordillera Occidental in every country from Mexico to Cape Horn), they form a northward continuation of the Atacama Desert range and, like it, are parched, treeless and desolate. Here is the second of the three Andean volcanic zones, but, with few exceptions, the towering firepeaks have long been extinct. Dominating the region is the huge truncated mass of Coropuna, 21,700 feet high, which rises in lonely grandeur from a bleak and savage wilderness. Coropuna was first climbed in 1911 by a small party led by Hiram Bingham, then a professor at Yale University and later United States Senator from Connecticut. The ascent required little skill in the technical sense, but appears to have been as punishing and exhausting a grind as mountaineers have ever undertaken.

Other great extinct volcanos of southeastern Peru include Ampato, more than twenty-one thousand feet high, and El Misti, the presiding deity of the city of Arequipa. El Misti was first ascended as long ago as 1878, and for many years there was an observatory on its summit ridge, maintained by astronomers from Harvard University. Although 19,165 feet in altitude, its snow-line is so high that the top can be reached on the back of a mule—provided, of course, that the mule is in the mood. In the black, ashy crater of another volcano near Arequipa archaeologists have unearthed ruined temples dating back to prehistoric times.

Of more interest to the mountaineer is the Cordillera Oriental of southeastern Peru, rising out of the rugged country around Cuzco and the famous ruins of Machu Picchu. This region was once the heart of the greatest Indian civilization in the New World, and the lower slopes of the mountains abound in terraces and trails and the remnants of watchtowers, centuries old. Higher up, however, is an almost untouched world of rock and snow: one of the truly Alpine regions of the Andes. Highest of all the peaks is the magnificent Salcantay (20,574 feet), which was first scaled in 1952 by a mixed group of American and French climbers. The ascent, mostly on snow and ice, was a difficult one, involving much maneuvering amidst avalanches, crevasses, crumbling cornices and hanging glaciers. No less than sixteen hundred feet of fixed rope were strung up the mountainside, and (apparently there was a statistician along) exactly 1,291 steps had to be hacked in the ice. But six of the party finally reached the tip of the slender white spire that is Salcantay's summit and returned in safety with a notable victory.

Beyond the southern cordilleras, to about the latitude of Lima, stretches a great conglomeration of ranges, crisscrossing one another in a tangle of so-called *nudos,* or "knots." This section has few outstanding individual mountains, but the central plateaus which form the core of the uplift are of enormous extent and elevation. It is an almost rainless world—brown, desolate and forbidding—yet among the most populous zones of the Andes, because it is the heart of the Peruvian mining district. The barren hills surrounding Cerro de Pasco, Oroya and Huancayo have for centuries been one of the principal sources of the world's supply of copper and silver. The Central Railroad of Peru, crossing the continental divide between Lima and Oroya at 16,500 feet, was regarded as one of the wonders of the world when it was opened in 1893 and remains today the highest standard-gauge railway line ever constructed.

The main range of the Andes is narrower in this region than at any other point between the Caribbean and southern Chile, scarcely 150 miles separating Lima, on the Pacific, from the jungle tributaries of the Amazon to the east of the divide. Farther north, however, the highlands spread out again, and the peaks rise sharply in the great massifs of central Peru. Like the Cordillera Oriental, these are ranges of granite and ice, non-volcanic in origin, and abound in rock-spires, precipices and glaciers of almost Himalayan proportions. Pre-eminent among them are the Cordillera Blanca, the Raura and Huagoruncho Range and the Cordillera de Huayhuash.

Of these, the Cordillera Blanca is both the largest and the best known, containing, among a host of other peaks, 22,200-foot Huascarán, the highest summit in Peru. Huascarán holds an interesting place in mountaineering history as being one of the few major peaks in the world to be first ascended by a woman. Its conqueror was Miss Annie S. Peck, a remarkable and indefatigable lady from Providence, Rhode Island, who for nine months of the year taught Latin at Smith College and Purdue University and during the other three went big-mountain hunting among the far-flung ranges of Europe, Mexico and South America. In 1904 Miss Peck reached a height of 20,500 feet on Sorata, in Bolivia. In 1908, at the age of over fifty, she visited the Andes again and this time fought her way successfully to the northernmost of Huascarán's formidable twin peaks.*

Little other climbing was done in the Cordillera Blanca until 1932, when a large party of Germans conducted an exhaustive exploration of the region. Besides reascending Huascarán, they climbed some twenty virgin peaks between sixteen thousand and twenty-one thousand feet in height and established the highest astronomical observatory in the world at twenty thousand feet on the summit ridge of the snow-peak Hualcan. In 1939 there was a second German expedition, during which Huascarán was climbed once more, as well as other major peaks; and during the postwar years there has been considerable activity in the area by parties of various nationalities.

The other ranges of central Peru are not nearly so well known and, indeed, were almost wholly unexplored until recent years. Few of the Raura peaks have been climbed or attempted, and the Huagoruncho massif, which consists principally of the 18,860-foot mountain of the same name, is to date also unconquered. The Cordillera de Huayhuash, however, was, a few years ago, the scene of one of the most spectacular ascents in modern mountaineering.

King of this uplift, a small compact range only fifteen miles in length, is 21,770-foot Yerupajá, also known, more expressively, as Carnicero—The Butcher. It was first challenged in 1936 by the same German climbers who explored the near-by Cordillera Blanca; but their attempt fell some two thousand feet short of the goal, and it remained

---

* The veracity of Miss Peck's claim has been the subject of much discussion, but for want of conclusive evidence to the contrary she is generally given the benefit of the doubt.

for an American party, in 1950, to forge a way to the top. That they did so was testimony not only to their skill and endurance, but to their luck as well. For Yerupajá proved to be one of the most difficult and dangerous of mountains, and the top climbers faced hazards which only by a miracle did not cost them their lives.

The group, though from various parts of the states, was organized as the Harvard Andean Expedition. Significantly, perhaps, only one of the members was over thirty, and most were of that highly specialized and daring school of climbers often self-described as "rock engineers." On Yerupajá, however, it was not rock they had to deal with, but snow and ice—and in their most dangerous forms. The peak was immensely steep; each day its white flanks caught the full melting heat of the tropical sun, and its walls and ridges were a deathtrap of plunging avalanches and crumbling cornices. The climbers had to worry not only about falling off the mountain themselves, but about the mountain's falling on them or disintegrating beneath their feet.

Nevertheless, they made steady progress. The weather held good. Following the general route pioneered by the Germans fourteen years earlier, they worked their way up the great ice-cliffs of the east face: hacking out their steps, stringing fixed ropes, hauling up their packs, establishing their upper camps. After some three weeks the highest one was pitched at 20,600 feet, within striking distance of the summit. But, though there had been no climbing mishaps, *soroche* (the Andean version of altitude sickness) and other ailments had taken a heavy toll, and by this time only two of the men were in condition to go on. They were David Harrah, of Stanford University, and James C. Maxwell, of Harvard, each twenty-four years old.

After several days at the highest camp, they too were having their troubles—particularly with their feet, which were constantly close to freezing. But they did not let this stop them, and on July thirty-first, after two previous false starts, they made their bid for the top. There was only one possible route: along the white spine of the summit ridge to its highest point, which was about a quarter of a mile distant. The angle of the ridge itself was not steep, and at the beginning it was fairly broad, but it was as yielding and unstable as a slack wire. A full half of their footway, as the climbers well knew, had no solid base at all, but was merely the top of a cornice overhanging the precipice of the west face. And on the other side the east face dropped away in an almost sheer wall. A half step too far in either direction would have meant instant disaster.

Slowly and warily they inched their way upward. For a hundred yards a crevasse in the east face paralleled the ridge, just below its crest; and, lowering themselves, they tried to move along its bottom— only to find the snow crumbling ominously beneath their feet. Regaining the ridge, they came at last to the base of a sort of summit pyramid and for the first time had a brief stretch of climbing on solid rock. Then, as they topped the rock, they came again to snow and ice: a final length of ridge sloping gently up to the topmost pinnacle. "It was very narrow and everywhere corniced," Harrah reported afterward. "Since we were so near the top and in so dangerous a place, we should have called this point the summit. We decided, mistakenly, that careful belaying would justify a traverse to the highest point."

They tried it—and they made it. At five-thirty in the afternoon they stood precariously, one at a time, on the tiny, dizzying snow-crest that is Yerupajá's summit.

Then, a few minutes later. . .

They were working their way down the ridge toward the highest rocks. Roped together, they stopped on a small snow-platform while Maxwell prepared to take a photograph. "The platform," wrote Harrah, "was about seven feet wide, appeared to be solid, but seemed as subject to avalanching on the east as to cornice-fracturing on the west."

It was the latter that happened. Without warning, the snow gave way under Harrah's feet, and the next instant he was plunging down the western precipice. The rope that joined him to Maxwell was a hundred and twenty feet long, and he fell the whole length of it, straight through the air. As it turned out, though, it was the very distance of his fall that saved both of them, for it gave Maxwell time to throw himself prone and drive his ax, with the rope around it, into the ridge. For him, providentially, the snow held. There came a sickening jerk, and a second, and a third. Providentially, too, the rope was of nylon and its elasticity absorbed some of the shock; otherwise Harrah would have all but been cut in two or Maxwell would have been pulled off. As it was, the third jerk, as Harrah bounced at rope's end, dragged him to within inches of the rim, and a fourth would have done for him.

The fall was stopped. But down below Harrah hung in space, four thousand feet above the distant glacier. It is better left to the imagination what the fall had done to his ribs and lungs, let alone his faculties. Maxwell could not pull him up, and he himself could not reach the concave mountainside. For ten feet he had to climb straight up on the rope—an amazing feat after what had happened to him—before the ice-wall bulged out enough for him to touch it, and from there on it took him forty-five minutes to scrape and claw his way back to the ridge.

Shaken and close to exhaustion, they struggled on down the long incline. A few minutes later there was almost a second accident, as a section of snow broke away before Maxwell's feet, but he was able to leap back just in time to avoid falling. Soon after, night closed in; but though they kept going until midnight, they were unable to reach their high camp and spent the rest of the night huddled in a small cave in the ice. Here they realized that their exploit was likely to have an even more serious consequence than the fall, for their feet were now frozen numb, and long hours of rubbing and warming failed to restore proper circulation. The next morning they crept on to the camp and rested for twenty-four hours, but it did them little good. Their feet grew steadily worse, swelling until they could scarcely force them into their boots, and when they started off again they were barely able to hobble. Fortunately their companions intercepted them as they were nearing the end of their tether and helped them the rest of the way down the mountain.

The Butcher had been conquered, but it claimed its pound of flesh, for subsequently Harrah lost all his toes and Maxwell parts of three toes. In this connection, it is perhaps interesting to note that the Yerupajá venture took place only a few weeks after the French climbers of Annapurna had come down from their mountain on the other side of the world—after a similar victory and at a similar price. Whether, in cases like these, the one is worth the other is a question that will be argued as long as there are mountains and men.

As the air age advances and the earth continues to shrink, mountaineering activity is sure to increase in the high and remote Andes. Some of it will be the sort of dogged slogging that has marked the ascents of Aconcagua and the great volcanos; but more, it seems likely, will be the difficult and precarious type of work that has more recently been done in Peru. In that country alone, it is estimated, there are still some twenty unclimbed peaks of twenty thousand or more feet. Most of them are extremely formidable, and two—Jirishanca, in the Cordillera de Huayhuash, and Chacraraju, in the Cordillera Blanca—are, like the Mustagh Tower in the Karakoram, ranked as "unclimbable," at least for this generation. Huagoruncho, too, though slightly lower, is considered one of the most difficult virgin peaks remaining in the world.

For many years to come mountaineering in South America will continue to have elements of exploration as well as of pure climbing, for large areas are still imperfectly known. The unscaled summits still far outnumber the scaled ones, and, among the latter, scarcely any have been tried by more than one route. Second only to the mountains of Asia, the Andes offer wide and high horizons to the climber of the future.

9

ICE ON THE EQUATOR

The Mountains of Africa

DARKEST AFRICA IS NO MORE. Or at least not what we used to mean by Darkest Africa. For better or worse, the old continent of mystery has become part of the modern world.

Over the past hundred years all but a small fraction of its area has, at some time, been owned or dominated by white men. It has been penetrated by railroads, girdled by airways. It has been mapped, mined, dammed, cultivated—and despoiled. If today we think of Africa as "dark," it is not in terms of wild beasts and painted savages but of race riots in Johannesburg, Mau Mau terror in Kenya, political strife in Egypt, Morocco, the Sudan.

But in Africa, as elsewhere, human history is made in the lowlands. Changeless amid constant change, its mountains remain as they have always been: high and remote above the world of men. Kilimanjaro, Kenya and Ruwenzori, the continent's three greatest uplifts, are little different now from what they were when primitive tribes ruled the grasslands and jungles and the rounding of the Cape was only a gleam in a mariner's eye. To be sure, all three have been climbed—as have many of the lesser peaks—but the expeditions to them have been few and far between, and for the most part they have been left to their lofty solitude. There are no longer many directions in which one may go in Africa and find himself a pioneer; but there are a few. And one of them is *up*.

There is nothing on the continent comparable to the Rockies or Andes of the western world. The great peaks do not form a long, continuous chain, but are widely separated and unconnected, and each mountain region differs greatly from the others in surroundings, structure and climate.

In the extreme northwest of the continent, in Morocco and Algeria, is the extensive uplift known as the Atlas Mountains. Beginning only a few miles from the Straits of Gibraltar and the Mediterranean Sea, the Atlas are more closely connected with Europe, both geologically and historically, than with any of the other ranges of Africa. They came into being millions of years ago in the same great earth-movements that created the Alps, and almost from the beginning of recorded history they have been known to the traders and sailors of southern Europe. Indeed, it was from Greek mythology that they received their name: the ancient navigators of the Mediterranean, marveling at the great snow-peaks in the desert to the south, associated them with Atlas, the Titan who supported the heavens on his shoulders, and named them for him.

Close as they are to western Europe, the Atlas are infrequently visited. The six groups of mountains which form the range rise out of wild, inhospitable country, and for centuries their foothills have been the home of fierce nomadic tribes. In addition, the surrounding plains and valleys—outposts of the Sahara—are among the hottest and driest regions in the world. In recent years, however, most of the high peaks of the Atlas have been climbed, and several English and French expeditions have surveyed the terrain. The loftiest group of the range is the High Atlas, farthest inland from the Mediterranean; the highest single peak, Djebel Toubkal (13,653 feet), which is snowcapped for most of the year, in spite of the waterless furnace that spreads around it.

Beyond the Atlas the great deserts of Africa spread endlessly away, and only sand dunes and low ridges break the parched monotony of the land. To the southeast, almost the entire breadth of the continent intervenes before the earth again buckles upward into the wild, little-known ranges of Ethiopia. To the south, along the west coast, there are five thousand miles, almost to the Cape of Good Hope, with only 13,350-foot Mount Cameroon rising to the height of a true mountain. The Sahara, the Congo forests and the great grasslands of Central Africa present one of the longest continuous flat stretches to be found anywhere in the world.

South Africa, however, is essentially a mountainous country. Cape Town itself lies in the shadow of the famous Table Mountain, and ranges extend northward from it, along both the Atlantic and Indian Oceans. For many years this has been the most Europeanized region of the continent, and it is therefore not surprising that it has seen considerable mountaineering activity—more, probably, than in the rest of Africa combined. Largest and most interesting of the ranges is the Drakensberg group, which extends several hundred miles from southwest to northeast through Natal, the Orange Free State and the Transvaal. The Drakensberge—so named by the Boers—consist of several chains of rugged, rocky peaks, notched by deep valleys and gorges. Most of the principal summits are between ten and eleven thousand feet, and the culminating point, the Mont-aux-Sources, rises 11,250 feet above the sea. There is no permanent snow or ice anywhere in the range, and very little at any time; but the far-ranging mountaineer may find rock-climbs, of every degree of difficulty. Some sections, notably that surrounding Mont-aux-Sources, have been opened up by the installation of roads and lodgings and are frequently visited. Others, however, are still isolated by miles of wild country, and there are many peaks which have not yet been scaled or even attempted.

The Atlas, the ranges of Ethiopia and the Drakensberge are the most important of the lesser uplifts of Africa. There remain the big three: Kilimanjaro, Kenya and Ruwenzori. These great snow-giants of the tropics rise within a few hundred miles of each other in British East Africa. They are, however, not part of one range, but rise as distinct and separate masses, each with its own individual topography, climate and history.

Kilimanjaro, soaring to an altitude of 19,565 feet, is the highest of the three and the loftiest point in Africa. It was also the first of the three to be discovered and climbed, and—thanks largely to Ernest Hemingway—is now the best known, at least by name. Situated less than two hundred miles inland from the Indian Ocean, its existence was known to white traders and missionaries as early as 1848, and, before long, adventurous men were pushing in from the coastal villages toward the great white wedge that hung in the sky to the west. The exploration of East Africa was accomplished about equally by England and Germany, and during the 'sixties and 'seventies of the last century expeditions representing both of these nations approached close to the mountain and investigated its approaches. Its topmost summit, known as Kibo, was reached in 1889 by Hans Meyer, a German scientist and mountaineer, who had devoted many years of study to the mountain and made no less than four visits to it.

Kilimanjaro is one of the most impressive peaks in the world. An extinct volcano, it rises in a magnificent sudden sweep from the flat surrounding wilderness, rivaled only by its own sub-peak, Mawenzi, some seven miles to the east. Its base rests in tropical grasslands—the famous big-game country of Northern Tanganyika. Higher up is a belt of dense forest and, higher still, the hardier vegetation of a colder climate. At fourteen thousand feet the lowest reaches of the glaciers are encountered, and the summit of the mountain rears into the clouds in a vast expanse of gleaming snow. From base to top, in a distance of a few thousand feet, Kilimanjaro presents a panorama of climate and vegetation that would ordinarily embrace thousands of miles—a vertical progression, in effect, from Equator to Pole.

The mountain has been repeatedly visited by geologists and botanists during the past fifty years, and many parties have ascended to the summit crater. Like most volcanos, it offers few climbing difficulties, other than those of distance and altitude, and after its various routes had been established and charted it lost much of its attraction for expert mountaineers. Mawenzi, however, first conquered in 1912, is a jagged rock-peak with steep ridges and precipices and offers more challenge than its larger neighbor.

Mount Kenya, the second highest mountain of Africa, (17,040 feet), is situated in Kenya Colony, about two hundred miles due north of Kilimanjaro. It was discovered in 1849, a scant year after its greater rival, and, like it, its approaches were first opened up by missionaries and traders. Attempts to scale it were made in 1887 and 1893, but it was not until 1899 that its summit yielded to an attack by a party of mixed nationalities under the leadership of an Englishman, Sir Halford Mackinder. This expedition not only encountered great climbing difficulties, but was constantly harassed by the savage native tribes of the region. It is probably the only major mountaineering party in history that has had to fight men as well as nature on its way to its goal.

Like Kilimanjaro, Kenya is of volcanic origin, but, unlike it, it bristles with crags and precipices. It, too, has twin peaks—Bation, the highest point, and Nelion—but they are only forty yards apart and the drop between them is a mere two hundred feet. All the routes to the summit, leading over both rock and ice, are extremely difficult, and, although several parties during the early 1900's tried to follow in the footsteps of Mackinder, the second successful ascent was not accomplished until 1929—a full thirty years later. Since then it has been scaled on several occasions, but only by highly skilled climbers.

The third of the three great mountains of Africa was also the third to be conquered. But in every other respect its story and that of its ascent stand first in the annals of African mountaineering. For the whole history of climbing and exploration has few stories more fascinating than that of the discovery and ascent of Ruwenzori, or The Mountains of the Moon.

The Mountains of the Moon! A name to conjure with, to set beside Atlantis, and Eden in the geography of a lost, legendary world. And, indeed, a legend was exactly what they were for upward of two thousand years. For, although their name has been known to the geographers of Europe since the fifth century B.C., no white man actually laid eyes on them until 1888.

The river Nile was the great waterway of the ancient world, and its lower reaches had since the beginning of history been a crowded highway of men and goods. But its origins were shrouded in darkness—the darkness of the vast, unknown continent of which Egypt was the outpost. All that men knew were the rumors that filtered through to them from far-ranging traders and wandering Arab tribes, and on these they built their theories and fancies. The dramatist Aeschylus wrote of "Egypt nurtured by the snow." Aristotle spoke of the Nile flowing from "a silver mountain," and Herodotus of its rising between "sharp-pointed peaks" in farthest Africa. Ptolemy, the great geographer of the second century A.D., declared that the great river flowed from "The Mountains of the Moon."

This, substantially, was all the ancient world knew. In the Dark Ages that followed even that much was forgotten, and for seventeen hundred years The Mountains of the Moon were remembered, if at all, only as creations of legend and imagination. Then at last, toward the middle of the nineteenth century, the interior of Africa began to be opened up, and the ancient mountains of fiction became suddenly mountains of fact.

The credit for their discovery—or rediscovery—belongs to the explorer, Henry Stanley; and even he was a long time finding them. Again and again during his extensive travels he passed close to their snow-capped peaks, but although he heard many reports of their existence, months and years went by without his catching a glimpse of them. The reason for this was that these legendary mountains are almost completely hidden by nature from the eyes of men. In contrast to the surrounding lowlands, which have four climatic seasons, two wet and two dry, the uplands of the range have only one—and that is wet. Indeed, the region is now known to be one of the wettest spots in the world, and it has been estimated that rain falls on as many as 350 days a year. Even on the rare occasions when it is not raining the warm air rising from the forests and plains below condenses in heavy mist about the snowpeaks. A dozen times a year, perhaps—and then for only a few hours—the mountains shake loose their cloudy blanket and stand forth, clear and dominant, against the tropical sky. At all other times they are, literally, invisible.

Stanley first visited the interior of Africa in 1871, but it was not until 1888 that he became, so far as is known, the first white man ever to gaze upon The Mountains of the Moon. One day in that year, traveling along the shores of Lake Albert, in western Uganda, his eye was caught by what at first he thought to be a fantastically striking cloud formation in the sky to the southeast. "I saw a peculiar-shaped cloud of a most beautiful silver color," he wrote later, "which assumed the proportions and appearance of a vast mountain covered with snow." Even then he could not quite believe his own eyes. The air below the white apparition appeared black and menacing, and he believed he was witnessing merely the weird displays of a distant tropical storm. It was not until he had stared into the southeast for hours that he realized he was actually looking at a vast, solid range of mountains.

Stanley gave The Mountains of the Moon a new and appropriate name: Ruwenzori—The Rain-Maker. Upon his return to civilization he made his discovery known to the world, and the fight for exploration and conquest began.

It was to be a fight lasting many years and involving great struggles,

A WORLD OF ROCK AND ICE

The wilderness of the St. Elias Range, in Alaska, cut through by the great twisting avenues of the glaciers. Mount Bona in the distance.

CAPSTONE OF THE WESTERN WORLD

The vast mass of Aconcagua, towering above the desolate valleys of the southern Andes.

hardships and disappointments. The first actually to penetrate into the unknown terrain was one of Stanley's own men, Lieutenant Stairs, who in 1889 ascended Ruwenzori's mist-hung slopes to a height of over ten thousand feet. During the next fifteen years scattered individuals and expeditions followed in his footsteps—explorers, scientists, missionaries, mountaineers—in the last group several of the most distinguished European climbers. They came, if they were lucky they saw, and they turned back in frustration. Without exception they bogged down in the steaming wilderness of rain and fog, many of them without even being vouchsafed a single glimpse of the peaks they had journeyed so many thousands of miles to challenge. The Mountains of the Moon were reluctant to give up the remoteness and secrecy which had shrouded them for two thousand years. The major problem was not so much to climb them as to reach, or even find them.

Among those to try their luck was the indefatigable Douglas Freshfield. In 1905 Freshfield was a man of sixty, but still an active climberexplorer, and early that year we find him setting out for Ruwenzori with his friend and climbing colleague, A. L. Mumm. The two Englishmen penetrated more deeply into the range than had any of their predecessors, reaching as far as the snouts of the great glaciers; but in the end they too were turned away from the heights by the remorseless weather. In 1906 the same fate befell A. F. R. Wollaston and a group of scientists from the British Museum, who were all but washed off the range by torrential downpours. Climbers began to despair of ever conquering this will-o'-the-wisp among mountains . . . when, suddenly, in the very same year, it was conquered.

Prince Luigi Amadeo of Savoy, Duke of the Abruzzi, was a member of the royal house of Italy and an admiral of the fleet. He was also one of the foremost explorers and mountaineers of his day. In 1897 he had accomplished the first ascent of Mount St. Elias, in Alaska, and two years later had led an arctic expedition that got to within two hundred miles of the then undiscovered North Pole. Now, in April of 1906, he set sail from Naples to find, explore and climb the last great unconquered mountain of Africa. In all three objectives he was completely successful.

The Duke's expedition was organized on the grand scale. In addition to a group of mountaineers and sportsmen he took with him a small army of scientists and technicians, writers, photographers, physicians,

Alpine guides and porters. Among them were two men who, by virtue of the Ruwenzori exploit and the Duke's later expedition to the Himalayas, were to win enduring fame in their own right: Filippo de Filippi, one of the foremost writers on mountains and mountaineering, and Vittorio Sella, who to this day remains an unsurpassed master of mountain photography. There were also many other men distinguished in various fields. What gave the expedition its unique character, however, was not so much the individual talents of its members as the fact that it was organized in a manner new to mountaineering. Theretofore the typical climbing party had been simply a group of friends, with or without professional guides, casually bound together in a common purpose. The Abruzzi venture, on the other hand, was a planned, integrated organism, in which every member had his specialized functions and responsibilities. As such, it was to accomplish far more than the conquest of an individual peak: it was to set the style for most ambitious mountaineering expeditions of the future.

The Duke and his men, like the other adventurers before them, pushed in toward Ruwenzori from the east coast of Africa. From Mombassa they traveled by rail to Nairobi and thence to Port Florence on Lake Victoria, passing in turn through the dense coastal jungles, the Taru Desert, home of the death-bearing tsetse fly, and the great grasslands of the Athi Plateau, swarming with lion, giraffe, zebra, antelope and buffalo. The journey across Lake Victoria to Entebbe was made by steamer, and for a day and a night they were out of sight of land on this huge inland sea that ranks second only to Lake Superior among the world's bodies of fresh water. From Entebbe they marched along jungle trails a distance of almost two hundred miles to Fort Portal in Uganda, the last outpost of civilization in the wilderness surrounding Ruwenzori.

During this stage of the journey the army-like expedition became an army in fact. The black tribes of Uganda were at that time among the most savage in Africa, and the British colonial government, concerned for the safety of its royal visitor, supplied him with a troop of native soldiers as escort. These, in addition to the original party and the multitude of porters, guides and camp-followers who had been picked up en route, swelled the total number of men to more than four hundred. By day they wound slowly across country in a single file five miles in length; at night they built stockaded encampments that were larger by far than any town or village for miles around. The whole journey, indeed, was something of a circus parade in reverse—with the lions, elephants and naked savages of Uganda as pop-eyed spectators and the representatives of western civilization as performers.

Beyond Fort Portal the real work began. The mountains which they sought, now less than fifty miles away, were, as usual, shrouded in their veil of mist, and only once in their entire journey did they catch a glimpse of shining snow-peaks high in the sky to the southwest. Still they pushed on, following the Mobuku River, which flows down through the labyrinth of Ruwenzori to Lake Albert Edward. This was the route that had been followed by the earlier expeditions, and Freshfield and Mumm had reported the existence of great peaks and glaciers near the head of the Mobuku Valley. As the Duke and his men advanced slowly they could see nothing of what lay ahead, but the gradually rising ground told them that they were at last approaching their goal.

The region into which these climber-explorers now penetrated was one of unimaginable weirdness and savagery—a nightmare-world of jungle, mist and rain. The gorges of the Mobuku were a tangled wilderness of dead and rotting vegetation, through which they had to hack their way, foot by foot. Men and pack-animals floundered to their knees in muck and mold, and through the high foliage of the treetops the rain beat down upon them incessantly. As they gained altitude the temperature fell, but the new coolness was, if anything, more oppressive than the full heat of the tropical sun. The sweating dampness of the forests pressed in upon them like a physical weight. No wisp of air stirred. It was as if they were moving along the bottom of a stagnant lake—a watery, choking world without light, sound or motion.

Day after day, however, the Duke and his men struggled on, and at last they came to the apex of the valley, at an altitude of about nine thousand feet. Here they laboriously cleared away a few hundred feet of jungle and pitched their base camp on the mire and broken rock. The Europeans in the party were close to exhaustion. The native porters shivered in the unaccustomed cold and huddled in their tents, chanting to keep away the hostile demons of the mountain. They refused to use the warm clothing and blankets which had been brought for them, preferring to huddle about the campfires where they could feel the warmth of the flames on their bare skin.

These days and nights at the base camp were the low point of the expedition. The rain never stopped; the mist never lifted; and beyond the radius of the little mud clearing lay an impenetrable veil of ghostly gray. The only thing that saved them from defeat, then and there, was the thoroughness of their organization, that resulted in there being enough food and supplies on hand to last even through several weeks of delay. A less well-equipped party, if it had not been flooded off the mountain, would have been starved off. The Duke and his men were prepared not only to labor, but to wait.

And at last their waiting was rewarded. Days came when there were short intervals between downpours. The mists thinned for an hour or two in the twenty-four, and above them they could see vague, towering battlements of rock and ice. With shouts of relief and joy the men sprang into action. In a few short marches they fought their way through the remaining miles of tangled vegetation and emerged on the upper slopes of the mountain.

Here they came into a world no less strange and fantastic than the jungle below. Between the uppermost trees and the glaciers spread a vast expanse of flowers. They were not, however, the usual tiny flowers of high mountain pastures, but huge dazzling blooms that put to shame the richness of the tropical foliage below. Close under the ice-fields were vivid banks of color, countless varieties of plants and shrubs magnified to many times their natural size by the equatorial rains: violets, geraniums and ranunculi, lobelias and senecios twice the height of a man and so densely packed that the guides had to slash their way through them with axes.

Some of the party remained behind to explore and catalogue this marvelous alpine garden. The Duke and his strongest climbers pushed on, ascending a great glacier to its source near the summit of a jagged ridge. From here they were at last able to see the whole sweep of the Ruwenzori Range—a lifeless, soundless snow-world in the tropical sky on which no men had ever looked before. Directly ahead of them, to the west, was a towering white mass of peaks that glittered through the mist, and they knew at once that these were the pinnacles which they sought.

The conquest of these topmost summits was accomplished by the Duke and three Swiss guides. Packing their tents and provisions on their backs, they worked their way slowly up glaciers and across snowfields to the slopes of the loftiest peak. This, upon closer inspection, proved to consist of two sub-peaks, connected by a long snow-ridge. The climbers established their last camp in the snow some two thousand feet below, spent an almost sleepless night anxiously watching the weather, and began their assault at dawn.

The lesser of the twin peaks seemed to offer the more practicable approach and they climbed it first, encountering no great difficulties on the way. As they reached it, however, great banks of cloud rolled in upon them, and for an hour and a half they were marooned on their lofty perch, straining their eyes for even a glimpse of the higher summit, only a few hundred yards beyond. At last they detected a white glint of snow through the grayness and set out toward it along the icy knife-edge of the connecting ridge.

Step by step they walked a tightrope through the clouds. All they could see was a few yards of the ridge before them; on either side the mountain fell away in sheer precipices, and the gulfs below were wrapped in impenetrable murk. Finally, however, the sharp rising of the ridge told them they had reached the walls of the higher summit. It became necessary to hack footholds in the glazed snow. Only one man moved at a time, the others meanwhile attempting to find a secure stance and paying out the rope that extended between them.

The last fifty feet of the mountain called for climbing skill of the first order. A smooth ice-gully cut vertically to the summit, with no hold of any kind within reach. One man stood at the base of the gully while another climbed to his shoulders, swung his ax into the ice above and pulled himself up by it. From a position on a narrow shelf he was then able to lend a hand to the other three. The process was repeated again—and once more. Then, suddenly, the Duke realized that there was no longer any ice-wall rising above them, but only a billowing wilderness of clouds. He and his companions had reached the topmost summit of The Mountains of the Moon.

They had won out. They had accomplished with complete success what they had set out to do and stood at last atop the legendary mountains of Africa. But the mountains had conquered too. Instead of a vast and majestic panorama spread out beneath them, all they could see were the tiny white knob of snow on which they stood and their own muffled figures outlined in the mist. Nature had permitted another of her great strongholds to yield to the courage and skill of man, but not to his eyes. The Duke had come and he had conquered. But in the moment of triumph he could scarcely see his hand in front of his face.

As has been indicated, the Abruzzi party was an expedition in the fullest sense of the word. Not content with merely climbing their mountain and rushing down to tell the world about it, they spent weeks in the mysterious tropical arctic which they had discovered. They climbed a half-dozen secondary peaks, made maps, took photographs, collected geological and botanical specimens, and the result was that, upon their return to civilization, the world was supplied with as great a body of new information as has ever been brought back from a journey of exploration. Not the least interesting fact was that the ancient geographers had been right—or almost right. The Nile *does* rise in The Mountains of the Moon. Their snow and rains, draining down to the east, pour into the waters of the great lakes, Victoria, Albert and Albert Edward, which are in turn the sources of the famous river of Egypt.

The Duke named the 16,793-foot summit of the range Mount Stanley, in honor of the explorer who had first seen it, and to its two snow-peaks he gave the names of the then-reigning queens of Italy and England, Margherita and Alexandra. In the past half century they have been climbed on various occasions. Two or three English expeditions followed, soon after, in the footsteps of Abruzzi, and in more recent times most of the lesser peaks of the range have been ascended and explored. With the opening up of East Africa they have become far more accessible—if no less invisible—than formerly. For several years now there has been a Mountains of the Moon Hotel at what was once the isolated frontier post of Fort Portal, and in 1953 the reported discovery of uranium in the region brought a sudden influx of scientists and prospectors.

As far as mountaineers are concerned, however, Ruwenzori has largely been left to its solitude of rain and mist. The Duke's successful venture not only brought to a close the period of first ascents in Africa and cleared up an age-old mystery, but also demonstrated how great mountains should be attacked. Instructed and encouraged by his example, climbers began turning their eyes toward Asia—and the greatest mountains in the world.

10

"HIGHEST YET"

The Challenge of the Himalayas

"SURELY THE GODS live here. This is no place for men!"

So spoke Kipling's Kim as he stood on the plains of northern India and raised his eyes to the Himalayas. In the years since, men of many generations and many lands have stood where Kim stood, staring, and all of them, like him, have felt the surge of awe and wonder in their hearts.

For the Himalayas are without rival among the mountain ranges of the earth. Their stupendous white rampart, curved like a bow along the frontier of India and Tibet, is composed of hundreds of peaks higher than the highest summits of Europe, Africa and the Americas; its topmost pinnacles—Everest, K2, Kangchenjunga—soar more than a mile farther into the sky than any other mountains, anywhere. Mount Washington piled upon Aconcagua, Fujiyama upon Ruwenzori, the Matterhorn upon a second Matterhorn would barely match the altitude of these giants of Central Asia. When one considers that most of the passes and glaciers of the range lie at elevations between fifteen and twenty thousand feet above the sea, it becomes literally true that where other mountains leave off is where the Himalayas begin.

The name Himalaya is derived from two Sanskrit words—*hima* and *alaya*—and means The Abode of Snow. Since the beginning of recorded history the range has played a dominating part in the lives of millions of Asiatics. Both the Hindu and Buddhist religions have wrapped it in legend and peopled it with gods and demons, and for centuries the remote Himalayan sources of the great rivers of India— the Ganges, Indus and Brahmaputra—have been the supremely holy places of pilgrimage to men of the eastern faiths. In a more worldly sense, too, the Himalayas may be said to be almost the determining factor in the whole pattern of civilization in Asia. Their crags and snows, peaks and glaciers, have formed an almost impenetrable historic barrier between the Mongolians and Tibetans of the north and the Hindus of the south. The dry, desolate plateau of Tibet and the teeming valley of the Ganges, lying only a few hundred miles apart on either side of the range, are in every other respect as remote from each other as if separated by continents and oceans. Not only the climate, but the history and present civilization of both China and India would be vastly different without the great white wall of mountains that stands between them.

The main range of the Himalayas is some fifteen hundred miles long and between one hundred and one hundred and fifty miles wide. Unlike most of the major mountain chains of the world it runs from east to west; unlike them, too, it is not an isolated and independent uplift, complete in itself, but part of a greater uplift of gigantic proportions. The continent of Asia, roughly speaking, is built on two levels. The lower is composed of a vast margin of almost unbroken lowlands, sweeping through Siberia, on the north, China, on the east, India, on the south, and Turkestan, on the west; the upper consists of the high central plateaus of Mongolia and Tibet. Highlands and lowlands are, for the most part, separated from each other by huge mountain ranges: the Kunlun, the Nan Shan, the Tien Shan, the Altai, the Hindu Kush, the Pamirs, and—greatest of all—the Himalayas. The plains of India, from which the southern slopes of the Himalayas rise, are scarcely five hundred feet above sea level. The plateau of Tibet, two hundred miles to the north, has a mean elevation of sixteen thousand feet—the veritable "roof of the world." The range may be likened to a prodigious wall supporting that roof and its highest peaks to steeples rimming its southern edge.

One reason why the Himalayas are the highest mountains on earth is that they are the youngest. It was not until comparatively recent geologic times that a great buckling of the earth's crust forced them upward out of the prehistoric ocean that once covered what is now southern Asia, and the slow process of erosion has not yet had time to wear them down. As a result, they are not only the loftiest of mountains, but the most fearsomely jagged and precipitous as well. Peak crowds upon peak in a wild, crumpled confusion of rock and ice. Glaciers snake downward from them into valleys so deep and narrow that they lie in perpetual shadow. And, still lower, the headwaters of great rivers have cut abysmal gorges through the very backbone of the range —their beds a mere four or five thousand feet above the sea, while the snowpeaks on either side tower a full four vertical miles above them into the clouds. The day will come, to be sure, when the patient, endless work of wind and snow and running water will reduce the Himalayas to gently rolling hills; but its coming can be reckoned in millions and tens of millions of years.

The highest peaks of the range are distributed fairly evenly along its 1,500-mile sweep. In the extreme east the Himalaya proper are considered as beginning at the bend of the Brahmaputra—the point where the great river cuts down from Tibet into the plains of India. From here the crest-line runs due west, crossing the independent state of Bhutan in a wilderness of peaks between twenty and twenty-five thousand feet in height, of which even today very little is known. In Sikkim, however, and further west, along the border between Tibet and Nepal, are found the greatest and most famous of all Himalayan giants —among them Everest, Kangchenjunga, Lhotse and Makalu, respectively the first, third, fourth and fifth highest mountains in the world. In interior Nepal the range is dominated by the great trio of Dhaulagiri, Manaslu and Annapurna, and three hundred miles farther west is the magnificent Garhwal group, topped by Nanda Devi and Kamet. This is the region sacred to Hindus through countless centuries as the source of the River Ganges.

Beyond Garhwal the Himalayas bend gradually to the north and sweep across the fabled province of Kashmir. Here, near the northernmost outposts of India and Pakistan, rise Nanga Parbat and the colossal sub-range of the Karakoram whose culminating point, known both as Mount Godwin Austen and K2, is topped only by Everest among all mountains. Actually, the Karakoram uplift rises on the far side of the River Indus, which, like the Brahmaputra on the east, flows down from Tibet into India and is considered to mark the farthermost extremity of the Himalayas. Nevertheless, the Karakoram are usually designated as a sub-division of the greater range and are, next to the Everest-Kangchenjunga uplift, the greatest mountains of the Himalayan system.

Northward and westward from the gorges of the Indus, two other huge chains of peaks spread out through Russian Turkestan and Afghanistan, but these ranges, known respectively as the Pamirs and the Hindu Kush, are not generally regarded as parts of the Himalayas.

For centuries the mountain wilderness between India and Tibet was a blank space on the map. Its only inhabitants were scattered herdsmen and small colonies of Buddhist lamas who dwelt in lonely monasteries beneath the sacred snows. Its only visitors from the outside world were occasional caravans, threading up the deep jungle valleys of the south and across the high, wild passes beyond. The great peaks were wrapped in the silence and desolation of the ages, unvisited and unknown.

Then, in the early years of the last century, the English conquerors of India began the systematic exploration and surveying of the vast domain which they had acquired. In the beginning, their investigations were principally concerned with the populous regions of the southern plains; but, as time passed, they began also to turn their attention to the great mountain rampart in the North, and gradually the structure and topography of the Himalayas were discovered and made known to the world. By the 1850's most of the important peaks had been named or numbered and their heights determined trigonometrically with a fair degree of accuracy. In 1852 Mount Everest was discovered and recognized as the highest mountain in the world.

The earliest recorded Himalayan ascents were made in the course of these surveys. As early as 1818 two Englishmen named Lloyd and Gerard reached a height of more than nineteen thousand feet on Leo Pargyal, near Simla—a record climb at the time—and during the succeding decades scores of virgin peaks fell to the surveyors and map-makers, chiefly in the more accessible regions abutting on the Ganges Valley. In 1851 a party of climbers reached the summit of Shilla, a 23,000-foot peak in the same region as Leo Pargyal. This was a particularly notable achievement on two counts: it established an altitude record that was to endure for many years, and it proved that men could live and work at theretofore undreamed-of heights. During the 1860's much further light was shed on high-altitude conditions by a member of the India Survey named Johnson, who made a remarkable series of climbs above twenty thousand feet and even slept for several nights at a height of almost twenty-two thousand.

The first purely mountaineering expedition in the Himalayas occurred in 1883, when a party led by W. W. Graham made numerous ascents in Sikkim. Foremost among Graham's exploits was that on Kabru, a 24,000-foot neighbor of Kangchenjunga. His account of the ascent, however, was so vague and incomplete that many doubted his claim that he had gained the summit, and the controversy has not been settled to this day. If Graham actually did reach the top he performed a truly notable feat, for no loftier summit than Kabru was climbed until 1930, although several expeditions went higher on greater peaks. It is unfortunate that the story of the first major Himalayan ascent, like that of Mont Blanc, a century before, should be marred by argument and suspicion.

Graham's expedition was an isolated, pioneering venture, but with the coming of the 1890's the full tide of Himalayan exploration and climbing was on. The Alps by this time were an old and familiar playground. The Caucasus, the Andes and the ranges of North America and Africa had been opened up. Mountaineering had come of age, and its practitioners began turning their eyes toward Central Asia and the greatest antagonists that the earth had to offer. The vast chain of peaks that forms the dazzling backdrop of India has at one time or another during the past fifty years been the goal of virtually every ranking climber in the world.

One of the first on the scene was Sir William Martin Conway, whom we have already glimpsed in Spitzbergen and among the Andes of South America. Conway, at the head of an expedition from the Royal Geographical Society of London, made a journey to the Karakoram in the summer of 1892—the first time that any large party of Europeans had penetrated into that ice-locked wilderness of the northernmost Himalayas. The purpose of the party was exploration rather than pure mountaineering, but they included among their exploits the ascent of the 22,500-foot Pioneer Peak—the "highest yet" since the climbing of Shilla, if Graham's claims on Kabru are disregarded.

During the next two decades there was much activity in almost all sections of the range. Douglas Freshfield made a difficult and adventurous circuit of Kangchenjunga, bringing back the first close-up description of that third greatest of Himalayan giants. A thousand miles away, in northern Kashmir, the peerless Mummery pioneered the approaches to Nanga Parbat and lost his life in an attempt to scale its lower walls—the first of many great climbers to find his grave in the snows of Central Asia. The Karakoram and adjoining ranges were explored by Dr. and Mrs. William Hunter Workman, a remarkable American couple who became mountaineers in advanced middle age and made no less than six major Himalayan expeditions between 1899 and 1912. Dr. Workman's highest ascent—23,400 feet on Pyramid Peak—was made when he was fifty-six years old, and Mrs. Workman, at forty-seven, set a world's climbing record for women at twenty-three thousand feet, which stood unchallenged for twenty-eight years.

In 1909 the Karakoram were the scene of another expedition—one of the largest and most elaborate which has ever been organized in the field of mountaineering. It was led by the Duke of the Abruzzi, who, encouraged by his recent success on Ruwenzori, marched up the great glaciers of the range and laid siege to the gigantic pinnacle of K2. Although unsuccessful in their principal objective—they barely penetrated the outer defenses of the giant—the Duke and his party added greatly to the knowledge of the region, and, before returning to civilization, accomplished the most noteworthy of Himalayan climbs up to that time. This was an attack on Bride Peak, a snow-mountain of 25,100 feet, rising across the glacial valleys in the shadow of K2. The very summit escaped them, blizzard and fog descending when it seemed almost within their grasp; but before turning back they reached an altitude of 24,600 feet—the highest any climbers were to go until the second Everest expedition of 1922.

Meanwhile other climbers were forging up into the unknown along the entire 1,500-mile rampart of the range. Dr. A. M. Kellas, a London physician and chemist, made dozens of ascents in Sikkim and Garhwal over a period of many years. Freshfield continued his far-ranging explorations, and other noted British climbers—A. L. Mumm, J. Norman Collie, C. F. Meade, Dr. Thomas Longstaff, C. G. Bruce, to name only a few—climbed and reconnoitered the peaks and passes of the gradually opening wilderness. Some of the expeditions were on the grand scale, as Conway's and Abruzzi's had been, whereas others were comparatively simple affairs. Dr. Longstaff's ascent, in 1907, of 23,260-foot

Trisul, one of the most famous of early Himalayan climbs, was accomplished with the aid of only two Italian guides and required merely one day of actual climbing on the peak. This feat was doubly remarkable in that Trisul—again discounting controversial Kabru—was then the highest summit ever reached, and remained so until 1938.

By 1914 the principal features of most sections of the Himalayas were at least roughly known to mountaineers. True, not one of the scores of summits over twenty-five thousand feet had been conquered, and giants like Everest, Makalu and Dhaulagiri had not even been approached. But the pioneering had been done, the way to the heights opened. After a five-year interim caused by the First World War mountaineers at last felt themselves ready to set their sights for the highest peaks of all.

Before going on to the stories of the great Himalayan climbs of recent years, it is necessary to have at least a general understanding of the unique problems with which the climbers have been confronted. Like all high mountains, the Himalayas present formidable obstacles of rock and ice, precipice and avalanche, enormously magnified, however, by sheer size. Also, they rise from the heart of a remote and inaccessible wilderness, necessitating not only great physical endurance in those who would even approach them, but elaborate arrangements for supply, transportation and communication.

Then, once the mountain is reached, there is the ever-present question mark of weather, and Himalayan weather is probably the most changeable and violent on earth. The climates of India and Tibet are almost as unlike as those of Equator and Pole, with the result that the lofty peaks between are the everlasting battleground of conflicting winds and storms. Central Asia pours down a relentless, icy gale from the west and north, while from India and the tropical seas beyond come the warm, damp air currents that culminate each summer in the monsoon. The monsoon is perhaps the most treacherous and relentless enemy which Himalayan climbers have to face. Every year from June through August, the months which would otherwise be the best for mountaineering, it drenches the northern Indian plains with great rainstorms and turns the heights beyond into vast deathtraps of fog and melting, crumbling snow. In the southern and eastern Himalayas, which catch the monsoon head-on, the climbing season is usually limited to a mere few weeks in the late spring and early fall. All winter the peaks are ringed with icy, blizzard-laden storms, all summer by fresh snow-banks and roaring avalanches; and even in the supposedly "safe" seasons they are subject to violent changes in weather, which time and again have meant to climbers the difference between triumph and disaster.

As if such objective difficulties were not enough, there is the subjective one of simply living and functioning at altitudes where the air contains only a fraction of the oxygen which human lungs are accustomed to breathe. On the one hand, a man must undergo a period of gradual acclimatization before his organs can operate properly at great heights; but on the other, it has been found that if he spends too long a time in a rarefied atmosphere, serious bodily deterioration sets in. Individuals vary greatly in their speed and degree of acclimatization, and neither age, strength nor general physical condition has proved a particularly reliable criterion of performance. Even more unpredictable are the mental reactions of men transplanted from their natural lowland habitat to the bitter, almost airless heights of the sub-stratosphere. Perception becomes dulled, judgments faulty, emotions unstable, the will atrophied; and extinction itself sometimes seems preferable to the next gasping, stumbling step. Even the employment of bottled oxygen is not the whole of the answer, for it cannot be used twenty-four hours a day, and often the carrying of the apparatus has proved almost as great an ordeal as breathing without it.

Still another problem in Himalayan climbing has been the lack of trained guides and reliable porters. Like primitive people everywhere, the vast majority of Hindus and Tibetans have from time immemorial looked upon their mountains with awe and superstitious fear, peopling them with demons and dragons and refusing even to approach their dread domain. Such early explorers as Conway, Freshfield and Abruzzi were therefore compelled to rely largely on Swiss and Italian guides, whom they brought with them from Europe, and were lucky if they could persuade native helpers to advance even as far as the outlying foothills of the peaks. In recent years, however, tremendous progress has been made. As expedition followed expedition, from 1920 on, the history of climbing in the Alps began to repeat itself in the East, and gradually a new and remarkable type of mountaineer has made his appearance—the native Himalayan climber. Or, more specifically, the Sherpa.

The Sherpas are a remarkable tribe of hillmen, Mongolian and Buddhist, whose original home was in southern Tibet but who have gradually migrated to Nepal and the vicinity of the Indian climbing center of Darjeeling. Alone among the indigenous people of the Himalayas, they have proved themselves to be true mountain men: not guides to be sure, in the special Alpine sense of the word, but far more than mere porters or coolies. As the Gurkhas have taken to soldiering and the Sikhs to policing, so have the Sherpas adopted mountaineering as their proud hereditary profession. Over the past thirty years scarcely a major Himalayan expedition has been undertaken without them, and in many cases they have gone with their loads as far up the great peaks as the climbers themselves. Pasang Kikuli, Pasang Lama, Lewa and Angtharkay—to name only a few—are names as honored in Himalayan history as those of the *sahibs* who employed them. And it was supremely fitting that the greatest of them, Tenzing Bhotia, was to stand at last, triumphant, upon the summit of Everest.

If, thanks to the Sherpas, the porterage problem has been largely solved, there is another problem that has not. This—prosaic but formidable—is politics. Tibet, Nepal and Bhutan, which together contain some two-thirds of the whole Himalayan range, have always been difficult of access for westerners, and it was these restrictions, rather than any natural obstacles, that kept mountaineers away from Everest until as late as 1921. During the 'twenties the British succeeded, to a degree in opening up Tibet and the northern Everest route, but the other two remained tightly closed. And since the last war, while Nepal has partially opened its gates, Tibet has withdrawn completely behind the Iron Curtain. Kashmir, the approach to the Karakoram and Nanga Parbat, is perennially torn by internal strife. India and Pakistan proper require formal permission before an expedition can enter their border ranges. The great white peaks are no longer merely the frontier between Central and Southern Asia, but between the Communist world and our own, and the international struggle for power has cast its shadow even on the once-remote Himalayas.

The climbing of great mountains is—and should be—primarily an adventure. But it is adventure wedded to hard work, patient organization and experiment, unwavering devotion to an end. Nowhere is the fact better shown than in the history of Himalayan climbing—more than a hundred years old and, yet, in terms of final accomplishment,

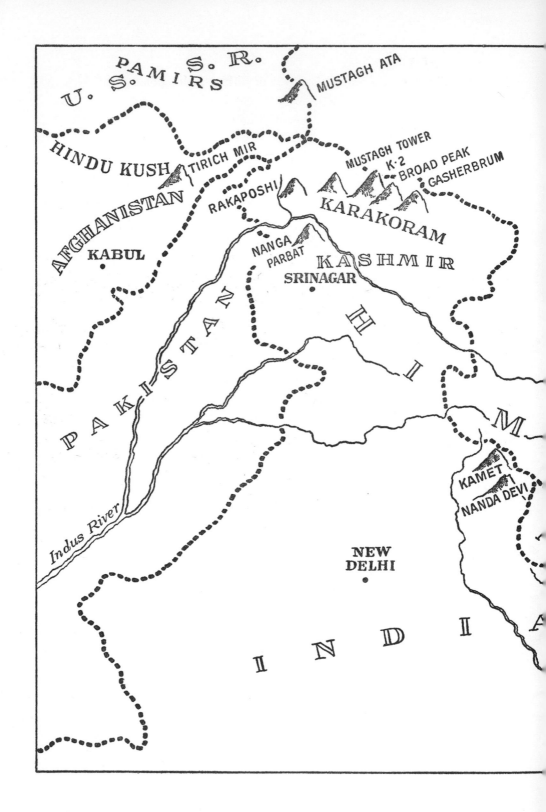

barely begun. In this and the succeeding chapters are related the stories
of assaults on various mountains, separated by many miles and many
years. At first glance they may appear to be unrelated stories, each complete in itself; but fundamentally they are merely parts in one continuing and unfinished story—a long, slow accretion of knowledge, skill
and achievement. Mountaineers today are finally winning the summits
of the world's highest peaks only because earlier mountaineers pioneered
the way to those peaks, explored and mapped the routes, struggled
against precipice and avalanche, altitude and monsoon, suffered exposure
and hunger and all manner of hardship, made endless mistakes and
learned from them. The final victories belong not only to those who
physically achieve them, but to the gallant ranks of those who went
before them—and dared and fought and failed.

The 1920's were a curious period in the history of Himalayan climbing. These were the years of the first great Everest expeditions, and the
attendant world-wide publicity had the effect of bringing mountaineering for the first time into the spotlight of public interest. There was,
however, comparatively little other activity. The nations of the world
were still licking their wounds of battle. Most of the famous climbers
of the older generation had reached an age where they could no longer
face the rigors of great heights, and the new generation, growing up in
the midst of war, had had scarcely any chance to learn the craft of
mountaineering. Except for Everest, the great peaks of Asia were left
to their immemorial solitude.

The end of the decade, however, saw a resurgence of activity which
continued without break until the beginning of the Second World War.
This second period of Himalayan climbing differed from the first in
many respects. Expeditions, for the most part, were larger and more
elaborately equipped; there was less exploration of unknown terrain and
greater concentration on the attainment of summits; and the summits
sought were higher than men had dared hope for before. Also, the field
was at last wide open in a national sense: in the early days the Himalayas had been almost the exclusive preserve of English climbers, but
now for the first time they began to attract men of other nations.

Mountaineers—at least most of them—are only human, and it is
natural that most of the ventures were directed at the highest peaks of
all. Kangchenjunga, K2 and Nanga Parbat—these three, together with

Everest, were, during the years between the wars, stormed again and again, and the struggles, failures and disasters of their attackers combine to make one of the most dramatic chapters in the history of mountaineering. Not all Himalayan climbing, however, was focused on the giants. Peaks of slightly lesser altitude were challenged too, and here the record changes from one of spectacular failure to one of hard-earned success. No one matched the 28,000-foot altitude record set by the defeated Everest climbers of 1924. No one reached the summit of Kangchenjunga, Nanga Parbat or K2. But year by year new peaks of twenty-three thousand feet and more were being conquered, and the magic figure of "highest yet" crept skyward.

One of the first notable ascents of latter-day mountaineering was the climbing of 23,300-foot Mount Kaufmann,* in 1928, by a party of Germans. Strictly speaking, this peak is not in the Himalayas at all, but in the rugged Pamir Range to the northwest; but the Pamirs are so closely connected to the larger chain that the rare expeditions to them may be considered part and parcel of Himalayan mountaineering. Depending on the status of Kabru, Mount Kaufmann may or may not have been the loftiest summit yet climbed to the top. In 1930, however, the ghost of Kabru was at last laid to rest and a new and undisputed record established. This was on Jonsong Peak, 24,340 feet high, which rises to the north of Kangchenjunga on the border of Sikkim and Nepal.

The conquerors of the Jonsong were members of an international expedition to Kangchenjunga, led by Professor Gunther Dyhrenfurth, a noted Swiss geologist and climber. Defeated in their main objective, they longed for a worthy, if lesser, victory and selected the impressive snow-dome to the north as the highest near-by mountain offering any chance of success. This secondary undertaking was blessed both with good management and good luck. Although it was already early June when they began the attempt, the dreaded monsoon held off; the Sherpa porters performed splendidly in establishing the high camps; and the long weeks on Kangchenjunga has resulted in all hands being thoroughly acclimatized to great altitudes. The siege was climaxed by two summit dashes, a few days apart, in which no less than six Europeans and two Sherpas reached the top.

---

* Mount Kaufmann lies in Russian territory and has long since been renamed Pic Lenin by the Soviet Government.

The struggle for the heights, however, was now on in earnest, and Jonsong Peak was "highest yet" for only one year. Then, in 1931, an English party won its way to the top of Kamet (25,447 feet) in what was then British Garhwal, and still another new mark was established. This expedition was led by Frank S. Smythe and Eric Shipton, who were then in the early days of their long Himalayan careers. Smythe, the previous year, had been one of the conquerors of the Jonsong, and both he and Shipton were later to become among the most famous of Everest climbers.

Accompanied by six Sherpas and a large company of local porters, the Kamet party approached their mountain along routes pioneered years earlier by Longstaff, Kellas and Meade. Base camp was made at 15,700 feet on the Raikana Glacier, to the east of the mountain, and a chain of higher camps established on the upper glaciers and the slopes of the peak itself. A large part of the ascent was up precipitous ice-walls, under the constant menace of avalanches from above; but after two weeks of strenuous work the fifth and highest camp was finally established within twenty-one hundred feet of the summit. From here Smythe, Shipton, one other Englishman and two Sherpas made the first try for the top. Although blessed with fine weather, they found the going underfoot extremely difficult, consisting alternately of sheer ice-slopes, up which they had to chop their way with axes, and huge drifts of powder snow, in which they floundered to their armpits. Halfway to the goal one of the two Sherpas collapsed and had to turn back to Camp V. The others, however, toiled on, hacking and clawing, needing six gasping breaths for every upward step, and after a nine-hour struggle came out at last on the narrow, tilted snow-ridge of Kamet's crest. Lewa, the remaining Sherpa, who had performed magnificently throughout the expedition, was given the honor of being the first actually to set foot on the summit.

Two days later a second group, consisting of two climbers and one of the Garhwal porters, also reached the top, and in another three days the entire party was safely off the peak and back in their base camp—a battered and exhausted band of conquerors. Ironically it was Lewa, the bright particular hero of the venture, who was to pay the severest price for his triumph. His feet had been so badly frostbitten on the summit dash that he subsequently lost most of his toes—the revenge, so his fellow-Sherpas believed, of the violated snow-gods of the mountain.

Kamet remained for five years the loftiest conquered peak. During this period, however, several noteworthy lesser ascents were accomplished, both in the Himalaya proper and in various adjacent ranges. Outstanding among the latter was the climbing, in 1932, of 24,900-foot Minya Konka, in remote Sikang Province of western China. The expedition, consisting of Terris Moore (known for his Alaskan ascents), Arthur Emmons, Richard Burdsall and Jack Young, was the first American party to climb in Central Asia in more than twenty years. The attainment of Minya Konka's summit was a remarkable feat in its own right, particularly since the ascent was made during October, in raging storms and fearful cold. It served, moreover, to whet the interest of Americans in the great peaks on the other side of the world, with the result that our own climbers were soon to be as active in the Himalayas as those of any other nation.

Another important expedition took place in 1934, when Gunther Dyhrenfurth, four years after his exploits on Kangchenjunga and Jonsong Peak, visited the Karakoram at the head of a second large international party. K2 was not attempted, but several ambitious climbs were made on neighboring peaks, among them an unsuccessful attempt on Gasherbrum I—also known as Hidden Peak—and complete ascents of Queen Mary Peak (c. 25,000 feet) and one of the five summits of the Golden Throne. Perhaps the most notable feat of all was the attainment by Mrs. Dyhrenfurth, who was a member of the expedition, of Queen Mary's 24,000-foot west summit—a woman's altitude record that endures to this day.

The same year also saw the first major Russian venture in the ranges of Asia: the climbing of Mount Stalin, in the Pamirs, which, at 24,590 feet, is the highest peak in the Soviet Union. The ascent was part of an elaborate survey of the region, which was broadly scientific in nature rather than a strictly mountaineering project. And the names given to various other summits—Red Army Peak, Peak Ogpu, Communist-Academy Peak and German-Communist-Party Peak—indicate that politics were not altogether left at home.

Some fifty miles southeast of Kamet, in the heart of Garhwal, stands a beautiful ice-sheathed peak known variously as The Blessed Goddess, the Goddess Nanda and Nanda Devi. For ages past it has been the holiest mountain in India. And for fourteen years, from 1936 to 1950, it was the highest mountain in the world that had been climbed to the top.

Nanda Devi's history is straight out of the pages of romance. Its white twin-peaked summit, piercing 25,660 feet into the sky, has been known to the inhabitants of the north Indian plains since the beginnings of recorded history. Uncounted generations of Hindu pilgrims have journeyed into the neighboring wilderness to worship at the sources of the sacred Ganges, and since the earliest days of British rule in India explorers and mountaineers have striven toward the mountain, longingly. Yet, before 1934, not one human being had ever even reached its base.

The reason for this is that Nanda Devi stands within a unique natural fortress. Around it rises a great ring of mountain walls, seventy miles in circumference, which shut it off from the outside world like the rugged battlements of a medieval castle. Many of the peaks of this barrier tower to a height of twenty-four thousand feet, and, except at one point, there is no gap or pass between them lower than eighteen thousand. But this is only the mountain's first defense. Within the enclosure of the outer walls there rises a second rampart, equally formidable, cutting the basin straight across from outer wall to outer wall and dividing it into two lesser basins. It is from the second of these, known to mountaineers as the Sanctuary, that Nanda Devi rises—a remote, inaccessible citadel at the heart of its double-walled castle.

Only one break exists in these monstrous fortifications of rock and ice. This occurs to the west where a raging mountain stream, called the Rishi Ganga, cataracts down from the glaciers and knifes through both inner and outer walls in a series of terrific gorges, on its way to join the Ganges far below. So wild is this torrent, however, and so deep the canyons that contain it, that for years it formed as impassable a barrier as the neighboring peaks and ridges. Besides, no devout Hindu would even approach it. For among those gloomy caverns and frightful precipices, so the legend went, dwelt the demons who guarded Nanda Devi, the blessed goddess of the secret snows.

Such a fairy-tale mountain as this could not but hold an irresistible lure for men with adventure in their blood. Graham, Longstaff, Bruce, Hugh Ruttledge, T. H. Somervell—these were only a few of the many noted Himalayan explorers who over a period of fifty years had set their hearts on Nanda Devi and struggled mightily to find the key to its hidden domain. Some had tried to force a way up the fearsome gorges of the Rishi. Others had stormed the barrier walls, and Long-staff, as early as 1905, had reached a point of nineteen thousand feet from which he had a glimpse—the first granted to any man—of the Promised Land beyond. But none of them had been able to penetrate even the outer of the two unexplored basin valleys. Behind its double curtain of rock and ice the Goddess Nanda remained as mysterious and unapproachable as she had been since the beginning of time.

Then finally, in the middle 'thirties, there were launched two ex-peditions to the mountain which were successful in every respect. The first broke through both outer and inner guardian walls and carried to the lower slopes of the great peak itself. The second, following after two years, climbed Nanda Devi to the top.

Of the two, the earlier exploit was in many ways the more remarka-ble, in that it was accomplished by a party of only two mountaineers. These were Eric Shipton, of Kamet fame, who since that ascent had further distinguished himself on the Everest expedition of 1933, and H. W. Tilman, another young Englishman, with a notable record of climbs in the Alps and Africa. Accompanied by three Sherpa porters, they left Ranikhet, in Garhwal, in the late spring of 1934, pushed through the wilderness flanking Nanda Devi's western ramparts, and launched an assault on the gorges of the Rishi Ganga. Day after day they crept along a mile-deep gash in the mountain walls. At times their route lay high on the faces of great cliffs, at others deep down beside the bed of the torrent. False trails were followed and abandoned; preci-pices grew more perpendicular, forcing retreat and detours; food and supplies had to be raised and lowered by ropes. But they kept going, and at last came out into the rolling forest-land of the outer basin. Here they set up their base camp, near the junction of the Rishi and another roaring glacial stream.

The outer rampart of Nanda Devi was now behind them and they were already in a virgin world where no human being had ever stood before. Their real difficulties, however, had scarcely begun. Ahead, on the far side of the basin, loomed the vast "inner curtain" that guarded the Sanctuary—a second rock-wall thousands of feet high and broken only by the deep, jagged slot of the Rishi canyon. Into this second series of gorges the explorers now threaded their way. For hours their route carried along foot-wide ledges in the cliff side, a skyscraper's height above the river. Then, presently, the ledges petered out into smooth vertical walls, and they were compelled to descend to the shadowy, roaring canyon floor. Time and again they had to battle their way across the Rishi, struggling not to be swept away in the icy torrent, heaving their soaked baggage back and forth on ropes. Then, to add to their woes, it began to snow, and a knife-edged wind beat down into the canyon from the heights above.

Now at last came the greatest obstacle of all—a gigantic buttress of black rock sweeping straight up from the bottom of the gorge to the towering ridges overhead. At first inspection it seemed impassable, but Shipton and Tilman knew that pass it they must, if they were to cherish any further hope of reaching their goal. They named it Pisgah, for they were confident that if it could be surmounted the way to the Promised Land beyond would at last be open.

The explorers went about their labors systematically. While Tilman and one Sherpa investigated the southern cliffs, Shipton and another reconnoitered the northern, climbing high on its sheer black walls, searching patiently for the tiniest shelves and gullies that would take them higher still. Time after time, possible routes seemed to present themselves, but in every case they proved false hopes, and in the end Shipton turned back, defeated. Descending to their camp by the river he waited disconsolately for Tilman to return from his exploration of the far side; but the hours passed and night came on, and still he did not appear. Shipton began to fear that his companion had met not only with disappointment, as he had, but possibly with an accident as well. Then, suddenly, there was an exultant cry in the darkness. Tilman and his Sherpa appeared, struggling across the swirling current of the Rishi—done in, but with their faces shining with excitement. They were shouting that they had found a way.

And they had. The next day the whole party, with all their baggage in tow, began the laborious ascent of the southern cliffs of Pisgah. Gully led to gully, chimney to chimney, ledge to ledge, as men and loads inched upward between the precipices and bulging overhangs of the canyon walls. Late in the afternoon they passed the crest of the great black buttress, and before night fell the angry roaring of the Rishi, which had dinned in their ears for so many days, was only a whisper in the remote depths below. Camping that night among juniper bushes beside a softly bubbling brook, they could scarcely believe what they knew to be the truth: that they had at last passed the great inner curtain of the basin and were in the very Sanctuary of Nanda Devi itself.

The world in which they now found themselves was lovely and serene beyond the dreams of men. On all sides the encircling mountain walls tiered above them like an enormous amphitheatre, their flanks dark with long slopes of fir and spruce. Lower down, the valley floor was a rolling alpine meadow, carpeted with springy turf and great banks of wildflowers, the grazing ground of wild herds of sheep and goats. Here and there the green expanse was studded with tiny lakes of cobalt blue, and from the surrounding heights descended the gleaming fingers of many glaciers. It was a landscape out of a fairy-tale, a lost, secret Eden from the days when the world was young. And in its very center, white and majestic, rose the citadel itself—the turrets and cliffs and battlements of the sacred mountain Nanda.

For three weeks Shipton and Tilman explored this virgin paradise. Together with their Sherpas, they traversed the spreading meadows, worked up to the crests of surrounding ridges and studied the great central peak from all sides. Then they threaded their way up the maze of glaciers to the lower slopes of Nanda Devi itself. Their small expedition was not equipped to launch an actual assault on the heights, but they carefully studied the possibilities of routes and campsites, which might be used by future parties, and came to the conclusion that the mountain was by no means unassailable.

It was now late June, and presently the monsoon broke. (Even the hidden Sanctuary of Nanda Devi is not exempt from the rigors of Himalayan weather.) The explorers therefore beat a hasty retreat down the gorges of the Rishi, barely escaping disaster in its now snow-swollen waters, and spent the next several weeks exploring in the lower altitudes of the Garhwal hills. At the end of the monsoon, however, they again returned to Nanda Devi, to reconnoiter further in the Sanctuary and on the crags and ice-fields above. Finally, they found a gap in the precipitous southern walls of the basin, and, crossing it, descended to the outer valleys and the inhabited world, proving that the Rishi canyon was not the only possible key to the mountain.

Thus the secret of Nanda Devi was solved—on two separate occasions and by two different routes. Throughout the following year the mountain was left to its age-old isolation; but there was small chance of climbers long neglecting this alluring and now accessible prize, and in the summer of 1936 a second band of adventurers set out to climb and conquer. This expedition, far more elaborate than the first, was composed of eight climbers—four British and four American—with Tilman to lead the way. Shipton did not return, being on that year's assault on Everest, but his place was taken by Noel Odell, an old "Everester" from the 'twenties. Among the Americans was Dr. Charles Houston, the young physician who had already climbed Mount Foraker, in Alaska, and was later to lead two expeditions to K2.

The observations of Shipton and Tilman had indicated that the best time to attack the mountain proper would be in the late summer, toward the end of the monsoon period. Accordingly, the end of July saw a long cavalcade of men and supplies moving up the roaring gorges of the Rishi; but they had scarcely entered this forbidding domain when a severe blow was dealt them. Thirty-seven Dotial porters, who had been enlisted in Ranikhet, refused to attempt the crossing of the swollen mountain torrent, dropped their packs on the spot, and returned home en masse. The climbers and their few remaining helpers were now confronted with the task of carrying sixty-two loads, averaging sixty-five pounds each, over the most difficult part of the route. It seemed at first an impossible assignment, but by dogged, backbreaking work it was finally accomplished. Slowly they crept on—clinging precariously to the canyon walls, crossing and recrossing the river—through the gorges of the outer wall, the outer basin, the inner gorges, and, at last, up and over the black bastions of Pisgah. By the end of the first week in August they were established in their base camp in the Sanctuary, at the very foot of Nanda Devi.

From this point the twelve remaining local porters were sent back home, their job well and faithfully accomplished. The party was now stripped to its essential members—eight white men and six Sherpas—and after a few days of rest in the soft, flowering loveliness of the meadows the real work of mountaineering began.

They were not long in discovering that, although Nanda Devi's valleys might be a paradise, the mountainside above them was something quite else again. Hour after hour, day after day, they struggled across endless slanting wastes of ice and mud and broken, sliding boulders, while a bitter wind slashed down at them from the frozen heights. They entered a belt of gray, impenetrable mist. When finally they passed that, it snowed, and soon they were floundering about in drifts up to their thighs. But they kept grimly going, up and down, up and down, back-packing food and supplies; and gradually the chain of high camps began to take form.

The general line of ascent was along the north ridge of the mountain, a great twisting spine of rock and snow that climbed skyward some eight thousand feet above the base camp. In many places, however, the ridge disappeared into smooth snow-covered slopes of ice, tilted at a fearsome angle and necessitating the kicking and hacking of thousands of steps. During this exhausting part of the siege the condition of all the white men held up remarkably—the result, they believed, of their long weeks of acclimatization during the passage of the Rishi gorge. The bad luck with the porters, however, continued. The most dependable of them all, a remarkable Sherpa named Pasang Kikuli, came down with snow-blindness in the early stages of the ascent. Then in turn, the others succumbed to maladies of various kinds, with the result that only one Sherpa of the six ever got higher on the mountain than Camp II. Severest blow of all was the death of one of them, several weeks later, from dysentery—the only casualty to mar an otherwise supremely successful venture.

Faced with the necessity of doing all the load-carrying, the climbers made slow progress. Base camp had been established August fifth at seventeen thousand feet, and it was not until eleven days later that Camp III was pitched at 21,200, less than halfway to the top. But the work went on with systematic doggedness. First, an advance party—usually two men—would reconnoiter upward from the highest camp already established. Their job was to find a feasible higher campsite, dump their loads there and return to the lower camp, all in one day's climbing. The next day they would rest, while a second party went up, carrying more loads; and on the third day, if all went well, the higher camp would be ready for occupation. Then the whole operation was repeated between the new camp and another still higher.

During the expedition's first two weeks on the mountain the weather had been almost freakish in its consistency—still, humid and, in the hours around midday, actually warm. On the night of August twenty-first, however, the long-expected storm caught up with them. Great black monsoon clouds piled up over the southeastern horizon, the wind rose in a shrieking crescendo, and mountain and men were soon wrapped in the fierce embrace of a blizzard. For the next forty-eight hours all activity was paralyzed. The climbers huddled in the various camps, cut off from communication with each other and barely able to restrain their tents from blowing off the mountainside in the fury of the gale. Camp III, the highest occupied at the time, was struck the worst. Snowdrifts were soon piled so heavily upon the two tents that the men inside had to support the canvas roofs with their hands, and on the morning of the third day it required a half hour's strenuous work to dig their way up to light and air.

By dawn on August twenty-fourth the blizzard had at last blown itself out, and a period of glorious weather set in. Nanda Devi's slopes and ridges were now, however, deeply sheathed with fresh, loose snow, and to the endless task of step-cutting was added the exhausting labor of floundering through deep drifts. Kicking and cutting their way, the climbers established Camp IV at 21,500 feet and Camp V, their highest, at 23,500, scarcely more than two thousand feet below the summit. Set on a tiny, tilting platform above a mile-high chute of ice, this last was so precarious a perch that even an eagle would have eyed it askance. But mountaineers are a more adventuresome breed than eagles, and these were happy that they had been able to find any campsite at all.

Odell and Houston were selected as the first pair to make a try for the summit. Deciding on a day of reconnoitering before the actual final push, they worked up the ridge to within one thousand feet of the top, found no obstacles worse than those encountered below and returned to Camp V, confident of success on the morrow. For Houston, however, it was not to be. At supper that night he ate from a tin of corned beef that was later found to have been punctured, and the next morning, far from being ready for the summit dash, he was violently ill from ptomaine poisoning. All thoughts of the top had to be temporarily dismissed, while Odell communicated with their companions below and the miserable Houston was helped down to the lower camps.

A council of war followed, and it was decided that Tilman should take the sick man's place. The following day he and Odell moved Camp V some five hundred feet higher than its original location and, on the next, set off at six in the morning for the summit. All the members of the party felt that it was now or never, for storm clouds were again appearing to the south and supplies in the upper camps were beginning to run low.

Moving slowly but steadily, Odell and Tilman crept up the mountainside through the long hours of the morning. The way lay first up steep snow-slopes, similar to those below; then along a gently rising rock ridge, sheathed in snow and ice; finally up deep gullies in the face of the summit pyramid. Here great billowing drifts engulfed them to the waist, but they managed to keep going and finally, at mid-afternoon, stepped from a small rock-rib onto a gentle ridge of snow. As they did so, there was a sudden ominous shuddering beneath them, and the drifts below plunged downward in a hissing avalanche. For a terrible, paralyzing moment it seemed that the ridge would go too. But it held. A careful probing with their ice-axes, a few more steps upward, and they stood together upon the flat white summit of Nanda Devi.

Except for the unfortunate fatal illness of the one porter, the descent of the mountain was accomplished as safely and successfully as the ascent. Two climbers had reached the top. Six others, who had hoped and striven for it as much as they, had not. But it is the very essence of the mountaineering spirit that victory for one is victory for all, and the band of adventurers who, a few days later, turned their backs at last on the sacred mountain consisted of eight supremely weary but happy men.

The natives of the surrounding valleys, however, were not so easily satisfied.

"Was the Goddess Nanda beautiful?" they asked eagerly. "And what did London look like from the top?"

11

BITTER VICTORY

Annapurna — Nanga Parbat

FOR FOURTEEN YEARS after the conquest of Nanda Devi no higher mountain was climbed to its summit. The late 1930's were a period of wide activity in the Himalayas, but the greatest peaks—Everest, K2, Nanga Parbat and the like—continued to repulse every challenge.

On somewhat lesser mountains, however, there were a number of successful ascents. Siniolchu, a beautiful 22,570-foot snow-spire in Sikkim, and its slightly lower neighbor, Simvu, were climbed in the same year as Nanda Devi by Paul Bauer and Karl Wien, two Germans who had previously won fame on Kangchenjunga. In 1937 Siniolchu was topped again, by a second German party; and another notable eastern Himalayan peak, Chomolhari (23,996 feet) yielded to an Englishman, F. Spencer Chapman. Several climbs were made by another British explorer, Marco Pallis, in Sikkim and Tibet and by the Swiss team of Arnold Heim and August Gansser in Garhwal.

Also during this period, the Karakoram were the scene of two ambitious, though unsuccessful, attempts. Gasherbrum I (26,470 feet) was challenged for the second time in 1936 by a French party, in one of the largest and most elaborate expeditions in Himalayan history; but, as with the earlier Dyhrenfurth effort, the assault fell short of the goal, and the climbers barely escaped disaster from the ravages of storm and cold. And two years later there was a near miss on 25,660-foot Masherbrum, when a British expedition was turned back within a day's climb of the summit. Last of the big prewar ventures, in 1939, was a second challenge of Nanda Devi, this time by a group of Poles. They were successful in reaching their objective, the 24,390-foot east peak of the mountain, which had not previously been attained; but the venture ended in double disaster, when two men were lost in an avalanche and the rest, because of the German invasion of their homeland, were unable to return home.

For several years thereafter almost the only westerners to see the Himalayas were airmen flying the "Hump" between India and China. By the late 1940's, however, climbers were again ready and able to return to the high mountains, and when they did it was in greater numbers than ever before. Pre-eminent among them were several of the prewar veterans, notably Eric Shipton and H. W. Tilman, who resumed their wide-ranging exploits in many sections of the range and, in 1947, almost reached the summit of the remote Mustagh Ata, a 25,200-foot peak in the Pamirs of Chinese Sinkiang. Also in 1947, a Swiss expedition made a number of ascents in Garhwal, and in the two following years parties from various European countries were active throughout the Himalayas, from the Kangchenjunga region in the east to Afghanistan on the west. It was not until 1950, however, that there was another feat that gained world-wide attention. This was the climbing of Annapurna, the tenth highest mountain in the world.

Many circumstances combined to make the Annapurna venture a landmark in mountaineering history. For one thing, it was the first major ascent in many years. For another, it was the first ever to be made in Nepal, which had theretofore rarely permitted a climbing party to cross its boundaries. The climbers were French, and France had, at the time, never won a major Himalayan victory. The expedition's experiences were dramatic and sensational, the subsequent book that told of them an international best-seller. And most important of all—at least from the strictly mountaineering point of view—was that Annapurna, at the time, was not only the highest peak to have been climbed, but the only so-called "Eightthousander."

Eightthousanders is the name given by Europeans to the world's tallest mountains: the small group of super-peaks which rise more than eight thousand meters, or roughly 26,250 feet, above the sea. As far as is now known, there are fourteen of them in the Himalayas (with none anywhere else), and their rank, location and altitudes * are as follows:

Everest	Nepal-Tibet border	29,028 feet
K2 (or Godwin Austen)	Karakoram	28,250
Kangchenjunga	Nepal-Sikkim	28,146
Lhotse	South peak of Everest	27,890
Makalu	Near Everest	27,790
Dhaulagiri	Nepal	26,811
Cho Oyu	Near Everest	26,750
Manaslu	Nepal	26,668
Nanga Parbat	Kashmir	26,658
Annapurna	Nepal	26,493
Gasherbrum I (Hidden Peak)	Karakoram	26,470
Broad Peak	Karakoram	26,400
Gasherbrum II	Karakoram	26,360
Gosainthan	Nepal-Tibet	26,290

Of these unconquered giants, some, before 1950, had been challenged many times, others once or twice, still others never. Annapurna was one of the "nevers"—indeed, even its name and location were scarcely known to the outside world—and still another remarkable aspect of its ascent is that it marked the first, and only, time that a great unknown mountain has been both reconnoitered and scaled by one expedition.

The French team consisted of nine men. As leader there was thirty-one-year-old Maurice Herzog, by profession an engineer, by avocation a brilliant and experienced climber. Also as climbers were five young men still in their twenties—Louis Lachenal, Lionel Terray, Gaston Rébuffat, Jean Couzy and Marcel Schatz—the first three professional guides, the last two amateurs, but all outstanding among the postwar crop of Alpine mountaineers. Rounding out the group were three men for specialized jobs: Dr. Jacques Oudot as physician, Marcel Ichac as photographer, and Francois de Noyelle, attaché at the French Embassy in New Delhi, as

---

* As with the Andes—according to the best available sources; for a great and remote mountaintop is not easy to survey, and with each succeeding exploration there is apt to be "growth" or "shrinkage." Even for Everest itself, there is still doubt about the correct figure. The original computation by British surveyors in India was 29,002 feet; but in the 1920's this was amended to 29,141, and in the 1950's, following a survey by the Indian Air Force, it was again amended to 29,028. This last is the currently (1964) accepted figure, but on past performance it is likely to remain so only until the *next* survey.

RETURN TO LIFE

The climbers of Annapurna being helped down the mountain. In the foreground, Terray, snow-blinded, supported by a Sherpa, with Schatz holding the rope. Behind them is Lachenal, led by two Sherpas, and higher up, the two dots are Couzy and his Sherpa.

From the book "Annapurna" by Maurice Herzog. Copyright, 1952,
by E. P. Dutton & Co., Inc., Publishers

THE NAKED MOUNTAIN

Nanga Parbat, climbed in 1953, the same year as Everest. All the expeditions
that attempted it ascended diagonally across this northern face toward Rakiot
Peak, the white hump on the skyline to the left; thence along the ridge toward
the summit. The highest point visible in the picture is the North Peak (25,550
feet). The top of Nanga Parbat, more than a thousand feet higher, is hidden
behind it.

transport officer. Plus, of course, the usual complement of Sherpas. It was to prove a strong, well-balanced team, and luckily so; else all of them would not have returned alive.

Back in France—once permission to enter Nepal had been granted—it had been decided that the expedition would have two alternative objectives: first Dhaulagiri, the huge and fabled citadel of central Nepal; second, if that proved impossible, the neighboring and slightly lower snow-peak of Annapurna. Accordingly, Dhaulagiri was investigated first, but it was soon decided that, if not impossible, it was too formidable to hold out hope of success, and the climbers forthwith turned their attention to Annapurna.

"The Goddess of the Harvests," the Nepalese call her, watching high in the sky above the fertile plateau of Pokhara. But there was nothing woman-like, nothing soft and fruitful, about the grim world of rock and ice through which the climbers struggled in their circuit of her flanks. The southern side of the mountain was unclimbable. The eastern and western sides—unclimbable. All presented either vertical precipices or cliffs of ice that daily crumbled down in gigantic avalanches. Only on its northwest face, a huge but not impossibly steep ramp of glacier and snow-slope, did Annapurna appear at least potentially vulnerable; and here, at the snout of the glacier, the Frenchmen set up their base camp and launched their attack on the heights.

The all-important task, of course, was to establish a chain of higher camps. The first was pitched on the lower glacier, some two thousand feet above the base, the second near the head of the glacier, and the third on the snow-slope beyond, at a height of more than twenty-one thousand feet. No serious climbing difficulties were encountered. The principal danger was from the avalanches that were forever rumbling and crashing down the mountainside, but the climbers chose their routes and campsites carefully and succeeded in keeping out of their paths. Best of all, the weather held good—or at least good by Himalayan standards. Every few days, to be sure, the wind rose and snow beat down, pinning them in their tents. But the storms did not last long; soon the wind fell and the sun blazed out again, and once again, on the dazzling ice-walls, men moved up and down like a column of ants. High up above the glacier was the only exposed rock on this side of the moun tain—a huge, curving arc of cliffs that supported the snow-dome of the

summit. And it was at the edge of these cliffs that they established Camp
IV.

Throughout the ascent the climbers had for the most part worked in
parties of two: Herzog and Lachenal as one team, Terray and Rébuffat
as a second, Couzy and Schatz as a third, with the other three expedition
members in support below. Now, as the time for the final thrust approached, this alignment was maintained, and Herzog and Lachenal
moved up ahead as Team No. 1. Circling the great cliffs above Camp
IV, they threaded their way through a glittering chaos of ice and snow
and set up a final camp at 24,300 feet, on a precariously slanting rib of
rock that they described as a mere "wrinkle in the snow."

Here they spent a night alone—a night in which they thought only
of the morning. The summit slope above them appeared of itself easy,
a mere twenty-two hundred feet of gently rising whiteness. The two
great imponderables were the weather and how they would react to the
now-tremendous altitude. At first light they crept from their sleeping
bags, pulled on their frost-stiffened boots and set off for the top. Simultaneously, below them, the two supporting teams moved upward, according to plan: Couzy and Schatz from Camps III to IV, Terray and
Rébuffat from IV to V. The day to which all their preparations and
struggles had been directed had come at last.

"June third. Sun in a clear sky. But the wind is blowing, whipping
clouds of icy dust around the summit. . . ." Step by step, hour after hour,
Herzog and Lachenal plodded on, as if up the tilt of a blazing white
roof. The tilt was not steep, and they climbed unroped; but at every
step their feet broke through the thin crust into deep powdery snow,
and soon their hearts were pounding and their lungs burning from the
exertion. Every fifty paces they alternated leadership, so as to share
equally the strain of opening up the track.

They felt themselves all but drowned in the glaring light of the
tropical sun. Their heads seemed on fire, yet at the same time the cold
stiffened their clothing and pinched their fingers beneath their gloves.
Half-suffocated, they stopped again and again to suck the raw, bitter air
into their lungs, but it gave them only a fraction of the oxygen they
needed. Minutes blurred into hours, and hours into eternity. Then at
last a black patch danced before their eyes—a final band of rock directly
beneath the summit dome. Here was the last great question. Was there
a way up the rock? As they approached it they saw a cleft splitting its

center. . . . One foot forward, then the other. One foot. The other. . . .
A blast of wind struck them, coming from the *other* side of the mountain, and even in their dazed and exhausted condition they knew what
it meant. Another few gasping steps, and they stopped—for the last
time. Maurice Herzog reached out and touched a delicate icy crest that
changed shape before his eyes as the wind swirled over it. Annapurna
was theirs: 26,493 feet high—the first Eightthousander ever climbed.

The day may come when men will scale a mountain and be lifted
gently from its summit by a helicopter. But that day is not yet, and, until
it arrives, getting down a mountain will remain almost as difficult—and
invariably more dangerous—than getting up it. Herzog and Lachenal
had won a great victory. Now they were to pay the great price.

Even while they stood on the summit, the sun receded and gray veils
of mist streamed in on an icy wind. There was no view. The world beneath them was blotted from sight. But there was one traditional act that
had to be performed, and, removing his gloves, Herzog opened his
pack and took out his camera and a small French flag. Handing the
camera to Lachenal, he fastened the flag to his ice-ax and then held the
ax above his head while his companion snapped the shutter. That was
all. In a few minutes flag and camera had been put away, and the two
men were inching down the snow-slopes, bent almost double against the
still-rising wind. By now both their bodies and brains were sluggish
from fatigue and lack of oxygen, and it was not until long afterward
that Lachenal, bringing up the rear, noticed something wrong about
Herzog. "Maurice—Maurice!" he shouted, and when the other turned
he pointed.

Herzog looked down in dull surprise and saw that his hands were
bare. He had lost his gloves.

This was the first in a long chain of mishaps that was now to plunge
the expedition into near-tragedy and almost into total disaster. Herzog
and Lachenal descended unroped, as they had climbed, and the former,
now all too aware of his already-numb hands, went as fast as he could
and reached Camp V ahead of his companion. Terray and Rébuffat were
waiting there, according to plan, and had just begun to minister to
Herzog when there was a sudden cry from outside the tent.

Within a few steps of camp Lachenal had slipped and fallen, and
now he lay among an outcropping of ice-hummocks almost three hundred feet below. Terray made his way to him and found that, while he

had broken no bones, he was suffering from shock and scarcely knew where he was or what had happened. With the utmost difficulty Terray got him back up to the tent, and for the rest of that day and all night he and Rébuffat tended the two battered men. Not only Herzog's hands, but his and Lachenal's feet, were badly frozen, and for a time the two others almost despaired of restoring their circulation. In the end, however, they were successful; and during the night, happily, Lachenal's mind cleared. He and Herzog told of the day's great victory. Congratulations were passed around. The worst seemed over.

But the worst had not even begun. For no sooner had the four started their descent the next morning than the storm, which had threatened all the previous afternoon, burst in full fury. In clear weather the down-trip from Camp V to IV would have taken no more than three hours; but now all landmarks were effaced in a cauldron of boiling snow, and for hours they groped and stumbled through white nothingness—numbed, blinded and lost. Once, they discovered later, they passed within two hundred yards of Camp IV, but neither could they see it nor could Couzy and Schatz, who were awaiting them there, hear their desperate snow-muffled shouts.

All day they wandered, and as darkness approached they knew that they would have to go face that dreadful, and usually lethal, Himalayan ordeal: a night in the open. Finding no shelter, they were beginning to dig a hole in the snow, when Lachenal, standing a little apart from the others, suddenly disappeared before their eyes. For a moment it seemed certain that tragedy had been added to catastrophe, but then they heard Lachenal's voice, telling them that the crevasse into which he had fallen was only a few yards deep. Investigation proved that its floor was solid and that its walls gave good protection from the wind; and, climbing down, the others settled themselves as best they could. What had seemed certain disaster was turned for a while into a stroke of luck.

But only for a very short while; for no sooner did they stop moving than the cold, even in their windless cavern, began gnawing through to their very bones. Taking off their boots, they put their feet into a bag and lay practically one on top of another to generate such warmth as they could. So the night passed, without sleep, without surcease from the cold. And shortly before dawn came the worst blow of all. A mass of snow, near the lip of the crevasse above, worked loose and plunged down, burying them in a white shroud.

Stifled and stunned, they struggled and managed to fight free. But everything they had had with them—their packs, climbing equipment and, most important, their boots—remained buried under the white tons of snow. For more than an hour, in stockinged feet, the exhausted, half-frozen men dug and groped with the last frantic desperation of the will to live. And at last they uncovered the four pairs of boots. Almost simultaneously day broke above them—a day bright with sunlight—but it was nearly too late. Both Herzog and Lachenal had again lost all feeling in their feet, and Herzog's hands were as cold and hard as blocks of ice. By now Terray and Rébuffat, too, had begun to suffer from frostbite, and all four were partially snow-blind from the effect of invisible ultra-violet rays when they had removed their goggles the previous day to find their way through the blizzard.

They were lost. Their legs could scarcely support their weight. They could not open their eyes against the white stab of daylight. Creeping to the rim of the crevasse, Lachenal and Rébuffat stood up where they might be seen and shouted for help. Ironically, they were seen and heard by Ichac, the photographer, almost four thousand feet down the mountainside at Camp II, but from Camp IV, only a few hundred yards away, both their figures and voices were blocked off by an intervening ice-cliff. Herzog and Terray struggled up from the crevasse beside them. All shouted. No answer. Half limping and half crawling, they began working their way down the snow-slopes. If they were going to die, they were going to die trying.

Then at last, after all their bad fortune, came the one great stroke of good. At eight o'clock that morning Marcel Schatz began to climb upward from Camp IV. Having seen no sign of the higher men the previous evening, he assumed that they had decided not to make the descent during the storm, but would be coming down that day; and now he was making a track to guide them on the last stage of their journey. Not more than a few minutes above camp he stopped and stood staring at the four apparitions who stood swaying, blind and crippled, on the white slope above him. Then he went up to them and led them down.

That was the end of the ordeal of climbing, but not of that of the climbers. Led by Schatz and Couzy, with Sherpa porters assisting, the descent from Camp IV to II was made all in that same day. Just above Camp III the mountain struck its final blow at them, hurling down an avalanche that almost swept Herzog, Rébuffat and two Sherpas to destruction. But they came out of it alive, and toward evening the whole straggling, exhausted caravan limped into Camp II.

From then on it was the doctor, Oudot, who was the key man of the expedition. Of the four climbers who had spent the night out, Terray was all right, and Rébuffat, though slightly frostbitten and suffering greatly with his eyes, would obviously suffer no permanent effects. But with Herzog and Lachenal it was another matter. The toes of both had turned blue-black, and on Herzog's feet the leaden color extended to the middle of the soles. His hands, from which shreds of rotted skin were hanging, were numb as far as the wrists. In a cramped, dimly lit tent, Oudet worked through the night and all the next day over the two men, administering novocaine to relieve their suffering and injecting them repeatedly with acetylcholine to stimulate the circulation of their blood.

One day, however, was all that could be spared at Camp II, for the monsoon was now due, and at any moment torrential rains would begin turning the mountainside into a deathtrap of melting snow. Sledges were improvised out of skis and stretched canvas and the crippled men roped onto them for the descent. Inching down the white slopes, their eyes blindfolded, their arms and legs swathed in bandages, they seemed less living men than mummies—except that mummies feel no pain.

Almost miraculously, the operation was accomplished without mishap, and a few days later they set off from base camp toward civilization— the mountain at last behind them, but a month's nightmare ahead. Herzog and Lachenal had to be carried every step of the way: over glacial moraines, high passes, steep ridges, swollen rivers, and finally through the underbrush of the lowland jungles. Instead of bitter cold there was now cloying, sweltering heat. The two crippled men stank of putrefying flesh, and their pain became so great that Oudot kept them almost constantly under morphine. Herzog, with septicemia, was often delirious, and one day his fever reached 105.6 degrees and it was touch and go whether he would live or die. Massive doses of penicillin pulled him through, however, and the weary caravan struggled on.

Rain beat down incessantly. The wet earth smoked. And almost every day, amid swarms of flies and crowds of curious villagers, Oudot did the grim work that had to be done on Herzog and Lachenal. For by now it had become obvious that the toes of both men—and Herzog's fingers as well—would have to go; and one by one, the doctor amputated them, before the lethal rot could spread farther into their bodies. By the time the journey was over Lachenal had lost all his toes and Herzog all his toes and fingers.

What price victory? . . . It is a question that will be asked and argued as long as men climb mountains, and the only definitive answer is that there is a difference of opinion. To the Annapurna climbers themselves —by their own statements—the game was well worth the candle. To Frenchmen generally it was worth it, for Herzog and his companions were welcomed home as heroes. To a country humiliated in war and distracted by peaceless peace the conquest of the mountain was a thing for high pride and deep emotion. On that white Himalayan summit the tricolor had flapped higher than any flag before it—unaided, triumphant, free.

In retrospect, indeed, it is this strongly nationalistic element, more than anything else, that distinguishes the Annapurna venture from most other postwar climbs. But happily, it was at least not carried to the blatant excess that marred the German exploits of the Nazi period. The French knew that they were human beings, not Wagnerian demigods; and though they took chances not usually considered warrantable in mountaineering, they did so with humility as well as pride. If they were foolhardy men, they were also dedicated men. They were brave and modest men. And from their struggle and ordeal they brought back a shining prize.

The year 1950 also saw another ascent, which, if less spectacular than that of Annapurna, was still a notable mountaineering feat. This was the climbing of Tirich Mir, monarch of the Hindu Kush Range, on the Pakistan-Afghan frontier, by a small expedition from Norway. Following a route reconnoitered the previous year, the climbers reached the 25,260-foot summit and descended safely, making a signal success of the first Norwegian venture in the mountains of Asia. In 1951, Nanda Devi, still exerting its potent lure on mountaineers, was challenged once again—on this occasion by a French party, whose objective was the ascent of both its main and eastern peaks. Like the Poles in 1939, they reached the lesser summit (one of the two top climbers being the Sherpa Tenzing, of later Everest fame); but like them, too, they lost two men, the leader and a companion disappearing during an attempt at the double ascent. As in the preceding years, there were also, from 1950 through 1952, ascents too numerous to list of peaks in what might be

called the secondary Himalayan bracket. And to these were added recurrent reports—though few details—of much Russian activity in the
Pamirs and Tibet.

1953, of course, will go down in climbing history as the Year of
Everest. But it was also the year of another great Himalayan victory,
which could have been overshadowed only by the conquest of the King.
This was the ascent of Nanga Parbat: the world's ninth highest summit
and the third of the Eightthousanders to be scaled to the top.*

The history of Annapurna is of one ascent. That of Nanga Parbat is
of a long, grim campaign, dating back almost sixty years. Standing in
the wild border country or northern Kashmir, it has long been known
to men, not only as one of the greatest, but as the most murderous,
mountain in the world. Almost as many lives have been lost in the attempts to gain its 26,660-foot summit as on all the other great Himalayan peaks combined.

Although some twenty-five hundred feet lower than Everest, Nanga
Parbat yields nothing to it as an individual mountain-mass. Rising in
isolated splendor at the far western end of the main Himalayan chain,
it has no neighbor-giants to dispute its supremacy, no lofty plateaus or
foothills building gradually up to its base. The great bend of the River
Indus, only a few miles away, is a scant three thousand feet above the
sea. From the hot, dry plains through which it flows the northern ramparts of the peak soar upward in an almost unbroken sweep of four and
a half miles—the highest single mountain face on earth. A world in itself is this white colossus, a frozen, lonely world above the clouds, without mercy. The Kashmir tribes, gazing up at it with awe and fear, gave
to it long ago its ominous name: Nanga Parbat—The Naked Mountain.

Nanga Parbat is nothing if not consistent. From the very beginning
disaster and tragedy have stalked its would-be conquerors and the first
venture into its forbidding domain resulted in the death of the foremost
mountaineer of his time. This was in 1895, when A. F. Mummery, fresh
from his triumphs in the Alps and Caucasus, pushed in to the base of the
mountain with two English companions and a small group of porters
and attempted to find a way up its lower battlements. Meeting with no
success on the southern side, the party worked its way around to the

---

* Annapurna, of course, was the first. Everest, climbed a few weeks before Nanga
Parbat, was the second.

northwest. Camp was established close to one of the great glaciers, and a few days later Mummery, accompanied by two of the porters, set off to reconnoiter on the heights above. None of them was ever seen again. Although no clue to their fate has been found, the generally held belief is that they were caught and overwhelmed by an avalanche.

Thirty-seven years passed before men again set foot on Nanga Parbat. Then, in the summer of 1932, came the second challengers, a well-equipped German-American expedition, which included among its members some of the ablest mountaineers of the day. The leader was Willy Merkl, of Munich, and most of his compatriots were also Bavarians. The Americans—the first ever to attempt a major Himalayan peak—were Fritz Wiessner, German-born, who ranked at the time as one of the foremost climbers in the United States; Rand Herron, a young sportsman who had made many ascents on mountains all over the world; and Elizabeth Knowlton, of New York, who, although an accomplished climber, served the party principally as newspaper correspondent.

This first of the latter-day expeditions was the most successful of all —until the final scaling of the peak in 1953. Making their attack from the north (the route followed by all succeeding parties), they worked their way diagonally upward under Nanga Parbat's frontal precipices and, after three weeks of struggle with steep snow and ice, came out high on the main eastern ridge. Here they were already at an altitude of over twenty-three thousand feet, and all but a fraction of the vertical part of the ascent lay beneath them. But a long tortuous stretch of ridge still separated them from their objective. Pressing toward it, they surmounted Rakiot Peak, one of the mountain's secondary summits, pitched their seventh camp on an icy saddle beyond, and began packing up their supplies for the final assault. The saddle, however, was as far as they were to go: for, all at once almost every affliction that can plague an expedition descended upon them. One climber was stricken with appendicitis. Another contracted frostbite. The porterage system broke down. And worst of all, a great eight-day storm descended howling upon the heights. Far from reaching the top, they were lucky to get down to base camp through the driving, billowing snow.

The 1932 party did important pioneering work and was one of the few to escape from Nanga Parbat without disaster; but their venture was still to end on an ironically tragic note. Sightseeing in Egypt on the journey home, Rand Herron slipped while descending the Second

Pyramid, fell three hundred feet and was instantly killed. It was almost as if the Naked Mountain, regretting its leniency, had belatedly reached across thousands of miles to claim a victim.

Two attempts. One disaster and one near-disaster. But the giant of Kashmir had not yet even begun to show its hand. The next two expeditions to Nanga Parbat, in 1934 and 1937, are, as sheer horror stories, unmatched by anything in the history of mountaineering.

Both ventures were by Germans, and on that of 1934 Merkl was again the leader. His companions were all experienced mountaineers: some, like him, veterans of the earlier attempt, others old hands who had won their spurs on Kangchenjunga and other Himalayan giants. Misfortune was not long in striking, for scarcely had they reached the base of the mountain when one of their number died of pneumonia. The others, however, pushed on, following the general route of the 1932 party, and reached the east ridge, near Rakiot Peak, without untoward difficulty. Camp VII was established on the saddle between Rakiot and the summit and Camp VIII still farther along, at a height of almost twenty-five thousand feet. On July sixth two climbers, Peter Aschenbrenner and Erwin Schneider, went on to a point which they estimated to be not more than eight hundred feet below the top, and perhaps four hours' climbing away. Returning to Camp VIII, they reported happily that no obstacles intervened. All that remained was one easy day's march to victory.

Then Nanga Parbat turned on them with malignant wrath.

That night a violent storm broke over the mountain. For thirty-six hours the men in the highest camp were pinned in their tiny tents, while all the world beyond a ten-foot radius was blotted from sight behind driving walls of snow. A hurricane wind tore at them, snapping the tent poles and ripping the canvas to shreds. Their portable cookers refused to function. Their meagre supply of cold food dwindled and disappeared. By the morning of July eighth the storm had shown no sign of abating, and only two alternatives faced them: to attempt to descend or to die where they lay.

Aschenbrenner and Schneider, with three porters, started down first and managed to cover the entire distance to Camp IV in one day. The others—Merkl, Welzenbach, Wieland and nine porters—were to have no such good fortune. Following a few hours after the first party, they were able to do little more than creep along through the driving bliz-

zard and monstrous banks of snow. After a while one of the porters
collapsed from exhaustion and soon after died. The others struggled
on, but darkness overtook them halfway between Camps VIII and VII,
and they spent the night on the open ridge. In the morning the storm
was still raging, and the frozen, enfeebled men were barely able to
move. One after another, the porters dropped in their tracks. Toward
midday, Wieland sat down in the snow and never got up again. Food
and sleeping bags had to be dropped as they staggered on, or were
blown off their backs by the fury of the wind.

By evening the survivors reached Camp VII, to find it stripped of
bags and provisions—scarcely a shelter at all. The following day five
of the remaining porters went on, two of them eventually reaching the
lower camps and safety, three of them dying of exposure and exhaustion
on the way. Merkl, Welzenbach and three men remained in the camp,
where, after two days, Welzenbach died. The others lay there for a
third day, the fifth since any of them had had a mouthful of food; then
they made their last supreme effort to get down. Merkl, however, was
so weak that he could go only a little way, and when night fell they
dug a hole in the snow and crawled in. When morning came only one
of the porters was strong enough to stand. He continued the descent
and at last came staggering, less than half alive, into Camp IV. Merkl
and the two others crept on hands and knees as far as their strength
would take them; then they lay down in the great drifts and died.

So the 1934 venture ended, in a disaster that shocked the world. Men
had at last climbed to within a few hundred feet of Nanga Parbat's
summit. Until that fateful night of July sixth the expedition had promised to be one of the most brilliantly successful in the history of mountaineering. And a week later the record stood: Nanga Parbat still
unconquered; eleven men dead on its icy flanks.

It almost passes belief that a catastrophe such as this could be followed by another still worse, yet such is the dark history of the Naked
Mountain. Terrible though the 1934 disaster was, at least an appreci-
able number of the climbers escaped with their lives. The expedition
of 1937 was literally annihilated.

The leader of this attempt was Dr. Karl Wien, a veteran of the 1931
Kangchenjunga venture, and the climbing party was again composed
of the pick of German mountaineers. The route of ascent was the same
as before: across the great snow-slopes below the northeast face and

then on up toward the east ridge. The weather held, the transport arrangements worked smoothly, and within a few weeks the main party found themselves well established in Camp IV, on a fairly level ice-terrace a few hundred feet below Rakiot Peak. The plan was to push on to the ridge at once, but more supplies were needed for the higher camps. Accordingly, Lieutenant Smart, the British liaison officer of the expedition, started down with a group of porters on the morning of June fourteenth, leaving seven of the nine German climbers and nine porters at Camp IV.

He was the last man to see any of them alive.

A few days later Ulrich Luft, one of two Germans who had remained below, went up with a small band of porters to join his companions. Reaching what he knew to be the site of the fourth camp, he was stunned to find the entire terrace buried under an immense avalanche of ice and snow. Not a vestige of human occupancy, or of any living thing, remained.

From the first there was not the slightest hope that any one of the sixteen men had survived. Luft, Lieutenant Smart and the other surviving German, however, did what they could to find the vanished men, and as soon as news of the tragedy reached civilization a relief party flew all the way from Munich to Kashmir to help them. After days of searching and excavating, the remains of the camp were at last discovered, buried ten feet deep in the debris of the avalanche. All the bodies that were found lay in their sleeping bags, showing no sign of struggle or panic. Several diaries were located, all of them complete through June fourteenth. Three watches, crushed with their owners, had all stopped at a few minutes after twelve. From this grim evidence, and that of the mountain itself, it was obvious that the climbers had been overwhelmed as they slept. An enormous hanging glacier had apparently plunged down from Rakiot Peak in the early morning hours of June fifteenth, swept across the terrace in a cascade of ruin and blotted the men out before they could so much as budge.

The 1934 and 1937 disasters on Nanga Parbat are unparalleled, even in so hazardous a field as Himalayan mountaineering; and the question inevitably arises—how and why could such things happen? Partly, to be sure, they happened through the agency of the blind forces of nature, over which men have no control. But no one who has had experience with great mountains and their hazards can escape the conviction that the two unfortunate parties contributed materially to their own destruction. Even more than the Frenchmen on Annapurna, several years later, they were motivated by national pride, and in their case it was pride of the particularly virulent Nazi variety. They came to the mountain less as sportsmen than as warriors, and, like the young "suicide climbers" in the Alps, they were prepared to gamble high for victory. It is always easy to point the finger of blame after the event. Yet the fact remains that men whose ambition was more tempered by caution would not have pushed as high as the 1934 party with such inadequate supplies and lines of communication, or have pitched camp, as did the 1937 party, without first testing the soundness of the slopes above. The Germans were engaged in all-or-nothing assaults. They were after the laurel wreath, and the end was all that mattered. And while feeling sorrow for the brave individuals who lost their lives, one cannot but feel that collectively they met a fate that was not undeserved. Blind, reckless force is no more the key to the conquest of a great mountain than to the conquest of the world.

Crushed by Nanga Parbat as no climbers had ever been crushed on a mountain before, the Germans were still not done with it, and in 1938 we find Paul Bauer, the leader of the 1929 and 1931 Kangchenjunga expeditions, heading still another venture up the northeast face to the saddle beyond Rakiot Peak. High on the mountainside they found the bodies of Willy Merkl and one of his porters, almost perfectly preserved after four years in the ice and snow. Subsequently, the party pushed on to about twenty-three thousand feet, but here they were driven back by a series of fierce storms. Even in defeat, however, they accomplished what in the light of previous events must be considered a remarkable feat: they came down off the mountain with every man still alive.

Again in 1939 a German expedition returned to the scene, but it was merely a reconnaissance to find possible new routes for an attempt the following year. Because of the war, it was an attempt that never came off, and it was 1950 before the Naked Mountain was again approached. This time there was a change in cast: instead of Germans, the climbers were three young Englishmen. But there was no change in Nanga Parbat. Although the threesome had no serious designs on the top, but intended only to investigate its lower slopes, it struck them down almost before they started. Two of them reached a height of about eighteen thousand feet and were swallowed up in a blizzard, and the third, suffering from frostbite, was barely able to make his way back to civilization.

Seven expeditions. Thirty-two lives lost. . .

Then follows an intermission of two years, and the curtain rises on the last act. It was to be an act as spectacular as any before it, but now the protagonist and victor was to be, not the mountain, but man. Specifically a man named Hermann Buhl.

The 1953 expedition to Nanga Parbat was again German—their first major Himalayan venture since the war. Known as the Willy Merkl Memorial Expedition, it was headed by Merkl's step brother, Dr. Karl Herrligkoffer, a Munich physician, and had as field leader Peter Aschenbrenner, one of the few survivors of the 1934 debacle. The climbing personnel included the top men that postwar Germany—and Austria—had to offer: notably the afore-mentioned Buhl, a slightly built, twenty-nine-year-old Tyrolean who divided his time between Alpine climbing and clerking in a Munich sporting goods store. In the previous few years he had won a fabulous reputation in Europe. Many of his ascents had approached the incredible, and for skill and daring, speed and endurance, he was ranked among the greatest climbers who ever lived. Tremendous things were expected of him on Nanga Parbat. But it is doubtful if anyone expected as much as what happened.

In its early phases, the 1953 campaign followed the general pattern of the earlier ones. The great snow-slopes were climbed, camps established, an icy route hacked out to the high skyline of the east ridge. As always on Nanga Parbat, the weather threatened—and sometimes broke; but this time the party was prepared to withstand it, and though there were a few temporary retreats, there was no rout or disaster. In due time the vanguard had skirted Rakiot Peak and were dug in on the slopes below the Silver Saddle, the name the earlier expeditions had given to the great snow-col between Rakiot and the summit. Once again, as so often before, the goal seemed well within reach. If. . . Always if. . .

Buhl, as had been anticipated, was up with the leaders, and on July second he and one companion, Otto Kempter, moved up to the highest camp as the first assault team. This camp was only at about twenty-three thousand feet, more than thirty-six hundred vertical feet, plus a great horizontal distance, from the top. But they believed—or at least Buhl believed—that it could be made in a single sustained effort, without the necessity of pitching another camp still higher. On the evening of the second the wind rose and a storm seemed to be brewing. But it did not materialize. By midnight the air was still, the sky brilliant with stars and a thin sickle moon. And an hour later Buhl crept from his sleeping bag and prepared to set off.

Exactly what happened next is part of the controversy that has since raged about this strange expedition. But at least it is obvious that the two men did not work as a team. Kempter felt in poor physical shape. Or he thought it was too early to start. Or he was slow in making ready. Or all three. Whatever the details—by two-thirty Buhl was ready to go, and Kempter was not. And Buhl set out alone. Whether or not he expected his companion to follow him has also been a matter of dispute, but in any case he left behind for him almost all of their food supply. At three o'clock Kempter left the tent and followed Buhl's tracks up through the snow. Four hours of climbing brought him to the plateau of the Silver Saddle, and from there he saw Buhl, high on the white slopes above him, still moving on strongly. Kempter himself, however, was at the end of his strength. Sitting down to rest, he fell asleep, and when later he awoke, he knew he could not go on. Buhl had now vanished in the frozen wilderness above. Kempter spent the rest of the day waiting on the saddle and toward evening descended to the high camp.

Meanwhile Buhl moved up and up, on his solitary way. Past giant ice-towers and deep crevasses—across the white plain of the Silver Saddle—up the steep, twisting ridge beyond. Here the snow was hard packed and slippery, and he used his steel-pronged crampons. A short rest. On again. A rest. On again. He was not equipped with oxygen; with each foot gained the going was harder, and he needed two deep breaths for every upward step. Originally he had hoped to be on the summit by noon, but by that time, as far as he could judge, he was barely half the way. By two o'clock the margin of time for a descent by daylight was running dangerously low, and the average climber would have stopped and turned back. But not Hermann Buhl.

The weather held good. Some of the time it was almost warm. But he was growing hungry and was afraid to consume his meagre food supply. Instead, he resorted to pirvitin, a capsuled heart stimulant that he carried with him, and this gave him at least the illusion of renewed

strength. Toward midafternoon he was faced with the hardest climbing
he had yet encountered—a battlement of rock rising out of the snow
and ice—and for some two hours, alone at twenty-six thousand feet,
he struggled with sheer cliff-faces and beetling overhangs that threatened at any instant to flick him off into the abyss below. At last, at six
in the evening, he came out above them, onto a shoulder close below
the summit. From here on the going was easier: again the familiar
slopes of hard-packed snow. But even Buhl's fantastic endurance was
now weakening, and his progress was no more than an agonized crawl.
The final few yards, indeed, were actually accomplished on all fours;
then at last there was nowhere to crawl but down—and he jerked himself upright. At seven o'clock, after sixteen and a half hours of solitary
struggle, he was standing on the top of Nanga Parbat.

Another climber would probably have died there. But once again,
not Buhl. Like any Sunday hiker on Knob Hill or Old Baldy, he first
dutifully admired the view. He took pictures. He unfurled the flags of
the Tyrol and of Pakistan. And as the sun set behind the western
ranges, he turned and began the descent. If it strained belief that he had
reached the top successfully, few mountaineers would have taken a
hundred to one that he would get back down again alive.

In the fading light he negotiated the topmost snow-slopes. But on
the cliffs below, night closed in on him. For a while he tried to grope
his way down; then stopped, in the certain knowledge that the slightest misstep would plunge him from the mountainside. There was no
level space anywhere, no ledge more than a few inches wide nor crevice
more than finger-deep. Leaning against the wall of rock, he planted
his feet as best he could and found a protruding knob for a handhold.
And there he stayed. Few men have survived a night out, high on a
Himalayan peak. None had ever survived alone, or with *nowhere
even to sit down*. But Hermann Buhl did. Hour after hour he remained
there in the darkness—knocking his frozen feet together, swallowing
his last rations and pirvitin tablets, praying that no storm would rise—
a tiny speck of life in that savage world of rock and space. And in the
morning, miraculously, he was still there. Still living.

And still able to move. . . . Starting at first light, he again began
lowering himself down the precipitous cliffs and by full daylight was
past the worst of the rocks. But the point at which he had spent the
night was only some five hundred feet below the summit, and another

three thousand remained to the high camp and safety. Through the endless day he descended the ridge toward the Silver Saddle: weaving,
stumbling, slipping, resting when he had to, then going on again, down
—always down. Sometimes he was conscious of his hunger and exhaustion, sometimes only of enveloping numbness. At intervals he experienced the familiar high-altitude illusion that he heard voices, or that
others were with him. Beneath him, what he thought were solid landmarks appeared and vanished like mirages.

His pace grew slower. The rests grew longer. Even going downhill
he was having great trouble breathing, and then the ridge dipped to
a low point and he had to climb *up*. He took his last three pirvitin,
and went on. He reached the Silver Saddle, crossed it, floundered down
the snow-slopes beyond. Finally, on the slopes there was a dark speck—
many specks—and this time it was no mirage. It was a tent, and men
coming out to meet him. As the sun set, his forty-hour odyssey came
at last to an end, and his companions stared at him, unbelieving, as at
a revenant from the dead.

Indeed, so astonishing was Buhl's feat—and so contrary to the usual
tenets of mountaineering teamwork—that it promptly split the expedition into warring factions. Was his sensational solo exploit justi-
fiable? Had he specifically disobeyed instructions of the leader, Dr.
Herrligkoffer? Had he done a grave wrong in leaving Otto Kempter
behind, or was it Kempter who had been at fault in failing to hold up
his end of the task? Instead of rejoicing in victory, the homecoming
party was torn by argument and recrimination, which culminated in
Munich in injunctions and threats of lawsuits.

To the German public, however, the exploit had been magnificent,
and mass opinion soon influenced the heroes to behave as such. The
hatchets were buried, at least from general view. Buhl paid tribute to
the others, and they paid tribute to him. It was agreed that, whatever
the ethical nuances, his feat was one of the greatest in mountaineering
history, and that the important thing was not how, but simply that,
Nanga Parbat had been climbed. For twenty years Germans had struggled and died for the prize of its summit. *"Unser Berg,"* they had
called it: "Our Mountain." And now it was theirs at last.

Surely no victory has ever been harder won.

12

HIGH DEFEAT

Kangchenjunga — K2

Two Eightthousanders climbed. With Everest, three. But eleven remain that have yet to feel the tread of boots upon their summit snows. By and large, the greatest Himalayas are still the unclimbed Himalayas.

Since the beginning of exploration in the range each of these giants has had a history of its own. Or, in some cases, no history, for five of them have not yet even been attempted. These are Lhotse and Makalu, near Everest; Broad Peak and Gasherbrum II, in the Karakoram; and Gosainthan, on the Nepalese-Tibetan frontier. Gasherbrum I, as we have seen, was challenged twice during the 1930's; and in more recent years, with the opening up of Nepal, there have been first attempts on three of the highest peaks in that region. Cho Oyu, eighteen miles to the west of Everest, was tried in 1952 by a British party that included Eric Shipton and Edmund Hillary, but the climbers were turned back far short of the goal by impassable ice-cliffs. In 1953, Dhaulagiri, first reconnoitered by the French Annapurna team, was scaled to within a thousand feet of the top by a group of Swiss, the final effort failing because of the lack of suitable high campsites. And near-by Manaslu, after investigation by H. W. Tilman in 1950, was the goal of two large Japanese expeditions in '52 and '53: the first a reconnaissance, the second an attempt that carried to twenty-four thousand feet before being stopped by wind and blizzard.

In addition to these, two Eightthousanders remain—the two greatest after Everest—and both have been subjected, unsuccessfully, to assault after assault. These are K2 and Kangchenjunga, the second and third ranking mountains in the world.

Kangchenjunga is the showpiece of the Himalayas. Everest hides its splendors from the eyes of men behind protective ranges of lesser peaks. K2 and Nanga Parbat, Annapurna and Nanda Devi reveal themselves only to explorers who have toiled through miles of wilderness to reach them. But the third highest mountain stands out proud and bold for all the world to see.

Indeed, "Kangchenjunga from Darjeeling" is one of the celebrated sights of India. Perched on a spur of the Himalayan foothills, 250 miles north of Calcutta, the famous hill-station is a natural observatory facing to the north. Immediately beyond the town the ground falls away, and for more than forty miles the eye can range without obstruction over the wild little border-state of Sikkim, a crumpled world of forested ridges and deep tropical canyons. On the far side of this low-lying green bowl rises the main range of the Himalayas. Peaks without number crowd the horizon in an unbroken sweep: India's dazzling northern battlement, five miles high. Seen from Darjeeling through the intervening mists, it appears less a solid mountain wall of rock and snow than a huge white wave transfixed in the sky.

At the very center of this gigantic panorama is Kangchenjunga itself. Rising on the border between Sikkim and Nepal, it spreads its ramparts for miles into both countries, a mass of many mountains rather than a single, soaring peak. It culminates in five summits, known to the people of the foothills by the lovely name of "The Five Treasures of the Snow." The highest of all, and the true summit of the mountain, is 28,146 feet high. Beside it, the wilderness of surrounding peaks, themselves higher than any mountain in North America, seem to sink into insignificance.

Favored by such a spectacular stage-setting, it is small wonder that Kangchenjunga has long worked its lure on adventurous men. As early as 1848 the botanist explorer, Sir Joseph Hooker, pushed northward through the jungle and gorges of Sikkim, to explore its southern approaches. Other expeditions followed, mostly for surveying and mapmaking, and in 1883 came Graham's climbs on Kabru and other near-by peaks—the first purely mountaineering ventures in the district. It was Douglas Freshfield, however, who was the greatest pioneer on Kangchenjunga. Setting out from Darjeeling in the fall of 1899 with the photographer, Vittorio Sella, and a few other companions, he made a complete circuit of the mountain, thus becoming the first westerner to look upon it from any but its southern side. The journey required seven weeks and was fraught with difficulties and hardships; but the investigation of terrain and routes was so thoroughly and accurately carried out that Freshfield's Circuit remains today a classic model for mountain exploration. As to the possibility of climbers actually ascending Kangchenjunga, Freshfield was less than optimistic. "It is guarded," he reported, "by the Demon of Inaccessibility."

For thirty years most other mountaineers were disposed to take his word for it. Between 1899 and 1929 more climbing was done in Sikkim than in any other region of the Himalayas—notably by the tireless Dr. A. M. Kellas—but the giant among giants was left to its towering solitude. The sole exception occurred in 1905, when a small party of Swiss climbers launched a short-lived assault on the summit. They reached a height of about twenty-one thousand feet on the southwest face, but there their luck gave out. The mountain hurled an avalanche down upon them, taking four lives.

The second attempt on Kangchenjunga, twenty-four years later, can scarcely be called an attempt at all. A young American climber, E. F. Farmer, of New Rochelle, New York, set out from Darjeeling in May of 1929 and, accompanied only by a few porters, began the ascent of the same southwest face. The porters, realizing the hopelessness of the attempt, soon gave up, but Farmer continued on alone. The next morning the others had a glimpse of him—a tiny moving speck on a snowslope far above. Then the clouds closed in, and he was never seen again.

Kangchenjunga could brush off efforts like these as a man brushes off flies. Only a few months after Farmer's disappearance, however, the mountain was to be subjected to an assault of far different calibre. This was the first of two attempts by the so-called "Bavarian Expeditions," led by Paul Bauer of Munich and composed of the most brilliant German climbers of the time. The giant defeated them in the end, as it had the others, but not until after a siege such as had never been waged before on any mountain. Indeed, the English *Alpine Journal,* which rarely indulges in superlatives, subsequently described the 1929 and

1931 Bavarian attempts on Kangchenjunga as "feats without parallel, perhaps, in all the annals of mountaineering."

The expedition of 1929 had to reconnoiter as well as climb. Setting out from Lachen, in Sikkim, in early August—they had selected the post-monsoon period for their attempt—they approached the mountain from the east and after ten days pitched their advance base camp at about seventeen thousand feet on the Zemu Glacier. This great river of ice was enclosed by the main north and east ridges of Kangchenjunga, but days of exploration failed to disclose any possible route up their mile-high walls. The only chance seemed to be on an eastern spur of the north ridge, a steep saw-edge of gleaming ice that climbed diagonally across the face of the mountain and joined the north ridge about two thousand feet below the summit. Freshfield, thirty years earlier, had observed and described this spur, but so formidable had it appeared to him that he had not even mentioned it as a possible way to the heights. Yet it was the way the Bavarians selected.

The next six weeks saw climbing such as had never before been attempted on any mountain. There were no rocks anywhere, no bare straightaway slopes of ice or snow. Instead, the spur climbed skyward for thousands of feet in one unending spine of broken, twisted ice. There were towers piled upon towers, cliff upon cliff, huge vertical columns which tapered like church-spires, and shining curtains, festooned with icicles, hanging down the precipices from cornices above. There were great bulges and chasms, wrenched by the wind and cold into fantastic mushroom shapes and grotesque likenesses of monsters from a nightmare. And, as if all this were not enough, the whole broken, tortured expanse was swept incessantly by avalanches. Gigantic blocks and bergs of solid ice, breaking off high above, swept down the chutes and spirals of the spur in two-mile drops of thundering destruction.

Up through this toppled, frozen world the climbers slowly forced their way. To do so they were compelled to improvise, as they went, a new technique of mountaineering. Time and again they came to towers and cornices which could not be surmounted by ordinary step-cutting. They bored shafts through them or hacked them away entirely. When they found themselves at the end of a day in a place where it was impossible to pitch the tiniest tent, they slept in caves which they dug in the ice. Up the whole terrible spur there was scarcely a stretch of more than a few yards which did not have to be chopped, tunneled or excavated before the porters could struggle up with their loads.

This labor went on not merely for days, but for weeks. Thirteen days alone were required to push a track up from Camp VII, at 20,700 feet, to Camp IX, at 21,700—a distance which on an ordinary mountain usually requires between one and three hours. But slowly they gained altitude, and toward the middle of October the day came at last when the worst seemed to be behind them. Camp X was established in an ice-cave at twenty-three thousand feet, and Bauer and two companions, scouting still higher, reported that the expanse above appeared free of serious obstacles. There was jubilation among the climbers in the highest ice-cave that night, for victory seemed only a few days away.

Kangchenjunga, however, had other plans. For a month and a half it had merely toyed with the intruders—harrying them with precipice and avalanche, but allowing them to creep ever higher toward its heights. Now, rising in wrath, it struck.

During the afternoon of October sixteenth the sky turned a baleful sea-green, and wild gusts of wind shrieked down from the summit ridge. By nightfall a blizzard was raging. Digging themselves out of their cave the next morning, the climbers at Camp X saw that the whole mountainside was buried under seven feet of fresh, loose snow. All vestiges of the track below were gone, all communication with the lower camps wiped out: they were marooned on a frozen perch in the sky. Another twenty-four hours they waited, while the blizzard howled on. All thoughts of the summit had been abandoned, but to stay longer where they were meant sure starvation. As for getting down, it was a feat that seemed humanly impossible; yet the attempt had to be made.

The hardships and dangers which had beset the Bavarians on their long push up Kangchenjunga were as nothing compared to the ordeal of their descent. First they had to batter their way through snowdrifts so huge that the furrow they cut was deeper than their own height. Then they came to steeper slopes, which peeled off in avalanches under their feet. At one point disaster was averted only by the miraculously quick action of one climber. A sudden downrush of snow caught the first three men on one of the ropes and hurled them off the side of a ridge. The fourth man, realizing that in a split second he and the others on the rope would follow them, leapt off the ridge in the opposite direction and, by acting as a human counterweight, stopped the fall of his companions.

That night they reached Camp IX and dug their way to the buried cave entrance through seven feet of snow. But the days that followed were even worse than the first. There were more avalanches, more slips and falls, more driving wind and bitter cold. New stairways had to be cut in the hanging ice-curtains and new tunnels and shafts in the great cornices and towers. One pitch was so steep that half the packs had to be thrown over the precipice before the porters could move a step. And —after all this—the whole of the third night had to be spent on the open ridge without shelter of any kind.

By now several of the men were so severely frostbitten that they could no longer walk. The others, themselves exhausted, took turns carrying them, sometimes on their backs, sometimes on rudely improvised stretchers, and at last they came out upon the Zemu Glacier, at the mountain's base, with every man still alive. Even here, however, Kangchenjunga was not done with them. A second storm now burst down, as violent as the first; snow and rain lashed the lower camps for three successive days; and landslides and mud-avalanches roared across their path. Not until they reached the village of Lachen, twenty miles away, were the battered, crippled climbers finally safe from the fury of the mountain.

So ended the first Bavarian attempt on Kangchenjunga—not merely in defeat, but in rout. It was a rout, however, in which the feats achieved outranked those of most successful climbs theretofore accomplished. Bauer and his companions had been subjected to an ordeal such as few men have ever undergone, anywhere; but every man among them came down from the mountain to tell the tale. More remarkable still, almost all of them would be ready, two years later, to go back for more.

Before the second Bavarian attempt of 1931, however, another group of men were to try their luck. Gunther Dyhrenfurth, the Swiss geologist-mountaineer, had long had his eye on the third highest of the world's mountains, and in the spring of 1930 he set out for it from Darjeeling at the head of a formidable expedition. The climbers who accompanied him included experts from half the countries of western Europe, including the Englishman, Frank Smythe, who was later to win fame on Kamet and Everest.

Having received permission, rarely granted at that time, to enter Nepal, the expedition attacked Kangchenjunga from the northwest. On this side the mountain soars up from its skirt of glaciers in three giant steps—successive tiers of ice-cliffs and sloping, snow-choked terraces, piled one on top of another across the whole expanse of a mile-wide face. Above the highest terrace the main north ridge of the peak slopes gently upward toward the summit cone. This was the ridge up whose eastern spur the Bavarians had struggled the previous year, and the 1930 climbers, also believing that it held the key to the mountain, now attempted to reach it from the opposite side.

They fared even worse than their predecessors. After days of arduous and dangerous work they succeeded in hacking out a track up the lowest of the ice-walls and were ready to establish the first of their upper camps on the terrace above. But before they could occupy it, catastrophe struck. One fine May morning, just as a large party of climbers and porters were starting up the cliff, there was a sudden shattering explosion high above, and an instant later what seemed to be the entire upper half of the mountain came toppling down in ruins. It was an avalanche such as few men have ever witnessed before or since. Millions of tons of ice and snow peeled loose from the underlying rock—whole hanging glaciers and bergs as big as houses—plunging and roaring thousands of feet down the mountainside, to land on the glacier below with a crash that seemed to split the earth. Even there, the maelstrom did not stop. Carried by its own momentum, a vast tide of snow and ice-blocks went careening over the almost level glacier for a full mile before it came to rest at last scarcely three hundred feet from the expedition's lower camp.

If the column of climbers had been directly in the avalanche's path they would have been wiped out in a twinkling. Fortunately, however, all except one were a little to the side of its main line of descent and, though stunned and battered, escaped with their lives. The unlucky one was Chettan, one of the outstanding Sherpa porters. Last in the column, he was caught beneath a crumbling ice-wall and crushed like an insect.

The Dyhrenfurth climbers were brave men, but they were not would-be suicides. Saddened by the death of Chettan and realizing it was only by the grace of God that any of them were still living, they turned away from the northwest face and launched an attempt on the ridge which enclosed it to the west. Their luck, however, was little better there, for,

with their diminished strength and resources, they found it impossible
to get the needed supplies up the steep, rotten rocks. After a few days
they gave up the hopeless struggle and marched off to Jonsong Peak
and a comforting consolation prize.

The second act of the Kangchenjunga drama had been played out.
The third was soon to follow.

Mid-July of 1931 saw Bauer and his fellow-Bavarians again hacking
and tunneling a track up their terrible northeast spur. The storms of
two years had festooned the mountain with new monsters of snow and
ice, and, as in 1929, almost every foot of the ascent was a bitter struggle. Bauer himself, in his subsequent account of the expedition, gives
a vivid picture of one day's ordeal on that savage mountainside. "On
the crest of the spur," he wrote, "towered successive mushroom-shaped
pinnacles, one above the other. At least five of these, each twenty to
thirty feet high, had to be demolished altogether. . . . Every blow had
to be carefully struck, each was a real technique in itself. We were
poised like wild animals, crouching beneath the cornices, balancing
between earth and sky, sometimes on the party's respective heads, to
try to avoid a simultaneous fall when the overhang collapsed."

In the midst of this arduous work tragedy struck—as sudden as lightning out of a blue sky. A group of climbers and porters, roped together,
were ascending a steep snow-gully over the lip of a precipice, some four
thousand feet above the Zemu Glacier. Hermann Schaller, one of the
strongest members of the party, was in the lead, clearing and enlarging
the steps in the tight-packed snow. One of the porters followed immediately after him, while a third stood at the foot of the gully paying
out the rope. Suddenly the first porter slipped and shot down the groove.
Schaller was jerked violently from his steps and flew over him through
the air in a great curve, while clouds of snow poured down the gully.
The rope spun downward, went taut—and broke. An instant later both
men disappeared into the abyss below.

The shock of the disaster stunned climbers and porters alike. For a
week all thought of the summit was abandoned, and the whole party
descended to the base of the mountain. The bodies of Schaller and the
porter were found beneath the cliffs and were buried on a rock-islet
rising from the glacier.

"But the continuance of the attack on Kangchenjunga," said Bauer,
"was for us a foregone conclusion and duty." Again the climbers bent

to the struggle against columns and spires and curtains of ice. Again men and supplies began moving up, and at last, on September tenth, almost two months after they had first come to grips with the mountain, they succeeded in establishing Camp X at an altitude of twenty-three thousand feet. This was about equal to their highest point of 1929, and, as they had observed then, the worst part of the mountain now seemed to be behind them. Above them the northeast spur swept upward in a comparatively unobstructed snow-slope to its junction with the main north ridge.

For a while their luck held. In spite of lashing storms and sub-zero cold, they contrived to pitch an eleventh camp at about twenty-five thousand feet, and a few days later two of their number, Hans Hartmann and Dr. Karl Wien, pushed up the remaining distance to the very summit of the spur. It was a great moment—one of the greatest, surely, that mountaineers anywhere have been privileged to enjoy. The terrible ice-ridge, up which they had struggled so desperately through two long summers, had been conquered at last. They were standing at 26,220 feet—higher than men had ever gone before, except on Everest. And above them was only the gentle slope of the north ridge, rising less than two thousand feet more to the topmost of Kangchenjunga's five summits.

But the moment of triumph was also the moment of defeat. Between the crest of their spur and the north ridge proper was a steep slope of some four hundred feet, sheathed in ice and powdered on its surface with eighteen inches of loose, freshly fallen snow. In many places the snow had already slid off; in others it was clinging merely by the tiniest friction of its particles. Under a man's weight it would inevitably have peeled off altogether and plunged to the glacier eight thousand feet below. Hartmann and Wien returned to Camp XI with heavy hearts to report that they had encountered an impassable obstacle.

Nevertheless, on the following day, Wien and three other companions went up again for a final try. If only they could get by the slope and dig out a final Camp XII on the ridge above, the summit was theirs. But what they found confirmed their worst fears. The steep pitch of snow and ice was the only possible way to the ridge, and to have ventured on it would have meant annihilation. Fresh snow was falling daily; the great storms of the early Himalayan winter would soon be roaring out of the north, and there was no possibility of improvement in the condition of the slope. With victory so close, it was a bitter blow, but there was nothing for it: they turned back, again defeated. And since those grim October days in 1931 no serious attempt has been made on earth's third highest mountain.

Almost a thousand miles from Kangchenjunga, at the far north-western end of the Himalayan chain, rises the great Himalayan sub-range of the Karakoram. Spreading across the frontiers of Kashmir, Tibet and Chinese Sinkiang, in a region uninhabited by men since the beginning of history, this mountain wilderness is perhaps the most desolate and savage in the whole uplift of South-Ceneral Asia. Its glaciers are the largest in the world, outside Alaska and the polar icecaps. Its summits, rising in a vast maze of spires and domes, rock, snow and ice, present a challenge to climbers that could scarcely be exhausted in a thousand years of mountaineering.

Indeed, the Karakoram contain more peaks of the first magnitude than does the Everest region itself. Uncounted hundreds are over twenty thousand feet high, and at least thirty exceed twenty-four thousand. Scarcely any have been climbed, merely a handful attempted, and only the greatest even named. Among them are the Eightthou-sanders, Gasherbrum I (Hidden Peak), Gasherbrum II and Broad Peak; the huge massifs of Masherbrum and the Golden Throne; Bride, Mitre and Queen Mary Peaks; the steeple-like pinnacles of the Baltoro Spires; the incredible vertical obelisk of the Mustagh Tower; and greatest of all—and second only to Everest among the world's summits—K2.*

For long years after its discovery, in 1861, K2 was considered the classic example of an unclimbable peak. Partly, to be sure, this was because of its enormous height of 28,250 feet, but, in addition to its sheer size, it seemed also to be so built as to be hopelessly unassailable. Everest had its cols, Kangchenjunga its northeast spur, Nanga Parbat its east ridge, and these appendages, formidable though they were, at least held out a possibility of ascent. K2, however, towered twelve thousand feet above its glaciers in a sheer, unbroken pyramid of rock and ice. Its ridges appeared little better than cliffs; its gale-scoured faces bristled with precipices and overhangs; along its entire upward sweep

---

* The name derives from an old surveying designation, which caught the imagination of climbers and endured. In years past it was more often called Mount Godwin Austen, after one of the early explorers of the region; and there are also several native names for it—among them Chogori and Dapsang.

the eye could discern no single spot level enough to hold even the tiniest of camps. In the second highest of the earth's elevations nature appeared to have created a masterpiece: a truly invulnerable mountain.

The early history of K2 is therefore one of exploration and investigation rather than of actual mountaineering. Conway, in 1892, and Dr. and Mrs. Workman, between 1899 and 1908, toiled up the great glaciers and passes into the very heart of the Karakoram; but they confined their climbing to lesser peaks and were content to survey the monarch from a respectful distance. The first attempt on it was made in 1902 by a mixed party of English, Swiss and Austrian climbers, who were turned back after advancing a short distance up the northeast spur. And the second, in 1909, was by the Duke of the Abruzzi. His elaborate expedition had been organized for the express purpose of besieging K2, and, with the aid of Italian guides and a large corps of native porters, he made two tries for the heights. The first carried to twenty thousand feet on the southeast ridge—later to be known by his name; the second some eighteen hundred feet higher on the northwest. Beyond these levels, however, it proved impossible to pitch camps or carry supplies, and the Duke, like his predecessors, had to admit defeat. Turning away from the mountain, he devoted the rest of the summer to exploration of the surrounding country and his record-setting climb on Bride Peak.

In the years that followed there were many expeditions to the region. Notable among them were a second Italian venture in 1929, the Dyhrenfurths' in 1934, the French attempt on Gasherbrum I in 1936, and the English one on Masherbrum in 1938. But it was not until this same year, almost three decades after the Abruzzi expedition, that K2 itself was again tried—and at last subjected to its first serious challenge.

As Everest has been largely a British preserve, and Kangchenjunga and Nanga Parbat German, the king of the Karakoram has, by the same token, now become an "American mountain." In recent years there have been three attempts to climb it—in 1938, 1939 and 1953— and all have been by expeditions from the United States, sponsored by the American Alpine Club of New York. The 1938 party consisted of only five men, led by Dr. Charles Houston, veteran of the successful British-American Nanda Devi expedition of 1936. His companions were Richard Burdsall, of the 1932 Minya Konka venture, Robert Bates, of wide Alaskan experience, William House, one of the country's outstanding rock-climbers, and Paul Petzoldt, the chief guide of Grand Teton National Park and, at the time, one of the very few professional climbers in the country. On its arrival in India the group was augmented by a British transport officer, six Sherpa porters and the usual crew of locally recruited coolies.

Leaving Srinagar, the metropolis of Kashmir, in mid-May, the expedition trekked up from the green valleys into the bleak domain of the Karakoram and by early June was established at its base camp, 16,600 feet high, beneath the great south face of K2. Splitting into groups of two and three, the climbers surveyed the mountain from all sides, ascending and descending the glaciers, struggling across windswept passes, seeking patiently for a route upward that might offer at least a gambler's chance of success. But they were not long in learning that their predecessors were right: there was no "natural" way up the peak. Photographs and maps had indicated that the northwest ridge was perhaps the best possibility, but precipitous, snow-powdered ice-slopes stopped them when they had climbed a scant few hundred feet above its base. The situation on the northeast was even worse; and reluctantly they decided to try the southeast, or Abruzzi, ridge, on which the Duke and his men had tried and failed. Camp I was accordingly established near the foot of the ridge, and on July first the upward push began.

As had been anticipated, the greatest difficulty was in finding spots sufficiently level to be used as campsites. Combing the mountain diligently, they were lucky enough to find a tiny snow-pocket that served as an admirable location for Camp II; but above that they encountered no such protected nooks. At every higher bivouac it was necessary to construct platforms of loose rock on which to pitch the tents, and even with these artificial foundations the climbers found themselves each night tilted precariously over black space.

Unlike most Himalayan routes, the Abruzzi Ridge of K2 presented rock-climbing difficulties of the severest kind. Between Camps II and III the line of ascent was along a rough outcropping of stone, paralleling an almost vertical ice-wall, and so hard was the going that nine hundred feet of fixed rope had to be rigged up before the porters with their packs were able to make the ascent. Beyond III things were no better: the mountainside bulged out in a series of cliffs and overhangs, requiring both exhausting physical effort and the most delicate technique to surmount them. Also, to make matters worse, the rock itself was rotten, breaking away from walls and ledges at slight pressure and descending in a murderous cannonade onto the exposed camp below.

The hardest stretch of all, however, was encountered just above Camp IV, at a height of about twenty-two thousand feet. Here, according to House, "a vertical wall of yellowish rock stretched completely across the ridge. There seemed to be no way around it, and when we had cut our way up to it . . . we found the rock worse than we had anticipated. It was nearly vertical, and what had looked like promising ledges from below were in reality tiny sloping platforms. After much trouble Bates curled himself around a projecting tooth of rock and belayed me while I traversed into the bottom of a shallow chimney. It was difficult to stay in, as the walls flared out and the bed was formed of ice, but after a good deal of exertion and not a little swearing I reached the top, gaining about eighty feet." House's modest account, one is certain, scarcely does justice to his exploit. For those eighty feet had taken him four full hours.

It was impossible for men with loads to climb the chimney, and House and Bates therefore spent the next day rigging up a sort of aerial tramway along its side. Meanwhile Houston and Petzoldt came up, and Camp V was pitched near the top of the chimney. All hands were subsequently held there for a day by high winds and driving snow; but a major storm did not materialize, and soon conditions were such that they were able to move still higher. Finding the going here slightly less difficult, they gained altitude rapidly. Within a few days a sixth camp had been established at about 23,300 feet and a seventh at almost twenty-five thousand.

At the latter point the ridge was at last beneath them, and they had come out onto an ice plateau that swept like a great terrace across the upper face of the mountain. Beyond the plateau was a gently rising snow-slope, from which emerged, gaunt and black, the 2,500-foot summit pyramid of K2. The snow-section presented what was obviously the easiest stretch on the peak, and even the beetling rock above appeared to offer no obstacles worse than those they had encountered below.

But the time had now come when they were faced with a difficult decision. From the outset the expedition had traveled light—not only in personnel, but in provisions—and, with the long reconnaissance and subsequent slow going on the ridge, their food supply was beginning to run low. They were not, to be sure, in any actual distress, but the margin of safety had become precariously thin, and a great storm, catching them in a high camp and rendering retreat impossible, might well have spelt disaster. With the summit so close and beckoning, the temptation to take the chance must have been strong indeed, but they managed to resist it and conceded that the pinnacle of K2 was not to be theirs that year.

Before descending, however, they allowed themselves one final foray toward the heights. With House and Bates established in Camp VI as support, Houston and Petzoldt went up again to VII, spent the night there, and on the next day set out up the snow-slope toward the summit cone. There was no thought in their minds of reaching the top—an eighth camp would have had to be established for that even to be considered—but merely of going as high as they could in one day's reconnaissance. Accordingly, they reached the base of the summit pyramid at an elevation of 25,600 feet and even scrambled up its lower rocks some four hundred feet higher. The pinnacle of K2 loomed huge and clear above them, now only a short day's climb away. But it might as well have been an eternity, as with reluctant steps they began the descent of the mountain.

This first American attempt on K2 was almost a model exploit for a small expedition. The climbers had reconnoitered the peak, found a feasible route and followed it to within striking distance of the top. And in doing so they had met with not a single serious mishap or injury. . . . The 1939 party went even higher. But at a price.

The second expedition, like the first, was sponsored by the American Alpine Club, but none of the 1938 climbers participated. Fritz Wiessner, who had been on Nanga Parbat in 1932, was now the leader. His companions were Jack Durrance, a well-known American skier and climber, Dudley Wolfe and Eaton Cromwell, old hands at mountaineering in many parts of the world, and Chappell Cranmer and George Sheldon, who at the time of the expedition were still undergraduates at Dartmouth. Upon arrival in Kashmir the party was rounded out by the acquisition of the usual British transport officer, plus nine Sherpas and a battalion of local coolies. It was thus a slightly larger group than that of 1938, but still exceedingly small as Himalayan expeditions go.

As before, the long trek into the heart of the Karakoram was accomplished in remarkably short order, and on May thirty-first the site of the old base camp was reoccupied. Several days were spent in searching for a possible new route leading to the heights above; but the climbers soon reached the conclusion that their predecessors had made the only feasible choice, and the assault was therefore launched on the same southeast, or Abruzzi, ridge. Even before they started, however, it became apparent that they were not going to enjoy the unvarying good fortune that had favored the climbers of 1938. Cranmer, who, at twenty, was the youngest of the party, fell ill at the base camp and was unable to do any climbing during the whole duration of the expedition.

Missing their companion's assistance, and worried about his condition, the others nevertheless began the push upward, and gradually the long chain of camps began to take form on the savage, ice-sheathed mountainside. In every case the tents were pitched in the same locations as the preceding year, for the simple reason that there were no other possible locations. Along the walls and buttresses the climbers found much of the fixed rope which Houston and his companions had rigged up; but the storms of a Karakoram winter had scarcely improved its condition, and the larger part of it had to be replaced.

After some three weeks of work, an advance guard of Wiessner, Wolfe, Sheldon and five Sherpas were established at Camp IV, beneath House's formidable chimney. Here, however, they were overtaken by a storm, and for six days and nights they huddled in their tents, while the snow billowed down upon them and the wind roared against the canvas like machine-gun fire. Fortunately their food supply was ample, and when the storm at last subsided they found themselves cramped and battered, but at least able to go on. Camp V was set up near the top of the chimney, and a few days later they were ready to go higher still.

Nevertheless, it was a badly depleted high-climbing party that began working its way along the upper ridge toward the great ice-plateau. Cranmer was still ailing and lay in the base camp under the care of the transport officer. Cromwell had likewise remained below, to direct the stocking and maintenance of the lower camps. And now both Sheldon and Durrance were forced to descend—the former with frostbitten toes, the latter because of difficulty in breathing—leaving Wiessner and Wolfe as the only active climbers. The Sherpas, on the other hand, were standing up well under the ordeal. Paced by their headman, Pasang Kikuli, redoubtable veteran of Nanga Parbat, Nanda Devi and the first K2 venture, they toiled up and down the precipitous ridge, and day by

SHOWPIECE OF THE HIMALAYAS

Kangchenjunga, as seen from above the hill-town of Darjeeling on the northern border of India.

Photo Deane Dickason from Ewing Galloway

KING OF THE KARAKORAM

K2, second highest summit in the world, as seen from the northeast. The route of the recent American expeditions led up from behind the skyline ridge on the left to the snow plateau just beneath the summit pyramid.

Ewing Galloway

day the straggling column crept higher on the mountainside. The sixth camp was pitched just beneath the crest of the ridge; the seventh on the ice-plateau at about 24,700 feet; the eighth, on the snow-slopes above, at almost 25,500.

The bare, frosted rock of the summit pyramid now loomed close above them, and, with luck, it would require only two days' more climbing to reach the top. Storms pinned them in Camp VIII for thirty-six hours, but the morning of July seventeenth dawned clear. While two of the Sherpas descended to the plateau to bring up more supplies, Wiessner, Wolfe and the remaining porter, Pasang Lama, set off to establish a ninth and final camp on the rocks above. Before reaching the base of the summit pyramid, however, they were forced to plow their way through huge drifts of freshly fallen snow. At such an altitude this proved a terribly difficult task, especially for Wolfe, who was much heavier than the others and found himself sinking into the snow up to his armpits. After an hour of desperate effort, he was near to exhaustion and had to turn back. Wiessner and Pasang Lama, continuing the struggle, finally got through. That evening they pitched their tent well up on the summit cone's southeast ridge and the next day moved it still farther to a height of 26,050 feet.

On the morning of July nineteenth, in perfect weather, they started for the top. Neither of them, according to Wiessner's subsequent account, was particularly bothered by the altitude. The climbing, however, was of the stiffest order, even necessitating the use of pitons to secure the rope; and their progress was accordingly slow. All morning and all afternoon they toiled on—up cliffs and bristling cornices, through deep ice-coated gullies, along the crests of rotten ridges. They were now so high above the surrounding world that they seemed hardly to be part of it any longer. The glacier, eleven thousand feet below, might as well have been a hundred miles; they could see it only as a thin gleaming ribbon between the mountain-masses on either side. Finally, even the pinnacles of Gasherbrum and Broad Peak were swimming below them in the evening light.

A bold plan had taken form in Wiessner's mind. "It was 6 P.M. by then," he wrote in his diary. "I had decided to go to the summit in spite of the late hour and climb through the night. . . . The weather was safe, and we were not exhausted. Night climbing had to be done anyway, as it would take us a long time to descend the difficult route up which we had struggled. Much better to go up the summit slowly, with many stops, and return over the difficult part of the route the next morning."

But it was not to be. Pasang Lama, who had climbed strongly and uncomplainingly through the long hours of the day, halted when he realized that night was coming on. All Wiessner's arguments could not persuade him to go farther, and when the former made a move to start climbing again he refused to pay out the rope. To have gone on alone would have been madness, and in the end Wiessner gave in. At a height of 27,500 feet—seven hundred and fifty below the summit of K2—the two men turned back.

Through eight terrible hours of darkness they descended the cliffs and buttresses of the pyramid—feeling their way with frozen hands and feet, clambering, struggling, swinging at rope's end five miles high in the night. At last, at two-thirty in the morning, they reached their highest camp. There they spent the next day, resting, and on the morning of the twenty-first made their second bid for the summit. The Sherpa, however, had lost his crampons in a mishap during the first attempt and was unable to negotiate the steep ice-chimneys that grooved their route. They were turned back without matching their earlier effort.

Now began the long and complex chain of events that was to lead to defeat and tragedy. Wiessner had full intentions of making yet another try for the top, but food at Camp IX was running low, and he and Lama therefore descended to Camp VIII to renew the supply. There they found Wolfe, as they had expected, but there was no sign of the porters who had descended a week before to bring up fresh loads. By this time there were enough provisions at VIII to last for only three or four more days. There was nothing for it but for all of them to descend to Camp VII.

Arriving there, they had their second shock. The camp was deserted, much of the provisions and fuel had been removed, and they had only one sleeping bag for the three of them. After a miserably cold night only one course of action was open: to continue the descent to Camp VI. Both Wiessner and Wolfe, however, were still thinking in terms of another summit attack, and it was therefore decided that only Wiessner and Lama would go down, while Wolfe waited at VII, conserving his strength. The first two, according to the plan, would come back the following day with fresh porters, and the whole party would then re-ascend to the highest camps.

But what was in store for them was something very different, for when they reached Camp VI the next day, Wiessner and the porter were stunned to discover that this too had been evacuated. Realizing that something had gone seriously wrong, the two men continued the descent. Camp V was likewise deserted. So were IV, III and II. At Camp II they spent their second freezing night. They had left their one sleeping bag with Wolfe, and by morning both were badly frostbitten and close to collapse. Nevertheless they stumbled on down and by mid-afternoon reached the base camp—"as truly broken, mentally as well as physically," said Wiessner, "as it is possible for men to be."

What had happened was that, while Wiessner, Wolfe and Lama were at Camp VIII and higher, the rest of the expedition had broken down below. Cranmer was still sick, and Sheldon, with frostbitten feet, was hobbling about on crutches. Durrance and Cromwell had been unable to hold out for long periods at the altitudes of the higher camps and had had to descend to the base. Meanwhile the Sherpas, who had gone down from VIII to VII for more supplies, had been unable to get back up again. They had waited at VII for several days, and at the end of that time, having seen no sign of life from above, assumed that the summit party had met with an accident and been killed. They had therefore begun the descent and, as conscientious porters, had felt it their duty to clear out the various camps as they went.

Now Wolfe was alone, high on the mountain in Camp VII, and it was obvious that heroic measures would be needed to reach him. Wiessner was done in, so weak that he could hardly eat or speak. Durrance, therefore, took over and started up with three Sherpas. But upon reaching the fourth camp he again succumbed to the altitude and two days later returned to the base with one of the porters. The other two had continued on to Camp VI, but needed re-enforcements to go still higher. Accordingly, two other Sherpas, one of them the head-man, Pasang Kikuli, went up from the base and succeeded in reaching VI in one day's climbing—one of the most remarkable feats of endurance ever performed by men upon a mountain. The next day Kikuli and two others continued on to VII, where they found Wolfe alive, but apparently broken down both physically and mentally. He told them he was too weak to come down that day, but would be ready for the effort the next morning.

As there was only one sleeping bag at VII, the Sherpas descended to VI for the night. They were held there the following day by a storm, but on the next, three of them, led by Kikuli, went up again. That was the last that was seen of them. The fourth Sherpa in the rescue party waited at VI for three days, but no one reappeared from above, and finally hunger and cold drove him down to base camp. The following day, Wiessner, still very weak, made an effort to go up, but could get only as far as Camp II. Then storms closed in again, hiding the savage heights—and the bodies of four brave men.

In retrospect, the experiences of 1938 and 1939 would seem to prove one fundamental point: that, if nothing else, a high-mountain expedition must consist of a well-balanced group of climbers. In the former year, at least four of the participants were of roughly equal ability and stamina and worked as a smoothly integrated team. But in the latter, Wiessner far outstripped the others, and, as a result, the party became too widely strung out on the mountainside and the chain of communication broke down. All this—and its lesson—is perfectly true, but unfortunately knowledge and careful planning are not in themselves enough to insure victory, or even safety, on a peak like K2. The third American expedition was as balanced and co-ordinated a party as could well have been assembled: yet it too met with defeat and disaster.

This was in 1953, after fourteen years and a world war. But two of the veterans of 1938 were back: Charles Houston, again as leader, and Robert Bates, as second in command. With them were five younger men —George Bell, Robert Craig, Arthur Gilkey, Dee Molenaar and Peter Schoening—all with outstanding records in the Western Hemisphere, though without previous Himalayan experience. Their British liaison officer, Captain Tony Streather, however, was an old hand in the region and a high climber for good measure, having reached the summit of Tirich Mir with the Norwegian expedition of 1950. For political reasons—since K2 now lay in Pakistan—the expedition was unable to employ Indian-Nepalese Sherpas and had to substitute less experienced porters of the Hunza tribe of Baltistan. But there was at least partial compensation for this disadvantage in the assignment to them by the Pakistan Government of one Colonel M. Ata-Ullah, as general supervisor of transport and supplies. Throughout the attack on the peak, Ata-Ullah was in charge of the base camp, and one gathers that without his efficient management the climbers' misfortunes would have had even worse consequences than they did.

The expedition started off in true air-age style, flying in toward the

Karakoram in a few hours, over country it had taken the earlier parties
some two weeks to traverse afoot. Beyond the outpost town of Skardu,
however, their route was the same as before: along deep valleys and
roaring rivers, up the Baltoro and Godwin Austen Glaciers, to their
base at the foot of K2. By late June they were on the mountain proper,
pitching their chain of camps on the long steep spine of the Abruzzi
Ridge.

During the early stages all went well. Camp I to IV were established
on schedule and thoroughly stocked. From IV the Hunza porters were
sent down to the base, and the climbers themselves took over all of the
load-packing; but happily they were in the best of condition, and the
advance continued without interruption. For the difficult House Chimney they had brought along a prefabricated aluminum pulley, and with
its help they were able, in a day and a half, to haul up nine hundred
pounds of food and equipment. Camp V was pitched—then VI—the
latter at a height of 23,300 feet. Here they found the remains of two
of the 1939 tents, with sleeping bags, stoves, fuel and food neatly
stacked in the ruins. But there was no hint of the fate of Wolfe and the
three Sherpas who had gone after him.

It was about this time that their own troubles began. For the sky,
which had been steadily brilliant, now grew gray and sullen, bitter
winds blew up, and the sun withdrew beyond deep veils of mist. If they
had known what was in store for them, they would probably have descended there and then. But they had no way of knowing. In contrast
to the more southerly Himalayas, the Karakoram are considered too far
inland to be affected by the monsoon from the Indian Ocean. Mid-
summer is usually the period of the finest weather, and the climbers
confidently waited for the sky to clear. But it never cleared. From July
twenty-sixth on, there was not a single day without wind and snow.
As they were to learn too late, 1953 was the one year in which the
monsoon *did* reach the Karakoram, and from here on to the end they
were caught in its web.

Still they kept hoping. And trying. In the intervals between squalls
they succeeded in moving on and pitching Camp VII; then Camp VIII.
Now they were at 25,500 feet, on the great ice-terrace below the summit pyramid, and all they needed were two fine days: one to set up a
final tent part way up the pyramid, and the second to make their bid
for the top. Already they had performed a memorable—in fact, an un-

precedented—feat, in that every member of the party had reached the highest camp. And there was enough food and fuel on hand to last the lot of them for ten days.

They dug in. They waited. . . .

And the weather grew worse. The squalls rose into gales, and the gales into a protracted storm that raged on without respite. "It blew so hard," said Houston later, "that the flapping of the tents was like a fusillade, and the wind had a personal malignant impact that made us all feel that the mountain was trying to kill us." For the entire time they were at Camp VIII snow and cloud hid the slopes above them, and it was seldom possible even to leave the tents for more than a few minutes at a time. They spent the days as well as the nights in their sleeping bags. Cooking was almost out of the question, because of the gusts of wind that penetrated into the tents; they had to eat principally dried foods and suffered badly from thirst because of the resultant lack of fluids.

Still, day after day, they kept the spark of hope alive, and even discussed in detail how they would conduct the summit attack—when and if. At the outset of the expedition a unique agreement had been reached: that if any of them reached the top their identity would be kept secret, so that the whole expedition would share equally in the credit for the victory. And now a second unusual step was taken, for instead of the leader's appointing the summit teams, they were selected by vote. Whether the resolve on anonymous conquest could have held up under the pressure of world curiosity is open to doubt; but since no one did reach the top there was no point in secrecy, and the names were made known. Bell and Craig were chosen for the first attempt, Gilkey and Schoening for the second, if the first should fail.

As it turned out, there was not even one attempt. Nor so much as the chance to move a foot beyond Camp VIII. One of the four tents went down in the wind, and its two occupants had to crawl in with their already crowded companions. Snow continued to fall until they were surrounded by fresh three-foot drifts. Day by day the situation grew more hopeless, and then suddenly, on top of it, came the first intimation of real disaster. On August sixth, their sixth day at the high camp, Gilkey complained of pain in his right leg, and upon examining him, Dr. Houston found that he was suffering from thrombophlebitis, a circulatory disease that involves clotting of the blood. This would have been bad enough at sea level. In a freezing tent at more than twenty-five thousand feet, it was serious in the extreme. When Gilkey tried to stand he fainted from the pain, and it was obvious that he would not be able to walk.

That was the end of any thoughts of the summit. On the same day they tried to start down the mountain, but were stopped after a few hundred feet by wind, deep snowdrifts and the imminent threat of an avalanche. Returning to the camp, they dug in again—and waited. At least they had enough food on hand for several more days, and it seemed incredible that during that time the weather would not improve.

But it didn't. It stormed on. And Gilkey grew worse. On August eighth Houston's examination showed that a clot of blood had broken away from his leg and lodged in a lung; his condition was critical. And so too, by now, was the situation for all of them, for the storm still raged and the food supply was inexorably dwindling. Two more days they waited, hoping against hope. And then there was no longer any choice. Wrapping Gilkey as securely as they could in a sleeping bag, rubber mats and a tent, they struck camp and began the descent.

The going was extremely difficult—first through hip-deep drifts and then down a steep slope of ice—and though it was not actually snowing, the wind drove the fallen snow into their faces with a fury that all but froze and blinded them. Gilkey, on his improvised stretcher, had to be lowered with the utmost care, one or more of the others going beside him, to keep him steady, and the rest paying out the ropes from above. At one point the drag of the ropes started a small avalanche, and those below disappeared as if in a white wave. But the rush of snow passed over them without harm; the descent continued; and by midafternoon, after hours of grueling work, they reached the level of Camp VII. They were not yet, however, *at* Camp VII. For the problems of lowering Gilkey had forced them to veer off from the direct route of descent, and they were still separated from it by a hundred horizontal yards of steep ice.

It was a ticklish enough traverse for active climbers, but to get the sick man across required all manner of delicate maneuvers. Spread out on the fifty-degree slope, they began hacking steps in the iron-hard surface of the ice. Houston and Bates were on one rope. Bell and Streather were on another. Schoening, in a secure position behind an outcropping rock, was belaying Gilkey, who was suspended on the slope about sixty feet below him; and Molenaar, out on the ice, was tied to Gilkey by a second rope. Craig, alone, had already crossed to the campsite and was making it ready for their arrival. One moment they were all at work, shouting instructions back and forth through the howling of the wind. In the next, with sickening suddenness, came the accident.

Bell became fouled in a rope and slipped. His momentum pulled Streather from his steps, and the two plummeted downward. By a miracle that unquestionably saved their lives, their rope became entangled with that of Houston and Bates, and that in turn with the one joining Molenaar to Gilkey. One after another these were jerked like marionettes from the ice-wall and went tumbling after them. But the entanglement that caused them all to fall also linked them together, in effect, on a single lifeline, and at its upper end, wedged behind his boulder, was Schoening. Luckily the pull did not come all at once, but in a series of spasmodic shocks. Schoening took them on his own body, on the boulder, on his ax jammed tight against the boulder. The nylon of the rope stretched almost like a rubber band. For a moment it seemed that the boulder would be dislodged. But both rope and boulder held. Schoening held. In a belay unprecedented in climbing history, he was able to stop the fall of five men—and at the same time still hold Gilkey in position on his stretcher.

The five, however, had gone down a distance of between one hundred and fifty and two hundred feet, most of them stopping at the brink of a two-mile-high precipice. Houston was knocked unconscious. Molenaar had a broken rib. The rest were badly shaken and close to exhaustion. For a time, at least, some of them needed help even more than Gilkey, and the latter, still in his heavy wrappings, was left anchored to the slope by two ice-axes, so that Schoening and Craig could be free to attend to them. The injured men were brought up to the campsite. The tents were pitched, and they were made as comfortable as possible. Then, after about a half hour, Craig, with Bates and Streather, who had been the least seriously hurt in the fall, went back to get Gilkey.

He was gone. Wrappings, axes and all. On the white slope was only a smooth, shallow groove, left by an avalanche that had poured down and carried him away.

The subsequent night at Camp VII was a nightmare such as few men have ever had to endure. The ghost of Gilkey lay close beside them. Houston was semi-delirious, Molenaar in acute pain; and, most serious of all, Bell's hands and feet were found to be in an advanced stage of frostbite. But the next day, providentially, he was still able to walk. And Houston's head was somewhat clearer. If both had not made at least this partial recovery, it would have been the end for all of them, for the others could never have got them down the mountain. Indeed, they realized now, they could never have got Gilkey down either; and his loss, tragic though it was, had also, in a way, been a grim deliverance. Inevitably, he would have died anyhow before they succeeded in reaching base camp. And the others, more likely than not, would have been killed in the effort.

The next morning they continued the descent. Slowly. Painfully. Through the still-roaring wind. But it was not of wind or pain that they were thinking, but of one thing only: not to slip again. *Not to slip.* A thousand feet down they found one of the two axes that had been used to anchor Gilkey, and, near-by, a bag containing a pair of his glasses—unbroken. But of the body itself they saw no trace. That evening they reached Camp VI and were pinned down for thirty-six hours by a fresh storm. But on the day following they made Camp IV; on the next, Camp II, where they were met by the waiting Hunza porters. And at last, on August fifteenth, they staggered, worn and beaten, into base camp, after six days of descent and almost two full months on the upper mountain.

They had lost ten to twenty pounds apiece. All were exhausted and suffering from some form of injury. But only Bell's frostbite was serious. Like Herzog and Lachenal from Annapurna, he had to be carried out to civilization and on his return to America lost two of the toes on his left foot. "He will climb again," reported the expedition's final bulletin. And so will all of them—except Arthur Gilkey. "To climb the second highest mountain in the world," wrote Robert Bates, "is a challenge not many men would accept with eagerness, but to a special few it seems one of the most glorious goals on earth." To which Charles Houston added: "All of us feel the experience was so tremendous that we would do it all again if the opportunity presented, even knowing all that could happen."

This is how mountaineers are made. And how the world's great mountains are climbed.

13

EVEREST

1: *The Struggle*

At eleven-thirty on the morning of May 29, 1953, occurred one of the great moments in human history. High in the Himalayan sky, two men crept up a twisting ridge of snow, reached a rounded white hummock and stopped, because there was nowhere farther to go. They were standing on the crest of Mount Everest, summit of the world.

It was a moment of triumph. And more than triumph, of fulfilment. For the conquest of Everest was no stunt, no quick and showy splurge of derring-do, but the culmination of years of aspiration and struggle. Standing at last upon that ultimate white point, Edmund P. Hillary and Tenzing Bhotia knew better than anyone that they had climbed there on the shoulders of the ten expeditions and hundreds of men who had gone before them. And if there was pride in their hearts, there were humbleness and gratitude as well.

The story of Everest begins one hundred and one years earlier, in 1852, when a clerk in the office of the Indian Trigonometrical Survey looked up from a page of figures and announced to his superior: "Sir, I have discovered the highest mountain in the world!" A careful checking of his calculations proved him right. The remote Himalayan summit, listed on the charts as "Peak XV," was found to be 29,002 feet high—many hundreds of feet taller than its closest rival. Later observers corrected its altitude to 29,141 feet * and named it for Sir George Everest, first Surveyor-General of India. And what began as a prosaic exercise in higher mathematics was to become, as years passed, one of the great adventures of modern man.

For a half century after its discovery Everest was a mountain of mystery. Tibet and Nepal, on whose frontiers it rises, were both rigorously closed to outsiders, and, far from climbing it, men of the West were unable even to learn anything about it. All they knew were the tantalizing figures of the Trigonometrical Survey. All they could see was a remote pinnacle of rock and ice, one of thousands in the great sea of peaks to the north of the Indian plain. The mountain itself—its structure and appearance, its surroundings and approaches—was as unknown as if it stood upon another planet.

Then, in the late 1890's, the full tide of mountaineering interest and activity flowed toward the Himalayas. Soon a thin trickle of pioneers began to penetrate into the great passes and gorges where no white man had ever been before; adventurous spirits crossed the frontiers into forbidden territory, disguised as Hindu or Mohammedan traders; men like Freshfield, Kellas and Longstaff turned their attention from the Sikkim and Garhwal Ranges to the even greater peaks that lay beyond. Slowly the net closed in about the remote, secret place where rose the highest mountain in the world. Nepal, which offers the shortest route from northern India to Everest, continued its rigid closed-door policy; but a British military mission to Tibet, in 1904, succeeded in at least partially opening up that country, and it was therefore from this direction—the north—that all the early expeditions approached the peak. As early as 1913 it appeared that the way had been opened politically, and an exploring party was being organized by Freshfield. But the project was ended by the outbreak of the First World War, and it was not until seven years later that men were again able to turn their eyes toward the greatest mountain.

Then, in 1920, the Royal Geographical Society of London and the British Alpine Club joined forces to form the Mount Everest Committee and after prolonged negotiation secured permission for a series of expeditions to approach and, if possible, climb the peak. The first, in 1921, was designed only as an exploratory mission and was led by Colonel C. K. Howard-Bury, who had traveled widely in Tibet and knew it as

---

* See footnote on page 135.

well as any white man living. Next in command were Dr. Kellas, and A. F. R. Wollaston, who had won fame on Ruwenzori and many another far-flung range. Others were Harold Raeburn, a veteran Himalayan climber, Dr. A. M. Heron, a geologist, and Major Morshead and Captain Wheeler, army surveyors who had traveled among the great Asiatic peaks for years. To these mature and experienced hands were added two younger men with brilliant, if briefer, mountaineering records: G. H. Bullock, of the Consular Service, and George Leigh-Mallory, master at Charterhouse College, Cambridge.

It was Mallory who was to become the foremost of the early "Everesters" and the most famous mountaineer of his day. He was the only man to participate in all three of the great expeditions between 1921 and 1924, and although never the official leader (he was only thirty-eight when he died), his marvelous climbing accomplishments and flaming spirit made him the outstanding figure in every one of them. Everest became *his* mountain, as completely as the Matterhorn, sixty years before, had been Whymper's. His companions, to a man, believed that if any one of them was to achieve conquest of the highest summit on earth Mallory would be the one, and some of them, in later days, clung staunchly to the belief that he attained his goal before death overtook him in the clouds.

There was nothing of the conventional athlete about Mallory. Slight and slim, with a round boyish face, he was anything but the popular conception of a rugged outdoor man. Again as with Whymper, climbing was to him not exercise or amusement, but passionate devotion, and, as with all great mountaineers, less a physical than a spiritual adventure. His explanation of why men climb remains today the simplest, and at the same time perhaps the most profound, that has ever been given.

"But *why?*" he was once asked, as he set out for a renewed assault on Everest. "Why do you try to climb this mountain?"

Mallory's answer consisted of four words:

"Because it is there," he said.

"There," however, was a remote, unknown corner of the earth, and it required an arduous journey of many weeks before the Everesters of the 1921 reconnoitering party came even within sight of their goal. Beginning at Darjeeling in the middle of May their march carried them first through the tropical jungles of Sikkim, then up through great passes onto the desolate Tibetan plateau. In the straight line the distance from

Darjeeling to Everest is only a hundred miles, but they had to journey more than three hundred, threading their way among the great peaks and gorges of the eastern Himalayas.

These were days of toil and hardship, and they took their toll in sudden and tragic fashion. Dr. Kellas, whose health was no longer robust, strained his heart while crossing the high passes and died in the Tibetan village of Kampa Dzong. Soon after, Raeburn became seriously ill and had to return to India, with Wollaston accompanying him; and these two were not able to rejoin the expedition until the middle of the summer. Everest had begun to claim her victims even before they had had so much as a glimpse of her.

The others struggled on: only six white men now, at the head of a vast procession of Sherpa porters, Tibetan guides and helpers, ponies, donkeys, bullocks and yaks. Day after day they pushed northward and westward across as savage country as exists anywhere on the earth's surface—through sandstorms and glacial torrents, across vast boulder-strewn plains and passes twenty thousand feet above the sea. At night they camped under the stars or enjoyed the primitive hospitality of Buddhist monasteries and village headmen. Their passports from the Tibetan authorities in Lhasa assured them courteous treatment, but the announcement of the purpose of their journey elicited only a shaking of heads and a turning of prayer wheels. To these devout and superstitious orientals, Everest was more than a mountain. Chomolungma, they called it—Goddess-Mother-of-the-World. It was sacrilege, they believed, for mere mortals even to approach it.

At last, late in June, the expedition arrived at the Rongbuk Monastery, where an isolated colony of priests and hermits dwelt, some twenty miles north of Everest. And from here, at last, they saw their mountain head on, in its titanic majesty—the first white men ever to have a close-up view of the summit of the world. "We paused," wrote Mallory, "in sheer astonishment. The sight of it banished every thought; we asked no questions and made no comment but simply looked. . . . At the end of the valley and above the glacier Everest rises, not so much a peak as a prodigious mountain-mass. There is no complication for the eye. The highest of the world's mountains, it seems, has to make but a single gesture of magnificence to be the lord of all, vast in unchallenged and isolated supremacy. To the discerning eye other mountains are visible, giants between twenty-three and twenty-six thousand feet high. Not one of their slenderer heads even reaches their chief's shoulder; beside Everest they escape notice—such is the pre-eminence of the greatest."

The explorers set themselves at once to their tasks, reconnoitering, surveying, studying the colossal rock-and-ice mass that towered before them and probing the possible routes to its summit. They were already at an altitude of eighteen thousand feet—far higher than the highest summit in the Alps or Rockies—and the slightest exertion set their lungs to heaving and their hearts to pounding. The world around them was a trackless wilderness of peaks, ridges and glaciers, and wind and snow roared down from the heights with hurricane fury. And still there remained two vertical miles of mountain soaring above them into the sky.

Working slowly along its base, Mallory and Bullock discovered that Everest was constructed as an almost perfect pyramid, with three great faces and three main ridges sweeping downward from the summit like vast buttresses. The faces were all built up in tiers of precipices which no man could even dream of scaling, and the south and northwest ridges, miles in length and flanked by vertical ice-walls, appeared equally hopeless.

Climbing to a 20,000-foot pass called the Lho La, at the foot of the northwest ridge, Mallory and Bullock had an experience that, in the light of later events, was significant and ironic. For as they peered down its farther side they looked into a deep, snow-choked valley that was later to become famous in Everest history as the Western Cwm. Indeed, it was Mallory who then gave it this name—using the nomenclature of his favorite Welsh climbing grounds—but little did he realize, of course, that it would ultimately be the road to victory. "I do not fancy it would be possible," he wrote later, "even if one could get up the glacier." And besides, that section of the mountain lay in Nepalese territory and was therefore politically closed to them. Accordingly, he and Bullock turned their attention elsewhere, and no human eye saw the Western Cwm again for thirty years.

It was on the northeast that the 1921 party detected the best possibilities. Here, bordering the 10,000-foot wall of the north face, a jagged arête descended from a rocky shoulder near the summit to a high snow saddle on the east of the Rongbuk Glacier. The angle of the arête was steep, but not so steep that experienced mountaineers could not ascend it, and from the shoulder upward the main east ridge and the wedge-like summit pyramid seemed to present no insuperable obstacles. The first great question mark was whether a way could be found to reach the saddle.

A way was found, but the finding required two long months of planning and toil. The saddle—or North Col, as it came to be known—rose from the Rongbuk Glacier as an almost perpendicular ice-wall four thousand feet high, and even the dauntless Mallory doubted that it could be scaled from that side. His only hope was that the far, or eastern, side might prove more feasible. The next and greatest job was to get there.

The Rongbuk Glacier was a narrow avenue of ice walled in by mountains in which no break appeared to exist. Actually there was a break, and if Mallory had found it he would have been able to reach the far side of the col in a day or two. But it was so tiny and obscure a passage that he missed it. The result was a circuitous journey of more than a hundred miles, back across the plateaus and passes which they had traversed before, and then south and west again toward the base of Everest.

In the end, however, the explorers accomplished their purpose, reaching the top of a 22,000-foot pass called the Lhakpa La, from which they could see the eastern approach to the col. It was indeed as Mallory had hoped: the great saddle of snow and ice rose on this side to a height of only fifteen hundred feet above the glacier floor and appeared not impossible to scale. In that moment the hardships and frustrations of the past two months were suddenly forgotten, for they were confident that they had found the key to the mountain.

By this time it was late August, and the brief Himalayan summer was almost over. But the work of the expedition would not be done until they had reached the col, and so the three strongest climbers, Mallory, Bullock and Wheeler, pushed on over the Lhakpa La, down its far side and across the glacier below. On their way they made a second important discovery: that there was, after all, a passage from the Rongbuk Glacier to the eastern side of the col. It was of course too late now for it to be of any help to them that year, but the narrow defile was used by the subsequent Everest expeditions from the north.

Once found, the eastern wall of the North Col did not prove a particularly formidable obstacle—at least not in 1921. The outer surface of the wall was composed of frozen avalanche snow, and up it the three climbers hacked their way, slanting carefully to right and left to avoid the gaping blue abysses with which it was scarred. At noon on the twenty-fourth of August they stood upon the top, at an altitude of twenty-three thousand feet—higher than any mountaintop in the world outside of the Himalayas.

The pinnacle of Everest, however, was still six thousand feet above them and two and a half miles away. Scanning the northeast ridge, the shoulder and the summit pyramid, they saw that Mallory's earlier surmise had been right: the upper mountain slanted upward in a fairly easy gradient of rock and snow, seeming to present neither difficulty nor great danger. The temptation was strong to venture still higher, but they were almost done in from their exertions as it was and realized they could not hope to match their strength against the wild wind and blizzards of the heights. After taking as complete observations as they could they descended from the col, rejoined their companions on the Lhakpa La and began the long return journey to India.

The members of the 1921 expedition had never once actually set foot on Everest itself; their highest point on the North Col was where subsequent expeditions would begin their real work. Yet, except for the death of Dr. Kellas, the venture had been a complete and distinguished success. The trail to the mountain had been blazed, the weakness in its armor found. Everyone was agreed that, as far as actual climbing problems were concerned, the greatest mountain *might* be climbed. That "might" was all the Everesters needed. No sooner had the reconnaissance party returned to England than preparations for the real assault began.

On May 1, 1922, the first Mount Everest climbing expedition pitched its base camp within sight of the lamasery near the snout of the Rongbuk Glacier. It was composed of thirteen Englishmen, sixty hillmen from Nepal and northern India, a hundred-odd Tibetan helpers and more than three hundred pack animals—a veritable army in miniature. Remote and isolated Tibet had not witnessed such a sight in the thousands of years of its history.

In the preceding year the purpose had been to explore, reconnoiter and learn. Now, however, all else was to be subordinated to one great purpose: to reach the top of Everest. To this end, the personnel of the party had been almost completely changed, with only Mallory and Morshead remaining from the original group. The new leader was Brigadier-General Charles G. Bruce, a veteran of the British Army in

India and a far-ranging Himalayan explorer over a period of many years. Colonel E. T. Strutt, another noted mountaineer, was second in command, and Dr. T. E. Longstaff, although now too old for the highest climbing, was on hand to lend the benefit of his experience. The others included Lieutenant-Colonel E. F. Norton, Dr. T. Howard Somervell and Dr. Wakefield; Captains Geoffrey Bruce, George Finch and C. G. Morris; C. G. Crawford, of the India Civil Service; and, as official photographer, Captain John Noel. Of these, Norton, Somervell and Finch were climbers in the prime of their careers and were expected, together with Mallory, to make the final bid for the summit.

As we have repeatedly seen, the climbing of a great mountain is far more than a matter of putting one foot in front of the other and moving uphill. Indeed, in the case of a giant like Everest, climbing in itself may be said to be of merely secondary importance. Two-thirds of the 1922 expedition's battles had to be fought before a man set foot on the mountain proper.

First, there was the all-important problem of weather. No man, to be sure, could hope to prophesy the day-by-day variations of calm and storm in those wild Himalayan uplands, but the observations of the previous year had convinced everyone concerned that Everest was climbable, if at all, only during a very brief period of the year. Until early May the whole region was locked in savage, blizzard-driven winter; after the middle of June the eastern Himalayas received the full brunt of the Indian monsoon and remained through the summer a deathtrap of snow and sleet and rotten, melting ice. A period of only some six weeks intervened in which the climbers might hope for reasonably clear skies, a minimum of wind and at least a fighting chance for success. It was therefore not accident, but careful planning, that brought the 1922 expedition to the skirts of Everest on May first. Their next great task was to get onto the mountain itself as quickly as possible. The race with the monsoon was on.

For two weeks climbers and porters crept back and forth along the northern glaciers, transporting food, supplies and equipment. Mallory, in an analysis of the problems of Everest, had likened a climbing expedition to a ladder, in which the higher rungs were useless unless the rungs below were dependable and strong. It was these lower rungs which now had to be fashioned—a chain of camps, not more than an easy day's march apart, extending as high as human strength could take

them. Camp I was pitched between the Rongbuk and East Rongbuk
Glaciers, Camp II halfway up the East Rongbuk, and Camp III near its
head, close by the eastern wall of the North Col. The older and less
acclimatized members of the party were left behind to staff and maintain
communication between these lower stations, while the stronger climbers
and porters proceeded to the establishment of Camp IV on top of the
col.

This in itself was a feat more difficult than the ascent to the summit
of a lesser mountain. Mallory and Somervell led the way, chopping
countless steps in the glaring ice-cliffs, edging around bottomless, dark
crevasses and seracs vast as toppled buildings. The porters followed,
straining on the ropes, scarcely more than creeping under their loads.
It was on these early Everest expeditions that the Sherpas first proved
themselves as mountain men, and the Englishmen were unanimous in
declaring that, without them, they would have got nowhere. Unlike the
Tibetans, who refused even to approach Chomolungma, the haunted
mountain, these sturdy tribesmen climbed doggedly and cheerfully to
heights where no men had ever stood before and in 1924 achieved the
almost incredible feat of carrying packs and establishing a camp at an
altitude of more than twenty-seven thousand feet. "Tigers," the English
called them, and they richly deserved the name.

With a huddle of tiny green tents established on the col, the assault
on Everest proper was at last at hand. Mallory, Somervell, Norton and
Morshead were selected for the first attempt, and at dawn on May
twentieth, accompanied by a group of the strongest porters, they set out
for the untrodden heights. The cold was almost unendurable, the west
wind roared down upon them like an invisible avalanche, and their goal
was still a mile above them, remote and tantalizing in the sky. Hour
after hour the climbers toiled up the northeast ridge. The going underfoot was not technically difficult, but constant care was necessary to
guard against a slip on the steep, ice-coated slabs. The wind tore at them
relentlessly, and, worse yet, as they ascended it grew more difficult to
breathe. Later expeditions were to learn an important lesson from their
ordeal and allow more time for acclimatization before storming the almost oxygen-less heights.

They had hoped to pitch their highest camp close under the northeast
shoulder, but at twenty-five thousand feet cold and exhaustion forced a
halt. Sending their faithful Tigers down to Camp IV they pitched their

two tiny tents in as sheltered a spot as they could find and crawled into their sleeping bags. All night they lay there, while the wind howled and the mercury in their thermometer dropped to seven degrees above zero.

At first daylight they were moving upward again through thick mist and gusts of wind-blown snow. After an hour's climbing Morshead reached the limit of his endurance and had to turn back, but Mallory, Somervell and Norton still struggled on. Their progress consisted of fifteen or twenty minutes' slow, painful climbing, a long rest, another period of climbing, another rest. Before long their hands and feet grew numb and their mouths hung open, gasping for air. Even their minds and senses, they reported later, were affected by oxygen starvation: ambition, judgment and will disappeared, and they moved forward mechanically, like men in a trance.

By midafternoon they had reached a height of twenty-seven thousand feet. They had ascended two-thirds of the vertical distance between the North Col and the summit and were a full twenty-four hundred feet higher than any man had ever stood before. Physically they could have gone even farther, but to have done so at that late hour, without food or shelter, would have been suicidal. Too exhausted to feel disappointment, or any other emotion, they turned their backs on their goal and began the descent.

As it was they were lucky to return to their companions alive. At Camp V they found Morshead so crippled by frostbite that he had almost to be carried down to the col. Then, crossing a steep snow-slope lower down, one of them slipped, and the four were carried to the very brink of the precipitous north face before Mallory succeeded in jamming his ax into the snow and holding the rope fast. As a crowning misfortune, night overtook them before they reached the col, and it was past midnight when at last they groped their way into their tents.

The same day that the first attempt ended in failure, the second was launched. The climbers now were Finch, Geoffrey Bruce and Tejbir Bura, a Gurkha corporal who had proved himself a first-class mountaineer. Captain Noel ascended with them to the North Col camp, where he remained in reserve, and twelve porters set up a fifth camp for them at 25,500 feet—a full five hundred feet higher than where Mallory and his companions had bivouacked a few nights before. This headstart for the final push, added to the advantage that they were supplied with tanks of oxygen to aid their breathing, gave the second party high hopes of success.*

They were hopes, however, that were to be quickly shattered. No sooner had Finch, Bruce and Tejbir crawled into their tent for the night than a blizzard swooped upon the mountain. For more than twenty-four hours the wind shrieked, the snow drove down in an almost solid mass, and the climbers struggled desperately with ripping canvas and breaking guy-ropes. It was little less than a miracle that men, tent and all were not blown into the mile-deep gulfs below.

After two nights and a day the weather cleared, and the climbers made their delayed start in a still, frozen dawn. At twenty-six thousand feet Tejbir weakened and had to return to the tent, Finch and Bruce continuing. The oxygen which they carried spared them the particular form of torture their predecessors had endured, but this advantage was more than nullified by the thirty pounds of tank and apparatus which each carried on his back. Worse than this, Bruce's apparatus was almost the cause of his death, for, at an altitude of above 26,500 feet, something went wrong with it and the flow of oxygen stopped. Accustomed by then to artificial breathing, Bruce would have been able to live for only a few minutes without it. Finch, however, quickly connected Bruce's mouthpiece to his own tank, and between them they were able to make the necessary repairs.

Hoping to escape the full brunt of the wind, they left the northeast ridge a few hundred feet below the shoulder and headed diagonally upward across the smooth slabs and powdered snow of Everest's north face. They made remarkable progress and by midday had gained a point only half a mile from the summit and a scant nineteen hundred feet below it. But here they reached the end of their tether. Their bodies and brains were numb; their limbs were ceasing to function and their eyes to focus; each additional foot upward would probably be a foot that they could never return. They turned back defeated, like their companions before them, but in defeat they had set a new world's climbing record of 27,235 feet.

One more attempt the expedition of 1922 was to make. It was doomed to be the most short-lived and disastrous one that has ever been made against the king of mountains.

The dreaded monsoon came early that year, and already in the first

---

* This was the first time that oxygen was used in mountaineering.

days of June dark banks of clouds appeared above the mountains to the south and the snow fell in billowing drifts on the upper slopes of Everest. A final thrust, if it were to be made at all, must be made quickly.

The main base, at which the whole expedition now gathered, resembled a field hospital more than a mountaineers' camp; of the high climbers only Mallory and Somervell were fit for further work. Resolved on a last try, however, they again pushed up the glaciers and, with Crawford, Wakefield and a squad of porters helping, resumed the laborious task of packing supplies up to the North Col. A night of sub-zero temperature had apparently solidified the fresh snow on the great wall, and they had reason to believe the going would be comparatively easy.

Starting early one morning from Camp III, Mallory, Somervell, Crawford and fourteen heavily loaded porters began the ascent. The Englishmen were on one rope, cutting steps and leading the way; three roped groups of porters followed. All went well until they had reached a point some six hundred feet below the summit of the col. Then suddenly they were startled by a rumbling sound beneath them. An instant later there was a dull explosion, and the rampart of snow and ice to which they clung seemed to shudder along its entire face. An ocean of soft, billowing snow poured down upon them, knocked them from their feet and swept them away.

By great good fortune, Mallory, Somervell and Crawford were not in the direct path of the avalanche. Caught by its flank, they were carried down a distance of some fifty feet; but by striking out like swimmers they were at last able to struggle to the surface and gain a secure foothold. Not so the unfortunate porters. Struck by the full force of the snowslide, they were catapulted down the steep slope to the lip of a sheer ice-wall below. A moment before there had been a gaping crevasse beneath the wall; now it was filled by the avalanche. Hurtling over the brink, the porters plunged into the soft, hissing sea of snow, disappearing from sight one by one as thousands of more tons poured down after them.

Grim and heroic work was carried out on the ice-wall that day. Hour after hour the climbers floundered through the great drifts, burrowing, straining at ropes, expending their last reserve of strength to find and rescue the buried porters. One or two they found almost uninjured. A few more, who at first appeared dead from suffocation, they were able to revive. But seven were beyond help. To this day their bodies lie entombed in the snow and ice beneath the North Col, tragic victims of the wrath of Everest.

So the 1922 attack ended, not only in defeat but in disaster. Any further attempt on the peak that year was unthinkable, and it was a silent, saddened band of mountaineers who, a few days later, began the long trek across Tibet toward India and home. Behind them the summit of the greatest mountain loomed white and lonely in the sky, its snow-plume streaming in the wild west wind.

The curtain drops for two years on Chomolungma, Goddess-Mother-of-the-World. No attempt was launched in 1923, but the struggle was by no means at an end. The Mount Everest Committee continued with its work, and in late March of 1924 a third expedition set off from Darjeeling on the high, wild trail to the heart of the Himalayas. Before it returned it was destined to write one of the most famous chapters in the history of mountaineering.

Several of the old Everesters were back again: the indefatigable Mallory, of course; Somervell, Norton and Geoffrey Bruce; Noel with his cameras. General Bruce had been appointed leader, but early in the march through Tibet he was stricken with malaria and had to return to India while Norton carried on as first-in-command. New recruits included N. E. Odell, the geologist, who twelve years later was to reach the top of Nanda Devi; E. O. Shebbeare, of the Indian Forest Service, as transport officer; Major R. W. G. Hingston as physician; Beetham and Hazard, both experienced mountaineers, and Andrew Irvine, young and powerful Oxford oarsman. In addition to these were the usual retinue of native porters and helpers, among them many of the veteran Sherpas from the 1922 attempt. Almost three hundred men, all told, were in the party when at the end of April it set up its base camp beside the great moraines of the now familiar Rongbuk Glacier.

The preliminary moves of the campaign were carried out according to the same plan as before—but more methodically and rapidly. The first three advance camps were established a day's march apart on the glaciers, and within two weeks the advance guard was ready to tackle the North Col. The whole organization was functioning like an oiled machine; there were no accidents or illness, and the weather was fine.

According to their schedule they would be on the northeast ridge by the middle of May and have almost a full month for climbing before the arrival of the monsoon. Even the most skeptical among them, staring eagerly at the heights above, could not but believe that Everest at last was theirs.

This time, however, misfortune struck even before they reached the mountain.

Scarcely had Camp III been set up below the col than a blizzard swept down from the north, wrecking everything in its path, turning camps and communication lines into a shambles. The porters, many of them caught unprepared and without adequate clothing or shelter, suffered terribly from exposure and exhaustion. Two of them died. The climbers, who were supposed to be conserving their energies for the great effort higher up, wore themselves out in their efforts to save men and supplies. Two weeks after the vanguard had left the base camp, full of strength and optimism, they were back again where they started, frostbitten, battered and fagged out.

A major blow had been dealt their chances for success, but the Everesters pulled in their belts and went at it again. The porters' drooping spirits were raised by a blessing from the Holy Lama of the Rongbuk Monastery, and a few days later a second assault was begun. At the beginning all went well, and the three glacier camps were re-established and provisioned in short order. But trouble began again on the great ice-wall beneath the North Col. The storms and avalanches of two years had transformed its face into a wild, slanting chaos of cliffs and chasms. No vestige of their former route remained.

Then followed days of killing labor. Thousands of steps had to be chopped in the ice and snow. An almost perpendicular chimney, a hundred feet high, had to be negotiated. Ladders and ropes had to be installed so that the porters could come up with their loads. There were many narrow escapes from disaster, notably on one occasion when Mallory, descending the wall alone, plunged through a snow-bridge into a gaping hole beneath. Luckily his ice-ax jammed against the sides of the crevasse after he had fallen only ten feet, for below him was only blue-black space. As it was, his companions were all too far away to hear his shouts for help and he was barely able to claw his way upward to the surface snow and safety.

At last, however, the route up the wall was completed. The body of climbers retired to Camp III, at its foot, for a much-needed rest, leaving Hazard and twelve porters in the newly established camp on the col. During the night the mercury fell to twenty-four below zero, and at dawn a heavy snowfall began; but Geoffrey Bruce and Odell, nevertheless, decided to ascend to the col. They did not get far. Halfway up they encountered Hazard and eight of the porters coming down. They were near collapse after the night of frightful cold and wind on the exposed col. Worse yet, four of the porters were still up above, having refused to budge downward over the treacherous fresh snow of the chimney.

A sombre council of war ensued at Camp III. Snow and wind were now driving down the mountain in wild blasts, and it was obvious that the marooned men could not survive for long. All plans had to be set aside and every effort devoted to getting them down. Accordingly, Mallory, Norton and Somervell fought their way back up the ice-wall, coming out at last upon a steep snow-slope a short distance below the top and immediately above a gaping crevasse. At the top of the slope the porters huddled, half dead from exposure, but afraid to move. The snow between them and the rescuing party was loose and powdery, liable to crumble away at any moment.

At this point Somervell took the lead. Roping up, he crept toward the porters along the upper lip of the crevasse, while Mallory and Norton payed out behind him. But the rope's two hundred feet were not enough; when he had reached its end he was still ten yards short of the men. There was nothing for it but that they must risk the unbridged stretch on their own. After long persuasion two of them began edging across. And made it. Somervell passed them along the rope to Mallory and Norton. Then the other two started over, but at their first step the snow gave way and they began sliding toward the abyss below. Only a patch of solid snow saved them. They brought up at the very edge of the crevasse, gasping, shaken, unable to move an inch.

Now Somervell called into action all his superb talents as a mountaineer. He jammed his ice-ax into the snow and, untying the rope from his waist, passed it around the ax and strained it to its fullest length. Then he lowered himself down the slope until he was clinging to its last strands with one hand. With the other he reached out and, while the snow shuddered ominously underfoot, seized each porter in turn and hauled him up to safety. Within a few hours climbers and porters were back in Camp III, all of them still alive, but little more.

After this experience a few days' rest at lower altitudes was absolutely necessary, and for the second time in two weeks the Everesters found themselves driven back to base camp. Their situation could scarcely have been more discouraging. They had planned to be on the northeast ridge by the middle of May, and now it was already June and no man had yet set foot on the mountain proper. In another ten days, at most, the monsoon would blow in and all hope of success would be gone. They must strike hard and strike fast, or go down again to defeat.

Their plan called for an assault in continuous waves, each climbing party consisting of two men, each attempt to begin the day after the preceding one. The base of operations was to be Camp IV on the North Col. Camp V was to be set up on the ridge, near the site of the 1922 bivouac, and a sixth camp higher yet—as near to the summit as the porters could possibly take it. The climbers believed that the establishment of Camp VI was the key to the ascent, for the experiences of the previous expedition had convinced them that the top could be reached only if the final "dash" were reduced to not more than two thousand feet. In the first fine weather they had experienced in weeks the band of determined men struggled back up the glaciers.

Mallory and Geoffrey Bruce were chosen for the first attack. With Odell, Irvine and nine porters they reached the North Col safely, spent the night there, and the next morning struck out up the ridge, accompanied by eight of the Sherpas. Odell, Irvine and one helper remained on the col in support. The climbers made good progress the first day and set up their tents at 25,300 feet—a mere two hundred feet lower than the highest camp of 1922. A night of zero cold and shrieking wind, however, was too much for the porters, and the next morning no amount of persuasion would induce them to go higher. Seething with frustration, Mallory and Bruce were forced to descend with them.

Meanwhile, the second team of Norton and Somervell had started up from the col, according to plan. They passed the first party on its way down, reached Camp V and spent the night there. In the morning their porters, too, refused at first to go on, but after hours of urging three of them at last agreed to make a try. The work they subsequently did that day has seldom been matched anywhere for endurance, courage and loyalty. Step by gasping step they struggled upward with their packs—freezing, leaden-footed, choking for air—until at last Camp VI was pitched at an altitude of 26,800 feet. Their task completed, they then descended to the North Col, to be hailed as heroes by all below: Lhakpa Chede, Napoo Yishay and Semchumbi, greatest of all Tigers.

That night Norton and Somervell slept in a single tiny tent, higher than men had ever slept before. Their hearts now were pounding with more than mere physical strain. The long-dreamed-of summit loomed in the darkness only twenty-three hundred feet above them; victory was at last within their reach. Carefully, for the hundredth time, they reviewed their plans for the final day. There were two opinions in the expedition as to the best route to be followed. Mallory and some of the others were in favor of ascending straight to the northeast shoulder and then following the crest of the main east ridge to the base of the summit pyramid. Norton and Somervell, however, believed that by keeping a few hundred feet below the ridge they would not only find easier climbing, but also escape the full fury of the west wind; and it was this route that they now determined to take.

Dawn of the next day broke clear and still. By full sunrise they were on their way, creeping upward and to the west over steeply tilted, snow-powdered slabs. As they had hoped, they were protected from the wind, but the cold was bitter, and both men coughed and gasped in the thin, freezing air. They could take only a dozen steps in succession before pausing to rest. While moving, they were forced to take from four to ten breaths for each single step. Yet they kept going for five hours: to 27,000 feet—27,500—28,000—

At noon Somervell succumbed. His throat was a throbbing knot of pain and it was only by the most violent effort that he was able to breathe at all. Another few minutes of the ordeal would have been the end of him. Sinking down on a small ledge in a paroxysm of coughing, he gestured to his companion to go on alone.

With the last ounce of his strength Norton tried. An hour's climbing brought him to a great couloir, or gully, which cuts the upper slopes of Everest between the summit pyramid and the precipices of the north face below. The couloir was filled with soft, loose snow, and a slip would have meant a 10,000-foot plunge to the Rongbuk Glacier. Norton crossed it safely, but, clinging feebly to the ledges on the far side, he knew that the game was up. His head and heart were pounding as if any moment they might literally explode. In addition, he had begun to see double, and his leaden feet would no longer move where his will directed them. In his clouded consciousness he was just able to realize that to climb farther would be to die.

For a few moments Norton stood motionless. He was at an altitude of about 28,100 feet—higher than any man had ever stood before; so high that the greatest mountain range on earth, spreading endlessly to the horizon, seemed flattened out beneath him. Only a few yards above him began the culminating pyramid of Everest. To his aching eyes it seemed to present an easy slope—a mere thousand feet of almost snow-free slanting rock beckoning him upward to the shining goal. If only his body had possessed the strength of his will; if only he had been more than human—

Somehow Norton and Somervell got down the terrible slopes of Everest. By nine-thirty that night they were back in the North Col camp in the ministering hands of their companions, safe, but more dead than alive. Somervell was a seriously sick man. Norton was suffering the tortures of snow-blindness and did not regain his sight for several days. Both had given all they had.

Norton and Somervell's assault was the next-to-last in the adventure of 1924. One more was to come—and, with it, mystery and tragedy.

Bitterly chagrined at the failure of his first effort, Mallory was determined to have one last fling before the monsoon struck. Everest was *his* mountain, more than any other man's. He had pioneered the way to it and blazed the trail to its heights; his flaming spirit had been the principal driving force behind each assault; the conquest of the summit was the great dream of his life. His companions, watching him now, realized that he was preparing for his mightiest effort.

Mallory moved with characteristic speed. With young Andrew Irvine as partner he started upward from the col the day after Norton and Somervell descended. They spent the first night at Camp V and the second at Camp VI, at 26,800. Unlike Norton and Somervell, they planned to use oxygen on the final dash and to follow the crest of the northeast ridge instead of traversing the north face to the couloir. The ridge appeared to present more formidable climbing difficulties than the lower route, particularly near the base of the summit pyramid where it buckled upward in two great rock-towers which the Everesters called the First and Second Steps. Mallory, however, was all for the frontal attack and had frequently expressed the belief that the steps could be surmounted. The last Tigers descending that night from the highest camp to the col brought word that both climbers were in good condition and full of hope for success.

One man only was to have another glimpse of Mallory and Irvine.

On the morning of June eighth—the day set for the assault on the summit—Odell, the geologist, who had spent the night alone at Camp V, set out for VI with a rucksack of food. The day was as mild and windless as any the expedition had experienced, but a thin gray mist clung to the upper reaches of the mountain, and Odell could see little of what lay above him. Presently, however, he scaled the top of a small crag at about twenty-six thousand feet, and, standing there, he stopped and stared. For a moment the mist cleared. The whole summit ridge and final pyramid of Everest were unveiled, and high above him, on the very crest of the ridge, he saw two tiny figures outlined against the sky. They appeared to be at the base of one of the great steps, not more than seven or eight hundred feet below the final pinnacle. As Odell watched, the figures moved slowly upward. Then, as suddenly as it had parted, the mist closed in again, and they were gone.

The feats of endurance that Odell performed during the next forty-eight hours are unsurpassed by those of any mountaineer. That same day he went to Camp VI with his load of provisions, and then even higher, watching and waiting. But the mountaintop remained veiled in mist and there was no sign of the climbers returning. As night came on, he descended all the way to the col, only to start off again the following dawn. Camp V was empty. He spent a solitary night there in sub-zero cold and the next morning ascended again to Camp VI. It was empty too. With sinking heart he struggled upward for another thousand feet, searching and shouting, to the very limit of human endurance. The only answering sound was the deep moaning of the wind. The great peak above him loomed bleakly in the sky, wrapped in the loneliness and desolation of the ages. All hope was gone. Odell descended to the highest camp and signaled the tidings of tragedy to the watchers far below.

So ended the second attempt on Everest—and, with it, the lives of two brave men. The bodies of George Mallory and Andrew Irvine lie somewhere in the vast wilderness of rock and ice that guards the summit of the world. Where and how death overtook them no one knows.

And whether victory came before the end no one knows either. Our last glimpse of them is through Odell's eyes—two tiny specks against the sky, fighting upward.

For nine years after the 1924 assault no climbers approached Everest. Tibet again closed its gates to westerners, and it was not until 1933 that permission was once more granted for an expedition to try its luck. By this time most of the veterans of the previous attempts were too old for another ordeal on the mountain, but a capable team of younger men was assembled by the Mount Everest Committee. The new leader was Hugh Ruttledge, an experienced Himalayan climber. Among the others were Frank S. Smythe, Eric Shipton and Captain Birnie, whom we have met on Kamet, Kangchenjunga and elsewhere; Wyn Harris, L. R. Wager, J. L. Longland and T. A. Brocklebank—most of them still in their twenties, but all among the most capable mountaineers of their generation.

Following the traditional route, the 1933 party battled its way along the glaciers, up the ice-wall to the North Col, and established its higher camps close to the northeast ridge. From Camp VI, at 27,400 feet— six hundred feet above the highest previous bivouac—two successive assaults were made on the summit. The first, by Harris and Wager, carried across the brow of the north face to the far side of the great couloir and ended, with both men near collapse, at almost the identical spot at which Norton had turned back nine years before. The second, by Shipton and Smythe, got no farther. Shipton succumbed to the effects of altitude soon after leaving Camp VI, and was forced to descend, while Smythe, struggling on alone, reached the end of his endurance just beyond the couloir, as had the others before him. It seemed almost as if Everest were ringed by a magic wall a thousand feet beneath the summit, beyond which no man could venture and live.

A dramatic discovery was made by Harris and Wager an hour's climb above Camp VI. On the tilted slabs just below the summit ridge they came suddenly upon a solitary, rusted ice-ax. The name of the Swiss maker, still plainly stamped on its head, left no possibility of doubt as to how it had come there: it was either Mallory's or Irvine's. Some mountaineers have claimed this to be an indication that Mallory and Irvine reached the top. Odell, they argue, saw them at a point much farther along the ridge; neither climber, presumably, would have attempted to go on without his ax, and the logical supposition, therefore, is that it was dropped in an accident on the way down. Others merely shrug their shoulders. Whatever one chooses to believe, there is no proof. The ax is no more than a tantalizing hint at the fate of the lost climbers.

The 1933 Everesters were favored by no better weather than their predecessors. Immediately after Smythe and Shipton's attempt, the monsoon struck in a fury of blizzards and all further climbing was out of the question. The expedition had accomplished notable work and suffered not a single fatality or serious accident. But the world's climbing record was still some 28,100 feet, and Everest was still more than twenty-nine thousand feet high.

For many years men had looked longingly upward at the summit of the highest mountain. Now, in the same year as the third climbing expedition, they were to look *down* upon it.

Almost since the beginning of aviation airmen had been considering the possibilities of a flight over Everest, and in April of 1933 the first attempt was made. It was completely successful. Under the leadership of the Marquis of Clydesdale (later the Duke of Hamilton) and Air-Commodore Fellowes of the Royal Air Force two specially designed planes took off from Purnea, in northern India, and reached the peak in a mere hour. A down-current of wind almost crashed them against the slopes of the summit pyramid, but at the last moment they succeeded in gaining sufficient altitude to clear it. Then the weather improved, and they spent the next fifteen minutes circling the pinnacle, making observations and taking close-range photographs. In another hour they were safely back at their airport.

A remarkable flying achievement for the time, the flight was of importance to mountaineers chiefly in that it confirmed their belief that the topmost thousand feet of Everest did not present impossible climbing difficulties—provided a human being could reach them with any strength or breath left in his body. The highest pinnacle, viewed from above, was a gentle crest of white, wind-blown snow. No human relic could be seen.

The year 1934 saw only one short-lived attempt on the mountain—an attempt so foolhardy and hopeless that it appears less an actual climbing venture than an elaborate suicide. The would-be climber was Maurice Wilson, an English adventurer and mystic who had never been on a high peak in his life. Like the ill-fated Farmer on Kangchenjunga, he smuggled himself into the forbidden regions of the Himalayas, hired a handful of natives to pack his supplies and launched a one-man assault on the mountain. Somehow he succeeded in struggling up the glaciers, but cold and exhaustion caught up with him below the ice-cliffs of the North Col. His body was discovered and buried the following spring.

In 1935 and 1936 the real Everesters returned to the wars. Because of long delays in gaining the sanction of the Tibetan government only a reconnaissance was undertaken the first year,* but in late April of '36 a full-fledged climbing party was once more at the Rongbuk base camp, ready for battle. Ruttledge was again the leader, and the climbing personnel was virtually the same as in 1933.

The earlier expeditions had had bad luck with the weather; this one had no luck at all. Windstorms, blizzards and avalanches thundered down upon them from the first day on, and—final blow—the monsoon blew up from the south a full month earlier than expected. After a few hairbreadth escapes on the crumbling deathtrap of the North Col, the climbers were forced to withdraw without having even set foot on the mountain itself.

In 1938 came still another expedition—the seventh. The leadership had passed on to H. W. Tilman, of Nanda Devi fame, but several of the old guard were again on hand—notably Smythe, Shipton and the veteran Odell, now well on into middle age, yet back for another try after fourteen years. For a time, the venture was favored by slightly better weather than its predecessors. The North Col was reached in short order, the northeast ridge ascended, and Camp VI pitched at twenty-seven thousand feet. Beyond it, however, the climbers came up against the same invincible defenses that had defeated every previous effort; and with the same result. Two summit assaults were launched— the first by the old team of Smythe and Shipton, the second by Tilman and young Peter Lloyd, who had climbed with him on Nanda Devi. In each case, however, the climbers were turned back short of the final

---

* The 1935 expedition, however, performed many remarkable feats, among them the ascent of more peaks of over twenty-two thousand feet than had ever been climbed before.

pyramid by exhaustion, oncoming darkness and the slanting, snow-powdered slabs of the north face. Then, before they could reorganize their forces for still another try, the monsoon struck, putting an end to their hopes.

So stood the fight for Everest up to the time of the Second World War. Seven expeditions had come and challenged, struggled and failed. Many brave men, white and brown, had lost their lives. And the summit of the greatest mountain still soared into the sky, unconquered—perhaps unconquerable.

SUMMIT OF THE WORLD (I)

Mount Everest from the Rongbuk Glacier, to the north. All the early expeditions approached the mountain from this side, reaching it by way of the North Col, which is concealed behind the nearer peak on the left.

SHERPAS

Six members of the sturdy hill-tribe which has helped write the story of Himalayan mountaineering. Second from the left is Pasang Kikuli, who, in 1939, gave his life in trying to rescue an American climber on K2.

Photo by 1936 Nanda Devi expedition. Courtesy Dr. Charles S. Houston

14

EVEREST

2: The Victory

TWICE DURING the war years there was a roaring over Everest's summit that was not the breath of the west wind. In 1942 and again in 1945, planes, following the trail blazed in the 'thirties, passed close beside the mountaintop: the first piloted, solo, by an American airman, Colonel Robert L. Scott, Jr., the second carrying one British and one New Zealand officer of the Royal Air Force. Once more the shadow of wings touched the ultimate height. Cameras clicked. The R.A.F. fliers soared to within thirty feet of the summit. But they were no closer to *being there* than if they had been at the opposite end of the earth.

The first postwar climbing venture on Everest took place in 1947 and was another of those quixotic solo exploits such as Maurice Wilson had pursued to his death in 1934. This time the lone challenger was one Earl Denman, a Canadian resident of South Africa, and he was blessed with either better luck or better judgment than Wilson, for at least he returned from his sortie alive. Without political permission, and in disguise, he followed the old route from Darjeeling through Tibet, packed up the Rongbuk and East Rongbuk Glaciers, and presently made a try for the North Col. But he was poorly equipped, could not cope with the cold and altitude, and was forced back before reaching its crest. In retrospect, Denman's venture is noteworthy chiefly on two counts: his whole trip, Darjeeling to Darjeeling, was made in a

record time of five weeks; and one of the two Sherpas who accompanied him was none other than Tenzing Bhotia, who six years later
was to stand on Everest's summit.

As far as true expeditions are concerned, the Everest story had a
wartime and postwar intermission of three more years; and it was an
intermission that involved not only the passage of time, but a drastic
change of scene. For if the physical world remained as it had always
been, the political world had altered greatly. Tibet, which in earlier
days had provided the only route to the mountain, was again being
sealed off from the outside world—this time by the Chinese Communists. But Nepal, in a sort of rough counterbalance, was undergoing
pressures which made it somewhat less restrictive than before. The
road to earth's highest summit no longer led in from the north, but
from the south. And it is from this direction—almost as if it were another mountain—that Everest, in the past few years, has been challenged and at last conquered.

In 1950 no less than three expeditions were allowed to enter Nepal.
One was the French Annapurna party; the second a small British group,
led by H. W. Tilman and bent on general mountain exploration; the
third an equally small group that had permission to head north to
Everest. In terms of Everest history, the unusual feature of this expedition was that it was American, marking the first time that any westerners other than Englishmen were to have a close-up, non-aerial view
of the mountain. An informal party of only four members, including
the veteran Dr. Charles Houston, it was in no way equipped for an
actual climbing attempt, or even a thorough reconnaissance, but merely
hopeful that it could pioneer a way in to the southern base of the peak.
Starting out in the fall, it was presently joined by Tilman, who by
then was finished with his own explorations and was anxious to have
a look at his old antagonist from a new angle.

With a modest retinue of Sherpas and coolies the trail blazers worked
their way north and east across Nepal, following the ancient trade
routes that lead up across the Himalayas to Tibet. In sharp contrast to
the old Tibetan approach, their march lay through fertile and populous
regions: first in Nepal's great central valley and then up deep river-
canyons into the heart of the range. Along the way crowds met and
followed them curiously; for they were the first westerners ever to
enter this part of the country, and it was no more strange and unfamil-

iar to them than were they themselves to its inhabitants. To their surprise, however, they found that the English language had traveled
faster than its native speakers. At all the larger towns where they
stopped it was taught in the schools, and on one playground wall was
printed, in bold letters: *Gather courage; don't be a chicken-hearted
fellow.* Not a bad motto, the travelers thought—either for a schoolboy
or an Everester.

The trails steepened. The earth billowed upward. And after only
two weeks of marching (as against an average of six on the Darjeeling-
Tibet route) they were close in to their goal. Here, on the Dudh Kosi
River, that drains the southern slopes of Everest, they came to the outpost village of Namche Bazar and, a bit farther on, to an ancient lamasery called Thyangboche. This was the Rongbuk of the south, the last
human settlement on the trail, and beyond it the great peaks leapt skyward in a frozen wave. Everest itself, however, was barely visible, only
its very summit emerging from behind a vast 25,000-foot ridge that
joins its southern neighbor, Lhotse, with a second satellite-peak, called
Nuptse, to the west. And the first problem was to find a way to its base.

From Thyangboche, Houston and Tilman went on as a twosome,
accompanied only by four Sherpas.* At the outset they had entertained
the idea that Everest might be challenged by climbing the south wall
of the Lhotse-Nuptse ridge, but one close-up look at its monstrous
precipices was enough to dispell the notion. Accordingly, they skirted
the western flanks of Nuptse, bearing north, to investigate what lay on
its farther side. One thing that they knew lay there was the so-called
"Western Cwm," the mysterious and untrodden snow-basin beneath
Everest's southwest face that had been first seen and named by Mallory
in 1921. But how—or if—it could be reached was a question to which
no one yet knew the answer.

Their route took them up a steep valley called the Khumbu; then
across a dried lake bed and again up, over the tumbled moraines of the
Khumbu Glacier. Straight ahead of them, now, was the Lho La, the
20,000-foot pass from which Mallory, ascending from the far side,
had seen the Western Cwm. And on the right—or east—they could
see the upper glacier descending in a steep cascade of ice and snow

---

* It is interesting to note that, although northern Nepal is the home-country of
the Sherpas, all expeditions to the region have brought theirs with them from India.
Only the Sherpas who have migrated to the Darjeeling area have had training and experience as high-mountain porters.

through the narrow defile between Everest and Nuptse. This was obviously the entrance to the cwm; but the northwest buttress of Nuptse shut off the view of the upper icefall, and they still could not see if the entrance was passable.

Houston and Tilman were equipped for a trip of only six days out of Thyangboche. They were not able to conduct a thorough investigation, but merely what might be called a reconnaissance for a reconnaissance. Climbing to some nineteen thousand feet on the near-by peak of Pumori, they succeeded in getting a head-on look at the icefall, but they were not close enough to see the details of its structure. Nor were they able to see far into the cwm beyond, or anything at all of the huge slopes at the head of the cwm that led up to the high saddle between Everest and Lhotse. With a little information, and much tantalizing lack of it, the two men had to return to Thyangboche.

In general, they were not optimistic. On the credit side, the way they had pioneered was far shorter than the old Tibetan approach. And they were impressed by the autumn weather, which, though cold, was so dry and settled as to leave the upper reaches of Everest almost bare of snow. In terms of a practical climbing route, however, what little they had seen was discouraging, and Tilman in particular believed that the icefall and Western Cwm would present far more difficult going than the familiar North Col approach on the other side of the mountain. They therefore returned to the world with no blaring of anticipatory trumpets. If there was indeed a way to climb Everest from the southwest, it was a way that still remained to be found.

The following spring of 195⊸saw the third solo Everest attempt—by a Dane named R. B. Larsen—and though hopeless as far as reaching the top was concerned, it was a rather impressive exploit. As with the other lone adventurers before him, Larsen's journey was unauthorized and secret. But though he too started from Darjeeling, he avoided Tibet and traveled by a new route through Sikkim and eastern Nepal. Accompanied by several Sherpas, he then followed the Houston-Tilman route from Namche Bazar up toward the head of the Khumbu Glacier, but did not like the looks of the icefall and promptly retraced his steps. Then came the remarkable part of his venture; for, instead of giving up, he made a wide circuit to the northwest, crossed a 19,000-foot pass to the Tibetan plateau, and arrived in due time at the Rongbuk Mon-

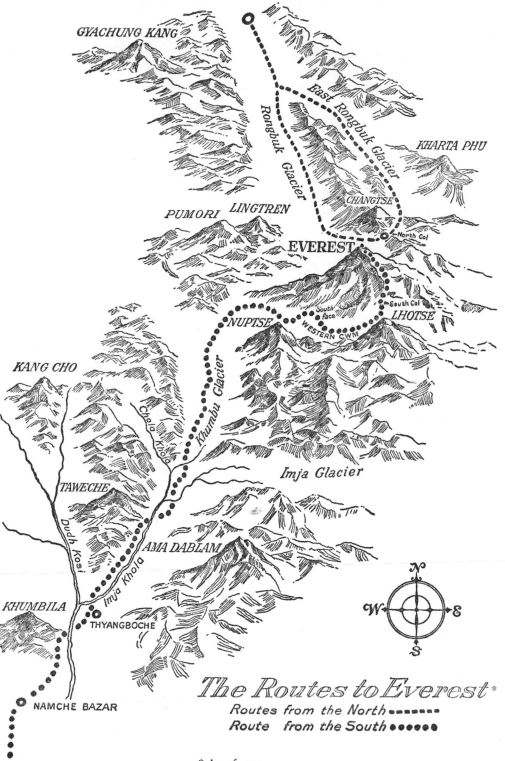

GYACHUNG KANG

East Rongbuk Glacier

Rongbuk Glacier

KHARTA PHU

PUMORI   LINGTREN

CHANGTSE

EVEREST

North Col

KANG CHO

Chola Khola

Khumbu Glacier

NUPTSE

South Face

WESTERN CWM

South Col

LHOTSE

TAWECHE

Dudh Kosi

Imja Glacier

AMA DABLAM

KHUMBILA

Imja Khola

THYANGBOCHE

N
W   E
S

The Routes to Everest
Routes from the North ------
Route   from the South ●●●●●

NAMCHE BAZAR

* As of 1953.

astery, thus becoming the first westerner ever to make the journey between the two opposite sides of Everest. From the East Rongbuk Glacier he attacked the North Col, and succeeded in reaching its top. But there his supplies began running low, his porters refused to go farther, and he was forced to turn back—the exploit ending with another remarkable semi-circuit of the mountain, back to Namche Bazar.

That was in April and May. In the fall of the same year the British returned with the first full-scale expedition since 1938. Tilman was missing, but his place as leader was taken by Eric Shipton, now back to Everest for the fifth time. The party included three other Englishmen—Tom Bourdillon, W. H. Murray and Dr. Michael Ward—and, for the first time, two New Zealanders—H. E. Riddiford and Edmund Hillary. They were prepared to climb high, if climbing proved feasible, but considered themselves primarily a reconnaissance expedition. And as it turned out, they were that and no more.

Passing through Namche Bazar and Thyangboche, they established their base camp beside the Khumbu Glacier and took up the job where Houston and Tilman had left off. Like these other two before them, Shipton and Hillary climbed one of the ridges of Pumori, seeking a view of the Western Cwm and the slopes beyond it. From their top altitude of nineteen thousand feet the earlier team had been able to form few definite impressions; but now the 1951 climbers reached a vantage point one thousand feet higher and were rewarded by a sight that filled them with hope. For from here they could see the whole sweep of the cwm, the west face of Lhotse that rose at its far end, and the high saddle, known as the South Col, that joined Lhotse to Everest. And nowhere did there seem to be insuperable obstacles. The cwm itself was an almost smooth plane of gently rising snow. From its head, the way, though steeper, appeared altogether feasible, offering "a perfectly straightforward route up the face of Lhotse to some 25,000 feet, whence it seemed a traverse could be made to the South Col." Once the floor of the cwm was reached, Shipton felt, a climbing party would have every chance of success.

But there was still the matter of penetrating the cwm, and on this score the outlook was far less promising. For its only entrance was up the great icefall that plunged some two thousand precipitous feet to the Khumbu Glacier, in a wild confusion of ridges and gullies, towers and chasms, that would obviously make the going not only difficult, but highly dangerous as well.

It was the icefall, though, or nothing; and accordingly the climbers pitched camp near its base and began working their way through the white wilderness above. The lower half proved less formidable than they had dared hope, and they made good progress. But the upper section was a far different proposition: an endless, trackless labyrinth of cliffs and crevasses, of huge ice-towers that threatened momentarily to collapse upon them, and soft, billowy drifts into which they sank to their waists. Their progress slowed; almost stopped. Then three of the climbers were caught in a minor avalanche and barely escaped disaster. Shipton—ever a cautious leader, to whom human lives were more important than victory—called a halt, and it was decided to wait a while to see if snow and ice conditions would improve.

For two weeks the party did exploratory work in the surrounding region; then returned to the icefall, only to find it worse than before. Nevertheless, they set to work doggedly, building a "staircase" of hacked steps and fixed ropes up the lower section and slowly threading their way higher into the maze above. "It was as if an earthquake had occurred," reported Shipton. "Over a wide area, stretching almost completely across the glacier, the cliffs and towers lay in a ruin of shattered ice-blocks. It reminded me of a bombed-out area in London during the war."

There was menace above in the toppling battlements, menace below in the snow-hidden chasms. At one point Hillary was in the lead, chopping a way through the ice-blocks, when a whole block tipped and plunged into a void beyond it. There was a deep roar, the whole surface on which the men stood began to shudder violently, and for a moment it seemed it would disintegrate entirely. Fortunately it did not. It held. And they were able to go on. But scarcely ever could they tell if they were on solid ice or simply on a thin crust above deep caverns of space.

There was another retreat; another upward push. Detouring, backtracking, zigzagging, they at last came almost to the top of the icefall, only to be confronted by a vast crevasse that split it across from side to side. There seems to have been a difference of opinion as to whether it could be crossed; but no attempt was made. The whole upper icefall impressed Shipton as too dangerous a proposition: not so much for the climbers themselves, who were reasonably mobile, as for the heavily

laden porters following in their tracks, who would have little chance
in the path of an avalanche or the sudden collapse of a snow-bridge.
A scant hundred feet or so short of the entrance to the Western Cwm,
the party turned back, leaving the rest of the trail blazing to those who
would follow them. The question of whether Everest could be climbed
from the southwest was still—a question.

Another year, another campaign. . .

But this was to be drastically different from any that preceded it.
For the political pressures that swung back the gates of Nepal had
opened them to many nations of the West, and now, for the first time,
a wholly non-British attempt was to be made on earth's highest mountain. 1952 was the year of the Swiss on Everest, and before they were
through they all but snatched the prize for which the English had been
struggling for thirty years.

For a time there had been talk of a joint venture, but national pride
and temperament on both sides caused the plan to fall through, and the
Swiss were left to go it alone. Organized in Geneva, the expedition—
or, rather, two expeditions, for there was one in the spring and another
in the fall—had almost wholly French-Swiss personnel; and from
within this category were chosen the best available climbers, both amateur and professional. For the first party the over-all leader was Dr.
Edouard Wyss-Dunant, the high-climbing leader René Dittert, and
there were seven others who were considered potentially capable of
reaching the summit, in addition to an expedition botanist and zoolo-
gist. Finally, of course, there were the indispensable Sherpas, led on
this occasion by Tenzing Bhotia, who was soon to make a spectacular
transition from hired porter to unexcelled climber. He alone was to
be a prime factor in all of the last three great expeditions to Everest,
and it is highly doubtful if the summit would yet have been reached if
it had not been for this little brown man of iron endurance and flaming
spirit.

Both in manpower and matériel, the Swiss were magnificently
equipped, and their siege of the heights was a model of mountaineering strategy. Starting from their first camp beside the Khumbu Glacier,
they worked their way up the great icefall, now following Shipton's
1951 route, now branching off on their own, as their judgment—and
the changes of the past year—dictated. Halfway up, they found a level,

ROCK ENGINEERING

Festooned with equipment, Fred Beckey, an expert American cragsman, performs a so-called tension climb in the Tumwater Canyon of Washington.
Note the rope, karabiner and piton which hold him to the overhanging rock.

Photo by Tom Miller

George Leigh-Mallory

Frank S. Smythe

Maurice Herzog

Sir John Hunt

MEN OF THE MOUNTAINS (II)

Portrait of Hunt is from the book "The Conquest of Everest." Copyright, 1953, by Sir John Hunt. Portraits of Hunt and Herzog printed by courtesy of E. P. Dutton & Co., Inc.

protected spot and established a second camp, so that climbers and porters would not already be worn out by the time they approached the more difficult upper section. And from here on, as had the British before them, they groped and hacked and twisted their way upward through the vast labyrinth of snow and ice. "The icefall was no mere inanimate obstacle," one of the men reported. "It was like some huge convulsed animal—a white prehistoric monster groaning and shuddering in its death throes."

But the snow-bridges held. The toppling towers did not fall on them. And at last they were almost at the top, facing the huge transverse crevasse that had stopped Shipton and his companions. There was no way around it: that was obvious. They tried swinging across, on a rope fastened to the lower rim, but neither ax nor crampon could find a hold in the smooth wall of the farther side. In the end, the bright particular hero was Jean-Jacques Asper, the youngest of all the climbers. At rope's end, while the others held him from above, he descended sixty feet into the maw of ice, manouvered from wall to wall across the narrower gulf below, and slowly worked his way up the almost-vertical pitches to the upper rim of the chasm. Once he was there, there was no further problem. Ropes were thrown across and secured. The other climbers and porters pulled themselves over. Within a few days, when the heavy loads began coming up, what had originally been a feat of great skill and daring was merely an oft-repeated routine operation.

Beyond the crevasse the Swiss were on new ground, moving up at last into the Western Cwm, where no man had ever stood before. The Valley of Silence, they called it—a still, ghostly corridor of sloping snow, with Lhotse monstrous at its head and the walls of Everest and Nuptse rising sheer on either side. It was four and a half miles long by two miles wide and rose in an easy gradient from some twenty thousand feet at the top of the icefall to 22,640 at the base of Lhotse. Other than scattered crevasses and ice-hummocks, which had to be avoided, it presented no climbing difficulties, and the three weeks the expedition spent there were a sort of entr'acte between the icefall campaign and the even sterner tests that were yet to come. This was the period of consolidating their position, of acclimatizing, of bringing up supplies. Camp III was established near the mouth of the cwm, Camp IV at about its mid-point, and V at the upper end, where the mountain walls leapt

skyward toward the high col between Lhotse and Everest. Some thirty-
two hundred vertical feet still separated them from this next great objective; but as they peered up their hearts beat high with optimism,
for they saw now with their own eyes that Shipton had been right:
there was indeed a straightforward and seemingly feasible route to the
heights.

They suffered, of course, from the ills that plague all Himalayan
ventures. Men fell sick; there were all manner of minor mishaps; the
wind lashed them; the cold gnawed at their bones. And always there
was the relentless pressure of time, pushing them on to the very limits
of endurance, so that they could be up and down the mountain before
the monsoon closed in with its lethal storms. Luckily, they were able
to respond to the pressure. No major storms materialized, and they
managed to hold to their schedule. By mid-May almost the whole party
was assembled in Camp V, at the foot of Lhotse's western face, and
the struggle for the South Col began in earnest.

From here on, Dittert was in charge of the day-to-day climbing operations, and under his direction the men worked in relays, slowly
probing their way up toward the frozen heights. The climbers had been
well chosen: all of them stood up under the ordeal. But one in particular now showed himself outstanding in strength and endurance.
This was Raymond Lambert, a thirty-eight-year-old professional guide
of long Alpine experience, whose performance was made even more
remarkable by the fact that he had long before lost, from frostbite, all
the toes of both his feet. More often than not, it was he, teamed with
the Sherpa Tenzing, who was out in the lead during the grim struggle
for the South Col, and it was gradually becoming apparent that, of all
of them, it was this pair who had the best chance of reaching the ultimate goal.

As always in the pioneering of a new route, there was much trial and
error. The ideal way, of course, would have been the most direct one
to the col; but mountains are rarely constructed according to men's
specifications, and constant reconnoitering was necessary. To the right,
to the left, back again, up again. Finally a great shallow gully, or
couloir, was selected as the best line of attack: first up over long sweeps
of snow and ice, then skirting a vast outcropping of bare rock that the
Swiss called the Epéron des Genevois, or Geneva Spur. As on the
northern side of Everest, the going was rarely difficult in a technical

sense. There was always a place for the next stance or hold—*if* the climber's strength was enough to reach it. For now they were reaching an altitude where every step was an effort, every exertion an agony. Hour by hour, foot by foot, they moved upward in slow motion: hacking their steps, installing fixed ropes, leading the porters, struggling always higher into the wind and the cold.

The two expeditions that followed them were to set up an intermediate camp between the Western Cwm and the South Col; but the first Swiss party had neither the time nor facilities, and the best they could do was to establish a sort of supply dump near the lower section of the Geneva Spur. Finally it was stocked. The route was ready. And on May twenty-fifth, after a three-day delay because of storm, the advance guard set out from Camp V to try the first complete ascent to the col. It consisted of Lambert, as deputy leader, René Aubert, Leon Flory, and Tenzing at the head of six other Sherpas.

They had hoped to make the whole climb in one day; but it was not to be. By nightfall, after some ten hours of labor, they were still struggling on the ice and rock of the Geneva Spur, and there they were forced to wait until morning. They were unable to make a proper camp —merely the flimsiest of bivouacs—and spent a freezing, sleepless night. Already, the previous afternoon, two of the porters had turned back, and with the coming of dawn the others, except for Tenzing, declared themselves unable to go on. So the three Swiss and the redoubtable Sherpa continued alone and, toward midmorning, reached the top of the spur. This, as it turned out, was somewhat to the south of the col, on the rising ridge of Lhotse, and, as a final punishing irony, they had to *descend* some five hundred feet to reach their objective. In the end, however, they made it and stood at last, the first of all men, on the southern threshhold of Everest's summit. Later that same day, Tenzing performed the remarkable feat of descending alone to their previous night's camping place and bringing up three of the porters to help in the establishment of Camp VI.

The South Col, at 25,850 feet, was a savagely desolate place—a bare sweep of ice pitted with small rocks and raked by the wild west wind. Above it, to the north, rose the last thirty-five hundred of Everest: close now—tantalizingly close—and yet appearing to the worn-out men almost as a second whole mountain standing on top of the mountain they had already climbed. Laboriously three tents were set up. Another mis-

erable night passed. It was the plan, the next morning, for all to go
on and pitch a final camp halfway up the summit ridge. But again the
porters were unable to continue, and Lambert, Aubert, Flory and Tenzing were once more on their own. Without the others, their try for the
top was virtually doomed before it began, for the four of them could
not hope to pack up enough equipment to establish an effective Camp
VII. Nevertheless, they carried what they could, including a single
tent, to set up at least the nucleus of a camp—if not for themselves,
then for the second assault party who would soon be following after
them.

From the level col the way led up moderately steep slopes of hard-
packed snow and then followed the line of Everest's southeast ridge.
For the most part, however, they did not stay on its crest, which was
too sheer and rocky, but worked out a route up a long gully that
roughly paralleled it. Here they were sometimes on rock, sometimes
on snow. The day was fine—in the full sun, the temperature almost
warm—and they were sheltered from the wind. On they went, on and
up through the hours, until toward midafternoon they had reached a
height of 27,560 feet. And here it was decided that at least a try
should be made for the top. Their single tent would not, of course,
accommodate four, but it would hold two; and the two who would use
it were Lambert and Tenzing. While Aubert and Flory descended to
the col, these two found a spot level enough for the tent, succeeded in
pitching it and prepared for still another sub-stratospheric night.

They had no stove, no sleeping bag and little food; and as soon as
the sun set it grew bitter cold. Sleep was out of the question, and the
night dragged on endlessly, while they thumped and rubbed themselves
to keep from freezing. At last, at six o'clock, it grew light, and they
were on their way again. Slowly—slowly—up the ridge. For a while
the climbing itself was easy; but the weather had deteriorated from the
previous day, and a weaving mist made it difficult for them to see where
they were going. Also, of course, at the height to which they had now
come, each step, each slightest movement, was an enormous effort. They
were carrying oxygen with them—three cylinders of it—but the apparatus required such manipulation that they could only use it while
standing still. They moved up three steps and stopped—three steps and
stopped.

Then the weather grew worse. The wind rose. Snow drove down.

Their pace grew slower and slower, and after five hours had passed they had gained less than five hundred feet above the high camp. Above them, through rents in the mist, they could see the ridge soaring on into space: perhaps another five hundred feet to the south summit of the mountain. The true and final summit was hidden behind it—still higher—but exactly how much higher no longer mattered. For now at last they were faced with the implacable fact that they could not make it. It was no one thing that made this so, but a combination of many things, and most of all, as Lambert later put it, that they had "reached some sort of physiological limit." Like the climbers on the other side of the mountain, years before, they had simply come to the end of their tether, and fortunately their minds were still clear enough to know it. At a height of some 28,250 feet, they called a halt to the hopeless effort and began the long descent back to the camp on the col.

Lambert and Tenzing had given all they had; Aubert and Flory only a little less. The next day they had to start down toward the lower camps, while Dittert led up the second assault party, consisting of four other climbers and five Sherpas. Unlike the first group, they succeeded in getting from Camp V to VI between one dawn and dusk. But once on the South Col, their luck left them, and they climbed no farther. Three days and three nights they stayed there, hoping for their chance. But several of the Swiss were now in bad condition. The porters could not and would not go on. The wind grew ever stronger, the cold deeper, and ominous monsoon clouds rose high on the southern horizon. Great as their effort had been, the game was now up, and on the fourth day they too began the descent of the mountain.

If ever an expedition won glory in defeat, however, it was this first Swiss venture of 1952. They had blazed a new route up eight thousand vertical feet of mountainside. Every man who had been rated as a high climber got as high as the South Col, and two to within a few hundred feet of earth's highest summit. There had been no fatalities, no serious accidents. It had been a signal achievement, and all that was missing was victory.

This time, not a year, but only a few months passed before the next attempt; for the Swiss had Nepalese permission for two expeditions in 1952, and the second took the field in October, as soon as the monsoon was over. The Everest region had often been visited and reconnoitered in the fall, but this marked the first time that an actual high-climbing attempt would be made at any season other than late spring. Though many imponderables were involved, the near-success of the earlier party made the Swiss hopeful of their chances. They were doomed, however, to bitter disappointment.

Only two members of the spring expedition returned: Dr. Gabriel Chevalley, who had been physician to the first group, as leader; and Raymond Lambert, eager for another try at the goal that had so narrowly eluded him. With them went five other men—four Swiss and one Swiss-American. This last was Norman Dyhrenfurth, son of the noted Himalayan explorer, who had long since been a United States citizen and thus became the first, and so far only, American actually to set foot on Everest. If the *sahib* personnel was largely different, however, the Sherpas were roughly the same group as before. And at their head, once again, was Tenzing, ready to team with Lambert for still another mighty effort.

For a while, all went well. The routes and hazards on the icefall were now familiar; fixed ropes put up in the spring were in many cases still usable, and a jointed aluminum ladder had been brought along to bridge the great crevasse. By the end of October the party had traversed the Western Cwm and were established in Camp V, at the foot of the west face of Lhotse. As they moved higher, however, the going became rougher. Though the weather held clear, it was colder and windier than in the spring. The hours of daylight were discouragingly brief. Then, with startling suddenness, tragedy struck—for the first time since 1924 in the campaigns for Everest.

One morning several of the climbers and Sherpas were at work on the ice-slopes above Camp V, hacking a way up the same steep couloir that had been used in the spring. At that time the route had proved itself safe from avalanches; but now, all at once, there was a roaring from above, and several huge blocks of ice came hurtling down on them. As it turned out, only one man was hit—Mingma Dorje, a veteran Sherpa. But he was hit badly. Several of his ribs were broken, one of them punctured a lung, and a few hours later he died. Then, as if this were not enough, there was a second accident within a few minutes of the first. Three other Sherpas, roped together and presumably shaken by what had just happened, lost their footing and went tumbling down the ice-slope for a distance of seven hundred feet. None of them, fortunately, was killed, but there were enough broken bones and bruises among them to incapacitate them for further work on the expedition.

The next day Mingma Dorje was buried in the Valley of Silence; the injured men were taken down to the lower camps; and that night a meeting was called of the remaining Sherpas to see if they were still willing to go on. The answer was a proud and stubborn yes, and accordingly the struggle for the South Col was resumed. The accident, however, brought about a change of route: no longer straight up the ice-chute toward the Geneva Spur, but following a wide detour to the right, up the seemingly safer slopes of the Lhotse Glacier. Because of the experience of the spring expedition, the fall party had from the beginning planned an intermediate camp between the cwm and the col; but now, with the lengthening of the climb, they established two of them. After long days of labor a new Camp VI was pitched halfway up the glacier, Camp VII near its head, at about 24,600 feet. From here, the way led almost horizontally back to the left, slanted across the ice-walls of the great couloir, and rejoined the old route near the top of the spur. Endless steps had to be hacked, hundreds of feet of rope affixed to the mountainside. But on November nineteenth ten men— Lambert, Ernest Reiss, Tenzing and seven porters—came out at last on the plateau of the South Col.

Once again the summit was near—and yet so far. For during their three weeks on the walls of Lhotse the weather had deteriorated steadily, and the col, once reached, proved an almost unendurable hell of wind and cold. They were barely able to pitch their tents on the site of the old Camp VI (now it was Camp VIII), and there they spent a freezing, sleepless night. In the morning they tried to go on: crossing the col and mounting the snow-slopes toward the summit ridge. But it was no go. Even while moving, and in their warmest clothing, they felt numbness spreading through their bodies. The roaring tide of air all but battered them to their knees. At a height of about 26,680 feet— a full fifteen hundred short of their spring record—they were fought to a standstill and had to turn back.

That was their first and last bid for the top. Fearful that they could not survive even one more night on the col, they continued down, that same day, to Camp VII, with climbers and porters alike on the verge of collapse. Around them, now, winter was closing in, murderous in its fury, and it was all they could do to get down to the cwm and the icefall, let alone resume the fight for the summit. Ruefully, the Swiss chose a word for what had befallen them. They had been "purged" from the mountain.

At roughly the same time—though the Swiss did not know it—another "purging" operation was in process on the far side of Everest. This was of the first Russian attempt on the summit of the earth.

For years it had been a standard joke among mountaineers that the Soviets would one day announce their conquest of the peak, to place on the trophy shelf beside their invention of the telephone and their discovery of antibiotics. But when they actually did make a try, no word of it reached the western world for almost a year thereafter. Even then, the news did not come from official Moscow sources, but filtered through Switzerland on the international grapevine; with the result that, to this day, few details are known. According to the reports, the expedition was a huge one, comprising no less than thirty-five climbers and five accompanying scientists, and was led by a Dr. Pavel Deshnolyan, reputed to be the foremost Russian mountaineer. The party made its attack by the old route from Rongbuk and the North Col and is said to have pitched its eighth camp near the northeast ridge at a height of some twenty-six thousand feet. Here, however, disaster struck, and six men, including Deshnolyan, were killed. According to the story, they were overwhelmed in an avalanche; but this is considered doubtful by old Everesters, who point out that the upper northeast slopes of the mountain have at all times been free from this particular type of danger.

Perhaps the whole story will come out in time. All we know now is that a Russian attempt was indeed made in the late months of 1952, and that their "purging" was a far more drastic affair than that of the Swiss.

Then came 1953. . .
And victory.
As all the world knows, it was the British again: back for the ninth time. And, win or lose, it appeared from the beginning that it might well be their last; for the Swiss had already staked their claim for a new try in 1954, and the French were making plans for '55. What further attempts the Russians might be contemplating was, of course,

a mystery. But, with or without them, the competition for the prize had become wide open, and it seemed inconceivable that Everest could continue much longer to withstand attack after attack. For the English, in 1953, it was almost a matter of now or never.

Accordingly, they made a supreme effort, putting everything they had into it, both in manpower and matériel; and though the end result was brilliant success, it was mixed, in retrospect, with a certain irony. This was the elimination from the party of Eric Shipton, who was originally—and logically—to have been its leader. For Shipton, throughout his long climbing career, had always been a partisan of the small, light-weight expedition, and over this he now found himself in strong disagreement with the other organizers of the venture. The upshot, in the fall of 1952, was that he stepped out, and his place was taken by Colonel John Hunt of the British Army. Hunt had never been to Everest, but, at the age of forty two, he had had wide experience both as a mountaineer and a leader of men, and, unlike Shipton, he was in favor of the largest and most powerfully geared expedition that could be put in the field.

Under him, as the project took shape, were thirteen men: George Band, Thomas Bourdillon, Dr. Charles Evans, Alfred Gregory, Edmund Hillary, George Lowe, Wilfrid Noyce, Dr. Griffith Pugh, Thomas Stobart, Dr. Michael Ward, Michael Westmacott, Major Charles Wylie —and, last but scarcely least, Tenzing the Sherpa, no longer ranked merely as *sirdar,* or headman, of the porters, but as a full-fledged expedition member. Of the others, two—Hillary and Lowe—were New Zealanders, and the rest English. Three—Hillary, Bourdillon and Ward —had been on the 1951 reconnaissance expedition, and the first two of these, plus four others, on Shipton's 1952 venture to the near-by peak of Cho Oyu. Professionally, there were among them two army officers (including Hunt), three physicians, three scientists in various fields, two schoolmasters, a travel agent, a photographer and—in the person of Hillary—a professional beekeeper. Ranging in age from forty-three to twenty-four, they were the strongest team of mountaineers and specialists that a fine-toothed comb could produce from the Commonwealth.

The approach to the heights followed the pattern set by the earlier parties. Up the Khumbu Glacier—the icefall—the Western Cwm. But their schedule allowed them three full weeks for practice climbs and general conditioning, with the result that they became more thoroughly acclimated than any Everesters had ever been before. In general, they used the Swiss routes and campsites—for which they later made grateful acknowledgment—and by the end of April were established in full strength at their fifth camp, below the great western face of Lhotse. Not only the porters, but the climbers as well, did a great deal of moving back and forth between here and the lower camps, both to carry the loads and to help bring themselves to peak condition. During this stage of the operations, Hillary and Tenzing, working as a team, once climbed from the Khumbu Glacier to the advance base and back in a single day—foreshadowing their feats of strength and endurance that were still to come.

Above Camp V, the British followed the route up the Lhotse Glacier that the second Swiss party had used after their accident. Working in relays, they hacked steps, strung fixed ropes and led the porters up for the establishment of the higher camps. All told, there were thirty-four Sherpas with the expedition (as distinguished from the hundreds of non-climbing coolies who had helped in the approach to the mountain), and, of these, twenty had been chosen for the hardest going beyond the Western Cwm. Almost all were veterans of the earlier expeditions, and their experience paid off in better porterage than any Everest party had enjoyed before.

Originally, only one camp had been planned between No. V and the South Col. But it was soon found that a second was necessary, if the men were to arrive on the col in shape to do anything more than collapse into their tents. Communication between the spread-out groups was maintained by portable radio-telephone, and, in spite of the inevitable storms and minor mishaps, their advance proceeded much according to schedule. The expedition was more plentifully supplied with oxygen than any of its predecessors, and, although they were not yet at an altitude where it was essential, it was often used experimentally by the climbers who were expected to go highest. There were two types of apparatus: one the so-called "closed-circuit," with which the user breathed oxygen only; the other the "open-circuit," in which the oxygen was mixed with the surrounding air. No one was yet certain which would prove the better; but both had a great advantage over the Swiss apparatus, in that they could be used while the climbers were actually in motion.

On May twenty-first, after three weeks of toil on the Lhotse face, the South Col was attained. First to reach it was Wilfrid Noyce, in company with a single Sherpa, and the sight they saw, as they came up over the crest of the Geneva Spur, must surely have been one of the most desolate and eerie in the world. For before them, in that wilderness of rock and ice, stood a tent—the skeleton of a tent—a gaunt, leaning pole and a few shreds of yellow canvas: the ghost of the Swiss Camp VIII of the previous year. But it was not long to remain so. The next day no less than twelve porters went up, the day after still more, and soon a new and living Camp VIII had taken shape on the wind-swept plateau. All the labors of the past weeks—grueling though they had been—receded into the background as mere preliminaries. Here, at 25,850 feet, was the base from which the final effort would be launched. And now, at last, all the complex activities and functions of the expedition were drawn together and directed to one single mighty purpose: to get a living human being to the top of Everest.

Following the traditional Himalayan practice, Colonel Hunt selected two summit teams of two men each. One, consisting of Tom Bourdillon and Charles Evans, was to make the first try direct from the South Col, using the closed-circuit oxygen apparatus. But though "first" in point of time, they were not the pair on which the highest hopes were placed, for the thirty-three hundred feet from col to summit seemed too much for mortal men to make in a single day of climbing. Their venture was given the name of reconnaissance-assault. They would go as far as they could; farther than Lambert, it was hoped; as far, if it was humanly possible, as the so-called south summit of Everest, a promontory on the sky-line ridge some five hundred feet below the final crest. This lesser peak shut off from below the approach to the true summit, and it would be the essential job of Bourdillon and Evans to reach the base of this approach and reconnoiter its problems and hazards. If they could go on to the top themselves—all right, so much the better. But it was not expected of them; and if they could not make it they were to descend to the col, and the lead would be taken over by the "second" team of Hillary and Tenzing. For them, a higher camp would be pitched, as far up the summit ridge as men could carry it. And from there, using open-circuit oxygen, they would make their try— *the try*—for the top. If this failed, the expedition might or might not be able to mount still another attack. But as far as current plans went, theirs would be the supreme and ultimate effort.

On the morning of May twenty-sixth, after a day's rest at Camp VIII, Bourdillon and Evans set off for the heights. With them went Colonel Hunt and one Sherpa, Da Namgyal, carrying a tent, food and fuel for the proposed Camp IX that would—probably—be used later by Hillary and Tenzing. At the very beginning two things went wrong. A second Sherpa who was to have accompanied them was sick and could not go, which of course meant heavier loads for the others; and Evans was having much trouble with the frozen valves of his oxygen set. But in spite of this they made steady, if slow progress: across the slopes of the col—up the steep snow-couloir that led to the southeast ridge —finally onto the ridge itself, where they passed the tattered remains of the highest Swiss tent. By this time, Bourdillon and Evans, who were less heavily laden than the others, were well in the lead. Hunt and Da Namgyal struggled on under their burdens and deposited them at a height of about 27,350 feet—not as high as the leader had hoped to go, but to the very limit of their strength. If the two men above them did not make the top, it would remain for the Hillary-Tenzing support party to carry Camp IX still farther.

Meanwhile, Bourdillon and Evans crept up toward the south peak. Following its usual pattern, the weather, fine in the early morning, worsened as the day advanced, and soon they were moving through gray clouds and squalls of snow. Evans was still having trouble with his oxygen, resulting in many stops for adjustment and the consequent loss of precious time. But the going underfoot was not too bad, and at last they came out upon the south summit, at 28,720 feet, and looked beyond it at what no human eyes had ever seen before. What they saw was not encouraging. The last few hundred feet of Everest soared up in a steep and savage pinnacle of rock and ice: climbable, perhaps; but not, they realized bitterly, for them. They might have made it—yes. But their strength would then be gone; their oxygen would be used up; darkness would close in. And death. On that day they had climbed the highest of all men. They had reached the south summit and seen the goal beyond. And that would have to suffice. As it was, they were so close to exhaustion that they suffered several slips on the way down and only narrowly missed disaster.

This had been the first challenge. The second was now to come. . . .

While Bourdillon and Evans descended to the col, Hillary and Tenzing moved up to it from the lower camps, and with them, as their support team, came Alfred Gregory, George Lowe and a young porter named Ang Nima. The New Zealander and the head-Sherpa had long since been picked by Hunt as the pair "most likely to succeed." During the weeks of labor on the lower mountain they had been kept largely in reserve: acclimatizing slowly, doing enough work to make them hard and fit, but never so much as might wear them out before the final assault was at hand. And now they were as ready as men could be for the great effort that lay before them. Hillary, at thirty-four, was at the very height of his powers as a mountaineer. Tall, rangy, habitually relaxed both in body and temperament, he had proved himself the best snow-and-ice climber on the expedition, and—even more important— was possessed of a sheer dogged endurance that seemed at times to approach the superhuman. Beside him, the slight wiry Tenzing appeared little more than a boy; but actually, at thirty-nine, he was the older of the two and, in experience, the senior Everester of them all.* By birth a simple oriental peasant, and unable to read or write, he knew little of the technical and scientific aspects of mountaineering. But what he lacked in training he more than made up for in strength and spirit. Alone among the men of his race, he had shown himself not only willing but eager—burningly eager—to climb to the heights; Everest was his dream, no less than of the *sahibs* whom he served; and, as he had pulled himself up from the rank and file of his fellows, so did it seem equally possible that he could raise himself, too, to that ultimate eminence. If not by legs and lungs alone, then by the very power of his desire and will.

Their companions knew that in both Edmund Hillary and Tenzing Bhotia lay the spark of greatness. Now it remained to be seen if it would kindle into flame.

At Camp VIII, on the night of May twenty-sixth, the exhausted Bourdillon and Evans told the second party what they had experienced and seen. It was the plan for the latter to be on their way the following morning, but a great wind blew in, shrieking, across the col and held them pinned in the tents for another twenty-four hours. When the next day dawned, clear and fairly calm, they started off. Hillary and Tenzing for the all-out challenge; Gregory, Lowe (Hillary's fellow-New Zea-

* For an outline of Tenzing's career, see Appendix II.

lander) and Ang Nima to pitch Camp IX as high as was humanly possible. All were using the open-circuit oxygen equipment, and each man carried on his back a weight of from forty to fifty pounds.

The route was the same as before: from the col to the snow-couloir; up the couloir to the ridge; up the ridge, past the old Swiss tent, to where Hunt and Da Namgyal had left their share of the Camp IX matériel. Now this was added to their burdens, making individual loads of up to sixty pounds, and their progress became necessarily slower. Little was left of the tracks made by their predecessors, and for much of the time Lowe and Gregory led the way, to spare the summit team the extra exertion of hacking steps in the snow. Thus hour followed hour. And by early afternoon all were tiring fast. Peering ahead for a possible campsite, they saw only the unrelieved steepness of the ridge; but at last Tenzing, remembering the ground from his climb with Lambert, suggested a traverse off the ridge to the left, and there they found a tiny almost level area in the lee of a cliff. This, at 27,900 feet, was to be the site of Camp IX, the highest habitation that men have ever built.

The support-team, their job well accomplished, dumped their loads and began the descent to the col, while Hillary and Tenzing set about the grueling work of clearing a platform and pitching their tent. At last it was done, and there they spent the long hours of dusk and darkness: checking their equipment, eating sparingly and drinking huge quantities of soup and lemon juice, sometimes holding for dear life to the sheltering canvas as it trembled and swayed in the gusts of wind. But theirs was not the ordeal that Lambert and Tenzing had suffered the year before. They were better equipped. The wind and cold were less savage. Once in their sleeping bags, they were almost comfortable, and with the aid of oxygen they were even able to doze.

It was well that it was thus, or the story that followed might have been a different one.

At four o'clock on the morning of May twenty-ninth Hillary opened the flap and peered from the tent—and this moment, rather than any that followed, may well have been the crucial one of that epic day. For the weather was clear, windless, perfect. Very slowly, so as not to exhaust themselves before they started, they set about their final preparations. Tenzing brewed up hot drinks, and Hillary adjusted the vital oxygen sets that would comprise almost their entire load from this point on. Thirty pounds each they weighed—a cruel burden at such an altitude; but burden or not, they were life itself. Finally, at six-thirty, Hillary and Tenzing were ready to go. They strapped crampons on to their boots. Over their down clothing went outer windproof jackets, and on to their hands they pulled three pairs of gloves: silk, woolen and windproof. Then they left the tent, roped up and started off.

For a while Tenzing went first, kicking steps in the soft snow that sloped up from their campsite to the southeast ridge. On the ridge itself, Hillary took over the lead, sometimes following its knife-edged crest, sometimes seeking firmer footing on the snow just below it. The sun was well up now, the sky pure and cloudless, and the mountain gleamed so dazzlingly that without their goggles it would have struck them blind. For an hour they plodded on. And another. Then the ridge dipped into a small hollow, and there they found the last, highest trace of their predecessors: two cylinders of oxygen left for them by Bourdillon and Evans. Scraping the ice from the gauges, Hillary saw that they still contained several litres—enough to get them down from this point to the col and to permit them to use up their own supply on the heights above.

Now, as they moved on again, the ridge steepened into a great snow-face, leading up to the south summit. Here, for the first time, the going was definitely dangerous, for the snow was loose and unstable, and a single false step would have plunged them into the abyss on one side or the other. Bourdillon and Evans had already preceded them here. But no vestige of tracks remained in the smooth whiteness, and they had to kick and hack their own steps as they cautiously zigzagged upward. It was nine o'clock when they reached the top and stood on the dome of the south summit, looking up at the final virgin stretch ahead. Their predecessors had described it as formidable, and that it was: a savage thrust of rock and ice clamped like a fang against the blue-black sky. "It was certainly impressive," reported Hillary, who was no hand for exaggeration—"and even rather frightening."

But it was this way or no way, and slowly the two men attacked the last four hundred feet of the mountaintop. It was still a ridge—the same ridge—on which they were climbing, but far steeper and more precarious than it had been below. On their left—the west—black precipices fell sheer to the distant cwm and icefall; and on the right, projecting out over twelve thousand feet of space, were wind-carved cornices of ice and snow that might crumble and fall at the slightest

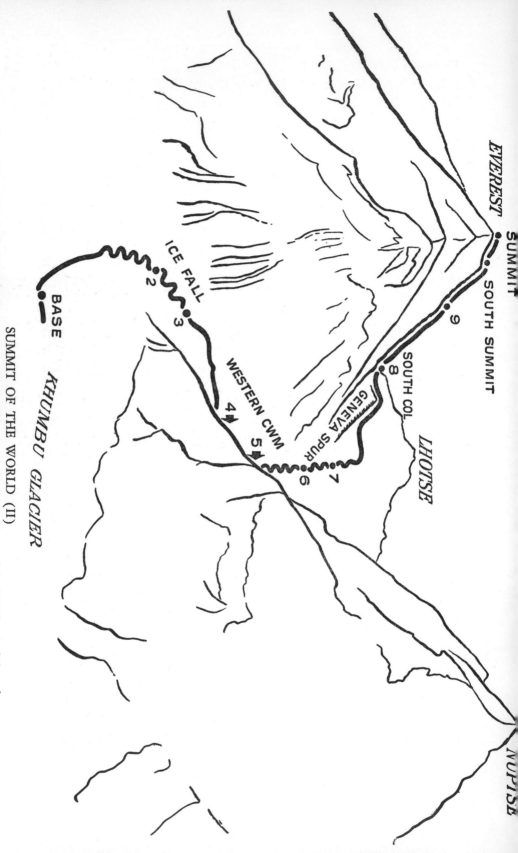

SUMMIT OF THE WORLD (II)

Everest from the southwest, and the route to victory. The camps shown are those of the British expedition of 1953.

Photo copyright by the Swiss Foundation for Alpine Research

ULTIMA THULE
The final stretch of Everest's southeast ridge, up which Hillary and Tenzing climbed to the top. This photograph was taken from the South Summit at a height of about 28,700 feet.

From the book "The Conquest of Everest." Copyright, 1953, by Sir John Hunt. Published by E. P. Dutton & Co., Inc.

pressure. Luckily, however, there was a middle route that proved feasible: a slanting, narrow catwalk between precipice and cornice that was composed of firm, hard snow. And it was up this that they now doggedly crept onward.

They moved one at a time: Hillary going first and cutting perhaps forty steps, and then stopping to rest and belay the rope while Tenzing came up after him. Again the manouver was repeated. And again and again. Sometimes great shoulders of the cornices blocked their way, and they had to slant off to the left—so close to the western precipice that their feet rested on its topmost rocks. But always they were able, in the end, to work back to the ridge and the sound snow. At this stage of the climb came a moment they had been eagerly anticipating. Each of them had been carrying two cylinders of oxygen, and now, almost simultaneously, their first cylinders ran out, and they were able to discard them, thus lightening their loads by a half. A bit farther on, both were bothered by the formation of ice in their breathing tubes, but they were able to clear them out and continued their progress.

After an hour of continuous step-cutting they came to the most formidable obstacle on the ridge: a vertical cliff of rock, forty feet high. They had seen this cliff, through binoculars, all the way from the distant Thyangboche Monastery, and there had been much speculation even then as to whether it might prove impassable. Now, seen from close up, it was a thing to chill the blood. The wall of rock itself was smooth and holdless. To the left was space. To the right a cornice— and space. But to the right, too, was the one possible route of ascent: a narrow crack running up the full height of the cliff between the cornice and the rock. For a long time Hillary studied it grimly from below. Then he made the effort of a lifetime. Wedging himself as far into the crack as he could, he strained and clawed upward for the tiniest holds, meanwhile kicking backward with his cramponed boots against the wall of the cornice behind him. At any moment he expected the wall to give, the hard-packed snow to crumble and fall from the mountainside—and himself with it.

But the wall held. His crampons grated upward. Foot by foot, he pushed and pulled and levered himself on, until at last he was able to get a hand over the rim of the cliff and wriggle up to its level summit. For a few moments he lay where he was, too done in to move. Then, his strength returning, he belayed the rope while Tenzing came up after him; and in ten minutes the Sherpa, too, was on top, collapsing on the rocks, as Hillary described it later, "like a giant fish that had just been hauled from the sea after a terrible struggle."

Thus these two indomitable men passed the last barrier of Everest's defenses. Even on an ordinary mountain, the climbing of that vertical pitch would have been no mean achievement. At a height of twenty-nine thousand feet it was all but miraculous.

The struggle behind them had been a thing of the grimmest reality. What followed now had more the form and texture of a dream. From the top of the cliff the ridge continued as before: the cornices on the right, the great precipice on the left. They went on cutting steps. They moved up into the steps. The ridge was now curving to the right, rising in a series of white hummocks, and as they worked their way around one, another appeared ahead. Then another and another. Always farther; always higher. The ax rose and fell, and the soft crunch as it struck the snow was the only sound in an immensity of stillness. They were tiring fast now and moving very slowly. "As I chipped steps around still another corner," Hillary recounted later, "I wondered, rather dully, just how long we could keep it up. And then I realized that the ridge ahead, instead of still rising, now dropped sharply away, and far below I could see the East Rongbuk Glacier. I looked upwards, to see a narrow snow ridge running up to a sharp summit. . . ."

A few moments later—at eleven-thirty in the morning on May 29, 1953—two men stood at last on earth's ultimate height.

Foolish people have since asked, "Who was in the lead? Who was first on top?" If they expected an answer, they do not know much about mountaineers—or about the human spirit when it rises to greatness. Edmund Hillary and Tenzing Bhotia were *together* on top—together in victory—together, grinning through their goggles and masks, clasping hands, thumping each other until forced to stop for lack of breath. "My initial feelings," said Hillary, "were of relief. Relief that there were no more steps to cut, no more ridges to traverse, and no more humps to tantalize us with hopes of success." For success was now theirs—success in the richest measure that has ever been given to men upon a mountain. And if relief was quickly followed by joy and pride, these were followed, in turn, by humility and gratitude.

Why climb Everest? . . . "Because it is there," said Mallory. . . . And now *they* were there: in the place of dreams, of hope, of aspiration.

The moments passed, as they stood silent and motionless on that crest of snow. Beneath them the world stretched endlessly to the horizon: range upon range of towering mountains, appearing now as no more than foothills; so remote and unreal that the two men seemed to be viewing them not from the same earth at all, but from a fabulous island in the sky. On that island they were alone—as alone as human beings can be on the surface of our planet. And at the same time not alone, for no two men by themselves could have been standing where they now stood. As surely as if they could have reached out and touched them, Bourdillon and Evans were there by their side. Hunt was there too, and all their other companions, far below, who had struggled as hard, and sacrificed more, for the common purpose. Mallory, of the flaming spirit, was there; and young Sandy Irvine. Norton and Somervell, Smythe and Tilman, Shipton and Lambert—the whole company of Everesters, white and brown, alive and dead—all of them were there, joined together at last at the ultimate goal. Geoffrey Bruce was there, muttering between cracked and frozen lips: "Just wait, old thing—we'll get you yet."

The ghosts faded. The world returned. Hillary turned off his oxygen, removed the mask and brought out his camera. From around his ice-ax, where they had been tightly wound, Tenzing unfurled a string of four flags—Nepalese, British, Indian and United Nations—and held them aloft, while Hillary snapped the picture that was soon to be known throughout the world. Then the New Zealander took more photographs, out and down from all sides of the summit, until presently his hands fumbled and his movements became unsure. Quickly he stowed the camera, replaced his oxygen mask and turned on the life-giving flow. Meanwhile the Sherpa, in a simple ritual of his Buddhist faith, had made a hollow in the snow and laid in it a few bits of biscuit and chocolate; and Hillary, joining him, placed beside them a small crucifix which Hunt had given him and asked him to take to the top. These they left there: offerings of gratitude to a God—the God of all men—Who had been merciful indeed.

Now fifteen minutes had passed, and it was time to start down. One final thing, however, remained to be done. Slowly, for the last time, their eyes moved over the snowy crest and the slopes below, searching for some sign, some possible hint, of the fate of Mallory and Irvine. But there was only the snow—only height and depth, space and stillness—and, hidden somewhere deep within them, the secret of the years.

Their descent from the summit was a race against time, exhaustion and their dwindling oxygen supply. But it was a race in slow-motion, for the journey was perilous, and they were resolved to return from their triumph alive. Down the ridge they went; down the vertical cliff; down more ridge, over the south summit, on and on along the white, twisting ribbon between the gulfs of space. On the way they picked up the extra oxygen cylinders that had been left by Bourdillon and Evans. And at two o'clock they reached Camp IX. Here they rested, brewed a hot drink and gathered up their equipment. Then started off again. After hours of perfect calm, the wind had now risen, blowing in savage gusts across the mountain and obliterating the snow-steps they had cut on the way up. But their strength was still sufficient to the challenge. Again the axes rose and fell; again the long stairway took form; and at last, in the fading light of early evening, they stumped down the lower slopes of the couloir into the arms of their companions on the South Col. . . . "Yes," said Hillary later, "the col might be the worst spot in the world. But to us, at that moment, it was home."

Good fortune prevailed to the end. For the next day the sun shone in splendor, and the descent to the lower camps was a triumphal procession. At the advance base—Camp IV—there were such demonstrations of emotion as to make a good stiff-upper-lipped Englishman blush with embarrassment; and by radio the news was flashed to a waiting world. There followed a brief, ugly interlude when small men tried to make political grist of it—to split white man and brown man in a mean wrangle over honors. But the conquerors of Everest were not small; they would have no part of this sort of thing; and soon the machinations of the troublemakers were forgotten. With happy timing, word of the conquest reached England on the very eve of the Queen's coronation, making that great day an even greater one. Hillary and Hunt were forthwith knighted, and Tenzing received the highest award that could be given a non-British national. From the Thames to the Ganges, from Nepal to New Zealand, there was rejoicing in the common victory.

And in the end, perhaps, it was this, above all else, that gave meaning and greatness to the climbing of Everest: that it *was* a common victory in a common cause. For a few magical minutes on a May morning in 1953 a man of the East and a man of the West stood side by side on the summit of the earth, bound together not only by a nylon rope, but by the bonds of brotherhood and high enterprise. In a world darkened by strife and fear, it was a thing to be remembered and cherished. For the triumph belonged not only to Hillary and Tenzing; not only to the ranks of the Everesters who fought and struggled toward the beckoning goal. It was a triumph for all men, everywhere, and the fitting end to a shining chapter in the sorry history of our century.

15

UNFINISHED ADVENTURE

The Himalayas of the Future

EVEREST CLIMBED. . .

Now the conquerors have come down from the heights, and the curtain has closed behind them on a whole era of mountaineering history. The "third pole" has been reached. The king has fallen. And as with every fall, the loud blare of triumph must be mingled with a softer note of regret. Once again, as so often in human experience, the magic of what-may-be has become the reality of what-is. Everest climbed will never be the same as Everest inviolate, and no other mountain will quite capture its place in the imagination of men.

But mountaineers, like other mortals, are built to look forward—not back. As one era closes, another has already begun to unfold, and it is safe to predict that the ascent of Everest will mark, not the end, but the beginning of the greatest period of Himalayan climbing.

What is left? In two words—almost everything. Of the fourteen Eightthousanders, only three have been conquered, and among the slightly lesser peaks the ratio is hundreds to one. The great exploits of recent years have focused attention on the roof of Asia. Everywhere there is more interest in mountaineering than at any time in the past. Climbing equipment has been enormously improved, transporation is easier, and the world is enjoying—if that is the right word—at least a facsimile of peace. From New York to Tokyo, from Norway and New

Zealand, plans are afoot for new expeditions to earth's highest places. "No end," said Mallory of Everest, "is visible or even conceivable to this kingdom of adventure." Applied to the whole of the Himalayas, this is as true today as ever before.

A question that cannot but enter the mind is whether Everest will be tried again. The answer is yes, inevitably—in time; but probably not until the memory of the first ascent has lost its immediate impact. One motive would be to scale it from another direction: by the old North Col approach on which so many men tried and failed, or by a new route not yet attempted. A second would be to climb it without the use of oxygen. On this score the opinions of mountaineers differ. But men have already gone to within a thousand feet of the top on their own lung-power, and it would seem likely that, with the right acclimatization and the right weather conditions, they will eventually go all the way.

For a while, however, Everest will probably recede into the background, and the focus will be on the Great Unclimbed. K2 and Kangchenjunga are, of course, the greatest prizes, and in the case of the former there is what amounts to an international queue waiting for a chance at the summit. With Kangchenjunga the situation is different, for there has been no serious attempt on it since the German expedition of 1931, and, as of 1954, there is none in the immediate offing. In part this is because it is generally considered the most difficult and dangerous of all the Eightthousanders; in part because the state of Sikkim, which provides the best approach, has since the Communist conquest of Tibet been rigidly closed to westerners. English, Swiss and Japanese groups have recently expressed interest in organizing expeditions, but permission has not been forthcoming, and the world's third highest summit remains in the province of the politician rather than of the mountaineer.

Westward from Kangchenjunga, in the Everest region, are three other unclimbed giants: Lhotse, Makalu and Cho Oyu. Lhotse, as we have seen, is very close to Everest, and for years it was considered its south peak (which is, indeed, what its name means) rather than a separate and individual mountain. More recent Himalayan climbers, however, have felt that it deserves a status of its own, and it is now generally ranked as the earth's fourth highest peak. Though its top has never been attempted, much of the route to Lhotse's heights has been traversed by the Everesters, and any future expedition would almost surely

follow their tracks across its western face to the high col between the
two summits. From there, observations have indicated, the way to the
top, though shorter, is even steeper and more difficult than that to
Everest's; and there has, to date, been no serious talk of trying to climb
it.

Makalu, fourteen miles to the east, is an isolated pinnacle that in
height ranks next after Lhotse and is sometimes known, because of its
cleft formation, as the Armchair Peak. Although it has been seen and
studied at a distance by all the Everest climbers, no man has yet set foot
on its slopes; but mountaineers from several nations have announced
their intention of challenging it. Makalu is huge, formidable, steeper
than Everest; and the details of its structure are unknown. Thus far,
Annapurna is the only Eightthousander to have been both reconnoitered
and climbed on the first attempt, and for anyone to do so on this even
loftier peak seems highly unlikely.

Cho Oyu, the third of the great outliers of Everest, has, unlike the
other two, been once attempted—by the Shipton-Hillary party in 1952.
According to them, the only feasible route appears to lead up from the
north, but this is in Tibetan territory and therefore now closed to western expeditions.

Farther to the west are the two unclimbed monarchs of central Nepal,
Dhaulagiri and Manaslu, almost unknown to the outside world until
very recent years. Both were challenged for the first time in 1953, the
former by the Swiss, the latter by Japanese; and if the usual, though
not inflexible, protocol of Himalayan climbing is observed, these nations
will have first chance at any further attempts. Off to the northeast of
this area stands Gosainthan, which is both the lowest and least known
of the Eightthousanders. Located in an almost unexplored section of
the range, it has never even been approached, much less attempted.
And since it is a Tibetan rather than a Nepalese peak, it is likely that
any expedition in the foreseeable furture will be from the far side of
the Iron Curtain.

The three remaining giants—all in the 26,000-foot category—are
Gasherbrum I (Hidden Peak), Gasherbrum II and Broad Peak, all in
the Karakoram, near K2. Gasherbrum I has been twice challenged, the
other two never. No definite plans for any of them have been announced; but with so many expeditions bidding for a chance at K2, it

TOP MEN

Sir Edmund Hillary and Tenzing the Sherpa, who together reached the summit of Everest.

Portrait of Hillary from the book "The Conquest of Everest." Copyright, 1953, by Sir John Hunt. Published by E. P. Dutton & Co., Inc. Portrait of Tenzing, Copyright by the Swiss Foundation for Alpine Research

THE "UNCLIMBABLE" CLIMBED

The Mustagh Tower, in the Karakoram Himalayas, scaled by two expeditions in 1956.

Instituto di Fotografia Alpina "Vittorio Sella"

seems probable that some of the overflow will be diverted to its lesser neighbors.

Lesser—greater. Except to a statistician the words are meaningless, for in the Himalayas all mountains are great, and altitude is by no means the only measure of their challenge. To take but one example, there is the Mustagh Tower, another of the Karakoram peaks.* For years, climbers moving up the Baltoro Glacier, at the heart of the range, have stared up in awe at its sheer monolithic grandeur; and though its height is a mere 23,860 feet, almost a vertical mile short of K2's, no one has yet dreamed of attempting it. Some have said that, if there is such a thing in the world as an unclimbable mountain, this is it. But so, too, was the Matterhorn "unclimbable," a hundred years ago. Time and again in mountaineering history, the impossible of one generation has become the accomplished fact of the next; and with the Mustagh Tower, as with the others, only the years and men's efforts will tell the tale.

Another tale still to be told—at least in its entirety—is concerned with one of the most fascinating mysteries in the history of exploration. To wit: Can there, just possibly, exist in the world a mountain even higher than Everest? The answer is, almost certainly not. But as of the middle of the twentieth century, the "almost" must still be included. Over the past fifty years or so there have been vague but recurrent reports of a vast uplift called Amni Machen—not in the Himalayas at all, but far to the north of them, in the little-known wilderness of far-western China. And the burden of most of them was that this was the world's highest summit. The story was given added impetus during the last war, when various airmen, flying the "Hump" between India and China, reported that from a 30,000-foot elevation they had looked *up* at a distant mountaintop. The human eye, however, is notoriously fallible in such matters. And even in our advanced scientific age, the altimeter is still an erratic instrument. Far more than this casual "look-and-run" type of surveying will be needed to dethrone Everest as the monarch of mountains.

In 1948, an American aerial exploration was organized by Milton Reynolds, a publicity-conscious Chicago businessman who had previously set a round-the-world flying record; but the venture bogged down in political difficulties and never got to within two hundred miles of its objective. Later in the same year, however, a Chinese party flew in to-

---

* Not to be confused with the Mustagh Ata, in the Pamirs. See p. 191.

ward the Amni Machen region and subsequently announced that, though it contained many big peaks, there was none even approaching the height that had been claimed. Since then, the Iron Curtain has closed in around the area, as around the rest of Central Asia, and the range has again vanished from the ken of western men. But if there were any chance of the Communists' possessing the world's highest mountain, they would by now almost certainly have known and announced it, and the recent Russian expedition to Everest indicates that this is not the case. As of our present knowledge, it would seem that Amni Machen may very well be an Eightthousander—the fifteenth. But anyone hungering for a loftier peak than Everest will probably have to wait a few million years, until geological forces turn dream into reality.

The theory of a new "world's highest mountain" has been pretty well exploded. But the remote roof of Asia is a prodigal in mysteries as in peaks and glaciers, and one, at least, remains—a particularly fascinating one—which must still be listed as unsolved. This is the existence, or non-existence of the *yeti,* or "Abominable Snowman." *

For years, in Himalayan history and folklore, there have appeared tales of strange creatures, reputedly half man and half ape, that roam the high, empty world beneath the great mountains, leading a will-o'-the-wisp nocturnal life and appearing to humans only at rare intervals. Almost all the Sherpas, as well as other natives of the region, accept their reality as established fact; and many insist that they have seen them—though usually at a respectful distance. Western explorers have of course discounted the fabulous and supernatural elements in the stories. But many of them, covering the range from Kangchenjunga in the east to the Karakoram in the west, have reported seeing footprints in the snow that belonged to no identifiable animal.

A few claim, like the Nepalese and Tibetans, to have had actual contact with the creatures. A strange story, told by Prince Peter of Greece to an Indian newspaper, relates that, during a recent expedition, several of his party became convinced that a Snowman was prowling about their camp at night and devised an ingenious method of capturing him. A large basin of *chang,* a strong native beer, was set out where the intruder would find it, and the next morning, as they had hoped,

---

* The intriguing name is a more or less accurate translation of an original Tibetan phrase.

he was lying near by in a drunken sleep. Quickly they trussed him up in heavy rope; but when the Snowman aroused himself he promptly broke his bonds and escaped, his captors being too frightened to try and stop him. A second story, told by a Norwegian engineer, Aage Thorberg, tells of an even more direct encounter—this time with two *yeti,* in the Kangchenjunga region in 1948. According to Thorberg, he and a companion, Jan Frostis, sighted a pair of the creatures on a snow-field, managed to close in, and were trying to lasso one of them, when the other leapt upon Frostis and mauled him badly. Both of the Norwegians had guns; but a quick shot by Thorberg seems only to have wounded the beast, and then the two of them ran off and disappeared.

Both of these accounts came from reputable sources. But at the same time they lacked any supporting documentary evidence and had so many earmarks of the tall tale that they failed to attract much attention. There was, however, a very different reaction when, in 1951, Shipton and his companions returned from their Everest reconnaissance expedition. For though they laid claim to no sensational confrontations, they brought back with them clear photographs of the footprints of an unknown animal, and their subsequent publication aroused an almost world-wide furore of controversy. Some zoologists expressed the belief that they were simply distorted bear tracks, others that they were those of a large and little-known langur monkey; and the general public had a field-day of fantastic speculation. The expedition members themselves, having seen no actual animals, prudently refused to commit themselves.

Similar tracks were subsequently seen and photographed by the Swiss Everest climbers in 1952, and Norman Dyhrenfurth, the American member of the autumn party, has stated his conviction that the *yeti* exists and is almost certainly a species of large ape. The footprints that have been encountered average some 10 to 12 inches in length, 4½ to 6 inches in breadth, and would seem to indicate a quadruped weighing between 130 and 175 pounds. Descriptions of the creature itself are still suspect, but it is worth noting that most of them agree in the essentials of dark furry body, hairless face and long heavy tail. In this last detail, however, the credibility of the stories wears thin, even in corroboration; for such a tail would presumably leave an occasional mark in the snow along with the footprints, and none has ever been found.

To the prosaic, factual mind, perhaps the most tantalizing question

is what the Snowman—or whatever it is—lives on. All its tracks have
been located on high glaciers and snow-fields, remote from any source
of food, either animal or vegetable; and the answer to date is simply
that no one knows. The footprints exist—that is certain. That *something* made the footprints is certain, too. But the rest is still mystery.
And, whatever the final solution, the authentic discovery of this strange
and elusive creature will be a major event in Himalayan exploration.

From Kangchenjunga to K2, from the climbing of the unclimbable to
the capturing of the *yeti*—the Himalayas still hold out their lure to
adventurous men. Even with Everest climbed, what has already been
done does not compare with what yet remains.

One thing that appears certain is that there will be more expeditions
in the future than ever in the past. Each year sees the coming of climbers
of new nationalities; the Indians and Pakistanis themselves are exhibit-
ing a swiftly growing interest in their own mountains; and with the
advance of the air age it seems not impossible that the Himalayas will
become a true world-center of mountaineering, such as the Alps have
been for a century past. Some expeditions will be large and ambitious:
aiming at the high goals, the unclimbed Eightthousanders. Many more
will be small and with modest objectives: simply a group of companions, with perhaps a few porters, out to climb and explore within the
limits of their capabilities. These latter will set no records. Their names
will not be blazoned in headlines. They will be following the mountain way only for the joy and satisfaction that they find in it.

And this is all to the good; for *the climb for its own sake* is the very
essence of mountaineering, and too many of the recent big expeditions
—great though their achievements have been—have been forced by
many pressures into a far different pattern. They have had to be organized almost like armies. The glare of publicity has beaten upon them.
Rivalries and jealousies have multiplied. Like so many other sports,
Himalayan climbing has become "big time," and in gaining the spotlight it has had to pay the inevitable price. Eric Shipton and H. W.
Tilman, two of the foremost mountaineers of our day, have long been
opponents of the outsized, high-pressured expedition, and, indeed, it
was largely disagreement on this score that led to Shipton's resignation
as leader of the 1953 Everest party. These men—and there are others
like them—believe that when a mountaineering venture expands beyond

a certain point it is bound to sacrifice too much, in human terms, to the mere fetish of success. Or as a certain climber put it, more pithily: "When the thing gets too big, it's just no damn fun."

Something like this was obviously in the minds of the Americans on K2, in 1953, when they discarded authoritarian choice for a general vote in the selection of who would have first chance at the top; and even more when they decided that, whoever got there, he would remain anonymous. The world loves a hero. An individual, not a collective, hero. All the pressures of publicity, of mass-psychology, of human nature itself, tend to create the hero-image and to raise up the one above the many. But the climbers on K2 wanted no part of this. They knew, as every climber knows, that this is a corruption and falsification of the very spirit of mountaineering. No man—not one in all history—has reached the summit of a great peak by his own strength and skill alone. Climbing is not a sport of "champions," but of human beings working together in selfless teamwork; and as often as not, the man who does not go all the way—who reconnoiters the route, carries the loads, pitches the tents, tends the sick and injured—contributes even more to success than the one who stands at last, victorious, on the top.

Competition, standardization, the aims and values of "big business" have little place in the mountain world. And even less does rabid nationalism. For years it has been a custom of climbers to set up the flags of one or more nations on the summits of newly won peaks, and up to a point the practice is natural and even praiseworthy. Surely all the world could look up with pride and satisfaction when the banners of Britain, India, Nepal and the United Nations flapped side by side on the crest of Everest. But when carried to extremes, as by the prewar Germans—and unfortunately by some more recent expeditions—flag-waving can become the ugliest of all the perversions of the mountaineering spirit. For the climbing of the earth's great peaks differs from the exploration of its continents and oceans, not only in external method but in its basic purpose and significance. There are no new domains to be carved out on the mountaintops. No gold to be won—no oil or uranium—no lands for settlement or bases for warfare. Mountaineering is not a means to an end, but an end in itself, and it is only cheapened and debased when it becomes involved with national aggrandizement and prestige.

Again, it has been outside pressures, rather than climbers themselves,

that have introduced the strident note of jingoism. A man actually at
grips with a great mountain is apt to be too concerned with the funda-
mentals of human living to care greatly if he is working for the greater
glory of England or Switzerland, Luxembourg or Afghanistan. The
challengers of K2, in 1953, were proud that the participation of
Streather, Ata-Ullah and their porters made them an international
rather a purely American expedition, and were uninterested in any
effort to give the Stars and Stripes a violent shaking. "Nationalism in
mountaineering is distressing," wrote Robert Bates on his return to
this country. "Climbing, we believe, should be a sport without national
boundaries or loyalties."

This is the belief, too, of a man of far different background—Tenzing Bhotia, of Everest. The one blot on the bright achievement of
Everest's climbing was the subsequent attempt of small-minded men
to turn it to the uses of political propaganda, with Tenzing, the oriental, as the key figure. But in the midst of the ugly turmoil, this simple
and unlettered Sherpa proved himself as great a man as he was a mountaineer. "Who reach top first?" he said to a questioner. "That make
much trouble. If I say Hillary first, Indian, Nepali people unhappy.
If I say I first, European people unhappy. If you agree, I like say both
got top together almost same time. If you everybody write that way,
no trouble. . . . Same trouble myself. Some people say I Nepali, some
say Indian. My sisters my mother living here. But now I live India
with wife daughters. For me Indian Nepali same. I am Nepali but I
think I also Indian. . . . We should all be the same—Hillary, myself,
Indian, Nepali, everybody."

These are noble thoughts, nobly spoken. They express—better, perhaps, than any practiced writer could manage—the *beau ideal* of mountaineering. But it is an ideal that is desperately hard to attain in these
years of the mid-twentieth century. One of the great imponderables of
the Himalayan future is the part that will be played in it by the Communist world, and one may be sure that, whatever part it plays, power
politics will be very much in the foreground. Virtually the whole range
lies on the frontier which separates that world from ours, and the Reds
have the same access to it from one side that we have from the other.
Already there has been much infiltration from the north into the valleys
of Nepal, Bhutan and northern Kashmir. At least part of the trouble-
making after the climbing of Everest came from identifiable Commu-

nist sources. And the Russians' own recent Everest expedition indicates that they are on the search for conquest—in mountaineering as elsewhere—and that they will be appearing with increasing frequency on the high peaks themselves. Indeed, it is conceivable that two expeditions, one from the West and one from behind the Iron Curtain, may someday find themselves converging on the same mountaintop at the same time; and one can conjure the startling and sinister image of the two parties coming face to face on a summit ridge.

Melodramatic? Perhaps. But a long way from impossible. For better or worse, we live in a world of politics, intrigue and struggle between nations, and that struggle has penetrated even to the remote fastnesses of the highest mountains. Climbers cannot ignore it, for they, like other men, are part of the world. But it is safe to say—at least for most climbers from the West—that their motives and goals will not be basically political. They will climb for the same reason that the true mountaineer has always climbed. Not for power, not for money, not to wave a flag or sample a cosmic ray or even to gain a victory as an end in itself. They will climb because of their love of climbing; their love of the mountains. Because—in the now famous phrase of George Mallory—the mountains *are there.*

Everest has been won. Well and good. So, too, have the poles been reached, the oceans spanned, the jungles threaded. But that does not mean that man's dreams are finished or that his race is run. "There are other Annapurnas," said Maurice Herzog, "in the lives of men." There are other Everests. Other trials and triumphs still ahead.

The vanquished peak of earth's tallest mountain does not block out the sky. Horizons, wide and bright, stretch beyond it. The high Himalayas are *there;* the challenge is *there;* a challenge not to physical or political conquest, but to one of the great unfinished adventures of mankind.

16

AX, ROPE AND TROUSER-SEAT

The Craft of Mountaineering

IN THE PRECEDING PAGES we have seen mountaineering in many and various guises—as a sport, as exercise and competition, as exploration and scientific research, as physical and spiritual adventure. In addition to all these it is a body of knowledge and experience and a technique based upon them. In short, a craft.

In the broad sense of the term mountain craft embraces an enormous field. It applies primarily, of course, to climbing as such, but extends far beyond it to include every aspect of how men live and act on the high places of the earth. It is concerned equally with ends and means, practice and theory, half-hour scrambles on a riverside bluff and Himalayan expeditions complete with oxygen tanks, two-way radios and three hundred porters. It encompasses such weirdly unrelated subjects as geology and acrobatics, meteorology and first aid, map making and bedmaking, paleontology and cooking. Within the limits of a single chapter it is obviously not possible to treat all these components in details; even less, to offer a manual on "how to climb." * Its purpose will be fulfilled if it simply makes clear how much more there is to mountaineering than a mere going uphill and down again and indicates in some measure the breadth and richness and infinite variety of the climber's world.

---

* For books of this nature, see the Reading List.

The Nature of Mountains

In the organic sense—insofar as plant, animal and human life are concerned—mountains are perhaps the "deadest" regions on earth. Geologically, however, they are the most alive. More than any other features of the earth's surface they present visible evidence of the immense physical forces which have molded, and are still molding, the face of our planet. These forces are of two kinds. The first consists of heat and pressure within the core of the earth, which result, over enormous periods of time, in the folding and buckling of the earth's surface and the thrusting up of great rock-masses into highlands and ranges. This may be called the creative force in mountain-making. The second, or destructive, force is found in the atmosphere, and manifests itself in the relentless leveling process of denudation and erosion. The geologic history and present form of the earth's high places are determined by these two agencies—the one building them up, the other tearing them down. Between them they create for mountains a life-cycle of vast duration and unvarying pattern.

The age of the earth's present ranges varies greatly. Some, like the Appalachians of the eastern United States, date back to remote geological times and show their antiquity in low, rounded outlines, molded by the winds and snows of uncounted eons. Others, like the Alps and Himalayas, are of comparatively recent origin—a mere two or three million years—and exhibit their youth in their height and striking boldness of contour. There are many evidences, indeed, that the Himalayas are still in active process of being built up and that Everest and its neighbors will, in spite of constant denudation, be even higher a thousand centuries hence than they are today. In terms of mountaineering, young, uneroded mountains always present a greater challenge than their older counterparts.

The actual physical structure of mountains also shows wide diversity. The rocks of the earth's crust are usually divided by geologists into three groups: (1) *igneous rocks* (granite, diorite, basalt, lavas, etc.), which have been formed directly by solidification of molten matter; (2) *sedimentary rocks* (limestone, sandstone, dolomite, clay, shale, etc.), which are formed from the sediment or fragments of other rocks; (3) *metamorphic rocks* (gneiss, schists, slates, etc.), a mixed type generally believed to be sedimentary rocks that have been subjected to great heat or pressure. All three types are found in mountains, sometimes in fairly simple form, more often in bewildering complexity. If any generalization can be made it is that the cores and upper reaches of most peaks are usually of granite or some similar igneous mass, their outer and lower slopes of stratified sedimentary or metamorphic rocks. A notable exception, however, is to be found in no less a mountain than Everest, which apparently is built up throughout of fossil-bearing limestone.

Because of their height and consequently exposed position, as well as the agency of gravity, mountains present a vast complex of natural phenomena which are not found elsewhere on the earth. They are not only subject to frequent and severe storms, but can also be the actual cause of storms, owing to their effect on the temperature and moisture of the atmosphere. Their climate is colder than that of the lowlands, their winds stronger, their air more rarefied. Also, every peak, whether or not it is still being pushed up from below, is falling to pieces at the top from the effects of weathering, with the result that rocks, ice and snow are forever pouring down its sides, sometimes in mere trickles, sometimes in vast avalanches. Truly high summits are almost invariably ringed with glaciers—great, creeping drainage systems whose behavior bears little resemblance to that of snow and ice at lower altitudes. Finally, the architecture of the peaks themselves is on a uniquely vast and complex scale. They are built of rock and snow and ice, to be sure. But they are built also of slopes, precipices, buttresses and ridges; gullies, chimneys, ledges and cornices; crevasses, gendarmes, névés and bergschrunds; humps, domes, spires and pinnacles. Seen from afar a great mountain may appear to be merely a sudden upward prolongation of the earth's surface; once approached, however, it becomes a world in and to itself.

Safety and Accidents

"In mountaineering," writes the climber-scholar, Geoffrey Winthrop Young, "there is only one principle: that we should secure on any given day the highest form of mountain adventure consistent with our sense of proportion. All else is more a matter of practice than of principle."

In other words, there are no immutable rules that apply to all moun-

tains and all mountaineers, no rigid formulas of "how" and "how not."
Indeed, it is a large part of the charm of the sport that it is infinitely
adaptable to the tastes and abilities of its followers. There are many
fine peaks which can be climbed in a matter of a few hours, others
which have been besieged for months on end, year after year, and still
have not been won. There are ascents requiring the utmost in daring
and acrobatic skill, others that are little more than a stiff uphill walk.
In fact, in frequented mountain districts such as the Alps a single summit will usually present several ways of approach, ranging from the
very easy to the all-but-impossible. Mountaineering, therefore, is not
an activity limited to "experts," or to young men, or to the physically
powerful. A remarkable number of the great ascents in climbing history
have been made by men well on into middle age, and self-knowledge
and self-discipline have time and again proved themselves of more
value than mere strength, agility or endurance. In the long run, judgment rather than muscle makes the mountaineer.

All climbing is concerned with two primary elements. The first is
reaching the objective. The second is getting there—and back—*safely*.
To say that mountaineering is a "dangerous" activity is meaningless;
so are skiing and sailing and flying and driving a car at sixty miles an
hour. What is true is that, more than in most sports, the element of
danger is always present, and the climber whose judgment or performance is faulty may well lose not only the game but his life. It is from
the recognition of this fact that mountain craft has developed as a science and an art. It cannot eliminate danger altogether—indeed, no true
mountaineer would wish it to if it could. What it can and does do is to
keep danger under control.

The hazards a climber faces are of three main kinds: that of falling
himself, that of being struck by other falling objects, and that of the
elements. All can take a great variety of forms. One can fall from rock
or ice or snow, over a precipice or into a crevasse, two yards or two
miles; the cause may be vertigo or a broken rope or improper balance
or rotten rock or the sudden, unexpected action of a companion. Falling
objects, too, can be either rock, snow or ice, ranging from a volley of
pebbles scuffed down by a careless climber above to a gigantic avalanche
peeling off the whole side of a mountain. The threat of the elements
can manifest itself in even more ways: in cold, storms and blizzards,
in bolts of lightning, in the effects of altitude, in swift changes in the

conditions of rock and snow, in the coming of night while a party is still far from shelter. These dangers are common to every high mountain, and no climber will get far on any range in the world if he is not prepared to meet and, in a measure, deal with them.

One of the first things which every mountaineer must learn is the distinction between *danger* and mere *difficulty;* for the two are by no means synonomous. On the one hand, let us take the example of an expert climber descending a steep cliff-face *en rappel.* All that the uninitiated will see is a man dangling in space supported by two slender lengths of rope, and he will jump to the conclusion that the man's situation is hazardous in the extreme. Actually, however, it is not hazardous at all. The climber is performing a standard maneuver; his rope is well belayed above, its coils are properly adjusted about his body; his landing place has been selected and he is descending with smoothness and co-ordination. What he is doing is difficult, in that its performance requires practice, but it is not dangerous. In contrast to this let us take the instance of a novice climber during an ascent. Two alternative routes have presented themselves—one a steep and jagged ridge with disconcerting drops on either side, the other a sheltered gully of moderate gradient with excellent hand- and footholds. He selects the latter, and to all appearances his choice is the wise one, for he encounters no climbing problems whatever. Actually, however, the innocent-looking gully is a funnel frequently raked by rock avalanches, and he will be lucky if he escapes from it with his life. In eschewing the ridge and its difficulties the climber has unwittingly exposed himself to an immeasurably greater degree of danger.

As mountaineering activity has increased in recent years, so too, of course, have accidents. On major expeditions and ascents of extreme difficulty a certain number are, perhaps, inevitable; but in the usual garden-variety sort of climbing almost all are avoidable if the proper precautions are taken. The New York chapter of the Appalachian Mountain Club compiled, not long ago, a so-called Climbing Code for the benefit of its members, which merits reading—and memorizing—by anyone who sets foot on a mountain:

The Ascent—No climb is worth the deliberate risk of life nor should it be judged successful if anyone is foolhardy. A judicious retreat is more admirable than a dangerous victory. Be confident that you can get up and down.

Judgement—Be alert to your responsibilities to others. Know their abilities and limitations as well as your own. Know the limitations of terrain, weather, and equipment. Good judgement means knowing these limits.

Margin of Safety—In the interest of speed, some compromise with safety may be wise, but more is needed than, "I almost didn't make it."

Companions—There must be mutual respect for the leader's orders to reflect safety. The essence of safe climbing is companionship and co-operation, not competition. Never climb solo.

Equipment—Be sure that it is the best both in type and condition. This includes clothing, food, and first aid equipment as well as climbing gear.

Belaying—Good belaying is the most important skill in safe climbing; a man's life may pass through your hands. Experience will show the value of dynamic technique and that he protects others best who protects himself.

Condition—Physical and mental condition should be adequate to your role as a climber. Hard work requires stamina. If you do not feel you can do it, Don't. Another day may be better for you.

Climbing Ability—Know and practice good form. This includes party organization, signals, rope handling, body co-ordination, rappeling, and all the details of rock, snow, and ice technique which make an expert mountaineer.

Leadership—Everyone is obligated to exercise leadership by promoting safety and discouraging extremism and spectacularity. Give beginners special attention and suggest they climb with an organized group of conservative tradition.

The life you save will be your own. In mountaineering, pride goes before a fall.

A climber's responsibility is not only to himself but to his companions, and, beyond them, to those who might have to risk their lives in rescuing him if he should get into trouble. A man who can reach the top of a mountain may be an expert technician. A man who also knows when to turn back is a mountaineer.

Rock-climbing

Rock-climbing is the most common form of mountaineering and involves a great variety of methods and techniques. In the strict sense of the term it may be said to begin where uphill walking ends—in other words, where the hands, arms, knees and body, as well as the feet, of the climber come into active play.

As in all other branches of the sport, the first requisite in a cragsman is sound judgment. Before beginning an ascent he must make his general choice of route (i.e., which side of the mountain he will attempt;

which main ridges, faces, chimneys, etc., he will aim for and which
he will avoid).* Once underway, moreover, he will find himself constantly confronted with the same problems and choices on a smaller
scale. In difficult rock-climbing virtually every movement requires a
decision as to how it can best be made, and the advance selection of
hand- and footholds can be fully as important as the physical maneuvers that follow. In this connection it is essential for the novice climber
to remember that a hold or stance cannot be judged by its outward appearance alone. Many rocks which look sound are actually rotten and
will crumble away when pressure is applied; many which seem firmly
fixed to the mountainside are in reality detached and precariously balanced, awaiting only the touch of hand or foot to break loose and topple
downward. In rock-climbing every hold should be carefully tested before the full weight of the body is entrusted to it. Probably more serious
mountaineering accidents have resulted from carelessness in this respect
than from any other single cause.

The ordinary type of rock-climbing is largely a matter of hand- and
footholds, requiring judiciousness of choice and good balance and co-
ordination when in motion. Not infrequently, however, a climber may
be confronted by a stretch of rock which cannot be negotiated by the
usual methods and for which special maneuvers must be employed.
Sometimes, as on a narrow ledge or steep slabs, the pressure of the body
against the rocks can give support which the hands and feet alone cannot supply. Other types of ledges, which offer no standing room at all,
may be crossed by what is known as a hand-traverse—a Tarzan-like
procedure in which the cragsman grasps the edge with his hands and
moves himself along by them, his body and legs hanging free below.
A knife-edged ridge, too narrow for standing erect or even for crawling,
will frequently yield easily to a climber who straddles it and pushes
himself along with his hands. Chimneys and cracks, in particular, lend
themselves to ingenious forms of cragsmanship, as Mummery first demonstrated on the fearsome walls of the Chamonix *aiguilles*. Thus a
narrow vertical fissure, though presenting no holds whatever, can often
be scaled if the climber jams an elbow and knee into it and levers him-

---

* Steepness alone is by no means the measure of the difficulty of a climb. The
slope of the rock strata is an important consideration, and a steep pitch on which the
strata slope upward will often provide a better route than a gentler one on which they
slope down. This fact is well illustrated by Whymper's experiences on the Matterhorn.

self up by them. Or, if the fissure is wider, but still has no holds, he may get his whole body inside and "chimney up" by the alternating pressure of back and feet against its two sides.

Two other climbing maneuvers often employed on difficult rock are those known as the "layback" and the *courte-échelle.* The "layback" is used on a steep stretch which offers no ordinary hand- or footholds, but where there is an underhold or vertical rock-edge within reach on which the climber can get a secure grasp. Pulling horizontally against the underhold or edge with his hands, he places his feet against the pitch to be climbed and, in effect, "walks" up it, his body meanwhile leaning out almost at right angles to the rock. In the *courte-échelle,* the first man of a party makes use of the bodies of his companion, or companions, to gain a stance or hold which would otherwise be out of his reach. The operation may consist merely of a boost from someone's hands, or it may involve the leader's climbing on the backs, shoulders or even heads of the other climbers. On occasion the ax is also brought into play to give additional artificial hand- or footholds.

One of the most remarkable developments in cragsmanship has been the perfection of a technique known as balance, or rhythm, climbing. It is based on the fact that equilibrium is much more easily maintained by a body in motion than a body at rest—a principle involved in many activities other than mountaineering. A dancer, skater or bicyclist, for example, is frequently in off-balance positions which he can maintain only because he is in constant motion from one to the other; if he were to attempt to hold one of them without moving he would immediately fall. So too with rock-scaling. A tiny fingerhold or quarter-inch ledge, which would afford no support at all to a stationary climber, can yet be made to serve his ends if he uses them but momentarily, for friction, on his way to another hold or ledge. Also, the climber himself can maintain equilibrium in otherwise impossible positions, if, while he is in them, he is already on his way to a counterbalancing position. The result is that by constant rhythmic movement and the ingenious use of friction an accomplished cragsman can often master short stretches of vertical or near-vertical rock which would be insurmountable by the ordinary methods of "stop-and-go."

In football and various other sports it is an oft-heard axiom that the best defense is a good offense. In mountaineering, however, the exact reverse is true. By far the most important aspects of the craft are those concerned with precaution and safety, and the climber who neglects them will inevitably come to grief, however great his strength, agility and daring.

Protective measures are nowhere more essential than in rock-climbing, for this branch of the sport is most often carried on in high and exposed places where a minor mishap may quickly turn into a disaster. In general, these measures are more a matter of common sense than of arbitrary rules and vary greatly according to the situation at hand. There are, however, a few which are almost always applicable. One is to avoid routes on which there is obvious danger of stonefalls and avalanches, even though the alternative route may present much harder climbing. Another is never, during difficult climbing, to entrust the entire weight of the body to one hand- or foothold. At every point in his maneuvering the climber should have at least two secure points of contact with the rock-surface, so that if one should break away or slip from his grasp he will still have the support of the other. It is also important that when strong pressure is applied to the rock with either hands or feet it is in a downward rather than an outward direction and takes the form of a steady push or pull rather than a sudden jerk. Ledges and protuberances which will support a two hundred-pound man moving easily and rhythmically can break away under the abrupt lunge of a small boy.

In almost every climbing operation there is a correct and an incorrect position for the body. Most novices, during their first experience on steep rock, are apt to hug the mountain too closely, fearing that if they lean back from it they may lose their balance and fall. More often than not, however, this merely results in a cramped and tense position, as well as in dangerous outward pressure on the rocks underfoot. The body should be kept in as near a vertical position as possible and sufficiently far out from the rock to permit easy movement and clear vision. Granted, clear vision down the wall of a cliff is not, for all people, an unmitigated blessing. But it is at least a lesser evil than not seeing at all; and it is to be hoped that the true sufferer from vertigo will not find himself on the cliff in the first place.

The Rope

The rope plays so important a part in mountaineering that it has grown to be the very symbol of the sport. In rock-climbing, in particular, it comes into almost constant use, and an understanding of its functions and manipulations is perhaps the most essential single requirement in any would-be cragsman.

The rope, properly employed, is *not* a substitute for good judgment or physical ability. Neither is it a leash for the stronger to lead the weaker, nor a sort of magic talisman insuring blanket immunity to the incompetent. It is, rather—again to quote Geoffrey Young—"the means by which the physical and moral efficiency of a party is pooled, and by which its margin of safety is extended so as to include all members of a party equally." The important words in this definition are "moral efficiency." For the rope's significance extends far beyond its mere physical function of tying the bodies of several climbers together; it ties them as well into a mental and spiritual unit and makes mountaineering, in the deepest sense, a collective rather than an individual enterprise. No climber, thus joined to his companions, can make snap decisions and take chances as he might if he were alone, for he is now, in everything he does, concerned not only with his own welfare but with that of others. The rope, on the one hand, may greatly increase his "margin of safety." But it increases his responsibility even more.

Unquestionably the greatest recent development in mountaineering techniques has been the introduction of the nylon rope. Supplanting the old-style rope of hemp or manila—and now used almost universally —it has proved itself superior in almost every way. For one thing, it is stronger; for another, more pliable and less subject to kinking and freezing; but its prime virtue is its elasticity, which enables it not only to hold a falling man, but to do it with a minimum of damage both to him and to itself. To take one spectacular example: it is extremely doubtful if David Harrah would have survived his 120-foot fall on Yerupajá in 1950 if the rope joining him to Maxwell had been made of the old materials. If it had not snapped from the tremendous jerk, it would certainly have crushed Harrah's ribs, and as likely as not would have pulled Maxwell off after him. The nylon strands, however, had so much give that Harrah, in effect, "bounced" at rope's end, and both men lived to tell the tale.

The rope commonly used in mountaineering is a half inch or so in diameter and between 80 and 125 feet long. There are a number of standard knots for tying it around the body—both for end and middle men—and the distance between climbers may vary according to the nature of the ascent. It is essential, however, that the rope be allowed neither to drag slackly nor pull jerkily between them. As many as a dozen men have been known to climb on one rope, and as few as two. In the early days of the sport large roped parties were in vogue (witness the seven all tied together on the tragic first ascent of the Matterhorn), but modern practice favors smaller groups, with three usually considered to be the ideal number.

The order of climbers on a rope is of great importance and should be determined carefully according to the dictates of common sense. The man highest on the mountain at any given time is obviously the one who can give the most assistance to his companions. Similarly he is the one who can receive the least. On an ascent, therefore, the strongest member of a party should always go first; on a descent, last. The weakest member should be last on the ascent, but in the middle on the descent, when it would be inadvisable for him to lead. On difficult horizontal stretches the correct place for the weakest is also in the middle, where both the leader and last man can assure effective support. Too great emphasis cannot be placed on the responsibilities of the top man on a rope. The anchor for all below him, he is himself without anchor (unless pitons and karabiners are employed), and a slip or misstep on his part can easily result in serious consequences.

In climbing of a routine nature, when the rope is employed merely as a general precaution, all the members of a party will ordinarily be in motion simultaneously. On difficult rock, however, the rope becomes an active protective device, and its proper use limits the movements of the group to one man at a time. At such times climbers make use of the protective maneuver known as the belay. The first step in belaying is for the anchor man on a team to take the most secure and protected stance available. He then passes the rope either around his own body or a projecting mass of rock, or both, in such a way that a slip or fall by the man actually climbing will put the least possible strain both on the rope and on himself. It is important that there be no slack between belayer and climber, for this would allow too much momentum to develop before the fall is stopped. But the belay should also be resilient— or what climbers call "dynamic"—so that there will be no tremendous jerk, but rather a gradual braking process.

When the going becomes exceptionally hard, it is essential for the top man, as well as the others, to have some measure of protection, and here the piton and karabiner come into play. As he climbs, the leader hammers pitons into cracks in the rock, affixes karabiner and rope, and the rope is then belayed by a companion below. The leader's protection, to be sure, is not as complete as if there were a belayer higher up, for once he is above his anchor he is subject to a fall. But at least the fall is stopped as soon as the rope goes taut in the karabiner, and usually this is in time to avoid serious consequences. For the most extreme types of climbing the "rock engineers" have developed many complicated refinements, both for attack and defense. Pitons are hammered in at almost every step. Auxiliary ropes are strung between them. And by an ingenious sling-and-pulley maneuver, involving so-called "prussik" knots, the cragsman is often able to hoist himself up otherwise unclimbable pitches.

"Prussiking" and such, however, are only for the highly specialized few. A far more common use of the rope is in the traditional technique of the rappel. Unlike the belay, this is an offensive rather than a defensive measure, and is employed only on descents, enabling a climber to lower himself down cliff-faces and overhangs which could not be negotiated by ordinary methods. For the rappel "roping down" would be the nearest English equivalent—a supplementary rope is used, thinner and usually longer than the standard one. This is passed around a rock-point or threaded through a firmly fastened rope-ring directly above the stretch to be descended, so that two equal lengths hang down the mountain. The climber then wraps a fold of the doubled rope around himself—under one thigh, diagonally across the body and over the opposite shoulder—and, facing in toward the mountain, proceeds to lower himself by letting the rope slip slowly first through one hand and then the other. The whole operation is based on the fact that the friction of the rope passing around the body takes almost all strain from the hands and arms. The weight of the rope itself acts as a brake, extremely powerful at the beginning of a descent when there are still two long strands dangling below the climber, becoming gradually less so as the strands shorten. In the case of steep or even vertical rocks the climber, in effect, walks backward down the mountainside, his feet gaining what purchase they can from such points of support as may exist, his body leaning outward against the braking power of the rope. On the descent of a bulge or overhang his body has no contact with the mountain at all, but hangs freely, supported in a sitting position by the rope under the thigh. In either case, however, the essence of the maneuver lies in the opposite pull of the body and the rope wrapped around it. The hands are the controlling but not the force-producing agency, functioning in much the same way as if they were manipulating the brake on an automobile.

More than any other aspect of mountaineering, the use of the rope requires close and constant teamwork. Each climber must know at all times exactly what his companions are doing, for it is the sudden surprise, the unexpected slip, that can carry not only one individual but a whole party to destruction. Often on steep rock the members of a rope-team are hidden from one another by intervening crags and bulges, and shouting is the only means of communication. For such situations most practiced climbers have developed a sort of shorthand code of speech, so that they can keep talk to a minimum and still exchange the necessary instructions and information.

Snow and Ice

Snow and ice, as found on high mountains, assume such a bewildering variety of forms that it is almost impossible to formulate a set of rules for dealing with them. If any generalization can be made, it is that climbing on them requires somewhat less agility than rock-clambering, but even greater experience and judgment.

The chief reason for this is that while rocks are more or less a constant, subject only to the slow influences of erosion and frost, snow and ice are in a constant state of flux, often changing both form and substance from day to day and hour to hour. Thus a cornice or snow-bridge high on a mountainside may provide a strong, safe highway during certain weather conditions, only to become during others a crumbling deathtrap. Similarly, a steep slope, perfectly safe for climbing in the cool of early morning, may well peel away in huge avalanches under the rays of the afternoon sun. Snow and ice—however massive and solid-appearing their outward forms—are not actually part of a mountain, as are the rocks, but merely a cloak or covering lying upon it. Freezing or friction may often hold them in position for long periods of time, but the downward pull of gravity is always there, and sooner or later every flake and crystal of them will complete its predestined journey to the valleys below. Glaciers, snow-slopes and ice-fields are not dead, changeless things. They are the drainage of the mountain, the source of streams and rivers, and a vital intermediate link in the endless living cycle of the watering of the earth. The mountaineer who has learned to think of them in terms of their functions—their "aliveness" —has taken the first great step in the mastery of snow and ice craft.

Most high peaks are flanked by glaciers, and these usually afford the most direct, sometimes the only, approach to the heights beyond. Basically a mountain glacier is a simple phenomenon—a large river of ice formed in high, cold altitudes and moving slowly down toward the lower, warmer altitudes along the path of least resistance. In the process, however, it is usually subject to so many variations of terrain and climate, and to so many forms of pressure and strain, that it becomes an organism of great complexity and many component parts.* Most important of these components are:

The glacier proper—the lower, and larger, section of the ice-sheet, generally located in a valley and having a comparatively gentle slope.

Moraines—broken rock and debris carried down by the glacier and deposited in long heaps along its margins. Those at the sides of a glacier are known as lateral moraines; one at its snout as a terminal moraine; one between two confluent glaciers as a medial moraine.

The névé—a snow-field lying above the snow-line which acts as the source or feeder of the glacier.

The icefall—the steepest section of the glacier, usually at the point where it flows down from the mountain proper onto the slopes and valleys below. Because of the enormous pressure to which the glacier is subjected at such points, the surface of an icefall is invariably a chaos of humps and fissures, high ridges and deep chasms.

Seracs—towers or pinnacles of ice, sometimes of great size, squeezed up out of the glacier by pressure below. They are formed not infrequently in icefalls and at points where crevasses intersect.

Crevasses—fissures and chasms formed by splitting of the glacier's surface. They can be either longitudinal or transverse, but most often lie roughly at right angles to the glacier's course.

The bergschrund—the great crevasse which separates the glacier proper from the upper glacier or icefall.

---

* The great majority of the world's glaciers are in the process of shrinkage—indicating that we are still moving away from the last ice age toward an ever-warmer climate.

Ice-fields—large, almost stagnant bodies of ice on high valley floors, which receive the outflow of several glaciers.

Hanging glaciers—small ice streams formed high on the mountainside, which terminate before reaching the lower slopes or valleys—frequently at the brink of a precipice.

All these glacial phenomena, with the possible exception of moraines, present important and complicated problems to the mountaineer. In certain instances, notably that of a steep and badly crumpled icefall, the actual climbing may be extremely hard, and in the case of very large glaciers the ascent may well prove to be the acid test of a climber's stamina and endurance. For the most part, however—to return to our former distinction—danger rather than difficulty is involved; and the safety of a party depends primarily on a knowledge of conditions and constant alertness. Seracs often topple, particularly in the heat of the day, bombarding the surrounding area with tons of falling ice. Hanging glaciers present a similar menace, not infrequently breaking away from the upper mountain in huge avalanches and pouring onto the main glacier below. Most dangerous of all are the omnipresent crevasses, threading the ice-surface like the lines of a jigsaw puzzle and waiting like traps to catch the ignorant or unwary.

On the lower reaches of a glacier, where there is apt to be little or no snow, crevasses are usually plainly visible, and the only problem is how either to jump or circumvent them. Higher up, however, and especially on the névé, they are often completely hidden. Thus a careless climber, imagining himself to be on perfectly solid footing, may actually be treading on a thin and unsupported bridge of snow and find himself suddenly plummeting through it into an abyss below. In such terrain elaborate precautions are a prime necessity. The climbing party should be roped together, preferably three to a rope, and widely enough spaced so that there is never too much weight on any one point of the glacial surface. The leader, on whom, as always, the chief responsibility falls, must advance slowly and cautiously, studying the texture and conformation of the snow for any hint of crevasses beneath and stopping at every suspicious point to sound with his ice-ax. If the haft of the ax plunges downward through the snow without encountering any resistance he will be wise in assuming that it is merely the unsupported covering of a crevasse and therefore to be given a wide berth. The shortest distance between two points on a glacier is seldom a straight line. Indeed a straight line is more often than not the shortest distance to disaster.

Even when every precaution is taken glaciers remain unpredictable and treacherous things, and falls into crevasses are one of the commonest of mountaineering accidents. In such a mishap the victim should immediately swing his ax into a horizontal position, in the hope that it will jam against the crevasse walls and arrest his fall. His companions should throw themselves down at once, to avoid being pulled in after him, and simultaneously thrust their axes into the snow and hitch the rope around them for anchorage. The difficulty involved in extricating a man from a crevasse depends on the nature of the crevasse itself, the degree to which the victim can help himself and the number of persons in the party. An extra rope is usually of considerable help, especially if the rescuing is being done by a lone individual. Great care must obviously be taken by the rescuers that in working around the edge of the crevasse they do not fall through themselves.

On the upper reaches of a mountain, above the zone of glaciers, snow and ice may be found in a great variety of forms. Crevasses are for the most part absent, but a host of new problems present themselves in the form of steep slopes and walls, ice-coated ridges and couloirs, overhanging cornices, avalanches and the like. Also, the snow and ice themselves may assume many different forms and combinations. One slope, for example, may consist altogether of solid ice; another of snow on ice; others of snow on rock, ice on rock, new snow on old snow, snow with a crust of ice, melting or freezing snow, melting or freezing ice. To make things still more difficult, conditions are never constant, but alter continually with changes in weather and temperature and the rising and setting of the sun.

In climbing steep ice- or snow-slopes the mountaineer's upward and downward progress is largely a matter of step-cutting with his ax. This can range from a fairly simple operation, in the case of sound snow, to an extremely laborious one, when the surface is of ice and scores of strokes must be made to effect one satisfactory step. On severe grades the staircase of steps is usually cut in zigzags rather than straight up or down, with an especially large step at each corner for security in turning. The tread of each step should slope very slightly inward and be deep enough to afford the climber support, not only for quick passage but also while engaged in cutting the next step. It is extremely important that the climber himself, in both step-cutting and step-taking, stand

as nearly erect as possible. Leaning in toward the slope may give the illusion of security, but the resulting outward pressure of the feet can
easily cause the snow or ice to break away beneath them. In the whole
operation balance and rhythm of movement count for far more than
strength.

Belaying is employed as a defensive measure in snow- and ice-climbing no less than on rock. Here, however, the rope is passed around the
haft of the ice-ax, which is then imbedded in the slope as firmly as possible and made to serve as the hitching point. The ax employed alone
can also be a most important protective device, for its prong, thrust
firmly into the slope, will generally check a slip before it develops into
an outright fall. Other useful articles of equipment are crampons, or
climbing irons. These consist of iron or steel frames, with projecting
spikes, that are fastened to the sole of the boot and permit the wearer
to gain a purchase on ice or hard snow which would otherwise be impossible. On long uphill trudges of not-too-steep gradient crampons
can take the place of step-cutting, but on extremely steep slopes they
serve merely as an additional safeguard against slipping.

If, in step-cutting, snow-slopes call for laborious climbing, they also
provide, in glissading, one of the most exhilarating experiences in
mountaineering. The glissade, as the name implies, is simply a slide,
and, as performed on long, smooth slopes, may perhaps be best described as skiing without skis. The climber, facing outward and throw-
ing his weight back on his heels, descends as rapidly as he can while
still keeping himself under control, his ice-ax, with spike thrust into
the snow on one side of him, acting as combination rudder and brake.
Stretches which would take two or three hours to descend by ordinary
step-cutting methods can in this fashion often be negotiated in a few
minutes. It is essential, however, that the snow be of the right consistency—firm but not ice-coated. If the surface is too slippery the climber
will be unable to control or stop himself; if it is too soft he will be
unable to gain momentum, and there will also be the serious danger of
his starting an avalanche. Unlike skiing, a fall in glissading will not
check one's speed, but increase it. It is therefore a maneuver that should
not be attempted by novices on steep slopes until they have first had
experience with it on gentler grades.

In gullies and chimneys the chief ice and snow hazards which a
climber faces are twofold—avalanches (which he may either start him-

self or which may descend on him from above), and slips on ice or *verglas*-covered rocks. On ridges the principal problem are cornices. Cornices, perhaps the most treacherous of all mountain phenomena, are masses of snow projecting from the main body of a ridge, usually on the side sheltered from the prevailing wind. Found for the most part in high and exposed places, they present two serious threats to the climber. The first is that of breaking away of their own weight and avalanching down upon him from above; the second is that of breaking away under his feet while he is moving along on top of them. Of the two dangers, the latter is more often encountered, and great care should be exercised in the climbing of any snow-ridge to make sure that one is actually treading the ridge itself and not merely a projecting shelf of unsupported snow. This is rendered doubly difficult by the fact that a cornice is seldom recognizable to a man who is actually on one; it must be located in advance and given a wide berth, even at the cost of the most difficult and arduous climbing. Indeed, there is no more important "must" than this in all the lore of mountaineering, for a corniced ridge, innocent though it may appear from above, is seldom anything but a white highway to destruction.

The variety of situations and conditions to be found in snow- and ice-climbing is almost limitless, particularly when winter and arctic mountaineering are taken into consideration; and it is impossible in a few paragraphs to do more than hint at a few of those most commonly encountered. In general, however, it may be said that climate and weather play a larger part than in rock-climbing and that the best time for an ascent is two or three days after a snowfall, in settled, but not melted, snow. Again and again the experiences of expeditions to the world's great ranges have shown that catching a mountain in the right condition is every bit as essential to success as the climbing abilities of the party itself. And time without number, on glacier and snow-field, ice-slope and cornice, the experienced and careful mountaineer has triumphed and survived, while his perhaps stronger, but more reckless, brother came to grief—if not to his death.

Clothing and Equipment

Along with the nylon rope, there has been one other great recent innovation in climbing equipment. This is new type of boot, soled with rubber, or synthetic rubber, cleats, which has almost completely re-placed the old nailed boot as the mountaineer's standard footgear. First introduced for military use during World War II, it has proven itself superior on almost all kinds of terrain, and today is accepted even by the guides of Switzerland, who ordinarily are as suspicious of change as a cat of water. For certain types of snow and ice work, as we have seen, crampons are often used in addition to the boots. On very steep rock, on the other hand, the boots are best discarded and rope-soled shoes or sneakers used in their place. This type of footgear is, indeed, absolutely essential on such delicate ascents as those of the Chamonix *aiguilles* and most of the Dolomites, as well as for cliff-climbing of the sort practiced by the "rock engineers." On snow or ice, however, or for long climbs over varied terrain, it is not only useless but dangerous.

The rest of a mountaineer's clothing varies, of course, according to locale, weather and the nature of the climb. In general, it should be warm and sturdy, but still so designed as to allow full freedom of movement; and experience has shown that several light- or medium-weight garments are usually preferable to one heavy, bulky one. In late years there has been great advancement in the making of windproof materials, and some of the down-lined jackets and coveralls used by recent Himalayan expeditions have been marvels of combined warmth and lightness. For high-altitude climbing, great improvements have also been made in boots and gloves, to give protection to those parts of the body most subject to frostbite. And dark glasses and skin lotions are essential to anyone facing the glare of high-mountain snow.

As for equipment, it has remained basically simple and can be re-duced to no more than the classic ax and rope—with perhaps a pair of crampons in reserve, if the route is to lead over snow and ice. This for the actual climbing itself. Add a knapsack with food and utensils, a sleeping bag, some extra clothing and a few first-aid items, and the average mountaineer is ready for his adventure. For a large expedition, of course, it is a different matter, and all manner of equipment may be brought into play, up to and including oxygen, radios and airplanes. Yet even here, it should be noted, most of the gear has little to do with climbing as such, but is rather concerned with the mere processes of keeping alive in a mountain wilderness. Recent expeditions have en-joyed a great advantage over earlier ones, in that the use of aluminum and other alloys have made much of their equipment far lighter than was formerly possible; and the development of concentrated and de-hydrated foods has also done a lot to ease the swaying, galling load on human backs.

It is not on the high-mountain expedition but in "rock engineering" —as the term implies—that special and elaborate climbing devices come into play. And the up-to-date cragsman approaching the base of his cliff is almost sure to have a supply of "hardware" clanking at his waist. If the climb is to be of only moderate difficulty, this may consist merely of pitons, piton hammer and karabiners. But if it is to be an all-out Sixth Degree affair, it will probably also include other more complicated instruments, such as rock drills for boring holes where no cracks for pitons exist, expansion and contraction bolts to fit into these, and rock anchors to hold the laboring cragsman in position. This is mechanized climbing in its most extreme form, and a cliff subject to such attack, festooned with iron and a maze of ropes, is apt to bear less resemblance to a mountainside than to a full-rigged ship or a sky-scraper under construction.

Climber and Mountaineer

To climb the unclimbable; to conquer the unconquered. This is part of mountaineering. But so too is an afternoon's scramble up Old Baldy or the ascent of an Alpine peak that has been surmounted a thousand times before. It is perhaps the greatest attraction of the sport that it offers to everyone exactly what he may be seeking, in terms of his taste, his ambition and his ability. This chapter will have served its purpose if it has merely indicated this boundless variety and, in some degree, made clear the fundamental distinction between a climber and a mountaineer.

Simple climbing proficiency is for the most part based on the same factors as proficiency in other sports. It demands good health and a measure of natural aptitude; strength, agility and endurance; co-ordina-tion of the body and discipline of the nerves; and a certain amount of technical knowledge derived from experience. It is concerned almost exclusively with physical activity, and its purpose is to take a man up a mountain and then back again, as quickly and safely as possible. In short, to climb is to go up or to go down.

Mountaineering, however, is something much more than this—some-thing both simpler and far more complex. In its broadest aspects it is concerned with every field of human knowledge and experience that bears any relation to life and activity on the high places of the earth. Time and again throughout the history of the sport—and, indeed, throughout almost any individual ascent—we see the mountaineer changing his role to fit the changing circumstances and situations in which he finds himself. One moment he is a cragsman, clinging to a dizzy precipice; the next he is a meteorologist studying the barometer; again a homesteader searching for a secure spot to pitch his tent and sleep. He is geologist, cartographer, trail-scout, botanist, cook, rope-splicer, photographer, explorer, guide, follower, philosopher, friend. He is not merely a climber, but a man at home on a mountain.

Yet the principle underlying all this activity is simplicity itself. It is —once again to quote Geoffrey Young—"the pursuit of the happiest kind of adventure which is consistent with the degree of one's experience, with one's sense of proportion, and with one's respect for noble scenery and a noble sport." In other words, the making of a mountaineer depends not so much on what a man does, as on what he is; not on what vertical cliffs and dizzy summits he has conquered, but on what he carries with him in his mind and heart.

17

BEHIND THE RANGES

Something hidden. Go and find it. Go and look behind the Ranges—
Something lost behind the Ranges. Lost and waiting for you. Go!
                                        —*Rudyard Kipling.*

SO MEN HAVE GONE— alone, in pairs, in small groups, in great expeditions—searching out the high, hidden places of the earth. They have climbed the cliffs of England, the rugged ranges of North America, the gleaming rock and ice spires of the Alps. They have journeyed thousands of miles to the Caucasus, the Andes, the lost peaks of Africa and the vast uplifts of Central Asia. They have sought out the summits of the Arctic and Antarctic and of the islands of the sea. Wherever in the world great mountains stand, there have been men who lifted their eyes to them and vowed that they would get to the top.

Some have got to the top; some have not. Some have found victory and fulfillment behind the ranges; others disappointment, defeat, and sometimes death. All have found danger and privation, long drudgery and backbreaking work. But all, too, have found in the struggle something profoundly worth the doing—for its own sake; and in the end it has always been the spirit of the climbers, rather than their achievement, that has given meaning and stature to their enterprises. Some of the finest exploits in mountaineering history have fallen short of their goals. Men have touched greatness no less in their defeats than in their victories. That is the mountain way.

In the preceding pages there have been many references to climbing as *sport*. And so it is—to a degree. But it is not a sport that can be fitted into one of the usual categories, complete with rules, schedules, contests and spectators. Perhaps this last is the most significant: that mountaineering, by its very nature, is almost never seen by anyone but its participants. There is the climber, his companions, the mountain. And that is all. Except in the rarest cases, as on a Matterhorn or an Everest, no one is following his progress. No one is umpiring or keeping score. As near as is possible in the modern world, he is a man on his own, and his rewards and penalties are known to himself alone.

Another much-used word has been *conquest;* but even more than *sport,* it is only a label of convenience. For a mountain is never "conquered." The Matterhorn today can hurl down murderous canonades of stones as fiercely as a century ago. The Jungfrau or Mount Rainier can still annihilate a man by the crumbling of a ledge or the tremor of a snowpatch. Even such domesticated little ranges as the White Mountains or Adirondacks can on occasion become formidable with wind and cold, snow, storm and darkness. There is no royal road to the high places, but only the road of skill and knowledge, care and enterprise, patience and hard work; and of no field of human activity can it be said more truly that a man receives according to what he gives. "Mountains are to be wooed and won," Robert Bates has written. "Not attacked and vanquished." The Nazis on the Eigerwand did not know this; there are foolish and reckless climbers today who do not know it; but it is the first of all things that must be understood by a true mountaineer. It is not love of conquest that brings a man to a great summit—and down again alive. It is love—and respect—for the mountain itself.

Mountaineering is more than a sport, more than conquest. And it is more than mere adventure, too, if by adventure one means only the facing of physical obstacles and dangers. Think back for a moment to the climbs and climbers that fill the pages of this book. To de Saussure dreaming, "with an aching of desire," of the white summit of Mont Blanc; to Whymper struggling, failing and returning to struggle, again and again, on the grim walls of "that awful mountain"; to Mummery inching his way up the slabs of the towering Grépon; to the Duke of the Abruzzi following the mountain gleam from horizon to horizon;

to Herzog and Lachenal stumbling back to the world of men from the white death of Annapurna; to Mallory and Irvine vanishing forever into the mists of Everest; to Norton, Smythe and Lambert bowed in bitter defeat with the goal so near, yet unattainable; to Hillary and Tenzing creeping up that ultimate ridge to stand at last, victorious upon the summit of the world. Their story has been indeed badly told if it is not clear that their motives are deeper than reaching this or that bump on the earth's surface; that all these are not merely scenes from an exciting melodrama, but part of a profound experience of the human spirit.

The mountain way is a way of life. An attitude and a response to life. A mountain is there; climb it. An ocean is there; cross it. A disease is there; cure it. A wrong is there: right it. On the surface, perhaps, these are very different things. But in essence they are identically the same thing. The various words, and a hundred more, could be erased, and a single word substituted. The word is *challenge.* . . . A challenge is there. Meet it. . . . It is the very act of meeting it that makes us more than animals—if somewhat less than gods.

In mountaineering the challenge is limitless. It does not have to be to Everest or a virgin Eightthousander. For every climber who blazes a trail to the unknown heights of the Himalayas or Andes there are thousands who follow the familiar routes up familiar peaks: to the summits of the Alps and Rockies, the crests of New England and Scotland, Norway and New Zealand, wherever mountains rise high and beckoning above the valleys. They set no records. They conquer no unconquerables. But they are no less mountaineers because the peaks they climb have been climbed before. They find adventure on their slopes, wonder and glory on their summits, whether they are the thousandth to stand there or the first. The heroes on Everest and the dubs on Old Baldy are not separated by so great a gulf as a statistician might think.

Men go to the mountains because they need the mountains; because they find behind the ranges things that are hidden from them in the life of the plains. "Our present world," the English writer, Frederic Harrison, once said, "is a world of remarkable civilization, but it is not very natural and not very happy. We need some snatches of the life of youth—to be for a season simply happy and simply healthy. We need to draw sometimes great draughts of simplicity and beauty.

We need sometimes that poetry should not be droned into our ears, but flashed into our senses. And man, with all his knowledge and his pride, needs sometimes to know nothing and to feel nothing, but that he is a marvellous atom in a marvellous world." These words of a man who knew and loved mountains were written a good many years ago. But surely they ring no less true today, in a world darkened by strife and hatred, doubt and fear.

Indeed, there has been no time in human history when mountains and mountaineering have had so much to offer to men. We need to rediscover the vast, harmonious pattern of the natural world of which we are a part—the infinite complexity and variety of its components, the miraculous simplicity of the whole. We need to learn again those essential qualities in our own selves which make us what we are: the energy of our bodies, the alertness of our minds; curiosity and the desire to satisfy it, weakness and will to master it. The mountain way may well be a way of escape—from turmoil and doubt, from war and the threat of war, from the perplexities and sorrows of the artificial world we have built ourselves to live in. But in the truest and most profound sense it is an escape not *from* but *to* reality.

Over and above all else, the story of mountaineering is a story of faith and affirmation . . . that the high road is the good road; that there are still among us those who are willing to struggle and suffer greatly for wholly ideal ends; that security is not the be-all and end-all of living; that there are conquests to be won in the world other than over our fellow-men. The climbing of earth's heights, in itself, means little. That men want and try to climb them means everything. For it is the ultimate wisdom of the mountains that man is never so much a man as when he is striving for what is beyond his grasp, and that there is no battle worth the winning save that against his own ignorance and fear.

Have we vanquished an enemy?
None but ourselves.

It is not the summit that matters, but the fight for the summit. Not the victory, but the game itself.

Topping a Pinnacle

A Rappel

MOUNTAIN CRAFT

Courtesy Swiss National Travel Office

Step-Cutting

Skirting a Crevasse

"HAVE WE VANQUISHED AN ENEMY?"

Courtesy Swiss National Travel Office

ADDENDUM:

Mountaineering, 1954-1964

THE YEARS MARCH ON. More than a decade has now passed since the first climbing of Everest. But that event, great climax though it was, by no means marked the end of an era, or of adventure in high places. Far from fading away, the age of mountaineering has continued at an ever-accelerating pace.

It has been a time of cold, but at least not hot, war. With the coming of jet planes the earth has shrunk more drastically than ever before. Almost everywhere, climbs and climbers have multiplied; techniques and equipment have been vastly developed; and the result is that even the mountains themselves seem to have shared in earth's shrinkage. On Old Baldies and Eightthousanders, on roadside cliffs and the heights of Everest, feats have been performed that a few short years ago would have been deemed impossible.

In the Alps, the birthplace of mountaineering, each successive year has seen more and more climbing of the classic peaks. And the fraternity of experts has achieved ascents by new and "special" routes that would have stunned the imagination of earlier generations. The north wall of the Eiger, of infamous history, has now been scaled by many climbers of many nations; and though it continues to take its grisly toll (the latest figure is a total of twenty-seven lives lost), it continues to attract

its challengers as the ultimate test of skill and daring. Other of the
"unclimbable" Alpine north faces—on the Matterhorn and the Grandes
Jorasses, in the Swiss Engadine and the Italian Dolomites—have been
subjected to attack after attack, many of them spectacularly successful.

Most such ascents take days to accomplish. With no ledges large
enough to hold even the tiniest tent, the climbers spend the nights sitting
or standing, lashed by their ropes to the mountain wall; and through
the daylight hours they wage an endless battle with verticality, with
rotten ice-glazed rock, with stonefall and avalanche, cold and storm. To
most mere humans—indeed to many mountaineers—such enterprises
smack more of self-imposed torture than of sport or adventure. But to
the elite of modern alpinism they represent the ultimate in challenge and
satisfaction; and there is no denying that here, in its special way, is a
demonstration of man pushing his skill and courage to their ultimate
limits. For the most ambitious, even such climbing, in the comparative
balm of summer, is not enough. Several of the most difficult of the
Alps' north faces have now been ascended in winter.

On our own home grounds, in the United States, there have also
been great advances in mountaineering skills and accomplishments. But
since we have few "faces" comparable to those of the Alps in size,
severity and variety of terrain, developments here have followed a rather
different course. Principally these have been in the realm of pure rock
climbing—in the perfecting of techniques and equipment for the scaling
of cliffs—and in the forefront has been a group of cragsmen known
as the Yosemite Climbers, whose laboratory has been the vast granite
walls of Yosemite National Park in California. Here there are no snow
and ice, no cold and few storms to contend with. But the smooth perpendicular precipices seem, to the groundling's eye, to be as "unclimbable" as is possible, and the scaling of them has been a marvel of skill,
daring and persistence.

As with the Alpine north faces, most of these climbs—on El Capitan,
Half Dome and such—take days to accomplish. But here the scale is
small enough so that retreat in case of trouble is usually possible, and
food and gear can, when needed, be hauled up from below. On the
less severe pitches climbing is "free," meaning without aids other than
a protective rope. When the going is harder—which is most of the time
—it becomes "artificial," an exercise in rock engineering, with a vast
assortment of pitons, bolts and rope slings called into use to make the

impossible possible. To the casual Yosemite tourist, staring up from the valley below, such climbing, of whichever genre, appears primarily as an elaborate form of suicide. But in actual fact it has led to few fatalities, or even serious accidents. Partly this has been because of the high level of proficiency attained by the cragsmen; partly because, as indicated, the scale and conditions of the ascents are such that an escape hatch is usually available when needed.

Still, such aerial acrobatics are for the specialized few. In the United States, as in Europe, most mountaineering is of a more conservative sort; and it is one of the heartening things in an often disheartening world that more and more Americans—not super-experts, but no dubs either—are being attracted to our country's high and hidden places. Membership in climbing clubs grows steadily in number and in level of performance. Mountaineering schools in Wyoming's Tetons and on Washington's Mount Rainier are now long- and well-established and boast an impressive roster of both teachers and clients. Though not yet as far along the mountain way as most European countries, America has at least reached the point of recognizing that a mountaineer is not, *ipso facto,* a certified lunatic.

Until recently, a schoolboy answering "What is the highest mountain in the United States?" with "Mount Whitney" would have received his full A. But no longer; for now that Alaska is a state, there are many that surpass it. Pre-eminent, of course, is "The Great One," Mount McKinley, and it is a measure of mountaineering progress that this sub-Arctic giant, which saw a lapse of nineteen years between its first and second ascents, is now, more often than not, climbed annually by several parties. This is not to say that—though three women have now reached its top—it has become "an easy day for a lady." North America's apex is still tall and vast, ringed with cold and storm. But, as with mountains everywhere, familiarity has bred knowledge, knowledge has bred competence, and the result has been dozens of recent successful ascents. Also as on other peaks, ambitious climbers have not been content merely to follow where others have led, and McKinley has now been scaled by many routes up its ridges and faces. (In the summer of 1962 alone, six parties reached its summit from three different directions.) Further, like Alps and Himalayas, it has become international climbing terrain, luring challengers from many countries, including Italy and Japan. Indeed, the most spectacular feat yet performed on its ice walls was the ascent of its theretofore virginal South Face in 1961 by a team of expert Italians.

Though visited far less often than McKinley, our continent's second and third highest summits, Mounts Logan and St. Elias, have in recent years each been reached for the second time. And each summer sees new attempts and ascents, first and otherwise, on many of the host of other peaks in Alaska and the neighboring Yukon. Each year, too, there are forays into the once sealed-off wilderness of British Columbia, and the time may not be distant when this region will be as familiar to climbers as the Tetons, the Cascades and the Canadian Rockies.

Farther from home, and second in scale only to the mountains of Asia, the Andes of South America have also been getting their full share of attention. Every year since World II there has been at least one, and often several, expeditions from the United States active somewhere in the huge range from northern Colombia to southern Chile; and there has been much climbing, also, by South Americans and by representatives of almost every nation in Western Europe. The focus of activity has been in the great cordilleras of Peru, where the scale and terrain of the mountains are roughly halfway between those of the Alps and Himalayas. So much so, indeed, that most of the major summits have now been scaled, and the future would seem to lie largely in the forging of new routes up old peaks. But outlying areas remain which have scarcely been touched by climbers, and it will be a long time before the great uplift from Caribbean to Cape Horn will be all *vieux jeu* to the explorer-mountaineer.

Elsewhere on the shrunken earth there has been the same pattern of more climbers, more climbs, more successful ascents. During the International Geophysical Year, of 1957-58, frontiers were pushed back to the point where many arctic and antarctic peaks were surveyed, and some even scaled, for the first time. And it is probably safe to say that there is today not a major peak left on earth with which mountaineers are not, at least to some degree, familiar. Further, the expansion has been not only geographical but human; for mountaineering, which a century ago was almost the exclusive province of a small, elite group of British gentlemen—and even until World War II was practiced only by small groups in Western, or highly Westernized, nations—has now been woven into the fabric of life in every civilized country. The Russians, in good totalitarian fashion, have taken to the mountains en masse, with crowds swarming to the Caucasus, as Western Europeans swarm to the Alps, and ambitious expeditions operating in the Pamirs and other ranges of Central Asia. The Chinese have begun to explore and climb their own mountains and have even launched a try for Everest. Most remarkable of all, in view of their long history of physical quiescence, the Indians have, since their independence, been extremely active in the Himalayas, conducting many expeditions, including two to Everest that came within a hairbreadth of success. It is not only earth's mountains that are international, but its mountaineers as well.

Nowhere is this more apparent than in the Himalayas, where in every year of the last decade a dozen or more nations have been represented in the struggle for the great peaks. And it is here, in what has been called The Golden Age of the Himalayas, that mountaineers have won their brightest triumphs. Disregarding for the moment all other peaks, take only the story of the Eightthousanders, those fourteen giants among giants which rise to a height of more than 8000 meters, or roughly 26,250 feet, above the sea. As of 1953, only three of them—Everest, Nanga Parbat and Annapurna—had been climbed to the top. But by 1960 all but one had been scaled; and that, the lowest of the lot, was missed because of political, not mountaineering, inaccessibility.*

First to fall, after Everest and Nanga Parbat, was K2, King of the Karakoram and second highest mountain on earth, which was climbed in the summer of 1954 by a strong party of Italians. Led by Ardito Desio, a geologist and university professor from Milan, the climbers attacked the peak by the same route up which American teams had struggled in 1938, 1939 and 1953. After almost two months of struggle they pushed on past the highest points reached by their predecessors. And on July 31 two of them, Achille Compagnoni and Lino Lacedelli, in an all-out push comparable to that of Hillary and Tenzing on Everest the year before, went all the way to the 28,250-foot summit. Thus the long campaign for K2, which the Duke of the Abruzzi had launched in the early days of Himalayan climbing, culminated in a great victory for his countrymen, almost a half-century later.

Like the victorious British on Everest, the Italians attacked with a

---

* For a listing, with locations and heights, of the Eightthousanders, see p. 192. Also the map of the Himalayas on pp. 176-77.

large and powerful task force. But in that same year of 1954 another Eightthousander was climbed by a party so small that it can scarcely be called an expedition at all. The mountain was Cho Oyu, 26,750 feet high, on the Nepalese-Tibetan border not far from Everest; and the team consisted of only three Austrians, headed by Dr. Herbert Tichy, and a small group of Sherpas. The peak had been attempted unsuccessfully in 1952 by a strong British party that included Eric Shipton and Edmund Hillary. In the autumn of 1954, shortly after Tichy and his companions had launched their campaign, still another expedition arrived at the base of the mountain, led by the Swiss Raymond Lambert and the outstanding French woman climber, Claude Kogan. These latter suggested that the two groups join forces. But Tichy, determined to put his strong belief in small expeditions to the test, declined; and subsequently he, Sepp Jöchler, and the redoubtable Sherpa, Pasang Dawa Lama, gained Cho Oyu's summit, in what must unquestionably be ranked as one of the great performances in Himalayan history. Conceding the Austrians' precedence, the Lambert-Kogan team waited at the foot of the peak until Tichy & Company had completed their exploit. Then they made their own try, but were defeated by the winds and blizzards of oncoming winter.

The following year, 1955, also saw two notable victories on earth's highest crests: by the British on third-ranking Kangchenjunga and by the French on fifth-ranking Makalu. Following the second German siege of Kangchenjunga in 1931, no climbers had challenged the mountain for almost a quarter of a century, and it had developed a reputation as a probably unclimbable peak. Then at last, in 1954, an English party conducted a new reconnaissance of its approaches, and the following spring a second group arrived for an all-out assault. Its success was spectacular. Led by Dr. Charles Evans, who had barely missed reaching the summit of Everest in 1953, the climbers made their attack from the southwest, a route never before attempted, and in a marvellously coordinated and effective campaign were presently within striking distance of their goal. On May 25 the "unreachable" summit was reached by George Band and Joe Brown, on the next day by Norman Hardie and Tony Streather, in a successful climax that astonished the mountaineering world. An interesting and unusual feature of the double ascent was that all four climbers, in deference to the feelings of the Himalayan hill people, to whom Kangchenjunga is sacred, refrained from setting foot on the utmost crest of the 28,146-foot peak. But the mountain had been climbed for all that, and the British were now the winners of earth's first and third highest summits.

Meanwhile, some hundred miles to the west, great deeds were also being performed by the French on 27,790-foot Makalu, a short distance southeast of Everest. The previous year there had been no less than three expeditions in the Makalu area: one American (which climbed the Southeast Ridge to 23,200 feet), one British (North Ridge to 23,000), and one French (which did not attempt the peak itself, but scaled its lesser neighbor, Makalu II). Now in 1955 only the French returned, their cap set for Makalu itself, and like the British on Kangchenjunga they scored a signal triumph. Choosing a route of their own, they followed a spiral course up the mountain from west to north; and it proved the right route, carrying them swiftly, indeed with almost astonishing ease, to the second French conquest (Annapurna had been the first) of an Eighthousander. Most remarkable of all, it was a conquest en masse; for, of leader Jean Franco's eight-man team, every one reached the summit—which, with one Sherpa added, made a record-setting nine men atop one of earth's highest peaks.

Two Eightthousanders in 1954. Two more in 1955. Then in 1956 came the bumper year, with a bag of three. Highest of this lot was fourth-ranking Lhotse, 27,890 feet high, separated from Everest only by the lofty saddle of the South Col. It had been unsuccessfully challenged the previous year by a mixed American-Swiss-Austrian expedition led by the noted United States climber, Norman Dyhrenfurth; but now, attempted again, it fell to an all-Swiss team during the course of the same expedition (*see later*) on which it made the second ascent of Everest. The feat was accomplished by two climbers, Fritz Luchsinger and Ernst Reiss, after a long and arduous struggle up one of the steep ice couloirs that furrow Lhotse's northwestern face.

A second success of the same year was that of a Japanese expedition to Manaslu, a 26,668-foot neighbor of Dhaulagiri and Annapurna in the great uplift of west-central Nepal. By now Manaslu was a thoroughly "Japanese" mountain, for this was the fourth team from that country to set its sights for it. In 1952 there had been a reconnaissance; in 1953 an attempt that carried to within 1250 feet of the top; and in 1954 the would-be climbers had suffered an extraordinary and frustrating experience when they were prevented from making their try by the opposition of hostile hillmen from the surrounding countryside. Now at last, however, perseverance was to have its reward. The mountain was reached without hindrance. A long string of camps was established on its icy slopes. And on May 9 and 11 two teams of two men each reached the long-sought goal, in a fine triumph for the first Asian nation to turn its serious attention to mountaineering.

The third of the "superpeaks" to fall in 1956 was Gasherbrum II, 26,360 feet, a thousand-and-more miles to the northwest in the Pakistani Himalayan subrange of the Karakoram. The venture was by Austrians and was almost routed at the outset by a ten-day blizzard and a huge avalanche. But the climbers managed to rally their forces and in the end put three men on the summit, to tally the tenth triumph in the battle for the fourteen Eightthousanders.

In 1957 only one victory was added to the list: on Broad Peak, 26,400 feet, which is also in the Karakoram. And this ascent, too, was made by Austrians, giving them a proud foursome of "firsts" (the others being Nanga Parbat, Cho Oyu and Gasherbrum II) on earth's highest summits. Among the four men who reached the top was Hermann Buhl, of Nanga Parbat fame. But a few weeks later, during the attempt on a nearby peak called Chogolisa (formerly known as Bride Peak), Buhl, climbing unroped, fell through a crumbling snow cornice and plunged thousands of feet to his death.

1958: Again one peak; again in the Karakoram. But this time—and for the first time—it was an American team that climbed an Eightthousander. Its objective was Hidden Peak, known also as Gasherbrum I, which at 26,470 feet ranks second only to K2 in the Pakistan Himalayas, and in its successful completion of mission it at last broke the long run of frustration that expeditions from the United States had encountered on the roof of the world. The venture was sponsored by the American Alpine Club; its prime mover and leader was Nicholas B. Clinch; and the other participants were Richard Irvin, Andrew Kauffman, Thomas McCormack, Thomas Nevison, Jr., Gilbert Roberts, Jr., Peter Schoening* and Robert Swift. Well planned and conducted—and with a better-than-average break from the weather—the expedition conducted its reconnoitering and camp-stocking in good order. And on July 5, after a stiff snow-and-ice climb, the summit was reached by Schoening and Kauffman.

---

* The same Schoening who did such yeoman work on K2 in 1953.

In 1959, for the first time in seven years, no Eightthousander was climbed to the top. But in 1960 one of the longest campaigns in Himalayan history reached a successful climax in the ascent of Dhaulagiri, the 26,810-foot monarch of west-central Nepal. This peak, it will be recalled, had been the first-choice objective of Maurice Herzog's French expedition of 1950, but after reconnaissance he and his men had deemed it too formidable even to attempt and turned their attention to nearby Annapurna. Others following after, however, had accepted the challenge, and from 1953 through 1959 no fewer than six climbing parties —two Argentine, two Swiss, one Swiss-German, one Austrian—had tried their luck on the mountain. But it had all been bad, with results ranging from near misses to utter routs. Called "the mountain of storms," Dhaulagiri was well on its way to being considered unclimbable.

Then came 1960, and again the classic end for "unclimbables." The victorious expedition, led by Max Eiselin, was predominantly Swiss, but included also a German, an Austrian, a Pole and an American—the last in the person of Norman Dyhrenfurth. It was notable, therefore, not only in its success, but for its international character, and also for the fact that it was the first, and remains the only, Himalayan expedition to use an aircraft to fly climbers and equipment in to its mountain. The pros and cons of the plane seem about to have canceled each other out. On the plus side, it made world-record landings as high as 18,700 feet, saving a vast amount of time and labor. On the minus, the swift transition from low to high altitudes caused serious acclimatization problems for several of the climbers; and further, in the course of operations, the plane cracked up twice—the second time for good—though fortunately with no resultant casualties. In any case, the actual climbing operations went better than ever before. On May 13 no less than six climbers, including two Sherpas, reached Dhaulagiri's theretofore inviolate summit, and ten days later two more followed after them, for an end result of total victory.

Thus, in eleven brief years from 1950 through 1960, thirteen of the world's fourteen Eightthousanders were first climbed to the top. Three of them—Everest, Cho Oyu and Nanga Parbat—have been reclimbed: Everest twice (*see later*), the other two once each: Cho Oyu by an Indian expedition in 1958 and Nanga Parbat by Germans in 1962. The last of the unclimbed Eightthousanders, Gosainthan (known also as Shisha Pangma), which lies wholly in Tibet, was, according to announcement from Peking, scaled by a Communist Chinese expedition in May, 1964. At 26,290 feet, Gosainthan ranks fourteenth among the world's peaks and is the lowest of those that are more than 8000 meters high.

The Great Himalayas, to be sure, consist of more than Eightthousanders. Over the past decade there have been expeditions by the score, and even hundred, to the slightly lesser peaks of the vast range—many of them no less formidable than the giants—and here too there has been a notable record of success. Most spectacular of all, perhaps, was the ascent, in 1956, of that "impossible of impossibles," the huge obelisk of the Mustagh Tower in the Karakoram; and the drama of the feat was compounded by the astonishing fact that it was climbed not once but twice, almost simultaneously, by two different routes. First up was a British team of only four members, who attacked the sheer rock and ice walls of the northwest ridge and gained the 23,860-foot pinnacle on the seventh of July. And a mere five days later a small French party, following the equally formidable east ridge, also forged a way to the top.

Other outstanding Karakoram climbs were those of Gasherbrum IV (26,000 feet) by Italians in 1958 and of Masherbrum (25,660 feet) by Americans in 1960. The latter was directed by Nicholas Clinch, who had headed the Hidden Peak expedition of 1958, with George Bell as climbing leader, and both reached the summit, along with William Unsoeld and Captain Jawed Akhter of the Pakistani Army—the latter becoming the first native of his country ever to scale one of the great peaks of his homeland. It was on Gasherbrum's summit that Bell delivered himself of what has since become one of the classics of mountaineering lore. His companion, Unsoeld, had knelt briefly in prayer on the topmost snows, and when he had finished and risen Bell inquired of him, "Well, Willi, shall we go down—or up?"

Elsewhere in the Himalayas there have also been notable ascents. To list only a few of many, these include climbs of Annapurna II (26,041 feet) by a British-Indian-Nepalese expedition in 1960; of Everest's neighbor, Nuptse (25,850 feet), by the British in 1961; of Pumori (23,442 feet), also near Everest, by Germans and Swiss in 1962—after six earlier attempts had failed; and of Jannu (25,294 feet) in the Kangchenjunga area, by the French in 1962. This last exploit, which followed after a reconnaissance of Jannu in 1959, was led by Lionel Terray, one of the 1955 conquerors of Makalu, and ranks as one of the most difficult climbs ever made in the Himalayas. But nevertheless the Makalu record for most summit climbers was broken, with eleven men —nine French and two Sherpa—reaching the top.

By no means, of course, were all expeditions successful. On the lesser peaks, as on the Eightthousanders, there have been far more defeats than victories, ranging from the narrowest near misses to rout and disaster. Among the distinguished "almosts" was a 1957 attempt on needle-sharp Machapuchare (22,958 feet) in central Nepal, in which a small British party was stopped by steep ice and foul weather less than 150 feet from the summit. Among the disasters was the fate that befell the International Women's Expedition of 1959 (all-female except for Sherpas), trying for a third ascent on Cho Oyu, in which four climbers, including the noted Madame Claude Kogan, were killed by avalanches. Indeed, no year has passed in which accident, illness and death have failed to take their toll on the great peaks; but at least the incidence of catastrophe is lower than it was during the 1920's and 1930's.

In addition to ventures wholly concerned with climbing, there have also, in recent years, been many Himalayan expeditions with other more general aims. There has been much surveying and mapping, research in geology and glaciology, investigation of fauna and flora. The search for the Abominable Snowman, or *yeti,* goes on apace—still with inconclusive, but largely negative, results. And in 1960-61 the Everest-Makalu area of northeastern Nepal was the scene of something new in Himalayan annals: a large multipurpose enterprise called the Himalayan Scientific and Mountaineering Expedition. Backed by the World Book Encyclopedia, led by Sir Edmund Hillary, and staffed by specialists from England, Australia, New Zealand, India and the United States, this conglomerate unit was in the field for nine months and included in its scope almost all the afore-mentioned activities, with a few others added. In mountaineering, there were two major ventures: (1) a remarkable first ascent of Ama Dablam, a spectacular 22,494-foot replica of the Mustagh Tower, by four climbers, including the American Barry Bishop; and (2) a semidisastrous attempt to scale Makalu without oxygen. On the latter climb, three men, in a tremendous effort, got to within a scant 250 feet of the summit; but all suffered severely from oxygen deficiency, barely escaping from the mountain with their lives, and one, badly frostbitten, subsequently lost both his feet.

Such, in brief outline, has been the chronicle of Himalayan adventure during the past decade—with one story still to be added: the story of Everest.

In Chapter 15 of this book, written soon after the 1953 first ascent of the highest mountain,* is the statement: "For a while, Everest will probably recede into the background." But unless a mere two years can be considered "a while," it was bad prophecy. From 1956 through 1963 no less than six subsequent expeditions have tried their strength, skill and luck on the King of Mountains.

First, in '56, came the Swiss, who had so narrowly missed the goal the year before the British; and this time they pushed on to a brilliant, if belated, success. Raymond Lambert and Tenzing Norgay † were no longer with them. But a strong new team, composed mostly of German-Swiss, had been assembled under the leadership of Albert Eggler; and following the tracks of their predecessors, they moved smoothly and powerfully up the mountain. In due time the South Col was reached; a highest camp was pitched on the southeast ridge above it; and from there, on May 24, Jürg Marmet and Ernst Schmied climbed on to the summit. The following day the performance was repeated by Adolf Reist and Hans-Rudolph von Gunten. Further—as already noted—two other climbers made the first ascent of neighboring Lhotse, thus giving the expedition the added distinction of being the first, and still the only, party to climb two Eightthousanders in the course of one campaign.

Following the Swiss ascent there was another two-year lapse in "Everesting"; and then, in 1960 and 1962, came two Indian expeditions, manned by climbers largely drawn from that country's armed services. Both were a blend of achievement and disappointment, for while they got high, neither reached the top. On the first try the lead climbers pushed to within 700 feet of the goal, on the second even slightly higher, only to be forced down by storms and the lack of suffi-

---

* There is no longer any doubt that Everest is earth's No. 1 peak. The ghost of Amni Machen has been laid once and for all by a Chinese survey which fixed its height at a mere 23,490 feet.

† Sherpas have no family surnames. During his early career, *the* Tenzing was usually designated as Tenzing Bhotia to distinguish him from many others of the same name; but after the climbing of Everest he opted for a change to Norgay.

cient manpower and gear to weather them out. They were heartbreaking defeats. But for a nation with no mountaineering tradition, and which a few years before had numbered scarcely a single mountaineer in all its vast population, India, in its almost-but-not-quite efforts, did itself proud.

It remained for another Asian nation, the Chinese, to place a third claim to going all the way. In 1960, they say—at the same time that the Indians were on the Nepalese side of Everest—an expedition of their own launched an attack on the Tibetan side, during the course of which three men gained the summit and left a plaster bust of Mao Tse Tung as a memento of their visit. Unlike the mysterious Russian venture of 1952, the Chinese climb is known to have taken place and to have carried fairly high on the mountain. But the account of it, as released to the world, was so saturated in Communist propaganda, so vague in moun-taineering detail, that most non-Chinese climbers (including Russian) have strong doubts that the summit claim is true.

In 1962 still another nationality entered the scene: this time Amer-icans. Our country's first go at earth's rooftop can scarcely, however, be called a true expedition, for it comprised only four men (one a Swiss) of very limited mountaineering experience, and in terms of organization and status was strictly a "bootleg" operation. The leader of the venture was Woodrow Wilson Sayre, a grandson of our former president and a philosophy professor at Tufts University. Making their approach through Nepal, he and his companions told Nepalese and American officials that they were bound for a peak called Gyachung Kang in the Everest region. But once in the wilderness, they crossed a pass into Tibet (i.e., Communist China), reached the northern base of Everest without being intercepted, and climbed to more than 25,000 feet, above the North Col, before coming to the end of their tether. Besides being little more than mountain novices, they were short on food and gear and had not a single porter with them. And, given the circumstances, theirs was a remarkable performance. But it is no less remarkable that they neither killed themselves ten times over nor triggered a nasty international "incident"; and, in any rational view, the attractive derring-do of the venture is far overshadowed by its irresponsibility.

Then came 1963. And a different story.

Americans, as we have seen, were comparative latecomers to ambitious mountaineering. In the Himalayas, during the 1920's and 1930's, our activities were scattered and mostly on a small scale (with the notable exception of the K2 ventures); but in recent years we have been busy making up for lost time—on K2, again; on Makalu, Lhotse, Hidden Peak, Masherbrum and other peaks, compiling a record that, if not superlative, is at least nothing to be ashamed of. It was not, however, until 1963 that our top climbers had their chance at the greatest prize of all.

The originator and leader of the American Mount Everest Expedition, 1963—or AMEE, as it came to be known—was Norman G. Dyhrenfurth, by then a veteran of four Himalayan ventures; and the labors of organization and financing occupied him full time for almost three years. In the end, however, all the threads were drawn together. A large and strong team of twenty men was assembled. They were supplied with the very best in food, clothing and equipment. A variety of scientific projects were mounted to augment and complement the actual climbing operations. And by late March AMEE was established at its Base Camp at the foot of Everest.

On the second day on the mountain tragedy struck. While helping forge a way through the Khumbu Icefall, John E. Breitenbach, an expert young climber from Jackson, Wyoming, was caught in the collapse of an ice cliff and instantly killed; and for the next few days his companions remained in a state of almost immobilized shock at the base of the peak. Then they pulled themselves together. The work of climbing went on. Following the route of the British, Swiss and Indians, the team pushed on up through the Western Cwm, up the Lhotse Face, to the South Col and beyond. And on May 1, James Whittaker and the Sherpa Nawang Gombu moved up through raging winds to earth's highest point, 29,028 feet above the sea.*

It was the hope and plan of AMEE, however, to do more than merely repeat, or less than repeat, what others had done before it. While operations had been proceeding on the conventional route, a reconnaissance had also been conducted on Everest's untouched and unknown West Ridge; and after the Whittaker-Gombu ascent an ambitious two-pronged assault was launched in an effort to climb the mountain simultaneously from two directions. One task force went to work again on the

---

* As has been noted earlier, Everest's height was first reckoned as 29,002 feet, later as 29,141. In a survey following the 1953 British ascent the figure was again adjusted, this time to 29,028 feet, and this is the height currently accepted.

old route. Another moved probingly up the West Ridge. And on May 22 two 2-man teams—Luther Jerstad and Barry Bishop on the South Col route, William Unsoeld and Thomas Hornbein on the ridge—arrived some two hours apart on the summit of the world. Unsoeld and Hornbein then traversed the peak and, following the others, began the descent toward the South Col. But darkness fell before either team could reach the shelter of tents, and, having joined forces, the four men spent the night in the open at more than 28,000 feet. Luckily, it was almost windless. They survived and got down the mountain. Two of them, Bishop and Unsoeld, had suffered frozen feet and later lost their toes. But both felt the game was worth the candle, for they had realized the ambition of a lifetime.

For the expedition, too, the enterprise was a dream come true; for though a stiff and tragic price had been paid, all that could conceivably have been hoped for had been accomplished on the mountain. With AMEE-1963, American mountaineering truly came of age.*

The question of course arises as to the cause of this great flowering of Himalayan climbing in recent years. And the answer is not that a new breed of supermen has appeared. Part of the reason for the wave of successes—at least after Annapurna and Everest—is unquestionably psychological. Once a barrier has been broken, its subsequent breaking is an easier affair, whether it be in space or the setting of track records or the scaling of mountains. But even more than this, in mountaineering as in astronautics, foot-racing or any other human activity, it has been a matter of increased experience and knowledge, of improved techniques and equipment. Latter-day climbers have the benefit of all manner of scientific and technological advances, with such end-products as concentrated foods, light but warm clothing, light but strong metals, efficient packaging, reliable instruments, effective medicines. Most important of all, they have had oxygen apparatus that *works;* and oxygen has often been the difference not only between success and failure but between life and death.

So men have gone to the top of the highest mountains. . . . And what is left for them now?

---

* *Editor's note*: For a detailed account of this venture, see *Americans on Everest,* by James Ramsey Ullman and other members of the expedition, also published by J. B. Lippincott Company.

For the Himalayas, the answer depends at least partly on politics; for the great range lies almost directly upon the borders of Communist China, and if China moves into them they will be lost, at least for a while, to the Western World. But, assuming that, happily, this does not occur—what then? The probability is that, although most of the giants have now been climbed, there will be more, rather than fewer, mountaineering expeditions in the years to come. Some will be to the great Eightthousanders, from Everest on down, in attempts to climb them both by old and new routes. Others will be to unclimbed lesser fry (if peaks of 20,000 feet and up can be called "lesser"), by parties smaller and more intimate than the large brigades usually needed for success on the topmost summits. In the vast arc of mountains, sweeping for more than 1500 miles from Assam to Afghanistan, the supply of first ascents—of adventure, exploration and discovery—cannot possibly be exhausted for years to come.

Among the hopes for the future is that there will be more international expeditions; for it is a cherished belief of most climbers that, just as earth's great mountains rise above the plains and valleys, so should mountaineering rise above the petty demarcations of the world of politics. As has been seen, a start in this internationalization has already been made. In areas other than the Himalayas it has been carried even further—as in two recent British-Russian ventures in the Caucasus and Pamirs. And it is a hope worth nurturing in our divided, fragmented world that this sort of joint enterprise will presently be occurring on the highest peaks of all.

"Everest is too great to belong to anyone. It is for all men," Tenzing Norgay has said. And so it should be for all mountains. And all mountaineers.

APPENDIX I

*One Hundred Famous Mountains**

WITH LOCATIONS, ALTITUDES AND DATES OF FIRST ASCENT

NORTH AMERICA

PEAK	LOCATION	ALTITUDE	FIRST ASCENT
McKinley	Alaska	20,300	1913
Logan	Yukon (Canada)	19,850	1925
Orizaba	Mexico	18,696	1848
St. Elias	Alaska	18,008	1897
Popocatepetl	Mexico	17,883	c. 1523
Foraker	Alaska	17,400	1934
Lucania	Yukon	17,150	1937
Fairweather	Alaska	15,300	1931
University Peak	Yukon	15,030	1955
Hunter	Alaska	14,580	1954
Whitney	California	14,500	1873
Rainier	Washington	14,408	1870

---

* This is not a list of the hundred highest mountains. It includes merely one hundred selected peaks which are either important in their own right or have played a significant part in the history of mountaineering. The altitudes of many summits—particularly those in remote and little-known regions—have not yet been exactly determined. In these cases, the figures given are the most commonly accepted estimates. The listing of first ascents has been updated through 1963.

		ALTITUDE	FIRST ASCENT
PEAK	LOCATION		
Longs Peak	Colorado	14,255	1868†
Grand Teton	Wyoming	13,766	1898
Waddington	Canada	13,260	1936
Robson	Canada	12,972	1913
Deborah	Alaska	12,540	1954
Washington	New Hampshire	6,290	1642

SOUTH AMERICA

		ALTITUDE	FIRST ASCENT
Aconcagua	Argentina	22,835	1897
Ojos del Salado	Argentina-Chile	22,590	1937
Tupungato	Argentina-Chile	22,300	1897
Huascarán	Peru	22,200	1908
Yerupajá	Peru	21,770	1950
Sajama	Bolivia	21,425	1939
Illimani	Bolivia	21,200	1898
Chimborazo	Ecuador	20,702	1880
Jirishanca	Peru	20,100	1957
Salcantay	Peru	20,000	1952
Chacraraju	Peru	20,000	1956
Cotopaxi	Ecuador	19,848	1872
Huagoruncho	Peru	18,800	1956

EUROPE

		ALTITUDE	FIRST ASCENT
Elbruz	Caucasus	18,480	1868
Dykhtau	Caucasus	17,050	1888
Koshtantau	Caucasus	16,875	1889
Mont Blanc	Alps	15,782	1786
Ushba	Caucasus	15,410	1903
Monte Rosa	Alps	15,217	1855
Dom (Mischabel)	Alps	14,942	1858
Lyskamm	Alps	14,889	1861
Weisshorn	Alps	14,804	1861
Matterhorn	Alps	14,782	1865
Täschhorn (Mischabel)	Alps	14,700	1862
Dent Blanche	Alps	14,318	1862
Grand Combin	Alps	14,164	1859
Finsteraarhorn	Alps	14,026	1812

† The first ascent by white men. Indians had possibly climbed it long before.

PEAK	LOCATION	ALTITUDE	FIRST ASCENT
Grandes Jorasses ...... Alps		13,806	1864
Jungfrau .... Alps		13,670	1811
Aiguille Verte .... Alps		13,520	1865
Mönch .... Alps		13,465	1857
Schreckhorn .... Alps		13,386	1861
Obergabelhorn .... Alps		13,365	1865
Eiger .... Alps		13,040	1858
Ortler .... Alps		12,802	1804
Wetterhorn .... Alps		12,149	1854
Etna .... Sicily		10,758	?
Olympus .... Greece		10,000	?
Mont Aiguille .... Alps		7,000	1492
Ben Nevis .... Scotland		4,406	?
Vesuvius .... Italy		3,891	?

ASIA

PEAK	LOCATION	ALTITUDE	FIRST ASCENT
Everest .... Himalayas		29,028	1953
K2 (Godwin Austen) .. Karakoram (Himalayas)		28,250	1954
Kangchenjunga ...... Himalayas		28,146	1955
Lhotse .... Himalayas		27,890	1956
Makalu .... Himalayas		27,790	1955
Dhaulagiri .... Himalayas		26,811	1960
Cho Oyu .... Himalayas		26,750	1954
Manaslu .... Himalayas		26,668	1956
Nanga Parbat .... Himalayas		26,660	1953
Annapurna .... Himalayas		26,493	1950
Gasherbrum I (Hidden Peak) .... Karakoram		26,470	1958
Broad Peak .... Karakoram		26,400	1957
Gasherbrum II ...... Karakoram		26,360	1956
Gosainthan .... Himalayas		26,290	1964
Nanda Devi .... Himalayas		25,660	1936
Masherbrum .... Karakoram		25,660	1960
Rakaposhi .... Pakistan		25,500	1958
Kamet .... Himalayas		25,447	1931
Jannu .... Himalayas		25,294	1962

PEAK	LOCATION	ALTITUDE	FIRST ASCENT
Tirich Mir	Hindu Kush	25,260	1950
Minya Konka	China	24,900	1932
Stalin	Pamirs	24,590	1934
Mustagh Ata	Pamirs	24,383	1956
Jonsong Peak	Himalayas	24,340	1930
Mustagh Tower	Karakoram	23,860	1956
Amni Machen	China	23,490	1960
Trisul	Himalayas	23,260	1907
Shilla	Himalayas	23,050	1851
Demavend	Iran	18,375	1837
Ararat	Turkey	16,946	1829
Fujiyama	Japan	12,395	?

AFRICA

Kilimanjaro	Tanganyika	19,565	1889
Kenya	Kenya	17,040	1899
Ruwenzori	Uganda—		
(Mountains of the Moon)	Belgian Congo	16,793	1906

ELSEWHERE

Mauna Kea	Hawaii	13,825	?
Mauna Loa	Hawaii	13,675	?
Erebus	Antarctica	13,300	1906
Cook	New Zealand	12,350	1894
Gunnbjornsfeld	Greenland	12,139	1935
Forel	Greenland	11,100	1938
Kosciusko	Australia	7,328	?

APPENDIX II

Glossary of Mountaineering Terms

(THE FOLLOWING LIST includes only the most common of the many special words and terms employed in mountaineering. F indicates French derivation, G German, W Welsh, I Italian.)

aiguille, F.—a rock spire or needle

alp—a mountain pasture

arête, F.—a ridge

belay—securing of a rope by hitching it over a projection or passing it around the body

bergschrund, G.—a large crevasse separating the main portion of a glacier from its upper slopes

bivouac—a temporary camp

boss—a knob of rock; a protuberance

cairn—a pile of stones set up to mark a summit or route

chimney—a steep, narrow cleft in a rock-wall

chockstone—a large block of rock wedged in a chimney

col, F.—a pass, or the low point of a ridge

cornice—a projecting mass of snow, as on a ridge

couloir, F.—a gully

courte-échelle, F.—clambering on the body or head of another climber

crampons, F.—climbing irons. Iron or steel frames, with projecting spikes, that are attached to the soles of the boots for use on steep snow or ice

crevasse, F.—a deep crevice or fissure in a glacier, caused by its downward movement *cwm,* W.—a hollow in a mõuntainside; a deep ravine

espadrilles, F.—rope-soled climbing shoes

gendarme, F.—a rock-tower, usually on a ridge

glissade, F.—sliding down a snow-slope

icefall—the steepest section of a glacier, usually taking the form of a wildly jumbled mass of ice

joch, G.—a pass, or the low point of a ridge

karabiner, G.—a metal snap-ring, usually used in conjunction with a piton, through which the rope may be passed for greater security during difficult climbing

kletterschuhe, G.—rope-soled shoes

moraine—rock and debris carried down by a glacier

névé, F.—a snow-field lying above the snow-line, usually the source of a glacier

pitch—a short, steep section of rock

piton, F.—a metal spike which may be driven into rock or ice to afford support for hand, foot or rope

rappel, F.—roping down. The maneuver of letting oneself down a steep place by means of a supplementary rope

scarpetti, I.—rope-soled shoes

scree—small stones and rock debris, usually found in the form of slopes at the foot of steep rock faces

serac, F.—a tower of ice, usually found on glaciers

snow-bridge—an arch of snow joining two sides of a crevasse

traverse—the horizontal or diagonal crossing of a mountainside. Also the crossing of a peak or pass from one side to the other

verglas, F.—thin veneer of ice on rock

APPENDIX III

Reading List

THOUSANDS OF BOOKS and articles have been written about mountains and mountaineering. They cover every imaginable phase of the subject and, together, comprise a vast treasury of factual information, technical theory and high—and true—adventure. The following list is in no sense a complete bibliography, but represents merely the author's selection of certain books which he feels would be of most interest to the general American reader. Highly technical and specialized works are omitted, as are all books written in foreign languages which have not been translated into English.

The list is divided into three principal sections, as follows: (1) books on mountaineering in general: (2) books dealing with specific mountains and expeditions; (3) journals and guides.

GENERAL

The American Alpine Club's Handbook of American Mountaineering, edited by Kenneth A. Henderson. A comprehensive, up-to-date guide to climbing techniques, mountain living and the principal ranges of this continent.

Mountain Craft, edited by Geoffrey Winthrop Young. A definitive English work and a "must" for any mountaineering library.

Mountaineering, edited by Sydney Spencer. An encyclopedia of the sport, with contributions by many authorities, mostly English.

Mountaineering, by Claude Wilson. A general consideration of climbing regions and climbing technique by a veteran of the English Alpine Club.

The Complete Mountaineer and *Modern Mountaineering,* by George D. Abraham. Mostly on technique.

Mountaineering Art, by Harold Raeburn. A pioneer Himalayan climber considers his craft.

Mountain Memories: A Pilgrimage of Romance, by Sir William Martin Conway. A record of thirty years of exploration and climbing in all parts of the world.

The Romance of Mountaineering, by R. L. G. Irving. A veteran English climber on the history and significance of mountaineering.

The Mountain Way, edited by R. L. G. Irving. An anthology of prose and verse about mountains and mountain climbing.

Ten Great Mountains, by R. L. G. Irving. A selection of famous adventure stories.

The Making of a Mountaineer, by George Finch. Experiences and observations of one of the early Everesters.

Mountains and Men, by Leonard H. Robbins. Tales of the great ascents (through 1930) by a popular American writer.

High Conquest, by James Ramsey Ullman. A general history of mountaineering up to the outbreak of the Second World War. The precursor of *The Age of Mountaineering,* it contains some of the same material.

The Story of Mountains, by Ferdinand C. Lane. An omnibus book treating of all the aspects of the earth's high places.

Challenge, edited by William Robert Irving. An anthology of mountaineering literature.

When Men and Mountains Meet, by H. W. Tilman. Climbs and explorations in Asia and, during the Second World War, in Italy and Albania.

On Top of the World, by Patricia Petzoldt. Adventures, mostly on mountains, from Wyoming to Kashmir, told by the wife of a leading American climber.

Nine volumes of pictures by Frank S. Smythe. Collections of outstanding photographs from England, the Alps and the Himalayas.

NORTH AMERICA

ALASKA

The Conquest of Mount McKinley, by Belmore Browne. The most complete and authoritative book on North America's highest mountain.

The Ascent of Denali, by Hudson Stuck. The story of the first ascent of McKinley by the man who accomplished it.

To the Top of the Continent, by Frederick Cook. Dr. Cook's concocted story of his "ascent" of McKinley.

The Ascent of Mount St. Elias, by Filippo de Filippi. The winning of the great Alaskan peak by the expedition of the Duke of the Abruzzi.

Travels in Alaska, by John Muir. Includes many descriptions of mountains and glaciers.

CANADA

The Glittering Mountains of Canada, by J. Monroe Thorington. History and description of the Canadian Rockies.

A Climber's Guide to the Rocky Mountains of Canada, by Howard Palmer and J. Monroe Thorington. The authoritative work.

In the Heart of the Canadian Rockies, by Sir James Outram. Exploration and first ascents by one of the foremost pioneers in the field.

Climbs and Explorations in the Canadian Rockies, by Hugh Stutfield and J. N. Collie. The adventures of two other noted pioneers.

Mountaineering and Exploration in the Selkirks, by Howard Palmer.

A Climber's Guide to the Interior Ranges of British Columbia, by J. Monroe Thorington.

Round Mystery Mountain, by Sir Norman Watson and E. J. King. Ski exploration in British Columbia, especially around Mount Waddington.

Where the Clouds Can Go, by Conrad Kain. Autobiography of a famous Austrian guide who made many of his greatest climbs in the mountains of Canada.

WESTERN UNITED STATES

Our Greatest Mountain, by F. W. Schmoe. Mount Rainier.

Mount Rainier: a Record of Exploration, by Edward S. Meany.

Wy' East "The Mountain," by F. N. McNeil. A chronicle of Mount Hood.

The Mountains of California; My First Summer in the Sierra; Steep Trails, by John Muir. Three of the many books written by the noted naturalist on the mountains of our West.

Mountaineering in the Sierra Nevada, by Clarence King. One of the earliest and most famous American mountain books, first published in 1872.

A Journal of Ramblings Through the High Sierras, by Joseph LeConte. Another early account of the mountains of California.

Guide to the John Muir Trail and the High Sierra Region, by Walter A. Starr, Jr.

The Teton Peaks and Their Ascents, by Fritiof Fryxell. Key to the best rock-climbing in the American Rockies.

Fourteen Thousand Feet, by J. L. J. Hart and Elinor Kingery. The Colorado Rockies.

The Rocky Mountain National Park, by E. A Mills.

The Call of the Mountains, by LeRoy Jeffers. Rambles among the mountains of the western United States and Canada.

Of Men and Mountains, by William O. Douglas. A Supreme Court Justice writes of camping and hiking in the Pacific Northwest.

EASTERN UNITED STATES

Appalachian Mountain Club White Mountain Guidebook. The definitive guide to the most important of our eastern ranges.

The Book of the White Mountains, by J. Anderson and S. Morse. One of the best of the recent books on the region.

Mount Washington Reoccupied, by Robert S. Monahan. A record of scientific investigation on New England's highest summit.

Bradford on Mount Washington, by Bradford Washburn. A boy's book.

The Friendly Mountains, edited by Roderick Peattie. Collected stories, sketches and essays about the White, Green and Adirondack ranges.

SOUTH AMERICA

Travels Among the Great Andes of the Equator, by Edward Whymper. The great climber's adventures and ascents in the mountains of Ecuador.

The Highest Andes, by Edward FitzGerald. The conquest of Aconcagua and Tupungato.

From the Alps to the Andes, by Mattias Zurbriggen. Autobiography of the famous guide who was the first up Aconcagua.

The Bolivian Andes, by Sir William Martin Conway. A record of exploration and climbing in the late 1890's by one of the foremost mountaineers of his day.

Aconcagua and Tierra del Fuego, by Sir William Martin Conway. Conway's expedition to the southernmost Andes.

A Search for the Apex of America, by Annie S. Peck. Exploits of a famous lady-mountaineer in Peru and Bolivia, including the conquest of Huascarán.

Inca Land, by Hiram Bingham. Includes an account of the first ascent of Coropuna.

The Butcher, by John Sack. The story of the 1950 ascent of Yerupajá, in Peru, by a group of young Americans who barely escaped with their lives.

EUROPE

EARLY DAYS IN THE ALPS

The Life of Horace Benedict de Saussure, by Douglas Freshfield (in collaboration with Henry F. Montaignier). The story of the father of mountaineering as told by an illustrious climber of later days. (De Saussure's own writings are not available in translation.)

Travels Through the Alps, by J. D. Forbes. Adventures of one of the foremost pioneer climbers of a century ago.

The Story of Mont Blanc, by Albert Smith. History of the mountain and an account of his own ascent (in 1851) by the first and greatest press-agent of mountaineering.

Mont Blanc Sideshow: the Life and Times of Albert Smith, by J. Monroe Thorington.

The Annals of Mont Blanc, by C. E. Mathews. A history of the mountain through the nineteenth century.

Where There's a Will There's a Way, by the Rev. Charles Hudson and E. S. Kennedy. A notable ascent of Mont Blanc in 1855.

Wanderings Among the High Alps, by Alfred Wills. Experiences of another noted pioneer.

Hours of Exercise in the Alps, by John Tyndall. Climbing adventures of the famous scientist, including the first ascent of the Weisshorn. (Other Alpine books by Tyndall are *The Glaciers of the Alps* and *Mountaineering in 1861*.)

The Alps in 1864, by A. W. Moore. Stories of many great ascents by one of the outstanding climbers of the nineteenth century.

Peaks, Passes and Glaciers, by the members of the Alpine Club of London. (Three series.) Famous Alpine ascents of mountaineering's Golden Age, described by the men who made them.

The Early Mountaineers, by Francis Gribble. Stories of the great first ascents in the Alps.

Pioneers of the Alps, by C. D. Cunningham and A. Abney. Biographies of the foremost Alpine guides of the early days.

Scrambles Amongst the Alps in the Years 1860-69, by Edward Whymper. The Alpine career of the greatest climber of his time, including the complete story of the Matterhorn. A mountain classic.

The Ascent of the Matterhorn, by Edward Whymper. The same as the above, but with Whymper's other climbs omitted.

Edward Whymper, by F. S. Smythe. A biography.

The Playground of Europe, by Sir Leslie Stephen. Another classic, the name of which has become synonymous with Switzerland.

The Alps in More Recent Times

Conway-Coolidge Climbers' Guides, edited by Sir William Martin Conway, W. A. B. Coolidge and others. Standard guides to the Alps for more than half a century.

Alpine Guides, by John Ball. Another famous series of guide-books. (In three large volumes.)

The Alps in Nature and History and *Alpine Studies*, by W. A. B. Coolidge. Two of the author's many books on various aspects of the Alps.

My Climbs in the Alps and Caucasus, by A. F. Mummery. The career of the man who revolutionized the technique of climbing. A veritable mountaineer's bible.

The High Alps Without Guides, by A. G. Girdlestone. A record of various exploits in the early days of guideless climbing.

The Italian Alps, by Douglas Freshfield. One of the earliest books by the great climber whose active career spanned half a century.

Above the Snow Line, by Clinton Dent. Mountaineering sketches by a well-known pioneer-climber of the Alps and Caucasus.

The Alps from End to End, by Sir William Martin Conway. Conway's "grand tour" of the Alps in the 1890's.

Peaks and Precipices, by Guido Rey. Records of many great ascents, mostly in the Dolomites, by a noted Italian mountaineer.

The Matterhorn, by Guido Rey. Whymper's mountain forty years after.

Alpine Pilgrimage, by Julius Kugy. The career of a distinguished German mountaineer.

Climbs on Alpine Peaks, by Abate Achille Ratti. The climbing adventures of the young priest who later became Pope Pius XI.

Adventures of an Alpine Guide, by Christian Klucker. Life story of one of the most famous professionals.

On High Hills, by Geoffrey Winthrop Young. Reminiscences of a life-time of climbing. An aristocrat of mountain books.

The Mountains of Youth, by Arnold Lunn. Contains much on winter mountaineering and skiing.

Climbs and Ski Runs, by F. S. Smythe. Mountaineering adventures in the Alps, Great Britain and Corsica by one of the foremost English climbers of the present day. (This is only one of several books on European mountaineering by Mr. Smythe.)

Climbs on Mont Blanc, by J. and T. de Lépiney. (Translated by Sydney Spencer.) New and precarious trail-blazing by two young French experts.

They Climbed the Alps, by Edwin Muller. Accounts of various famous ascents by a contemporary American writer.

A History of Mountaineering in the Alps, by Claire Eliana Engel. The most complete and up-to-date work on the subject, covering the whole span of Alpine climbing history.

ELSEWHERE IN EUROPE

British Mountain Climbs, by George D. Abraham. Deals with climbing districts and routes.

Rock Climbing in the English Lake District, by O. G. Jones. One of the best of many books on the region.

Norway: the Northern Playground, by W. C. Slingsby. The standard work on mountaineering in Scandinavia.

The Exploration of the Caucasus, by Douglas Freshfield. The definitive work on the subject and one of the great books of mountaineering history.

ASIA

EARLY HIMALAYAN EXPLORATION

Climbing and Exploration in the Karakoram Himalayas, by Sir William Martin Conway. Pioneering on the grand scale.

Climbing in the Himalayas and Other Mountain Ranges, by J. Norman Collie. Accounts of various Himalayan journeys including the Nanga Parbat expedition on which Mummery lost his life.

Round Kanchenjunga, by Douglas Freshfield. Narrative of a famous trip of exploration and a classic of its kind.

Five Months in the Himalaya, by A. L. Mumm. Adventure and exploration in the early days.

Karakoram and Western Himalaya, by Filippo de Filippi. An account of the K2 expedition of the Duke of the Abruzzi.

In the Ice World of the Himalayas, by Fanny and Hunter Workman. One of many books written by the remarkable American couple who were among the pioneers of the Himalayas.

Approach to the Hills, by C. F. Meade. Recollections of a veteran mountaineer who blazed many new Himalayan trails.

Wonders of the Himalaya, by Sir Francis Younghusband. Reminiscences covering many years and expeditions.

Himalayan Wanderer, Kulu and Lahoul, 20 Years in the Himalayas, by Gen. C. G. Bruce. Three books of mountain memories by one of the foremost explorers of the great range.

Mount Everest

Mount Everest: the Reconnaissance, by Lt. Col. C. K. Howard-Bury and others. Official account of the preliminary expedition of 1921.

The Assault on Mount Everest, 1922, by Gen. C. G. Bruce and others. Official account.

The Fight for Everest, 1924, by Lt. Col. E. F. Norton and others. Official account.

The Epic of Mount Everest, by Sir Francis Younghusband. A résumé of the expeditions of 1921, 1922 and 1924.

The Story of Everest, by Capt. John Noel. Account of the same three expeditions by the photographer of the 1922 and 1924 exploits.

After Everest, by T. H. Somervell. Reminiscences of a famous Everester.

George Leigh-Mallory, by David Pye. A memoir.

Attack on Everest, by Hugh Ruttledge. Story of the 1933 expedition recounted by its leader.

Camp VI, by F. S. Smythe. The 1933 adventure.

First Over Everest: the Houston-Mount Everest Expedition, 1933, by Aircommodore P. F. M. Fellowes and others. Over the top of the world by plane.

Everest: the Unfinished Adventure, by Hugh Ruttledge. Official account of the 1936 attempt.

Everest, the Challenge, by Sir Francis Younghusband. A discussion of the various expeditions up to the 1936 attempt.

Mount Everest: 1938, by H. W. Tilman. The story of that year's expedition, told by its leader.

Upon That Mountain, by Eric Shipton. Recollections of the author's climbs during the 'thirties.

Kingdom of Adventure: Everest, edited by James Ramsey Ullman. A chronicle of all the pre-World War II expeditions, told by the participants and with added material by the editor.

The Mount Everest Reconnaissance Expedition, 1951, by Eric Shipton. The first postwar Everest book, telling of the investigation of the southern approach to the mountain. Brief text and many photographs.

Forerunners to Everest, by members of the Swiss Expedition of 1952. An account of the two great attempts that forged a new route almost to the summit.

The Mountain World (annual): *1952,* by various authors. Mostly about the Swiss challenge in that year, with added chapters on climbing in the Andes and Greenland.

Everest: 1952, by Andre Roch. A book of photographs by one of the Swiss climbers.

The Story of Everest, 1921-1952, by W. H. Murray. A review of the mountain's history, through the penultimate Swiss attempts.

The Conquest of Everest, by Sir John Hunt. Victory at last, as told by the expedition leader, with a chapter on the reaching of the summit by Sir Edmund Hillary.

OTHER RECENT HIMALAYAN EXPLOITS

Himalayan Campaign, by Paul Bauer. Account of the great Bavarian attacks on Kanchenjunga in 1929 and 1931. Translated and condensed from the original German by Sumner Austin.

The Kanchenjunga Adventure, by F. S. Smythe. Story of the Dyhrenfurth expedition of 1930. Includes an account of the conquest of Jonsong Peak.

Kamet Conquered, by F. S. Smythe. The "highest yet" of 1931.

The Naked Mountain, by Elizabeth Knowlton. Account of the German-American Nanga Parbat expedition of 1932.

Nanga Parbat Adventure, by Fritz Bechtold. The disastrous exploit of 1934.

Himalayan Quest, by Paul Bauer. Includes accounts of several successful climbs of 1936 and of the Nanga Parbat tragedy of 1937.

Nanda Devi, by Eric Shipton. The discovery of the route to the mountain, in 1934, by the author and H. W. Tilman.

The Ascent of Nanda Devi, by H. W. Tilman. The conquest, two years later, of what remains today the highest mountain ever climbed to the top.

Blank on the Map, by Eric Shipton. Exploration in the farthest Karakoram.

Himalayan Assault, by Henri de Segogne and others. The French attempt on Gasherbrum in 1936.

Helvellyn to Himalaya, by F. S. Chapman. Climbing adventures in many lands, culminating in the first ascent of Chomolhari.

The Everlasting Hills, by J. Waller. Account of the 1938 attempt on Masherbrum, in the Karakoram.

The Throne of the Gods, by Arnold Heim and August Gansser. Story of a journey of exploration and scientific investigation.

Peaks and Lamas, by Marco Pallis. A subjective account of two Himalayan expeditions by a man who is both a mountaineer and a student of Tibetan Buddhism.

Five Miles High, by Members of the First American Karakoram Expedition. Edited by Robert Bates. The story of the 1938 attempt on K2.

Images de L'Himalaya. A portfolio of magnificent Himalayan photographs, mostly by Vittorio Sella. (Published in France, but available in this country.)

Nepal Himalaya, by H. W. Tilman. Three trips in 1949 and 1950 into almost unknown mountain country.

The Ultimate Mountains, by Thomas Weir. Four Scotsmen on an informal expedition in Garhwal.

Beyond the High Himalayas, by William O. Douglas. The Supreme Court Justice's story of his travels in remotest Kashmir.

Annapurna, by Maurice Herzog. The account of the spectacular French venture of 1950, which became an international best seller.

K2—The Savage Mountain, by Charles S. Houston and Robert H. Bates.

Nanga Parbat, by Dr. Karl Herrligkoffer.

ELSEWHERE IN ASIA

Men Against the Clouds, by R. L. Burdsall and A. B. Emmons. The conquest of Minya Konka, in Tibet, by a party of Americans.

The Ascent of Mount Stalin, by Michael Romm. A Soviet expedition to one of the great peaks of the Pamirs.

Mountaineering and Exploration in the Japanese Alps, by the Rev. Walter Weston. The definitive book on mountaineering in Japan.

Mountains of Tartary, by Eric Shipton. Exploring and climbing experiences, before and after the war, in Sinkiang Province of China. Includes an account on an attempt on Mustagh Ata, in the Pamirs.

AFRICA AND ELSEWHERE

Across East African Glaciers, by Hans Meyer. The first ascent of Kilimanjaro.

From Ruwenzori to the Congo, by A. F. R. Wollaston. Early exploration.

Ruwenzori, by Filippo de Filippi. Account of the great expedition of the Duke of the Abruzzi to The Mountains of the Moon.

Snow on the Equator, by H. W. Tilman. Experiences of fourteen years as a planter and mountaineer in East Africa. Includes ascents of Kilimanjaro, Kenya and Ruwenzori.

In Coldest Africa, by Carveth Wells. Travels among the high ranges by a well-known American explorer.

No Picnic on Mount Kenya, by Felice Benuzzi. A quixotic climb of the great East African peak by two escaped Italian prisoners during the war years.

The High Alps of New Zealand, by the Rev. W. S. Green. Adventures of a noted clergyman-mountaineer.

Climbs in the New Zealand Alps, by Edward FitzGerald. The conqueror of
Aconcagua on the other side of the world.

The Conquest of Mount Cook, by Freda Du Faur. The climbing of New
Zealand's highest peak.

Unclimbed New Zealand, by John Pascoe. A record of recent mountaineering
adventures.

Exploration of Mount Kina Balu, by John Whitehead. An expedition to the
great mountain of North Borneo.

The First Crossing of Spitzbergen, by Sir William Martin Conway. Mountaineering in the Arctic.

The Heart of the Antarctic, by Sir Ernest Shackleton. Contains an account of
the ascent of Mount Erebus.

JOURNALS AND GUIDES

Journals of mountaineering are published by scores of clubs and organizations all over the world. Among the most important, in English, are:

Alpine Journal, published by the Alpine Club, London. In existence since
1857.

Himalayan Journal, published by the Himalayan Club, of Calcutta.

Canadian Alpine Journal, published by the Alpine Club of Canada.

American Alpine Journal, published by the American Alpine Club, New
York. First issued in 1929.

Appalachia, published by the Appalachian Mountain Club, Boston. First
issued in 1879.

Trail and Timberline, published by the Colorado Mountain Club, of Denver.

Sierra Club Bulletin, published by the Sierra Club of San Francisco.

Mazamas, published by The Mazamas (climbing club) of Portland, Oregon.

The Mountaineer, published by The Mountaineers (climbing club), of Seattle.

In addition to their journals, most mountaineering clubs issue guidebooks
and maps of the regions in which they are particularly interested. In the
United States considerable material is also published by the National Park
Service of the Department of the Interior, the National Forest Service of the
Department of Agriculture, and the various state governments.

Addenda: 1954-1963

THERE HAVE, of course, been many mountaineering books published during the decade of 1954-1963. A brief noncomprehensive list of the most significant ones would have to include the following:

GENERAL

The Mountain World. A compendium of world mountaineering, now issued biennially by the Swiss Foundation for Alpine Research and available in English translation.

The Book of the Mountains, edited by A. C. Spectorsky. A comprehensive anthology of mountaineering literature.

The Mountains, by Lorus J. Milne, Margery Milne and the Editors of *Life* Magazine. A general presentation of mountains in their many aspects, only partially concerned with mountaineering.

Mountaineering, by Ronald W. Clark. A historical survey in text and pictures, with the focus largely on British climbing.

Conquistadors of the Useless, by Lionel Terray. The life and worldwide climbing career of one of the greatest of modern mountaineers.

EUROPE

THE ALPS

The Alps, by Wilfrid Noyce and Karl Lukan. A lavish text-and-picture book.

Starlight and Storm, by Gaston Rébuffat. A first-person account by the great French climber of six ascents of great "north faces" in the Alps.

The White Spider, by Heinrich Harrer. A history of the spectacular climbs on the north face of the Eiger, by a member of the party which made the first successful ascent.

North Face in Winter, by Toni Hiebeler. A first-person account of the first "out-of-season" ascent of the Eiger.

ASIA

MOUNT EVEREST

High Adventure, by Sir Edmund Hillary. The co-conqueror of earth's highest peak tells the story of his career and its great climax.

Tiger of the Snows, by Tenzing Norgay, with James Ramsey Ullman. In which Everest's other co-conqueror does the same.

The Everest-Lhotse Adventure, by Albert Eggler. The leader of the Swiss expedition of 1956 tells of his team's great double triumph.

Lure of Everest, by Brigadier Gyan Singh. The story, told by its leader, of the almost successful Indian expedition of 1960.

Americans on Everest, by James Ramsey Ullman and other members of the successful American expedition of 1963.

OTHER HIMALAYAN VENTURES

Victory Over K2, by Ardito Desio. The successful Italian climb of 1954.

Kangchenjunga: the Untrodden Peak, by Charles Evans. The successful British climb of 1955.

The Ascent of Dhaulgiri, by Max Eiselin. The successful international ascent of 1960.

Karakoram, by Fosco Maraini. A handsome volume in prose and picture centered on—and roundabout—an Italian expedition to Gasherbrum IV.

High in the Thin Cold Air, by Sir Edmund Hillary and Desmond Doig. The story of the Himalayan Scientific and Mountaineering Expedition of 1960-61, which was led by Sir Edmund.

To the Third Pole, by G. O. Dyhrenfurth. A general history of the Himalayas and their climbers.

Abode of Snow, by Kenneth Mason. A history of Himalayan exploration and mountaineering.

U.S.S.R.

The Red Snows, by Sir John Hunt and Christopher Brasher. The account of a British expedition to the Russian Caucasus in 1958.

Red Peak, by Malcolm Slesser. The story of a joint British-Russian expedition in the Pamirs in 1962.

INDEX

NORTH PLATTE COLLEGE LIBRARY
NORTH PLATTE, NEBRASKA